THE HISTORICAL APPROACH

TO THE BIBLE

TRUTH IN RELIGION, 2

The purpose of the Truth in Religion series is to present, on the popular level, the truth—in the institute's judgment—on religious topics about which much misinformation and misunderstanding are current.

The purpose of the Religion and Ethics Institute, Inc., as stated in its Illinois charter, is "to promote the discovery and distribution of sound historical and scientific knowledge in the fields of religion and ethics." The institute proposes to do this on both the research level and the popular level.

OTHER BOOKS BY HOWARD M. TEEPLE

The Mosaic Eschatological Prophet (Ph. D. dissertation)
The Literary Origin of the Gospel of John
The Noah's Ark Nonsense (Truth in Religion, 1)

THE HISTORICAL APPROACH
TO THE BIBLE

HOWARD M. *erle* TEEPLE

Religion and Ethics Institute, Inc.
Evanston

8726597

1-31-83 Jr

Copyright © 1982
by
Religion and Ethics Institute, Inc.
P. O. Box 664
Evanston, IL, U.S.A. 60204

LC: 81-85275
ISBN: 0-914384-02-3

Printed in the United States of America
by
BookCrafters
Chelsea, MI 48118

TO

the scholars who have had
the intelligence and the
courage to produce the
historical approach to the
Bible

CONTENTS

Preface   ix

Misunderstanding
1. Understanding the Bible   1
2. Why Is the Bible Misunderstood?   7
3. Unreliable Guides   23

History
4. Ancient and Medieval Interpretation   38
5. The Birth of the Historical Approach   60
6. The Nineteenth Century   83
7. The Twentieth Century—A   110
8. The Twentieth Century—B   126

Methods
9. Principles of the Historical Approach   147
10. The Original Languages   155
11. Establishing the Text   166
12. Types of Literature—O.T.   177
13. Types of Literature—N.T.   188
14. Literary Methods   202
15. Archaeology   213
16. The Background of the Old Testament   226
17. The Jewish Background of the New Testament   240
18. The Christian Background of the New Testament   258
19. The Gentile Background of the New Testament   272

Value
20. The Value of the Historical Approach   286

Appendixes
Notes   294
Bibliography: Pioneers of the Historical Approach   298
Personal Name Index   317
Subject Index   322

PREFACE

The most amazing aspect of religion in the United States is the prevalence of the fundamentalist and traditional approaches to the Bible, in spite of the abundance of decisive evidence against them. Both make the Bible the supreme authority in religion, and fundamentalism even maintains that the Bible is literally the infallible word of God. In sharp contrast stands the historical approach to the Bible, which studies it the same way historians study other ancient literature. This approach has evolved gradually through the centuries. First came study of the original languages of the Bible, then came study of the text, ancient literature, ancient history, archaeology, and other related subjects. Scholars asked, What did the words mean in the age in which they were written? What was the author saying, and why? What was the historical background? The attitude toward the Bible held by many Jews and Christians is somewhere between the two poles, between a strictly fundamentalist approach and a strictly historical approach.

Eventually the value of the historical approach was sufficiently recognized that it became—and still is—the standard way to interpret the Bible in the religion departments of most colleges and universities and to a large extent in mainline seminaries. Yet most laymen and the general public know very little about it. Many people are even unaware of its existence. Why?

There are several specific causes, in addition to the general fact that traditional religious views are slow to change. In the last few decades mainline Protestant churches have been coasting along, neither actively promoting the historical approach nor opposing fundamentalism. Their policy was just the opposite in the 1920s and 1930s, but thereafter they became too lenient in the interests of ecumenism, a policy which failed to produce either church unity or intellectual progress. The crisis situation in World War II was seized upon by conservative Jewish and Christian leaders to gain support for conservative religious views. The media have reported much more frequently opinions and discoveries that support conservative interpretation of the Bible than those which upset them.

The major cause of the prevalence of fundamentalism, however, is its zealous, aggressive promotion on the part of the adherents.   They have employed all conceivable means and tactics to advance their beliefs: tracts, door-to-door canvassing, Bible schools, Bible "universities," radio evangelism, television evangelism, private "Christian" schools, and establishment of their own publishing houses and chains of bookstores. Some members of this movement try to censor what is taught in public schools; some have tried to force unscientific "creationism" upon American children. An argument they have used for admitting creationism into textbooks is that children should have a right to know a different view. If that is the case, why do they refuse to admit the historical interpretation of the Bible into their schools and evangelistic activities? Incidentally, in the controversies over what children should be taught, a vital educational and moral principle is often overlooked: Every child has the inherent, human right to be taught the best knowledge that society has learned. If there is an unpardonable sin, it is that of deliberately concealing from children significant facts they should know and forcing them to believe false ideas. When this moral principle is applied to teaching the Bible, the injustice being done to youth—and adults too— is apparent. The historical approach to the Bible is the only reliable means of understanding and evaluating it. To deliberately deprive minds of that knowledge is an unethical act.

Considering the role of the Bible in religion and the influence of religion on society, the need to make the historical approach to the Bible generally known can hardly be overestimated. This book was written to help meet that need.

The Religion and Ethics Institute, too, was founded to help meet the need. Although its interests have broadened to include the whole spectrum of religion and ethics (past, present, and future), REI (the institute) still is deeply concerned about the tragic effects of the misunderstanding of the Bible. In addition to the publication of a few books, REI produces and distributes slide lectures for academic use; many of these, with their slides of archaeological sites and artifacts, supplement the information in the present book.

The purpose of this book is to guide laymen, students, and the general public to a better understanding of the Bible, to study it as historians study it. The book presents a concise survey of the causes of the misunderstanding of the Bible, and the development, application, and value of the historical approach. Occasionally these subjects have been published separately, but not in this combination. Every reader of the Bible should have knowledge of these fields; a view of "the whole picture" is essential for understanding and evaluating the Scriptures.

The main concern in the historical survey section (chapters 4-8) is to select the books that are landmarks in the development of the historical approach. The bibliography is unique in that it lists only the pioneering works which in some respect advanced the historical approach in a sound direction; works which made no new contribution or that were entirely off the track are omitted. So many books have appeared in recent decades that no claim is made for completeness of coverage of that period.

A special effort was exerted to make the book clear and readable. For assistance in this regard, I am deeply indebted to a team of readers who unsparingly criticized the first draft of the manuscript. Many thanks to the team: my wife Gladys, Paul Gehl, Richard Higginbotham, and Arnold Nelson. Gladys and I worked together on the typing and proofreading.

The biblical quotations are generally from the Revised Standard Version. The quotations from the Pseudepigrapha are from R. H. Charles, *The Apocrypha and Pseudepigrapha of the Old Testament*.

Evanston, Illinois   H. M. T.
November 1981

CHAPTER 1

UNDERSTANDING THE BIBLE

What do we have to do in order to "know the Bible"? Does knowing the Bible consist of quoting certain passages, citing chapter and verse? Or does knowing it require understanding it as a whole in the light of its historical origin? Historians and biblical scholars agree on the latter method.

Many people think they understand the Bible, but actually they misinterpret numerous passages in it. Usually they do not intend to misinterpret them, however, but sincerely believe that they are representing them correctly. Why does this happen? How can sincere people misunderstand a book which many of them regard as sacred and which they have read repeatedly?

Let us begin by asking ourselves some important questions. How was the Bible written? Why was it written? Under what conditions? What is the meaning of certain passages? Of particular words? When we encounter difficulties in understanding the Bible, how can we solve them? What facts pertaining to a passage should we know? What methods should we use in our efforts to understand it?

Perhaps we can see the problem more readily if we look at some specific examples. Here are some biblical passages that are often misunderstood. They require the application of certain methods which will be described in later chapters of this book.

A.   He who sacrifices to any god, except to the Lord only, shall be utterly destroyed (Exod. 22:20).

What is the meaning of the verb "sacrifice"? To what other gods were the Hebrews liable to sacrifice? Why? Should we sacrifice to the Lord?

B. 1.   In the beginning GOD CREATED the heavens and the earth. . . . So GOD CREATED the great sea monsters

and every living creature that moves, with which the
waters swarm, according to their kinds, and every
winged bird according to its kind. . . . And GOD
made the beasts of the earth according to their kinds
and the cattle according to their kinds, and everything
that creeps upon the ground according to its kind.
. . . So GOD CREATED man in his own image, in
the image of GOD he CREATED him; male and female he CREATED them. . . . And GOD said,
"Behold, I have given you every plant yielding seed
which is upon the face of all the earth, and every
tree with seed in its fruit; you shall have them for
food." . . . And on the SEVENTH DAY GOD finished his work which he had done, and he rested on
the SEVENTH DAY from all his work which he had
done (Gen. 1:1, 21, 25, 27, 29; 2:2).

B. 2.   In THE DAY that the LORD GOD MADE the
earth and the heavens, when no plant of the field was
yet in the earth and no herb of the field had yet
sprung up--for the LORD GOD had not caused it to
rain upon the earth, and there was no man to till
the ground; . . . --then the LORD GOD FORMED
man of dust from the ground, and breathed into
his nostrils the breath of life; and man became a
living being. . . . And out of the ground the LORD
GOD made [literally: caused] to grow every tree
that is pleasant to the sight and good for food, . . .
So out of the ground the LORD GOD FORMED every
beast of the field and every bird of the air, . . .
So the LORD GOD caused a deep sleep to fall upon
the man, and while he slept took one of his ribs
and closed up its place with flesh; and the rib which
the LORD GOD had taken from the man he MADE
into a woman and brought her to the man (Gen.
2:4b-5, 7, 9a, 21-22).

The story of the Creation is complete in Genesis 1:1-
2:4a; fish, birds, beasts, cattle, creeping things, man and
woman, plants, and trees have all been created. But the

passage which follows it, Genesis 2:4b-25, begins by stating that no plants and no man yet existed. Why is the Bible inconsistent at this point? The second passage continues by reporting that the Lord God caused trees and plants to grow out of the ground, and he made man, beasts, birds, and woman. Why is the story of the origin of life retold?

Important differences between the two passages exist too. In the first passage the Creation required six days, but in the second passage all living things were made in one day, the same day on which the earth and the heavens were made (2:4b). In the first, God is always--and frequently--referred to as "God," but in the second he always--and frequently-- is "Lord God." In the first passage the verb "create" *(bara'* in the Hebrew text) occurs often, but in the second passage other verbs are used instead for the same action. Why are there such linguistic differences between the two passages?

C.   For to us a child is born,
          to us a son is given;
      and the government will be upon his shoulder,
          and his name will be called
      "Wonderful Counselor, Mighty God,
          Everlasting Father, Prince of Peace."
      Of the increase of his government and of peace
          there will be no end,
      upon the throne of David, and over his kingdom,
          to establish it, and to uphold it
      with justice and with righteousness
          from this time forth and for evermore.
      The zeal of the Lord of hosts will do this
          (Isa. 9:6-7).

Who is this child? A Jewish king? Jesus? God? Whom does the description fit? And when does his reign over David's kingdom begin? Had he been born when the author wrote?

D.   Now after John was arrested, Jesus came into
      Galilee, preaching the gospel of God, and saying,
      "The time is fulfilled, and the kingdom of God is at
      hand; repent, and believe in the gospel" (Mark 1:14-15).

What is "the gospel" in this passage? What is "the kingdom of God"? When is the kingdom coming? What is the connection between the kingdom and repentance?

E.   Now when the Lord knew that the Pharisees had
        heard that Jesus was making and baptizing more
        disciples than John (although Jesus himself did not
        baptize, but only his disciples), he left Judea . . .
        (John 4:1-3).

Did Jesus baptize or not? What is the explanation of this
apparent contradiction?

F.   O Timothy, guard what has been entrusted to
        you. Avoid the godless chatter and contradictions
        of what is falsely called knowledge, for by pro-
        fessing it some have missed the mark as regards
        the faith (1 Tim. 6:20-21a).

What kind of knowledge is denounced here? Science?
College education? Seminary training? Bible schools' teaching? Radio and television preaching? Or something existing
at the time that the author wrote? If the last, what was it?

What are the correct answers to those questions? What
is our evidence? What is our method? How do we decide what
a particular word, phrase, or verse means? How do we explain the conflicting statements in the Bible? What is our basis for deciding why a certain word is used in one passage and
a different term is used for the same thing in an adjoining passage? Is evidence our guide, or does the desire to defend our
beliefs determine our explanation of the Bible? Or do we
evade the issues by saying that we cannot be bothered with little details, or that we should not criticize the Bible?

It is important to understand the Bible correctly when
we read it, whether we are Christians, Jews, or independent
thinkers. If the Bible is an important element in our religion,
the value of an accurate understanding of it should be obvious.
If it is not to us a religious guide, it remains a part of the cultural heritage of the Western world, a heritage which we all

should know, evaluate, and appreciate.

Accurate understanding of the Bible is valuable not only when we read it, but also when others try to persuade us to accept their interpretation of it. Suppose someone hands us a tract based on selected biblical verses. Or radio and television evangelists use Scripture as the basis of their efforts to promote their religion. Or our own clergyman or church school teacher interprets the Bible in a different way than we do. How do we judge whether or not they understand the Bible correctly?

Understanding the Bible is not an easy matter, however, although many people have believed that it is. During the Protestant Reformation Martin Luther claimed that the Bible is its own interpreter; that is, it is intelligible and interprets itself. According th this view, Christians do not need the church or anyone to interpret the Bible for them, because Scripture is self-explanatory when it is read. This sounds like a wonderful idea, but it does not work well in practice because the Bible is not that clear. Even Luther changed his interpretation of some biblical passages after he acquired more knowledge. In the dedication of John Calvin's commentary on Romans, he remarked: "yet a man might see at all times, how that even those who have godly, religiously, and soberly handled the mysteries of God [i.e., the Bible], have not always agreed among themselves." If the Bible is self-explanatory, why did the Reformers soon disagree among themselves on the interpretation of Scripture and why did their movement split into separate denominations over this matter? Why did the Protestants fail to reach agreement on their understanding of the Bible in the centuries following the Reformation?

Diversity in the interpretation of the Bible continues. The meaning of Scripture apparently is not self-evident, for various readers still emerge with very different views of a passage. Considering the wide divergencies and even contradictions among interpretations of the Bible, some persons must misunderstand at least parts of the book. Misunderstanding of the Bible is not new. Jews and Christians through the centuries have disagreed strongly among themselves and with each other over the interpretation of many passages. Other religions, too, have experienced difficulty in understanding their sacred writings. After the Bible has been read, studied, and discussed by millions of people for many centuries, we would expect that proper understanding would have been achieved and generally accepted by now, and that misinterpretation belongs only to the past. Regrettably, that is not the case.

The effects of misunderstanding the Bible have been tragic. Both Judaism and Christianity split into various groups, and the schisms were often accompanied by ill will and sometimes persecutions. Other results have been tensions between Jews and Christians, between them and the members of other religions, and between them and the secular world. The consequences have included personal controversies and hatreds, friction and even divorces in families, intolerance, wars, hindrance of the intellectual development of religion, and the fostering of a schism between religion and modern knowledge.

What are the causes of the widespread misunderstanding of the Bible? We will examine that question next.

CHAPTER 2

WHY IS THE BIBLE MISUNDERSTOOD?

Three factors have caused the Bible to be commonly misunderstood, in both the past and present. They are the nature of the Bible itself, the mistaken beliefs about it, and the unreliable guides which have led readers astray when they interpret the book.

THE NATURE OF THE BIBLE

Certain aspects of the Bible make it easy for readers to misunderstand it. The Bible was written in ancient times, in a cultural environment very different from ours. If we are unfamiliar with that environment, we are liable to think that the authors were saying something quite different from what they actually meant.

Its Date of Composition

Because the Bible was written in the distant past, in circumstances very different from those of the modern world, its readers today need much knowledge of ancient history and culture. A great deal of this information was lost and had to be rediscovered through archaeology and more careful study of documents already known, including the Bible itself. This process of rediscovery has occurred mainly in the last two centuries, as we shall see in later chapters. Some of this recovered information transforms our understanding of the Bible. Laymen generally, and even some biblical scholars, still lack sufficient knowledge of these discoveries.

The fact that the Bible was written so long ago also requires the use of historical principles of interpretation. To understand any ancient literature, reliable literary and historical ways of studying it must be found and employed. Study of other ancient literatures and religions has not only provided

more information about the Bible's environment, but has aided
development of dependable methods of biblical interpretation.
Above all, more careful study of the Bible itself has led to better methods of interpreting it. Unfortunately, many people do
not know these methods, and consequently do not use them.
Sometimes biblical scholars know of the methods, but religious bias prevents them from applying them.

Its Complexity of Thought

The Bible was produced by many hands over a period of
at least 1350 years, from about 1200 B.C. (the earliest portions existed first as oral tradition) to approximately A.D. 150.
Its books were written in many different environments and situations. Therefore we should not be surprised that it contains
not only a great diversity of topics, but even divergence of views
on the same subject. For example, Paul believed that gentile
Christians need not obey the Jewish law[1] (Gal. 3 and 5), but the
writers of the Gospel of Matthew (5:17-19) and the Epistle of
James (2:10) uphold complete observance of that law. If we
try to force all those passages to agree with each other, we
misinterpret Scripture.

Two other factors also contributed to the variety and complexity of thought in the Bible. In the days when the books were
being written, no organization existed in either Judaism or
Christianity that was strong enough to enforce uniformity of
thought. Also, those writers who believed that they were inspired by the divine Spirit did not hesitate to introduce their
ideas, even when the ideas varied greatly from the beliefs and
customs prevailing in their religion. Thus new and contradictory elements could enter the tradition.

Its Literary Complexity

A third source of the misunderstanding of the Bible is
the book's literary complexity. The Bible contains a wide
range of material: narratives, drama, sayings, proverbs,
poetry, songs, prophecy, letters, tracts, and apocalypses.
More difficult to recognize but equally important is the composite nature of many of these writings. At times a writer

combined two sources, perhaps inserting his own connecting links and comments. Sometimes a later editor, or redactor, composed and inserted his own material into a written source. Composite writing is common in ancient literature. If we assume that all the material in a composite book has come from a single pen, we are liable to miss the distinctive elements and points of view in the different sections. We also may try to force all the details to agree with each other, something that the original writers did not intend. Even the same word may have a different connotation in an inserted block of material than it has in an adjoining original passage.

Lack of Knowledge of the Nature of the Bible

Little of the historical, literary, and linguistic knowledge which is essential for understanding the Bible has been available to laymen until the present century. Even now, much of it is hard to find. Most of this knowledge was not known even to historians until the nineteenth and twentieth centuries. And some of it has not yet been assimilated into scholarship.

A good commentary which explains biblical passages can aid understanding, but commentaries are usually so brief that they cannot do justice to the subject. Most commentaries and handbooks are inadequate because the authors may not know enough of the historical background and/or may be biased in favor of traditional views. Other types of writings, however, are more prevalent sources of misinformation about the Bible. So many tracts, popular articles, and books by uninformed writers are printed annually that the lack of accurate information and the abundance of misinformation certainly handicap readers in their efforts to understand the Scriptures.

MISTAKEN BELIEFS

Readers' own beliefs are powerful influences in shaping their interpretation of Scripture. Unfortunately, they seldom realize this. They tend to assume that their knowledge is adequate and that their attitudes and beliefs are correct. Often they unconsciously force passages to agree with and support

their own beliefs and prejudices. Certain that they are right,
they are unaware that they are misinterpreting the Bible. Readers must recognize this danger in order to understand the book.
They should beware of certain beliefs which they have acquired,
and they should realize that they may need to obtain more knowledge.

At first glance, it seems that the historical approach
bears a negative attitude toward the Bible, but that is not the
case. Historians have a negative attitude toward the causes
of the misunderstanding of the book, but they have a positive
attitude toward the book itself. Although the historical approach
may not support some of the traditional values of the Bible, it
finds values in the book that tradition failed to discover.

Belief in the Inspiration of the Bible

According to the doctrine of the divine, literal inspiration of Scripture, God's Spirit, the Holy Spirit, directly inspired the prophets and apostles with God's words, and the
biblical authors wrote them down verbatim. In the seventeenth
century the Imagists, led by Johann Koch (latinized as Coc-
ceius) in Holland, taught that everything in the Bible, even the
punctuation, was directly dictated by God. This doctrine
reached its peak in the late nineteenth and twentieth centuries
in the so-called "fundamentalist" movement, which asserted
that the divine inspiration of the Bible is a "fundamental" doctrine.

Several beliefs naturally flow from the doctrine of verbal inspiration. If God's Spirit literally dictated the text of
the Bible, and only the Bible, that book must be unique. No
other book can be like it, for it alone is Scripture. Belief in
the uniqueness of the Bible was aided by the fact that for centuries, the Western world was not acquainted with other ancient literature. The biblical authors, however, knew many
of the ideas of their neighbors and used them, often adapting
them to their own religion. But later generations lost the
knowledge of those neighbors' beliefs and customs, which had
to be rediscovered in the classical literature found during the
Renaissance and in the Near Eastern documents and monuments
found subsequently through archaeology. After these writings

became known again, they were compared with the Bible and found to contain similar ideas and literary characteristics. They have provided valuable insights into the meaning of many biblical passages. Belief in the Bible's uniqueness had engendered the intolerant attitude that only believers in "our" religion are "saved." Discovery that there are parallels between Scripture and other ancient literature has not only aided understanding of the Bible, but has fostered tolerance and goodwill among peoples as well.

Exposure of the fallacy of the belief in the Bible's uniqueness was stoutly resisted by theologians for many years. Friedrich Lücke, professor of theology at Göttingen, denounced the idea in his book, *Outline of New Testament Hermeneutics and Its History* (1817). He asserted that the New Testament must be understood as a revelation of a unique religion and that therefore the New Testament should be interpreted only by "Christian" methods unlike those used with other books. Historians today, however, reject that policy, for it shuts out information needed to understand the Bible.

The Bible must also be a unity, say those who uphold its divine, literal inspiration. As God could not contradict himself, so the Bible cannot contradict itself. Thus, some contend that divergent points of view cannot occur in it, for all passages in the book must agree with each other.

Actually, there are divergent views in the Bible. Not only between the Old Testament and the New Testament, but even within each of these two bodies of literature. The Old Testament contains a great variety of concepts about the nature of God. The Lord partakes of part of the animal sacrifices according to Leviticus 3:9-11, but that primitive notion is rejected in Isaiah 1:11, for example.

Inconsistencies in the New Testament caused major controversies in the early church. In the second century, differences between the synoptic gospels and the Gospel of John in respect to the date of the Last Supper led to the Quartodeciman dispute over the date of the resurrection and therefore the date of Easter. In the same century the differences between the Christology in the synoptics and the Logos Christology in the Gospel of John was a factor in producing the Christian sect called the Alogoi, which denied that Jesus was the Logos.

One of my former colleagues in teaching Bible to college students used to remark: "They who say they believe the Bible from cover to cover, are simply not aware of all that is between the covers." Many persons imagine that they believe everything that is in the Bible, but actually that is impossible-- there are too many contradictions in it.

According to the doctrine of verbal inspiration, the Bible is literally the Word of God. That belief easily leads to the view that the book is inerrant; that is, the Bible cannot contain any errors of fact or any mistaken beliefs. It follows then, that all the events it relates must have happened, just as they are reported; also, narratives are considered historical accounts--never myths. Belief in an inerrant Bible was still widely accepted in the eighteenth century when even the prominent German biblical scholar, Johann Ernesti, stated that it is impossible for Scripture to err because the writers were divinely inspired.

The claim that the Bible is inerrant is untenable, however, no matter how often the claim is repeated and how zealously promoted. In Mark 1:2-3 the Old Testament passage quoted is all ascribed to Isaiah the prophet, but the truth of the matter is that only verse 3 is from Isaiah. The portion of the quotation that is in verse 2 is from Malachi 3:1. Another example of factual error occurs in the biblical statements about "the four corners of the earth" (Isa. 11:12; Rev. 7:1); the expression rests on the erroneous ancient belief that the earth is flat and has four corners. In 1730 Matthew Tindal, an English Deist, pointed out a major error. He observed that many New Testament writers expected Jesus to return in their lifetime, but Jesus did not come back to earth and thus the apostles were mistaken. [2]

The doctrine of divine inspiration automatically gave the Bible a position of great authority among believers. Some Protestant Reformers gave the book increased prestige by using it as the supreme authority in opposition to the authority of the Catholic Church. Also, soon after the Reformation, Protestants who were involved in theological disputes among themselves relied heavily on the Bible as the defense for their beliefs, and consequently they attached an exaggerated importance to it. The more heated the dispute, the more important the defense of the Bible seemed to be.

Bibliolatry is the inevitable result of full acceptance of the doctrine of the verbal inspiration of the Bible. So much authority is assigned to the Bible that, in effect, its devotees worship it. Bibliolatry is thus a form of idolatry.

The notion that the Bible is perfect is contrary to the attitude toward the Old Testament expressed in some passages in the Sermon on the Mount. The Old Testament saying, "an eye for an eye and a tooth for a tooth," is quoted and rejected (Matt. 5:38-39). In the preceding seven verses two other Old Testament quotations receive similar treatment. Thus some passages in the Bible explicitly disagree with and reject other passages. If Jesus uttered the Sermon on the Mount, he certainly did not regard Scripture as infallible.

Although the verbal inspiration of the Bible is a belief discarded by the majority of Christians today, a strong vestige of it remains in the minds of those who believe that, although the Bible is not perfect, it is still the primary authority. We must beware of assigning too much authority to the Bible, however. If we expect too much from it, we are liable to be reluctant to recognize the variety it contains, its composite nature, and the influence of environment on its formation--aspects essential for understanding it. Also, giving too much authority to the Bible shuts out other elements essential in mature religion.

Various "solutions" have been proposed to the problem of the divine inspiration doctrine versus the evidence that the Bible is not infallible. One response to the evidence is to ignore it and to condemn automatically any interpretation of the book that suggests error in Scripture. Not only the interpretation is denounced, but also the scholars who recognized the error. Sometimes thorough study of the Bible is intentionally discouraged by labeling such study as "picking the Bible to pieces." Under this policy, the accuracy of the whole Bible is stoutly affirmed, and the evidence to the contrary is carefully evaded.

Another solution is to reinterpret the offending passages to try to make the Bible entirely true. The usual result of such reinterpretation is misinterpretation. An example is the reinterpretation of the word "day" in the Creation story. When geology proved that the earth has been formed, not in a week, but through millions of years, some interpreters argued that a day in the story must mean a long period of time. That is utter misinterpretation, for when God blesses the seventh day as a day of rest (Gen. 2:3), the reference is clearly to a twenty-hour day: the Sabbath. In the nineteenth century, Christian rationalizations of the miracle stories in the gospels were also examples. A closely related tactic is to try to harmonize passages, to interpret them to make them agree with each other.

One solution used in the past is to conclude that only parts of the Bible are inspired. An early form of this was the view that only certain books thus qualify. Divine inspiration was one of the requirements for the admission of a book into the canon (the list of books officially accepted into the Bible), although religious authorities did not always agree on what books qualified. Later, some Christians maintained that not all the books admitted into the canon are of equal merit and inspiration. Theodore (350-428), bishop of Mopsuestia, denied that Proverbs and Ecclesiastes were divinely inspired. For doctrinal reasons, Martin Luther regarded Hebrews, James, Jude, and Revelation as secondary in importance.

A different form of this type of solution is the view that only certain passages in the Bible are inspired. Luther's solution to the diversity was not to try to harmonize the passages, but rather to distinguish between those with greater and those with lesser authority, or between those important for all time and those important only for a time in the past.

Yet another solution is to claim that, although the Bible is inspired, there are other sources of revelation also. Under this view, the word of God is not limited to the Bible. Religion does not stand or fall with the Bible, and therefore discrepancies are not so upsetting. This solution has appeared in several forms. One form is the traditional claim that the Catholic Church has transmitted the teaching of the apostles, some of which is outside the Bible in patristic writings. The Council of of Trent (1546) decreed that "this [divine] truth and this discipline are contained in written books [the Bible] and in unwritten traditions, which were received by the Apostles from

the lips of Christ himself, or, by the same Apostles, at the
dictation of the Holy Spirit, and were handed on and have come
down to us; . . . preserved by unbroken succession in the Catholic Church."

A second form of this solution is the belief in "continuing revelation"; that is, God continues to reveal his will by
means of his Spirit. This idea favors mystics, who believe
that the Spirit speaks directly to them. The Reformer Hul-
dreich Zwingli concluded that some of the sayings of Greek and
Roman authors are so noble that they, too, must have been inspired by the Holy Spirit. Under the doctrine of continuing revelation, new truth can supersede the old, including the Bible
itself. Johann Gabler (1800), professor of theology at Altdorf,
Switzerland, distinguished between "revelation" and "documents of revelation" (the Bible); he regarded the former as
superior and said that therefore the presence of myth in the
New Testament should not be a cause of shock. Further,
said Gabler, to defend as true history the myths that contain unworthy ideas about God would make "the whole Bible in
our day a laughingstock."

All the solutions which we have described tend to inter-
fere with accurate understanding of the Bible. Two other solutions lead to better results. One proposed nearly two hundred years ago is simply to ignore the question of divine inspiration when studying the Bible. Karl Keil, professor of
theology at Leipzig, in his book *On the Historical Interpretation of the Books and Its Necessity* (1788), maintained
that both sacred and profane writers should be interpreted by
asking what they were saying, and not by being anxious whether what they said is true or not. Johann Gottfried Eichhorn,
German scholar of the Old Testament and Near Eastern languages, maintained at the beginning of the nineteenth century
that investigation of the conditions under which the New Testament was written should disregard completely the question of
its divine inspiration.

Yet another solution to the problem of inspiration is to
recognize that the Bible is like other ancient books. It contains human thoughts, and therefore some human errors in it
should be neither surprising nor disturbing. The Bible and
other ancient writings are alike, not because they were in-

spired by the Spirit, but because all are human in origin and
reflect the conditions of their times, and because ideas and
customs often spread from one culture to another. Johann
Semler, in his *Treatise on the Free Investigation of the
Canon* (1771-75), denied that the Bible is inspired. His opinion, along with his historical interpretation of the Bible, a-
roused a storm of protest in those orthodox days. Other leaders in this interpretation were Hugo Grotius and Thomas
Hobbes in the seventeenth century, Jean Turretini and the
English Deists in the eighteenth, and Friedrich Schleiermacher in the nineteenth century. This is the solution generally accepted by historians today. The decisive evidence
is the similarity of the Bible to contemporary ancient writings. This evidence demonstrates that the Bible is not u-
nique, but is a product of its human environment in the past.

Belief in Traditional Authorship

When the writer of a book in the Hebrew Scriptures was
unknown, Jews sometimes gave the book authority by assigning
the authorship to a hero in the past. Thus the Pentateuch
was ascribed to Moses, and the Psalms were assigned to David. Early Christians ascribed the authorship of most of their
books to some apostle. The Christians had a special reason
for doing this: in the bitter controversy between the gnostic
heretics and the other Christians in the second century both
groups ascribed their writings to first-century apostles to give
their views more authority. The controversies between Jews
and early Christians further stimulated the Christian desire to
assign the authorship of their books to Christian leaders in the
apostolic period. Some Jewish and early Christian authors
wrote pseudonymously in the name of famous persons in the
past to give authority to their work. Examples are Daniel in
the Old Testament and the Pastoral Epistles, James, and 1
and 2 Peter in the New Testament.

These practices created erroneous traditions of the authorship of many biblical books. They misled biblical scholars into thinking that they knew who wrote them. Actually,
the only biblical writers known with any certainty are some
Hebrew prophets and Paul. Nevertheless, traditional author-

ship was taken very seriously, partly because it was a factor
in determining whether a book belonged in the canon. The un-
warranted importance attached to prophetic and apostolic authorship had a large impact on the history of the interpretation
of the Bible. For centuries men were afraid of evidence that
indicated that a canonical book was not written by its traditional
author, lest it weaken the book's authority and indicate that it
should not be in the canon. For many centuries the traditions
of authorship also blocked the recognition that many biblical
books are not by a single author, but are composite. As long
as biblical scholars were convinced that a book was written by
one traditional author, they interpreted it accordingly and excluded the evidence that more than one writer was involved.

Belief in traditional authorship often produces misunderstanding of the books or at least of passages within them. It
can cause readers to try to make the book fit a different writer
in a different situation in a different city or even country. By
preventing readers from realizing the composite nature of a
book, it can blind them to the distinctive aspects and shades
of meaning of passages written by different authors.

At first the idea that some biblical books were not written
by their traditional authors produced two different reactions
in respect to the canon. One response was to accept the idea
and reject from the canon the books not written by known prophets and apostles. As late as 1788 Johann D. Michaelis contended that the purpose of historical study of the New Testament is to determine which books were written by apostles and
thus belong in the Bible.

The second kind of reaction was to reject the idea and
stoutly defend the traditional canon: all the books in the canon
belong in the Bible, and any evidence that upsets traditional
views of authorship should be vigorously opposed. The Council of Trent in 1546 expressly condemned Cajetan's questioning
of the authorship of biblical books. The zeal to defend traditional authorship created a prejudice against any study of the
Bible which suggested that a book was written by a different
author or by several authors or at a later time. In 1873 Paul
de Lagarde recognized the prevalence of this bias and urged
that in biblical studies the question of the canon should be left
out of consideration in order that a fair-minded examination of

the Bible can be made.

Later there was an enlightened third reaction to the idea that some biblical books were not written by their traditional authors. This was the recognition that there is not a clear distinction in content between the books in the canon and those outside of it, and therefore the questions of authorship and canonicity are not crucial. As a result of this recognition, the heated controversies over the canon rightly belong to the past and the door has been opened wider for historical study. The books of the Apocrypha have been re-accepted into some Protestant editions of the Bible (they were in the original printing of the King James Version). Nevertheless, prejudice against evidence of non-apostolic authorship remains in conservative religious circles and interferes with understanding the Bible, even today.

Belief that the Old Testament Must Support Christianity

For many centuries Christians believed that the Old Testament must support Christian faith. The initial cause was the desire to prove that Jesus was the Christ, or the Messiah, that many Jews expected to come. Jews (except Jewish Christians) were not convinced by the Christian claim. Consequently, Christians eagerly sought support in the Jewish Scriptures, and they interpreted various passages there as prophecies about Jesus. Some of their interpretations of this sort are incorporated in the New Testament. For example, Hosea 1:1 reads: "When Israel was a child, I loved him, and out of Egypt I called my son. " This is a definite reference to the Hebrew exodus from Egypt; the Jewish nation is personified as "Israel" and God's "son, " which are common figures of speech in the Old Testament. Israel is called a "child" because the nation was young at the time of the exodus. In Matthew 2:5, however, the Christian author applies the word to the infant Jesus. The application apparently was suggested by the words "child" and "my son. " The interpretation is a misinterpretation, for in Hosea, God's "son" is the Jewish nation before Hosea wrote, but in Matthew, God's "son" is Jesus long after Hosea wrote.

New Testament writers tried to make the Old Testament forecast the coming of Christianity too. Jeremiah 31:31 predicts that the Lord will make a new covenant "with the house of Israel and the house of Judah." The author of Hebrews (8:8; 9:15) misinterpreted the passage by applying it to Christianity. Jeremiah clearly was referring to a righteous remnant of faithful Jews. Although the early Christians claimed that they were the new Judaism and that the new covenant was made with them, they did not fit the biblical passage. The Christian movement soon became predominantly gentile and soon abandoned Judaism. Both of these aspects of Christianity were quite contrary to what Jeremiah had in mind.

The belief that the Old Testament predicts Jesus and Christianity is a doctrine which continued in the patristic literature, the Reformation, and fundamentalism today. Luther claimed that the Books of Moses pertain to Christ, and even "all the stories of Holy Writ, if they are rightly regarded, refer to Christ." For fundamentalists the citation of Old Testament passages as "prophecies of Christ" is still standard procedure.

Many Old Testament verses that some Christians have applied to Jesus are not even speaking of a future Messiah; those that do are not speaking of Jesus--they simply do not fit him. The Christ of the Old Testament prophecies (e.g., Isa. 11; Jer. 23:5-6; Micah 5:2-4) is a victorious Jewish king who will overthrow foreign rule and establish the independence of the Jewish nation. With Jesus the opposite occurred; the Roman governor killed him and the foreign rule continued. Furthermore, the Christ of Christian faith, with a supernatural birth (or an incarnation), resurrection, ascension, and future return is completely absent from ancient Jewish expectation, both inside and outside the Old Testament.

It may seem surprising that there is misinterpretation of the Bible within the Bible itself. But that is the way it is! Jews and Christians in ancient times were not concerned with the context and the historical setting of passages or earlier writings, including the Bible. Often the historical setting was unknown to them. Frequently they misunderstood the meaning of a word or a phrase and made it the basis of their interpretation of the passage, as in the misinterpretation in Matthew of "my son" in Hosea.

After the New Testament books were canonized as part

of the Christian Bible, Christians became very concerned that
the Old Testament should agree with the New. This process
appeared among the Fathers and continued in the Reformation.
John Calvin frequently misinterpreted the Testaments to make
them agree. As Emil Kraeling expressed it, Calvin tried to
Christianize the Old Testament and Judaize the New Testament.
The Reformed churches followed Calvin's lead. In the present
century Karl Barth practiced a Christianizing interpretation of
the Old Testament that was popular with conservative Christian
theologians.

When the Old Testament is carefully compared with the
New and with the history of the early church, it is clear that
the two testaments disagree with each other on many points,
some of them major. The religion of the Old Testament is
primarily a religion for Jews and requires obedience of ancient Hebrew law. In general, the concept of God is quite
different in the two testaments--for example, in the New Testament God does not require the offering of cultic sacrifices.

As the history and characteristics of ancient Judaism became better known in modern times, the claim that Jesus and
Christianity are predicted in the Old Testament could not reasonably be maintained. The belief that the Old and New Testaments completely agree with each other was likewise exploded. By the end of the nineteenth century the Christianizing of
the Old Testament was rejected by historians and most biblical
scholars. Wilhelm De Wette was one of the leaders in demand-
ing that the Old Testament be interpreted independently of the
New Testament (1826).

Belief that Modern Knowledge Is Bad

When modern knowledge upset traditional theological beliefs and views of the Bible, religious conservatives concluded
that such knowledge is evil. This belief has produced negative
attitudes which hinder the understanding of the Bible.

One of those attitudes is a prejudice against thorough
study of the Bible. Accordingly, Scripture should not be examined closely, and traditional interpretation of it should be
accepted "on faith." One should never have any doubts about
the truth of anything in the Bible, because doubting the Bible

is doubting God (for "the Bible is God's Word"). This attitude is opposed both to detailed study and to comprehensive study-- in short, it opposes scholarship.

A peculiar form of the negative attitude toward thorough study is the attitude that happiness, peace of mind, and self-improvement are independent of truth and scholarship. An example is the recurrent popularity of inspirational and religious self-improvement books which ignore biblical scholarship. Such books are defended by asking, what does it matter if people misinterpret the Bible, as long as it makes them happy? The fallacy of that view is that misinterpretation of the Bible is not necessary in order to lead individuals to self-improvement and happiness, and in the long run the practice of ignoring known facts only breeds mediocrity in society.

Another negative attitude is that science and secularism are inherently bad. This attitude is usually accompanied by the assumption that the Bible and religion are automatically good. It draws a sharp distinction between the Bible and secularism. An objection to the attitude is that such separation of the Bible from secularism did not exist among the biblical writers, for religion and secularism were intertwined. The Israelite government was a theocracy, with God and king ruling together, and religion was deeply involved with the culture. Mundane subjects such as food and clothing are important features in both Testaments. The Bible and secularism are intertwined today too. Secular study of ancient history and literature has made tremendous contributions to the understanding of Scripture. This is true also of the secular field of archaeology. The historical and scientific methods of secularism have made possible the valid methods of biblical study.

A second objection to the religious belief that science and secularism are undesirable is that they are not necessarily bad, nor are the Bible and religion necessarily good. In fact, with respect to their effects upon civilization, all of these are mixtures of worthy and unworthy elements. To condemn science and secularism, as such, is popular--and foolish! It is often indulged in by theologians and evangelists who are trying to cover up the fact that their beliefs are contrary to, and can be exposed by, secular knowledge.

The development of the reader—whether layman, student, clergyman, or scholar—is the proper starting point for solving the problem of the misunderstanding of the Bible. If we acquire adequate knowledge and avoid the pitfalls which have led others astray, we can acquire a better understanding of history's most widely read book. The goal is well worth the effort.

In the next chapter we will discuss the third factor which has caused misunderstanding of the Bible.

CHAPTER 3

UNRELIABLE GUIDES

Unreliable guides which have often been used to find the meaning of Scripture constitute the third factor causing misunderstanding of it. The assumption that the Bible must agree with one or another of those guides has caused many readers to draw erroneous conclusions.

Tradition as Guide

The rabbis' comments on the Old Testament were collected in the Talmud and cited as authoritative in the Middle Ages. They still are authoritative for exegesis in Orthodox Judaism, but not in Reform Judaism. Similarly, the church fathers commented on the Bible, and through the Middle Ages their opinions were regarded as the correct interpretation of Scripture, although churchmen realized that individual Fathers disagreed among themselves at times and were liable to error. Church creeds and other conciliar decrees, as well as the decrees of the pope at Rome, also decided the meaning of Scripture. The combination of the Fathers' commentaries, the creeds, and the conciliar and papal decrees formed the tradition of the Western church and was the authoritative official guide for understanding the Bible. The procedure in finding the meaning of a passage was simply to learn how tradition had interpreted it in the past.

The Protestant Reformation broke away from church tradition as the basis of biblical interpretation. Luther at first accepted tradition as authoritative, but as he became involved in controversy with the Catholic church, he turned to the Bible for support. He and other Reformers interpreted it directly from the text, instead of using tradition.

Roman Catholicism reacted defensively by elevating still further the position of church tradition. When the Council of Trent at its Fourth Session (1546) reaffirmed the authority of Vulgate (the official Latin version of the Bible used in the Ro-

man Catholic church for many centuries), it decreed that the
church has the sole right to interpret the Bible. The Council
declared:

> Furthermore, in order to restrain willful spir-
> its, the synod decrees that no one, relying on his own
> wisdom in matters of faith and morals that pertain
> to the upbuilding of the Christian doctrine, may twist
> the Holy Scripture according to his own opinions or
> presume to interpret Holy Scripture contrary to that
> sense which holy mother Church has held and holds,
> whose right it is to judge concerning the true sense
> and interpretation of the Holy Scriptures, or con-
> trary to the unanimous consensus of the fathers, . . .

The French Catholic scholar, Richard Simon, reached a similar conclusion from a different standpoint. In the seventeenth
century he decided that laymen cannot understand the Bible by
their own efforts because it is complex and has many variants
in the text. Therefore, he declared, the Catholic church with
its tradition is needed as a guide for interpreting Scripture.

During the last hundred years an increasing number of
Catholic scholars became dissatisfied with tradition as the
guide. They began to study the text in its original languages,
Hebrew and Greek, instead of the Latin translation, and they
examined it in its historical setting. This new, direct study
of the Bible in Catholicism led to some untraditional conclusions. By the close of the nineteenth century Catholic officials were very disturbed by the progress of this movement,
which later was called "modernism." Pope Leo XIII, in his
encyclical "Providentissimus Deus" (1893), proclaimed that it
is the function of the church to judge the true sense of Scripture, and that the individual scholar is free to interpret the Bible only in agreement with the faith of the (Catholic) church.
Any interpretation that finds contradictions in the Bible or between it and the teaching of the Catholic church is either
"foolish or false," according to Leo XIII. The modernist movement received a further setback from Pope Pius X at the beginning of the twentieth century. He rigorously opposed the
activities of Catholics who were seeking the reform of church

dogma or who were studying the Bible historically. Some Protestants were equally disturbed by modern biblical study and tried to defend their conservative tradition against it.

The rising tide of modern knowledge exerted increasing pressure, however, and eventually popes themselves placed less reliance on church tradition. Pius XII and John XXIII encouraged fresh study of the Bible.

Linguistic and historical study of the Bible has demonstrated in passage after passage that tradition is unreliable. This knowledge was upsetting. The faithful wondered why tradition should suddenly be rejected, after it had been accepted for centuries.

The answer to this question is that we know much, much more about the subject than our ancestors did. Tradition was formulated long after the biblical books were written and often in cities far distant from the places of their origin. By that time, the situations in which the Bible was composed were unknown. The Fathers only guessed at the conditions in the biblical environment, and their interpretations were further weakened by their apologetic motives--they wanted to make the Bible support their views. Sometimes they even misquoted it to make it fit their ideas. Often their methods of interpretation were very unsound.

Modern historians, on the other hand, have the advantage of fuller information about the Bible's origin and a better comprehension of the origin and nature of church tradition. A vast store of historical facts and methodology is known to them that was unavailable to their predecessors. And thanks to the influence of scientific thought, we today can be far more objective and can let the Bible speak for itself more than the Fathers could. Sometimes we are not as objective as we should be, but the best scholars today far surpass the ancient interpreters.

Spirit as Guide

Devout persons have often relied on the Holy Spirit as a guide for biblical interpretation. In the third century the church father Origen insisted that because the Holy Spirit was the author of Scripture, it is the indispensable guide to its meaning. This idea was emphasized in the Reformation. The necessity

of faith and spiritual illumination was one of Luther's six rules
for the interpretation of Scripture. Zwingli rejected human
wisdom as a basis and made the Spirit of God the sole guide for
exegesis. He even lifted Psalm 36:9 out of context to try to
prove it! This is the verse: "For with you [God] is the foun-
tain of life; in your light we see light." Zwingli interpreted
"your light" as God's Holy Spirit, but there is no evidence in
the verse or in its context that "your light" means Spirit or
that the second occurrence of the word "light" pertains to the
interpretation of Scripture. Judging from the context, "your
light" in the verse is God's love. The Anabaptists believed
that the individual Christian could interpret the Bible for himself, provided he was illumined by the Holy Spirit. Later the
"Protestant scholastics," as the orthodox Protestants of the
sixteenth and seventeenth centuries have been called, insisted
that true interpretation of the Bible is impossible without the
"light" of the Holy Spirit. The Society of Friends, or Quakers,
and some mystic movements, have also relied on the Spirit as
the guide.

An offshoot from this old doctrine was Karl Barth's con-
tention that the Holy Spirit speaks the Word of God to man when
he reads the Bible. The Word centers in Christ, claimed Barth.
This Word has little or no relation to the literal meaning of the
text. For example, in Romans 12:9-10a Paul states: "Let love
be genuine; hate the evil; hold fast to the good. Love one another with brotherly love." The main idea that this (and the
Spirit?) suggested to Barth is that Christians should have "en-
mity against *eros*." Where did Barth get that idea? Out of his
own head. *Eros* is the Greek word for romantic, physical
love, and Barth's purpose was to denounce it and promote his
interpretation of *agape*, the Greek word for brotherly love. But
there is no evidence that Paul here is opposing *eros*; in fact,
the word does not even occur in Paul's letters or elsewhere in
the New Testament! Barth goes on to say that love *(agape)* of
men is love of them in their "existential existence," and he
adds: "Suffice it that Love in this passage does not in the end
refer to some general and directly visible neighbourly or brotherly love."[3] His remark is a direct contradiction of Paul's
statement, "Love one another with brotherly love." Did not
Barth here demonstrate the unreliability of his method based

on spiritual guidance?

The "Spirit," it should be recognized, does not have a good record as a teacher of the meaning of the Bible. Zwingli with all his devotion to the Spirit, often misunderstood Scripture. And the Spirit seems to have the bad habit of giving different people different interpretations of the same passage! The Anabaptists believed that the Spirit taught them the meaning of biblical passages, but there was a wide variety among their interpretations of the same passages.

Certainly everyone has the right to create new ideas that are suggested to him by reading passages in the Bible and other literature. But if he ignores the evidence, he has no right to claim that these ideas come from the biblical author or that the Holy Spirit has told him what the Bible means. The spiritual guide has often turned out to be an unreliable guide, and spiritual interpretation is liable to be only subjective interpretation.

It is significant that all the major discoveries in understanding the Bible have come, not through spiritual revelation or mysticism, but through the hard work of linguistic, historical, scientific study. The Bible says of false prophets, "by their fruits you shall know them" (Matt. 7:16). This is a principle which can be applied to guides for biblical interpretation. In biblical interpretation, the "Spirit" has failed to produce the fruits of consistency and accuracy.

Theology as Guide

Theology is yet another guide to understanding the Bible that has been tried. When this is used, the interpretation of Scripture must agree with the theology of the reader, which may be the reader's own, or a traditional one, or a prominent contemporary theology. Jews used this guide before the Christian era as well as during it, and Christians have used it through the centuries. Hundreds of instances occur in the writings of the church fathers. For example, Justin Martyr in the second century tried to prove that Jesus is the incarnate Word by citing from Proverbs 8 "the Lord created me from the beginning" (*Dialogue with Trypho* 129). The writer in Proverbs, however, was describing God's wisdom. Justin ignored the context of the verse and allowed current theology to decide for him that the passage refers to Jesus--which it obviously does not.

In the sixteenth and seventeenth centuries Protestants were not allowed to find in the Bible any evidence contrary to Reformation doctrines. Paul in Romans 12:16 wrote that the gift of prophecy should be used "in proportion to our faith." Protestants misinterpreted this to mean that everything, including biblical exegesis, must agree with the faith--Protestant faith, that is! Protestantism, however, contained within itself the seeds of future reformation of the Reformation. Protestantism could not long escape a major fact of its own history: it originated in dissent and in study of the Bible--a fact that was an inspiration to future Protestant investigators of Scripture and a defense for their activities.

After the historical approach to the Bible arose, it often led to an interpretation of a passage that was at variance with the interpretation determined by theology. Therefore theologians have often opposed historical biblical study because they feared its detrimental effects on their beliefs. In the first half of the twentieth century many theologians advocated a return to theology-centered biblical interpretation.

One of the first of those theologians to do so was James Orr in his book, *The Problem of the Old Testament* (1906). He opposed the modern reconstruction of Hebrew history because it upset traditional theology. Later the cultural crisis resulting from the First World War created the desire for the security of the old, stable religion, and this motive stimulated many theologians in Germany to return to the theological approach. Karl Barth, for example, set aside literary and historical criticism in his commentary on Romans. He contended that it is theology, not historical study, which really produces understanding of the text. Adapting to his own purpose Paul's doctrine of revelation by faith, Barth said that the Bible is a witness to "primal history," which is not really history but the revelation of the God who speaks in Christ. Barth tried to combine "the witness of Scripture" and "the witness of the church" in his conservative theological exegesis of the Bible. Rudolf Bultmann, although he used the historical approach, was influenced by Barth's theology. He asserted that historical understanding of the Bible is only a pointer to the Bible's witness, and the witness discloses itself only to faith.

Many other German theologians in the 1920s and 1930s minimized the historical approach to the Bible. Carl Steurnägel maintained that Old Testament theology must be free from the chains of the history-of-religions approach. Walther Eichrodt asserted that it is impossible by historical means to penetrate to the essence of Old Testament religion, and that theological interpretation is required to explain the eternal truths of the Bible. He ascribed to the whole Bible a unified, systematic theology.

In the 1940s and 1950s the German theological revival spread to Great Britain and America, where it became prominent. Once again confusion and discouragement after a world war fostered a return to theology. Biblical theology, Neoorthodoxy, and *Heilsgeschichte* (salvation history) were popular in many seminaries and among theologians.

Characteristically, in that period advocates of theology as the guide claimed that one must be a (Christian) believer in order to understand the Bible. British examples included E. C. Hoskyns and A. G. Hebert; American examples included Paul Minear and John Knox.

Fortunately, several biblical scholars, especially some Germans, disagreed with the theological approach. Adolf Jülicher (1920) denounced Barth's attitude and procedure. He commented that Barth was a man of two worlds at war with one another in his breast, with two different bases for interpreting the Bible; one was historical science, and the other was Barth himself with his theological obsession. When he interpreted Paul, Barth set himself above Paul and above historical science. Barth, stated Jülicher correctly, rejected history and forced Paul to speak Barth's ideas.

Ernst Lohmeyer (1927) repudiated Bultmann's demand for an existential type of theological understanding of the biblical text in addition to a historical understanding. He charged that Bultmann had eliminated the distinction between faith and knowledge, with the result that he provided dogmatics, not historical knowledge.

Theologians argue that the biblical writers wrote from

faith and viewed life through the eyes of faith, and therefore we should share in that faith in order to understand the Bible. Paul Minear once maintained that objective study only confuses the situation by using the modern writer's historical methods and "by transposing problems of life into problems of thought."[4]

On the contrary, theology, or faith, as the guide to the study of the Bible invariably causes misunderstanding of the book. It is not the historical methods, but the faith of the interpreter, that confuses the situation when theology is the guide. There are two reasons that this is so. First, theology as the guide shuts out objective information necessary for understanding and evaluating passages. The biblical writers did indeed write "from faith to faith," but it often misled them. Sometimes they emerged with superstitious and mistaken beliefs about life. In fact, the effect of theology on the biblical writers is strong evidence against faith as the guide. Their faith did not take into account important facts that are now known, and if we make their faith our guide, we are liable to be under the same handicap. To believe as the biblical writers believed, is to exclude the knowledge that history and scientific investigation have disclosed since they wrote. Without that knowledge, we cannot see the Bible in relation to human civilization as a whole or evaluate the worth of biblical thought for the modern world.

The second reason theology is an inadequate guide is that it deprives the mind of an objective attitude and compels the mind to defend its faith by forcing the Bible to agree with it. When our beliefs determine our biblical interpretation, we cannot see when the Bible disagrees with our faith. Our interpretation is liable to be eisegesis, a reading into the text of what we want to find there. The history of the interpretation of the Bible illustrates this abundantly. Examples of anyone's discovering true understanding of the Bible *because* he had faith are very hard to find. Examples of persons who misunderstood it because they made faith their guide are abundant. There is an inherent weakness in the attempt to understand the Bible through the eyes of faith: *the eyes of faith are blind!* They are quite unreliable.

Philosophy as Guide

Some interpreters of the Bible have used philosophy as their guide. They believed in a particular philosophy of life, and they assumed that the Bible must be in harmony with it. Therefore they interpreted the Bible accordingly. Usually the philosophy was one that was current in the interpreters' own day. The biblical writers, however, did not foresee later philosophy, and any similarity between the Bible and the particular philosophy was generally coincidental or contrived. Sometimes the interpreter wanted to promote the philosophy he *really believed in* and at the same time *appear to be orthodox* by claiming that the Bible supported it.

Philo, an Alexandrian Jew at the beginning of the Christian era, tried to harmonize the Jewish Scriptures with Greek philosophy. In the third century Clement of Alexandria and Origen zealously used the allegorical method (see next chapter) to reinterpret the Bible in conformity with Greek philosophy.

Later, rationalism was one of the philosophical approaches employed. A tenet in it was that truth is found by reason alone. This sounds fine, but the rationalists' omission of empirical evidence and scientific investigation was a fatal weakness. The rationalists combined their philosophy with the belief that the Bible is the authority in religion. Therefore they interpreted the Bible so that all its contents seemed "reasonable." The Socinians in the sixteenth century led the way. When they encountered biblical words which they did not want to accept literally, they said the words must be meant metaphorically--references to Jesus' blood as a ransom, for example. In the seventeenth century Baruch Spinoza used reason to try to explain biblical verses, while Thomas Hobbes asserted that though some things in the Bible are above reason, nothing in it is contrary to reason.

In the eighteenth century the Deists rationalized the biblical miracle stories. Miracles are contrary to the laws of nature, but the miracle stories were assumed to be true because they are in the Bible. The Deists therefore, rationalized them. They solved the problem by claiming that either a natural event was misunderstood and reported as a miracle, or the story was only symbolic. Actually, belief in miracles was very prevalent in the superstitious ancient world. Judging from other literature as well as the Bible, the miracle stories were intended literally as miracles, and there is no evidence that they were based on a misunderstanding of natural events. The Deists rightly rejected belief in supernaturalism, but they urged a return to "natural religion," which was the religion of their philosophy and which they erroneously claimed is the religion of the Bible. An example of this view is Matthew Tindal's *Christianity as Old as the Creation: or the Gospel a Republication of the Religion of Nature*. In the nineteenth century the most prominent exponent of Christian rationalism was Heinrich Paulus. A German professor who effectively refuted such use of rationalism was Albert Schweitzer (1906).

At times the guide employed is a philosophy of history. In Hegel's dialectical philosophy of history, an idea or event, a "thesis," occurs, which is followed by an opposing idea or event, an "antithesis"; in the ensuing conflict, aspects of the two are combined in a "synthesis." F. C. Baur, David F. Strauss, and others of the Tübingen school in the nineteenth century applied this theory to the early church, declaring that conflict between the Judaizing Christians (thesis) and Paul and his followers (antithesis) produced catholic Christianity (synthesis). They carried this theory too far by overlooking other developments in the early church that contributed to the formation of catholic Christianity. It is also a mistake to apply Hegel's theory universally by assuming that history necessarily develops in this manner; sometimes what emerges triumphant is not a synthesis but one or the other of the two forces, or one of them may combine with a third force.

The popularity of Darwin's theory of evolution caused some writers in the last half of the nineteenth century to use it as a philosophical basis for the interpretation of social history and the Bible. According to the theory of social evolution, history and culture develop in a straight line, steadily getting better. As applied to the Old Testament, the view was that Judaism improved steadily, with the best religion in the latest books. As applied to the whole Bible, all the New Testament automatically must be better than any of the Old, and the later New Testament books present a higher, more spiritual religion than the earlier works in the New Testament.

But the fact of the matter is that history and religion do not always move straight forward. Some of the later biblical books are inferior in religion to some earlier ones, and parts of the Old Testament are superior to parts of the New (and vice versa).

In the twentieth century existentialist philosophy has had a harmful influence on biblical interpretation. Existentialism, which has its roots in the theology of Sören Kierkegaard (19th c.), is concerned with the problem of human existence in a special sense of the term "existence." According to this philosophy man is in a state of anxiety because he cannot resolve the paradoxes of the universe, the tensions between the finite and the infinite. Existentialism is generally hostile to Western philosophy, secularism, and science. It is injurious to biblical interpretation because it opposes scientific attitudes and the historical approach.

Barth's guide to biblical interpretation was a combination of evangelical theology and existentialist philosophy. Influenced by Kierkegaard, whom he frequently quotes, Barth was obsessed with the notion of paradox. To both Kierkegaard and Barth, everything basic in Christianity is a paradox: the gospel, Jesus as the Christ, Paul as an apostle, and so on. Barth's interpretation of Romans 2:1 illustrates his forcing the Bible to support his existentialist view of mankind. The verse condemns judging another person, but Barth interpreted it as meaning that man is nothing and pride in anything human is condemned--a notion that is not in the passage at all!

Modern Life as Guide

Some readers of the Bible assume that all of it must be relevant for today and that therefore application to modern life should be the guide to understanding it. The effort to read current meaning into the Bible has been called "the modernizing method" of interpretation. The historian is primarily concerned with the time and situation in which the Bible was written, but the modernizer is primarily concerned with the time and situation in which he or she lives. Modernizing the Bible is a process that has been going on ever since the book was written. In fact, the process began before the Bible was finished, for the writers of some later books of the Bible tried to modernize earlier portions of it. The Book of Chronicles, for example, retells the story of the Israelites from earlier biblical books in order to give more authority and prestige to the Levites, the lower clergy of the Chronicler's own day. New Testament writers tried unsuccessfully to make the Old Testament predict Christianity according to the beliefs in New Testament times. We have observed that the Jewish writer Philo in the first century A.D. and the church fathers later read Greek philosophy into the Bible. Ernest C. Colwell observed that in the days of the Reformation, some interpreters of Genesis tried to show that Adam was a Lutheran!

The rationalists of the eighteenth and nineteenth centuries not only reinterpreted the miracle stories to make them fit their own philosophy, but they tried to modernize Jesus by eliminating some of the Jewish aspects of his life. Exponents of "nineteenth-century liberalism" continued this process, as we shall see in chapter 6.

The Protestant Kingdom of God movement in the nineteenth and early twentieth centuries modernized Jesus' preaching. In this movement the kingdom of God was believed to be not a supernatural kingdom established suddenly and miraculously by God, but a society of social justice which obeys God's will and is to be built through universal love of neighbor. The purpose of the church is to construct that moral society. The founders of the movement were Albrecht Ritschl and Adolf von Harnack in Germany, and from there it spread to England and the United States. In America it was known as the Social Gospel movement, and its leaders were the Protestant ministers, Washington Gladden, Lyman Abbott, George Herron, and above all, Walter Rauschenbusch. It inspired the founding of the Federal Council of Churches in 1908.

The Kingdom of God movement sprang from the noblest of motives--concern for social and economic justice, but in respect to interpretation of the Bible, it was a mixture of truth and error. It rightly recognized that the kingdom of God in Judaism and in most of the New Testament would be on earth and would be an ideal society in which there would be no sin, and love of God and of man would prevail. The movement failed to acknowledge, however, that Jesus expected the kingdom to come suddenly and supernaturally and that he or God would reign from Jerusalem. To the extent that it eliminated the eschatology (beliefs about the end of the world or age) and supernaturalism, the movement modernized the kingdom of God and Jesus' message. This misinterpretation contributed to the downfall of the Social Gospel in learned circles.

The Christian "liberal" lives of Jesus are also examples of modernizing the Bible. These are described in chapter 6. An unusual type of modernization of Jesus was the attempt to make him an ideal businessman and salesman. The advocate of this view was Bruce Barton in his book *The Man Nobody Knows,* published in 1925. According to Barton, Jesus decided at an early age that he would be a businessman--he said he must do his Father's business (Luke 2:49, Authorized Version; the word "business" is not in the original Greek text, however). Jesus understood advertising, claimed Barton, because he called his message "good news." Biblical scholars had better judgment than to accept this notion. The Bible is often modernized by those advocating Christianity as good for business or as the ultimate in modern psychology.

Modernizing is an error that is difficult to avoid, for the constant pressure to find lessons, morals, and theology in the Bible that are relevant for today readily leads to misinterpretation of the text. People easily make the error because they are not aware that they are reading into the Bible thoughts that are not there. One method of dangerous contemporization of the Bible is to translate it into current vernacular that puts modern ideas into it. An example is *Good News for Modern Man.*

The classic work that opposes the modernization of the Bible is Henry J. Cadbury's book, *The Peril of Modernizing Jesus* (1937). Cadbury, professor of New Testament at Harvard, exposed the error of various liberal lives of Jesus that described him to suit modern interests. He recognized that even quoting the very words of the text does not prevent modernization of the Bible; if the words are interpreted in a modern sense that differs from their original meaning, misunderstanding results. Cadbury called for honest historical interpretation of the gospels.

The Bible indeed has value for the modern world, but it

is too much to expect that it contains nothing but modern thoughts and actions that fit life today. The authors of the Bible wrote for the people of their own times, with the beliefs, problems, and customs that the writers knew. The authors did not know what kind of world we would live in, and they did not write for us. If they had written for our times, their readers seldom would have known what they were talking about!

Sensationalism as Guide

A guide which is certain to result in biblical interpretation that is both new and erroneous is sensationalism. The mode in which this is presented to the unsuspecting public is usually a book or an article in a magazine or in a newspaper Sunday supplement. The writer's motive is to produce something which will arouse intense curiosity, attract attention to the author, and make some easy money. The writer may be orthodox or unorthodox. He may be seeking a new way to defend the faith, or he may be interested merely in personal fame and fortune.

We are not talking here about sincere, careful efforts to investigate and make new discoveries, using sound methods. Such efforts are both desirable and necessary for the growth of knowledge. Rather, the type of guide we are discussing is that in which the interpreter of the Bible is so carried away by his eagerness to produce something new and profitable that he is not objective and careful in his work. Sensationalism, not truth, is his goal.

The thought of sensationalism in biblical studies quickly brings to mind two radical books published in recent years. The thesis of Hugh Schonfield's *The Passover Plot* is that Jesus did not really die on the cross, but planned the event so that he appeared to die and come to life again. This wild thesis is a combination of speculation and misinterpretation of the gospels. Schonfield accepts as historical the gospel traditions of Jesus' forecasts of his death, and then proceeds to use them as evidence that Jesus plotted his apparent death. Although Schonfield knew some modern scholarship, he did not know enough of it to understand the evidence. He illustrates the principle that one should have a thorough, not just a cursory, knowledge of a field before writing in it. "A little knowledge is a dangerous thing."

John Allegro's *The Sacred Mushroom and the Cross* is even worse. Although this author has done some good work on the Dead Sea scrolls, and this book displays considerable erudition, the thesis of the book is based on wild speculation. Obsessed with sex, fertility cults, and the drug in the "sacred mushroom" in the ancient world, Allegro imagines that early Christianity was just a "drug cult" in which the Christ figure of the New Testament was worshiped through the phallic mushroom.

It was sensational, irresponsible biblical interpretation that Professor Cadbury had in mind when he remarked, ". . . the ambition to say something new often outweighs the ambition to say something true."[5]

The unreliable guides invariably lead to misunderstanding of the Bible. Experience has taught that the only dependable guide to follow is the historical approach. We turn now to a brief survey of how it arose and who were some of the pioneers in discovering it.

CHAPTER 4

ANCIENT AND MEDIEVAL INTERPRETATION

Accurate understanding of the Bible has been achieved slowly. This is not surprising, considering that lack of knowledge, mistaken beliefs, and unreliable guides have so often blocked its advance, as we have seen. Nevertheless, progress occurred, because some scholars dared to think and to investigate, in spite of opposition and hostility.

ANCIENT INTERPRETATION

When people in the ancient world interpreted Scripture, they did not use the historical approach, at least not in the modern sense of the term. They did not try to discover the particular situation in which an author wrote or the cultural background of the passage. Nor did they realize that the words might have had a different meaning in biblical times than in their own day. Often they ignored the context.

Motives and Methods of Jewish Interpretation

Biblical exegesis in ancient Judaism consisted mainly of interpretation of the Hebrew Scriptures by the rabbis, beginning in mid-second century B.C. and extending through the fifth century A.D. These rabbinical interpretations were codified in the Talmud. The earliest portion of the Talmud is the Mishnah, which was the oral torah, or "oral law," of the Pharisees. The written Torah, or "written law," consisted of the Hebrew Scriptures (which Christians labeled as the "Old Testament), especially the Pentateuch. Jewish biblical interpretation was of two types: *halachah*, which is legalistic in form, and *haggadah*, which consists of narratives and maxims.

Several motives underlay the Jewish interpretation of Scripture. Sometimes an interpreter genuinely tried to determine what a passage meant, but sometimes he tried to interpret it to make it support his beliefs. Sometimes a sect tried

to make Scripture support its own history. The Essenes at
Qumran, for example, claimed that some biblical passages
refer to and predict the advent of their sect and its great
Teacher of Righteousness. Another motive for interpreting
the Old Testament was to clear up ambiguity on how to apply
the Torah more fully to current life. For example, the Hebrew Scriptures forbid work on the Sabbath, but the question
arose later, what is work? Therefore the Pharisees made de-
cisions on what is, and what is not, legal activity on the Sabbath. The rabbis also wanted to reconcile and to harmonize
conflicting biblical passages by reinterpreting them. (Some
Jewish scribes, and later many Christian scribes, used a more
direct method to reconcile passages; they changed the text of
Scripture accordingly when they produced new copies.) The desire to interpret Scripture to fit a subsequent period of history
and the motive to reconcile discrepancies invariably resulted
in misinterpretation.

The methods of biblical interpretation generally used in
ancient Judaism would not meet modern standards. One technique was to lift the passage out of its context. With this method an interpreter ignores what the surrounding verses are talking about, and thus he can read into the passage thoughts which
the author never had in mind. Here is an example from *Pirke
Aboth* (Sayings of the Fathers), a book in the Mishnah. A passage in the Psalms reads:

> Blessed is the man who walks not in the counsel of the
> wicked, nor stands in the way of sinners, nor sits in the
> seat of the scornful; but his delight is in the Lord, and
> on his law he meditates day and night (Psalms 1:1-2).

The interpretation in *Pirke Aboth* reads:

> Rabbi Hananiah ben Teradion [early 2d c. A.D.] said,
> "If two sit together and no words of the law (are spoken)
> between them, there is the seat of the scornful'" (*Pirke
> Aboth* 3.2).

Although this interpretation agrees with the psalm in empha-
sizing the necessity of thinking about the law, it reinterprets

the term "the scornful"; the term no longer refers to those who
scorn or scoff at others, but to any two men sitting together
who fail to quote and discuss the Torah. Thus Rabbi Hananiah
ignored part of the context and the literal meaning of a word.

In ancient times the two main methods of biblical interpretation in Judaism were the literal and the allegorical. In literal interpretation, the words in the text are accepted at face value; they are presumed to mean what they say. The interpreter
looks for the plain meaning of the passage. In the allegorical
method, details are not interpreted in their plain meaning, but
are said to represent something else. The Greek Stoics had
used this device to reinterpret the poems of Homer and Hesiod
to make them fit Stoic philosophy; the human traits of the gods
in the myths were removed in this manner. Although a few
Jews in Alexandria in the second and first centuries B. C. had
borrowed this method from the Greeks, Philo of Alexandria in
the first century A. D. was the first Jew to apply it extensively.
He claimed that Scripture has two meanings, literal and allegorical, but that the latter is more significant. Philo sought
to recommend Judaism to the pagan world (this was yet another
motive for interpreting the Bible), so he employed allegorical
interpretation to try to show that the Jewish Scriptures contain
Stoic, Platonic, and Neo-Pythagorean philosophy. In allegorical interpretation the alleged "hidden" meaning of letters,
numbers, words, and grammar could be virtually anything the
interpreter desired, and thus he could make the Bible say whatever he wanted it to say !

Occasionally Jews employed a third method of biblical
interpretation, the typological. In this method some event is
regarded as typifying something else; some similarity in the
pattern of both is assumed to exist.

Some Jewish interpretation of the Old Testament was
claimed to be obtained by direct revelation from the Spirit of
God. The Essenes, or Covenanters, at Qumran, who wrote the
Dead Sea scrolls, studied the written law every night, at which
time they believed that new interpretations were divinely revealed to them. Whenever a member of the sect received such
a "revelation," he was obligated to pass it on to others. The
revelations usually supported the eschatological views of the
sect. Those beliefs included the convictions that the end of the

present age was near, that the end would include a judgment day, and that the Essenes were God's chosen people, "Sons of Light," who would soon fight and defeat the other humans on earth, "Sons of Darkness." A major characteristic of their biblical interpretation was that they tried to make the Scriptures predict the history of their own sect; for example, they said that they fulfilled the prophecy that God would make a new covenant (Jer. 31:31-34). As we might expect, this spiritual approach to interpretation usually resulted in misinterpretation.

At the beginning of the first century A.D. the Jewish rabbi Hillel in Palestine listed seven rules for the interpretation of Scripture. Most of these exegetical rules are unreliable, but there is some merit in three of them. They are the rules that one may draw inferences that are based on a similar passage elsewhere, inferences from the context, and inferences from particular case to general rule and vice versa. Hillel did not create the rules, but he deserves credit for his effort to establish a set of objective guidelines. Other rabbis later expanded his list.

Objective rules for the interpretation of Scripture are necessary for accurate biblical study. Hillel's rules, however, were not adequate, and they failed to place rabbinic interpretation on a sound basis. The rabbis were generally unaware of the historical situation in which the Bible was written; they often ignored the context of a word or a passage; they failed to distinguish between the essential and the incidental elements; and sometimes their interpretation was very speculative. An example of their speculative exegesis is the opinion that because there are 613 letters in the Hebrew text of the Ten Commandments, there should 613 commandments in the Oral Law!

Motives and Methods of Christian Interpretation

The motives behind early Christian interpretation of the Bible were similar to those in Judaism. Occasionally a Christian interpreter really tried to determine what the passage meant. But often he wanted to make the Old Testament predict Christian history. And sometimes his purpose was to use Scripture to help solve a problem in the church. After the middle of the second century, Christians often desired to reconcile

differences within the Bible and to make the Bible agree with
Greek philosophy.

The earliest examples known to us of Christian exegesis
of Scripture are in the New Testament where quotations from
the Old Testament are interpreted. The early Christians were
just as guilty as the Jews of ignoring the context and original
meaning of biblical passages. In fact, the early Christian methods of interpreting Scripture were borrowed from Judaism.
Lifting a passage out of context and applying it to a very different kind of situation from that which the author had in mind is
known today as the "proof-text method" of interpretation. Regrettably, it is the most persistent method; it is popular because with it a person can make the Bible support any idea.

A few examples of interpreting passages out of context
will demonstrate the unreliability of the method. In Acts 2:27
a verse from the Psalms (16:10) is quoted as a divine prophecy
of Jesus' resurrection. The application to Jesus was suggested
by the statement "you (the Lord) will not let your holy one see
decay" (the quotation in Acts, with the main verb in the future
tense, is from the Septuagint (Ps. 15:10), not from the Hebrew
text). "Holy One" became a synonym for the Christ, and the
idea of not seeing decay was easily applied to Jesus' death and
resurrection. The quotation does not fit, however, because the
reference in the psalm is to the psalmist himself, not to Jesus.
The author of the Gospel of Matthew was especially prone to
quote and misinterpret the Old Testament. In 1:22-23 he claims
that Jesus' birth "fulfills" Isaiah 7:14. The passage in Isaiah
is not a reference to Jesus but to a child whose mother would
name him "Immanuel" and in whose day "all the land will be
briars and thorns" (Isaiah 7:24). The term "virgin" in the
Septuagint (the term is "young woman" in the original text in
Hebrew) caused the author of the gospel to connect the passage
with the virgin-birth story about Jesus. He disregarded the
facts that Jesus was not named "Immanuel" and that the context of the passage does not fit— all the land did not become
briars and thorns. In Matthew 2:17-18 a passage in Jeremiah
(31:15) is interpreted as a prophecy of the story of the slaughter of male babies by Herod (an event which never occurred,
judging from evidence both outside and inside the Bible), but
the passage in Jeremiah is not referring to such a situation.

In Jeremiah the reference is clearly to the past, but in Matthew the passage is misinterpreted as a reference to the future.

In some New Testament passages the Old Testament is interpreted more accurately. Mark 2:25-26 mentions the time that David and the men with him were hungry and broke the law by eating holy bread that only the priests should eat (1 Sam. 21:3-6). In the Marcan story the reference is used to support the breaking of the law by Jesus and his disciples when they picked grain on the Sabbath. In Matthew 9:13 the author quotes "I desire mercy" from Hosea in support of Jesus' association with sinners. In each of these two cases the Old Testament is quoted as expressing a principle which is then reasonably applied to the Christian situation. Although the Christian situation in each case is very different from the Hebrew situation, the Old Testament is not misinterpreted. These two gospel passages do not claim that the Christian situation "fulfills" Scripture or that the Scriptures are referring to or prophesying the Christian situation; the gospel authors are only applying to a Christian situation an idea or principle that is in Scripture. This is an important distinction. The examples cited from Acts and Matthew 1 and 2, on the other hand, claim that the Old Testament passages mention things that they do not refer to at all.

Occasionally Paul used the typological method of interpretation of the Old Testament. In 1 Corinthians 10:1-4 he regards the crossing of the Red Sea by the Israelites as a typology of Christian baptism, the manna in the wilderness eaten by them and the water drunk by them as a typology of the Lord's Supper, and the rock from which Moses miraculously obtained the water as a typology of Christ. Such interpretation is forced, to say the least. The crossing of the Red Sea corresponds to baptism only in that water happens to be involved in both; the analogy is especially weak because in the story of the crossing of the sea the Israelites were not touched by water, whereas a water baptism in which the baptized is not touched by water would be unthinkable. The only link between the Mosaic food and drink and the Lord's Supper is that in both cases the food and drink are associated with supernaturalism. The only symbolic connection between the rock and the Christ is that theoretically drink came from both (water from the rock;

blood from Jesus). The main connecting link, however, is Paul's imagination!

Some Christian gnostics in the second and third centuries indulged in very fanciful interpretation of the Bible. An example of their speculation is in the *Gospel of Philip* (71) where the author states that Adam came into being from two virgins, and therefore Christ was born from a virgin to rectify Adam's fall.

The allegorical method of interpretation became prominent in the church in the second and third centuries, especially in Alexandria. In this method letters and words are interpreted as symbolizing more than their plain meaning. Paul used it in Galatians 4:22-26 in his interpretation of Genesis 16:15 and 21:2; he even called the Genesis statement an allegory (which it is not). Christian gnostics in the second century were the first to freely allegorize the New Testament, although Marcion was an exception. Some church fathers did it too, especially Clement of Alexandria and his pupil Origin around the beginning of the third century. All allegorical interpretations— Greek, Jewish, and Christian— are utterly subjective and are misinterpretations of the text, usually to support the writer's own particular interests. The Christian Arnobius (ca. 300) attacked the allegorizing of their own myths by pagans, but did not object to Christian use of the same method. Tertullian (ca. 200) accepted the literal meaning except when it conflicted with the teaching of the church; when a passage did conflict, he interpreted it allegorically to make it orthodox. Jerome (ca. 400) in his later years turned more to literal interpretation, yet he continued to use the allegorical when the plain meaning seemed absurd or meaningless.

Linguistic and Literary Study

Movement in a scientific direction began slowly with linguistic and literary study. The earliest form was the use of grammar to obtain the plain meaning when the text was interpreted literally. Both Jews and Christians employed the grammatical method, in varying degrees, according to the knowledge and inclination of the interpreter.

A few scholars applied linguistic knowledge for another

purpose; namely, they translated the Bible into the language of those Jews and Christians who did not know the language, or languages, of their Scriptures. Translation made the Bible available to more readers for study. Equally important, the act of translation required very close attention to the grammar, syntax, and vocabulary of the text. Careful philological examination of literature is invariably conducive to fuller understanding of it.

The earliest work approaching translation of any of the Bible apparently was the oral paraphrasing in Aramaic of the Hebrew text when it was read in the synagogues of Palestine after the Exile (late sixth century B.C.). This was done for the sake of the congregation, because Jews in Palestine had adopted Aramaic as their language and no longer knew Hebrew. The paraphrases were not based on close examination of the text, however, and thus do not qualify as examples of the beginnings of scientific translation.

In the third and second centuries B.C., Jewish scholars in Alexandria translated the Old Testament into Greek, which is the version known as the Septuagint. This careful translation of the text was made for the benefit of the Diaspora Jews who lived outside of Palestine and spoke Greek, not Hebrew. In the second century A.D. some others too translated the Old Testament into Greek. The first was Aquila, who was born a pagan, converted to Christianity, was excommunicated for his astrological studies, and then converted to Judaism. He made a very literal translation directly from the Hebrew text (ca. 140). Sometime in the same century Theodotion revised the Septuagint, using the Hebrew text as a guide. Less accurate was the translation made late in the second century by Symmachus. His main concern was to produce a readable style and to modify the human characteristics of God in the Old Testament. He was a member of a Jewish-Christian sect, the Ebionites.

As Christianity expanded, it acquired many members who did not know Greek, and therefore the Bible was translated into their languages. Apparently the New Testament was translated into Latin by the end of the second century, and by the middle of the third the Greek Septuagint was translated into Latin—a translation of a translation. This version is known as Old Lat-

in, and may have originated in Carthage. In the middle of the
second century Tatian, an ascetic Gnostic, arranged the Greek
text of the four gospels into a continuous narrative, known as
the Diatessaron. It was soon translated into Syriac for use in
the Syrian Church. The whole Bible (except the Catholic Epistles and Revelation, which were not in the Syrian canon) was
translated into Syriac in the fifth century; this official version
replaced the Diatessaron in the Syrian Church. By the end of
the fifth century the Bible had been translated into the following languages also: Gothic, Coptic, Georgian, Armenian, and
Ethiopic. These translations were made not primarily for laymen to read, but so that clergy could read the Bible aloud in
church services and laymen would understand it when it was
thus read.

Jerome produced a new Latin translation of the Bible,
known as the Vulgate. Originally Pope Damasus commissioned
him to revise the Old Latin text of the canonical gospels, because there were many variant readings in the manuscripts cir-
culating in the churches. Jerome expanded his project to include the whole Bible. He began by comparing Old Latin manuscripts of the New Testament and by using the Septuagint for
the Old Testament. Eventually he recognized the principle that
it is necessary to go back to the original languages. The Old
Latin manuscripts varied so much among themselves that he
could not determine by examining them which, if any, represented the original text. Furthermore, Jews ridiculed translation from the Septuagint and insisted that translation of their
Scriptures should be made from the original language, Hebrew.
Consequently Jerome translated the gospels from the Greek
text and the Old Testament from the Hebrew text. Tradition
ascribed the whole Vulgate to Jerome, but is is very probable
that he translated only portions of it—in the New Testament,
only the gospels. [6] Jerome was wise to go back to the original
languages, but Augustine faulted him for using the Hebrew text
of the Old Testament instead of the Old Latin.

Another kind of linguistic and literary biblical study to
appear early was that which questioned the authorship of some
of the books. In chapter two we observed that erroneous traditions of authorship have caused misunderstanding of the Bible.
Correcting these mistaken traditions, therefore, is an impor-

tant field of study. In the second century A.D. the Christian
sect known as the Nazarenes, as well as the pagan philosopher
Celsus, rejected the tradition that Moses wrote the first five
books of the Bible. Celsus concluded that more than one writer must have written them. Origen questioned the traditional
authorship of the Epistle to the Hebrews on the grounds that it
lacks Paul's roughness of style and diction. Nevertheless, he
did not definitely reject the tradition, for he realized that most
churches in his day believed that Paul wrote Hebrews. Origen's pupil Dionysius compared the language, style, and thought
of the Book of Revelation with that of the Gospel of John. He
concluded that there are so many differences between them that
the two books could not have been written by the same "John. "
A few years later Porphyry, a pagan Neoplatonic philosopher,
demonstrated that the Book of Daniel was written in the second
century B.C. instead of in the sixth century B.C. as tradition
claimed.

          Textual criticism is primarily the effort to determine
the original text by comparing variant readings of it. Jerome,
as we have seen, started to establish the text of the Old Latin
version, but he abandoned the attempt in favor of manuscripts
in the original Greek and Hebrew. Origen, who preceded him,
was the outstanding pioneer in textual criticism of the Old Testament. He observed that copies of the Septuagint did not always agree among themselves and that various Greek versions
of the Old Testament sometimes differed from each other.
From Jewish scholars he learned that the Hebrew text at
times disagreed with the Greek versions. The Septuagint
was in general use in the churches, so Origen decided to produce an accurate Septuagint text. For this purpose he learned
Hebrew. Then he systematically compared the Septuagint with
other Greek versions and with the Hebrew text. Afterwards
he produced the *Hexapla*, an arrangement of the whole Old Testament in six parallel columns. The first column contained
the Hebrew text, and the second was a transliteration of that
text into Greek letters. The other columns contained four
Greek versions: the one translated by Aquila, the one by Symmachus, the Septuagint as revised by Origen, and the translation made by Theodotion. In some sections he used up to three
more Greek versions, making a total of nine columns. With

this arrangement scholars could readily compare the different texts. This project was a tremendous undertaking, and it has been estimated that the book consisted of about 6,500 pages.

Through the centuries certain types of written works were created which have proved to be useful tools for biblical study. One type is the commentary. The earliest verse-by-verse commentaries on a book of the Bible are those written by the Essenes at Qumran. These commentaries are included in the Dead Sea scrolls, written between mid-second century B.C. and mid-first century A.D. Fragments have been found of the Essenes' commentaries on Isaiah, Hosea, Micah, Nahum, Habakkuk, and the Psalms. In these commentaries the Essenes were determined to find scriptural prophecies of the history of their sect and its enemies. The Christian gnostic teacher Heracleon wrote a commentary on the Gospel of John in the second century A.D. He interpreted John to support Valentinian gnosticism. Only fragments of his book have survived, mainly in quotations from it in Origen's commentary on the same gospel. The commentary idea was adopted by some church fathers, including Origen, Theodore of Mopsuestia, and Jerome, who wrote many works of this type. None of these early commentaries meet modern standards, partly because all their authors were too concerned with eisegesis, reading into the Bible what they wanted it to say.

A second type of tool which can be useful for biblical study is the introduction to the whole Bible or to its individual books. The first recorded introduction to the Bible was *Introduction to the Divine Writings*, written by Adrianos of the School of Antioch around A.D. 450.

A different kind of aid to biblical study appeared when the four gospels were divided into numbered sections. Originally there were no chapter and verse divisions in the Bible, and the first step in that direction was the creation of sections. They have been called "Ammonian sections" on the assumption that they were the work of Ammonius Saccas. It is more probable that Eusebius produced them early in the fourth century for use in his "canons," or tables. The Eusebian canons list by their section numbers the parallel passages in the gospels. With these tables, readers using the Greek text could locate and compare the same narrative in whichever gospels con-

tained it. The sections were longer than the present verse divisions and shorter than the present chapters.

Schools

Ancient schools interpreted the Bible and were forerunners of the more enlightened work in schools centuries later.
Two famous rabbinical schools at the beginning of the Christian
era were those of Shammai and Hillel, both in Jerusalem.
They often disagreed, with Shammai teaching a strict interpretation of the Torah, and Hillel taking a more liberal view.

A Christian catechetical school was established at Alexandria late in the second century, with Pantaenus as its first
teacher. It was most influential under the leadership of Clement and Origen, and continued into the fourth century. After
Origen moved to Caesarea in 231, he established there another
school, which also became famous. These schools produced
theological treatises, commentaries, and Origen's *Hexapla*.

The best interpretation of the Bible in the ancient world
was conducted in the fourth and fifth centuries by the "School
of Antioch," as it was later called. This monastery school
was influenced by Greek rhetoric and philosophy and by non-
Alexandrian Jewish interpretation of the Old Testament. Consequently it rejected allegorical interpretation and insisted
that the Bible be understood in its literal sense. It paid attention to context, philology, and to a limited extent, the historical setting of a passage. The school's chief teacher was
Diodore of Tarsus, and his most famous pupils were Theodore
of Mopsuestia and John Chrysostom. This school recognized
that some parts of the Bible are of more value than others, and
it realized that human factors affected the writing of Scripture.
Theodore insisted on studying a passage as a whole instead of
using a collection of separate texts isolated from their respective contexts. He said that Old Testament prophecy prepared
the way for Christ, but it did not predict him. The Antiochene
School's interpretation of Scripture led it to emphasize the humanity of Jesus and the oneness of God. It was condemned
for heresy and disappeared. Allegorical interpretation became
dominant in Christianity for many centuries. The only lasting
influence of the school was through the writings of its leaders

and a few Fathers influenced by them, chiefly Augustine and
Jerome.

Thus in antiquity some forerunners of the historical approach appeared. A few Fathers preferred the literal interpretation of Scripture. Linguistic knowledge was applied light-
ly to interpretation and more fully to translation. Significant
work was conducted in textual criticism. Important types of
tools were constructed (though the quality of these tools was
quite unsatisfactory): a set of rules for the interpretation of
Scripture, commentaries on biblical books, and an introduction to the Bible. The School of Antioch tried to direct biblical interpretation in a sensible direction.

On the other hand, during this period some very regressive patterns were formed. The heated controversies with
heretics, especially gnostics, induced the Fathers to assert
that only the church has the right to interpret Scripture. Controversies with Jews and pagans made Christians zealous to
prove that Jesus was the Messiah, or Christ, and that the Old
Testament is a book of prophecy of Jesus and Christianity. After the downfall of the School of Antioch, allegorical and mystical interpretation of the Bible triumphed.

MEDIEVAL INTERPRETATION

In the West the Middle Ages (considered as A.D. 500-1500)
was a period of the spread and consolidation of Christianity, of
intense religious intolerance, and of the establishment of schools
and universities. It also was a time of gradual growth of linguistic knowledge and, in the fifteenth century, of rapid increase
in literary knowledge. All of those historical developments affected biblical interpretation, each in its own way.

Traditional Interpretation

In the first half of the Middle Ages both Jewish and Christian biblical interpretation was quite traditional. Jewish exegesis followed the rabbinic comments preserved in the Talmud.
However, the Karaites, or Qaraites, a Jewish sect founded in

the eighth century, was an exception; it rejected the talmudic
tradition and interpreted Scripture directly from the text.
Christian interpretation was largely a repetition of the orthodox exegesis of the Fathers; excerpts or summaries of some
of their comments were written in the margins of the biblical
texts to facilitate their use. These explanatory notes are
called "scholia." Christians in the West studied the Latin
scholia to find support for ecclesiastical dogmas. Even the
biblical commentaries produced in this period generally consisted of patristic quotations, repeated from one commentary
to another. In the eighth century Bede in England wrote commentaries consisting of a compilation of his own selection
from the comments of the church fathers, mainly the four
great Latin Fathers: Augustine, Jerome, Ambrose, and Gregory the Great.

Peter Abelard, a French dialectician and theologian in
the early twelfth century, arranged together contradictory
statements from the Fathers in his *Sic et Non* (So and Not
[So]). Although his purpose was to facilitate discussion and
to help resolve the seeming contradictions, the eventual effect
of pointing out the contradictions was to detract from the authority of patristic interpretation. From our perspective, the
decline of rabbinic and patristic authority was a forward step,
for the rabbis and church fathers did not understand Scripture
well enough to determine the meaning of the Bible. Release
from their authority gave Jews and Christians freedom to make
new interpretations.

Acceptance of the "fourfold sense" of Scripture was characteristic of Jews and Christians in the Middle Ages, at least
until the twelfth century. Biblical passages were believed to
have four different senses, or meanings: the literal, the allegorical, the moral, and the anagogical (mystic, spiritual).
There was considerable variety of thought on the subject, however, and some writers were concerned with only two or three
senses in the text. Cabalistic interpretation was prevalent in
Judaism in the late Middle Ages. This method was a mystical
approach in which each letter was assumed to contain sacred
mysteries which the interpreter discovered by rearranging letters, by using their numerical value, and by treating each letter as the initial of another word.

Gradually interest turned more toward the literal sense. In the thirteenth century the Dominicans Albertus Magnus and Thomas Aquinas and the Franciscan Bonaventure, strengthened the position of the literal by insisting that the senses of Scripture are not separate from each other, and that the literal sense must be found first and the others must be based on it. Nevertheless, their use of the literal sense was too theological to constitute a historical approach. Thomist influence fostered a shift toward emphasis on the literal sense in the fourteenth century, led by Pierre Auriol, a French Franciscan professor. Another Franciscan, Nicholas (or Nicolaus) of Lyra, who was a regent master in the Paris university, wrote a commentary on the Bible in which he tried to give a fully literal interpretation. It was entitled *According to the Literal* [Sense]. Later he wrote a biblical commentary according to the anagogical sense, but his main interest and influence was in the literal sense. In the same century Nicholas Trivet (or Trevet), a Dominican at Oxford, wrote literal commentaries on the Bible; John Wycliffe rejected authoritative and allegorical interpretations in favor of the literal. Yet literal interpretation declined in the fifteenth century—it was too unorthodox!

Rise of Schools and Universities

The rise of monastic and cathedral schools and the establishment of universities contributed to the decline of reliance on traditional interpretation of the Bible. Late in the eighth century Charlemagne energetically fostered education to facilitate the governance of his domain through an efficient clergy under his control. With the aid of two advisers, Alcuin of York and Theodulf of Orléans, he promoted schools in monasteries and cathedrals throughout his empire. With Charlemagne's support, Alcuin established a palace library at Aachen (renamed Aix-la-Chapelle) and, after he was appointed abbot at Tours, a library there. Charlemagne's widespread expansion of the number of schools helped to prepare the way for more learned study of the Bible in future years. Even more important was the founding of many universities in the twelfth to fifteenth centuries. Among these universities, the following later made significant contributions to understanding the Bible (listed in the order of founding): Paris, Oxford, Cambridge, Prague, Heidelberg, Cologne, Leipzig, Louvain, and Freiburg.

In the twelfth century the whole Bible was brought into the classroom and was taught in the cathedral and monastic schools. Hugh of St. Victor at the abbey of that name in Paris seems to have been a leader in the movement. Later the Bible was taught in the universities. The teachers were usually friars and monks. The classroom situation required lectures on the meaning of biblical passages. The lectures were on theology and morality and prepared the students for future preaching. Lectures and classroom discussion were conducive to fresh biblical study instead of the mere repetition of the old patristic comments.

Role of Philosophy

In ancient times the philosophy of Plato had influenced Jewish thought in the Wisdom of Solomon and the writings of Philo. Clement of Alexandria, Origen, and especially Augustine incorporated Platonism in Christian theology. The influence of Augustine's writings caused a widespread adoption of Platonic ideas in Christian mysticism in the medieval church; this is particularly true of the writings of Bernard of Clairvaux. This development tended to block the rise of historical study of the Bible.

Aristotle's philosophy, on the other hand, afforded a higher position to human reason and to realism. It was not popular in either Judaism or Christianity in ancient and early medieval times. Late in the twelfth century, however, a Jewish rabbi who was tutored by Arabs, Moses ben Maimon (called Maimonides), impressed with Aristotle's views, tried to harmonize Jewish faith and human reason in his treatise, *Guide for the Perplexed*. He interpreted the Old Testament rationally. He used reason to evaluate the Hebrew laws, and concluded that some of of them were suitable only for ancient times. Another Jewish scholar, Levi ben Gershon (called Gersonides) in the fourteenth century was a rationalist too, but with a significant difference. Maimonides assumed that Scripture agrees with reason, so he interpreted it accordingly; Gersonides, however, recognized the possibility that Bible and reason may disagree. He maintained that whenever they are not in harmony, the Bible "cannot prevent us from holding that to be true which our reason prompts us to believe." Thus the difference between the two men is that with Maimonides the Bible is the superior authority, whereas with Gersonides (as with Saadia ben Joseph, 10th c.) reason is superior.

Some Christian thinkers, too, absorbed Aristotelian philosophy. Peter Abelard in the twelfth century adopted a moderate realism, a middle course between extreme realism and the nominalism current in his time. He regarded Aristotle and reason as equal to the Bible and the Fathers. He distinguished between important and unimportant elements in Scripture, and between Scripture and "the word of God." In the next century Albertus Magnus made a synthesis of theology and Aristotelianism. He was influenced by Jewish and Arabian writers as well as by Aristotle. While teaching at the university in Paris, he taught Thomas Aquinas. Aquinas followed him in making a similar synthesis, but his was much more systematic than that of his teacher. Aquinas was acquainted with Maimonides' writing and often referred to him. Maimonides had contended that the two sources of knowledge of God are revelation and reason. Aquinas agreed, but added a third source, intuitive vision. He maintained that some Christian doctrines cannot be established by reason, yet they cannot be contrary to reason. Nevertheless, when faith and reason appeared to conflict, Aquinas chose faith. His writings had a major impact on Christian theology and, less directly, on biblical interpretation.

Numerous theologians in the Middle Ages were interested in the use of philosophy as a means to attain a fuller understanding of Christian doctrine. They were disturbed, too, by the disagreement at times between faith and reason. Although they continued to believe that Scripture and the Fathers are the main source of the knowledge of God, they were convinced that reason, enlightened by the Holy Spirit, could provide deeper insight.

Throughout the Middle Ages another important cultural contact was occurring. Arabs were passing on to Jews and Christians the tremendous scientific advances which Arabs had made in the Middle East. Scientific discoveries tend to create a scientific attitude or even a scientific philosophy of life. The psychological and intellectual effect of scientific thought is that it opens the way for further discoveries and the acceptance of new ideas. Thus the Arabs contributed indirectly to the rise later of a new approach to the Bible, namely, the historical.

Linguistic and Literary Study

Important constructive developments appeared which were forerunners of the historical approach to the Bible. The first advance was in the field of language. Linguistic study of the text was the main cause of the decline of those unreliable methods of interpretation, the allegorical and the anagogical. We saw that in the early Middle Ages Jews generally relied on comments in the Talmud, instead of making their own direct study of the Hebrew text. The Karaites, however, made grammar their guide in direct exegesis of Scripture. This sect, incidentally, survives today, with about 10,000 members in Egypt and Turkey. It was a threat to rabbinic Judaism because of its refusal to follow traditional rabbinic interpretation. Saadia ben Joseph, the Gaon (president) of the Jewish academy at Sura in Mesopotamia, rose to the rabbis' defense and employed the Karaites' own weapon, linguistic interpretation. He preferred the literal sense of Scripture and made Hebrew philology the means of finding it. His grammatical and lexicographical studies laid the foundation for the interpretation of the Hebrew Scriptures by Spanish and French Jews in the following centuries.

Christian interpretation of the Jewish Scriptures was another threat to rabbinic Judaism. Many Jewish exegetes opposed the Christian use of the Old Testament to support the claim that Jesus was the Christ and had replaced the Torah. At first Jews attacked and Christians were on the defensive, but by the time of the Crusades the Christians took the offensive. The controversy was manifest in various treatises and public debates as well as in scriptural interpretation. A motive behind Jewish exegesis at the time often was to fortify Jews against Christian proselytizing efforts.

After Saadia, founders of the science of Hebrew gram-

mar and lexicology were Menahem ben Saruk (10th c.), Ye-
huda Hayyuj (10th c.), and Abuwalid Ibn Janah (called Rabbi
Johan; 11th c.). They learned methodology from the Arabs.
Other prominent Hebrew grammarians were the French Jew
Solomon ben Isaac (called Rashi; 11th c.), the great Jewish
scholar from Spain, Abraham Ibn Ezra (12th c.), and David
Kimhi (known as Radak; early 13th c.), a Jew living in south-
eastern France. Kimhi wrote *Book of Completeness*, which
for many years was the leading Hebrew grammar, and *Book
of Roots*, a Hebrew lexicon, or dictionary.

For centuries Christians in the West knew the Hebrew
Scriptures almost exclusively in the Latin Vulgate. In contrast,
Christians in the East knew them only in Greek translation because Greek was the language of the Eastern Church. Contact
in the twelfth century with Jewish biblical scholars introduced
some Christians in the West to the Hebrew text of the Old Testament and to Hebrew grammar, and they, too, began to interpret directly from the Hebrew text. The monastic school of
St. Victor in Paris led the way in applying Hebrew linguistics
to interpretation. The school's most influential teachers of
Hebrew were Hugh of St. Victor and Andrew of St. Victor.
Early in the fourteenth century Nicholas of Lyra learned Hebrew grammar from Spanish Jews and acquired from them the
Hebrew text of their Scriptures; then he made his own studies
of the Hebrew text.

Until the thirteenth century, Christians in the West did
not study the text of the New Testament in its original language,
Greek. Then Robert Grosseteste of Oxford learned Greek and
carefully applied it to his study of the New Testament and the
Septuagint. Later in the same century Roger Bacon wrote both
Greek and Hebrew grammars, and advocated knowledge of
Greek and Hebrew as necessary for understanding the Bible.
In the fourteenth century the Council of Vienne (1311-12) de-
creed that chairs for the teaching of Greek, Hebrew, and other
Eastern languages be established and endowed in the principle
Christian schools and universities. This decree was not car-
ried out fully, but it demonstrates that there was a growing
recognition of the importance of knowing the languages essen-
tial for the study of the Bible, humanities, and science.

In Western Christianity contact with Greeks and Greek

literature did for New Testament studies what contact with Jewish scholars did for Old Testament studies. When the Turks
conquered Constantinople in 1453, Byzantine Christians fled to
Italy, bringing with them knowledge of the Greek language, the
Greek text of the New Testament, and the Greek classics. This
event was an important factor in the early Renaissance. The
Greek text of the New Testament had been almost unknown in
the West for centuries. Acquisition of the Greek language and
Greek text made possible the study of the text in its original
language. Like grammatical study of the text of the Old Testament, this study made literal interpretation inevitable and
exposed the fallacy of allegorical and spiritual interpretations.

Important work in translating the Scriptures into English
was accomplished in the medieval period. Portions of the Bible were translated into Anglo-Saxon in the tenth century and
into Middle English in the thirteenth century. The first complete translation of the Bible into English was the Wycliffe Bible (1382), a translation of the Latin Vulgate. Wycliffe did not
translate all of it himself, but his leadership was responsible
for the work. He urged that every humble and holy man should
be free to read and to interpret the Scriptures for himself.
Churchmen, however, took a different view of his work. They
regarded it as an attack on the doctrines of the church, and
they charged that the result was that "the pearl of the Gospel
is scattered abroad and trodden underfoot by swine."[7] Nonetheless, preaching directly to the English people from Wycliffe's translation was carried on actively by his followers, the
Lollards. The real significance of Wycliffe's version is the
motivation behind it. The translation was made, not for the
church or the clergy, but for the laymen. It prepared the way
for the Bible to become accessible to future generations of laymen, some of whom played an important role in the growth of
the understanding of the Bible.

After the invention of printing, vernacular Bibles (that
is, Bibles in the language of the people) were printed in the fifteenth century in Italian, Dutch, French, and German. These
Bibles were generally translations of the Vulgate.

The availability in the late Middle Ages of biblical manuscripts in the original languages stimulated the revival of textual criticism. Influenced by Origen's *Hexapla* and Jerome's

work, the Italian humanist Lorenzo Valla re-established Christian textual criticism in the fifteenth century. He wrote brief grammatical notes on the Vulgate New Testament text after critically comparing it with the text in at least three Greek manuscripts. He strongly objected to the Vulgate because of its inaccurate translation of the Greek text.

New tools for biblical study appeared occasionally. In addition to Hebrew grammars and lexicons, commentaries on the Bible were written. Rashi wrote a major commentary on the Hebrew Scriptures. Another Jew, Ibn Ezra, left Spain and traveled for twenty-seven years in Italy, France, and England, visiting scholars, then wrote the best Old Testament commentary (1140) that had yet been written. In it he noted inconsistencies in Scripture. The Christians Andrew of St. Victor and Nicholas Trivet wrote commentaries on the Old Testament after they learned Hebrew. Andrew's commentaries influenced other Christian scholars, including Roger Bacon. When Nicholas of Lyra's *According to the Literal* was printed in Rome (1471-72) a century and a half after it was written, it became the first printed commentary on the Bible. In the Middle Ages the content of commentaries gradually shifted away from rabbinic and patristic quotations toward the commentators' own remarks.

A few other aids to biblical study were produced in the late Middle Ages. Beginning in the thirteenth century, Christians wrote geographies of Palestine and concordances to the Bible and to patristic literature. The chapter divisions of the Bible probably were made in the thirteenth century by Stephen Langton, Archbishop of Canterbury. The first Jewish concordance to the Hebrew text of the Old Testament was compiled by Isaac Mordecai Ben Nathan in the fifteenth century.

A few courageous medieval scholars revived a movement begun in antiquity, that of questioning traditional authorship of some biblical books. In the ninth century a Jewish scholar, Chivi of Balkh, listed two hundred rationalistic, legal, and historical reasons against the tradition that Moses wrote the Pentateuch. For this act he was nicknamed Al-Kalbi, "the Cynic." In the twelfth century Ibn Ezra used literary analysis and concluded that at least parts of the "Five Books of Moses" were written later than the time of Moses. He decided also that the Book of Isaiah is in two sections written by two different au-

thors (chapters 1-39 and 40-66). In the same century Hugh of
St. Victor commented that the Wisdom of Solomon (in the Apocrypha) was not written by Solomon.

Historical Situation

At the close of the medieval period a historical principle
reappeared, namely, the necessity of knowing the environment
in which the author lived and wrote. It had been generally ignored since the School of Antioch. John Colet, who later became dean of St. Paul's Cathedral in London, gave a series of
lectures in 1497 at Oxford on Paul's letters, in which he tried
to interpret them in the light of Paul's time. The lectures
made him famous—and suspected of heresy! Otherwise, this
principle made slight progress in the Middle Ages because, unlike the linguistic field, little new knowledge of the subject became known.

Thus by the end of the Middle Ages the best biblical scholars had rejected the traditional comments by rabbis and church
fathers as the proper basis for understanding the Bible. They
also rejected the allegorical and mystical methods in favor of
the literal and grammatical methods of interpreting Scripture.
These trends resulted largely from new knowledge of the Hebrew language and biblical text, and later, knowledge of the
Greek language and biblical text. The linguistic knowledge
also led to the production of improved tools such as grammars,
lexicons, and commentaries. Wycliffe and the Lollards recognized the importance of making the Bible available to laymen.
Lorenzo Valla reestablished textual criticism in biblical study.
A very few scholars questioned the traditional authorship of
some biblical books. Colet recognized the value of knowing
the historical situation in biblical times.

The progress was mainly the result of new contacts between cultures, newly acquired linguistic and literary knowledge, and the establishment of schools and universities. Philosophy, formal and informal, played an indirect role: Aristotelianism suggested that the Bible and reason should agree, and
the attitude underlying Arabian science implied that some
change in ideas might be desirable.

CHAPTER 5

THE BIRTH OF THE HISTORICAL APPROACH

In the sixteenth, seventeenth, and eighteenth centuries biblical scholars developed further those few principles of historical biblical interpretation that their predecessors had discovered. Equally important, they found additional historical principles that must be applied in order to understand the Bible. Some of the progress came from within the church and synagogue; some of it came from "outsiders"; often it was regarded as heretical.

SIXTEENTH CENTURY

This was the century of the Protestant Reformation, a century of active biblical study. But it also became a century of dogmatism, both Catholic and Protestant, which inhibited understanding of the Bible.

Biblical scholarship continued to occur mainly in the fields of language and text. Again, contact between different cultures was an important factor, especially relations between Jews and Christians in respect to the Hebrew Scriptures. In spite of tensions and persecutions, some Jewish and Christian scholars maintained friendly relations and learned from each other, and Old Testament scholarship was the beneficiary. The relationship between Elijah ben Asher and a Christian cardinal at Rome, Aegidius of Viterbo, provides an illustration. Aegidius provided a living for Elijah and his family in exchange for Hebrew lessons from him. The cardinal also taught Elijah the Greek language.

Linguistic and Textual Study

The Dutch humanist Desiderius Erasmus read the classics and the church fathers, in Greek and in Latin, and he saw that ancient writings could be understood best by studying them in their original languages. Therefore he carefully studied the New Testament in Greek. He recognized that some words in the New Testament do not have the same meaning they have in classical Greek. Erasmus fought for the right of scholars to study the New Testament in Greek, and his English friends John Colet and Thomas More agreed with him. He also advocated scholarship in general as useful for the development of the Christian man (1504).

Erasmus was a leader in his time in the field of textual criticism. He recognized that the discrepancies between the Greek New Testament and the Latin Vulgate were probably the result of errors in translating the Greek into Latin. He observed, too, differences among the manuscripts of the Greek text, and realized that these differences must be the result of copyists' errors and alterations in transmitting the text. He was shocked that biblical scholars still relied on the Vulgate. With the aid of manuscript collations (records of the variant readings among the manuscripts) sent to him from England by Colet, Erasmus sought to establish the original text of the New Testament. His famous edition of the Greek text was based on a few late manuscripts. Johann Froben published it, along with Erasmus' Latin translation, in 1516 in Basel. It was the first published printed Greek New Testament (the Complutensian Polyglot was printed earlier, but published later). It was popular at Cambridge University, but some orthodox leaders denounced it because it omitted some late readings. After Erasmus' death it was placed on the Catholic Index of prohibited books.

Robert Estienne (Latinized as Stephanus), a royal printer in Paris, printed his *Thesaurus Linguae Latinae* in 1532, which became a standard Latin lexicon. He printed the Vulgate, the Hebrew Old Testament, and the Greek text of writings of some of the church fathers. His 1550 edition of the Greek New Testament was the first to contain a critical apparatus listing variant readings. His annotations to his editions of the Bible aroused so much hostility from the faculty at the Sorbonne that he fled to Geneva in 1551. There he published in that year another edition of the Greek New Testament; it was the first to contain the verse divisions used to this day.

Efforts to establish the Hebrew text of the Old Testament

continued in Judaism. The second edition of the Rabbinic Bible, edited by Jacob ben Chayim, a Jewish scholar in Tunis, was printed in Venice in 1524-25. Prepared from the first edition and additional manuscripts, it became the standard Hebrew text of the Old Testament until modern times. The Rabbinic Bible derived its name from the fact that it includes comments on the text by earlier rabbis.

The chapter divisions in the Hebrew Scriptures, made in the Middle Ages, were unnumbered. Arius Montanus, a Spanish Benedictine, added numbers in his printed edition of 1571, a Hebrew text with an interlinear Latin translation.

In 1538 the Jewish lexicographer Elijah ben Asher, also known as Elijah Levita, demonstrated in one of his books the validity of a theory proposed by Jewish scholars as early as the ninth century. Elijah established clearly the fact that the Masoretes early in the medieval period had invented vowel-points and had inserted them in the Hebrew text of the Old Testament. Before the sixth century, Hebrew was always written without vowels—and usually is today, outside the Bible. The Masoretes, who were Jewish grammarians, inserted "points" or marks in the Hebrew text to represent the vowels and thus preserve the traditional pronunciation, which was in danger of being lost. The vowels also made the meaning of the text more certain, for two different words can have the same consonants but different vowels. Thus the text since the early Middle Ages has not been precisely the same as the original, for the original did not have the vowels. This discovery shocked both Jews and Christians, for the orthodox doctrine with both was that the vowel points were in the original text, and the text has been divinely preserved unchanged. The discovery of variant readings in the biblical text in Hebrew, Greek, and Latin was similarly unsettling.

Two new translations of the Bible appeared in the vernacular and were widely influential. Although nineteen German versions preceded Luther's, his was the first German translation (1522) from the Hebrew and Greek texts. Luther made skillful use of popular speech, with the result that his version was instrumental in shaping both German religion and German language. Three years later William Tyndale, educated at Oxford and Cambridge and influenced by Erasmus, completed the first English version of the Bible that was translated directly from the Greek and Hebrew texts. Translation from the original languages instead of from the Vulgate was so unorthodox that ecclesiastical opposition in England forced Tyndale to move to Hamburg in 1524 to complete his translation in association with Luther. The printer Quentel in Cologne began to print it in 1525. When Cochlaeus, an enemy of the Reformation, learned of it, he reported it to the authorities at Cologne, who stopped the printing. Later that year the printing was finished at Worms. In 1526 the book was secretly exported to England, where the copies were quickly purchased by laymen eager to read them and by church authorities zealous to destroy them. Thomas More was among those who zealously attacked Tyndale's version for its unorthodox translation of some passages. On the other hand, Cromwell and Cranmer were so well impressed by it that they advocated an English translation of the whole Bible under the patronage of the king (Henry VIII). Afraid to return to England, Tyndale moved to Belgium, where in 1536 he was condemned for heresy, strangled, and burned at the stake. Yet the style and accuracy of his translation were so excellent that they largely determined the style and form of the Authorized Version (popularly known today as the King James Version), produced nearly a century later.

Increased knowledge of the original languages and text led to the production of improved tools for biblical interpretation. The tools were now in the form of printed books instead of manuscripts.

As in the Middle Ages, more grammars and lexicons were produced for study of the Hebrew text than for the Greek text. The German humanist Johannes Reuchlin studied the Hebrew language under learned Jews and wrote a combined Hebrew grammar and lexicon, published in 1506, which greatly stimulated grammatical study of the Hebrew text of the Old Testament among Christians in German lands. Reuchlin, like his contemporary Erasmus, was a linguist who was devoted to the cause of scholarship. When the Dominicans of Cologne and a Jewish convert to Christianity, Johann Pfefferkorn, wanted to destroy Jewish books, Reuchlin opposed them in the interests of scholarship.

Calvin wrote detailed commentaries on almost the whole Bible. The first concordance to the whole Bible in English translation was compiled by John Merbecke (or Marbeck), an English clergyman and musician. For this work he was condemned to the stake for heresy in 1544, but was pardoned through the influence of Bishop Stephen Gardiner of Cambridge University. The book was eventually published in 1550.

Interpretation of the Bible

New interpretations of the Bible appeared during the Reformation, particularly in the writings of Calvin and Luther, who used grammatical interpretation extensively. Like Erasmus before them, Calvin, Luther, and Zwingli recognized the principle that the context of a passage should be taken into consideration. Zwingli said that lifting a verse out of context is like breaking off a flower and trying to plant it without its roots.

Calvin's comments on the Bible were more thorough and scholarly than Luther's, and more grammatical and literal. He recognized that the prophecies in the Old Testament were meant for the times in which they were written. He rejected belief in the verbal dictation of the Bible by the Holy Spirit, as did Luther and Zwingli. Although he adopted these sound principles, Calvin had the disconcerting habit of reinterpreting Scripture to suit himself whenever a passage was contrary to his own beliefs.

Luther's interpretation of Scripture was Christocentric, or Christ-centered. He asserted that not all of the Bible is the Word of God, but only those passages that "preach Christ," for "Christ is the very Word of God." Luther's concept of the Word of God is a confusing mixture. He combined the ideas of (a) Word of God as any words revealed by the Holy Spirit, (b) the Word of God as the Bible itself, and (c) Jesus as the Word (Logos) of God in the Prologue of the Gospel of John. The last idea is his basis for limiting the Word of God in the Bible to the passages that "preach Christ." Luther's Christocentric approach resulted in the misinterpretation of many passages, which were forced to refer to Christ when actually they do not refer to him at all. Luther insisted on the right of each individual to interpret the Bible for himself. Whereas Luther believed that the final authority for religious knowledge is the

Bible, Zwingli insisted that it is the Holy Spirit.

In spite of his mistakes, Luther made important contributions to biblical scholarship. He dared to question the canon; he was free from Calvin's biblical fanaticism and intolerance; like Abelard, he recognized that scriptural passages varied in value and that some were important only for their own time. Like Rabbi Hillel fifteen centuries earlier, Luther recognized that a set of guidelines could be helpful for exegesis. He drew up six rules of interpretation. The first three are methods in the historical approach: (1) the necessity of grammatical knowledge, (2) the importance of taking into consideration the times, circumstances, and conditions in which the passage was written, and (3) the necessity of observing the context of the passage. Luther's last three rules, however, are sure paths to subjective misinterpretation: (4) the necessity of faith and spiritual illumination, (5) the necessity of keeping "the proportion of faith," and (6) the necessity of referring all Scripture to Christ (if a passage is not clear, it should be interpreted as referring to Christ). Erasmus rightly faulted Luther for relying on the Spirit as the guide in interpreting Scripture. Luther and other Reformers applied the fifth rule in the sense that biblical interpretation should agree with Christian faith. Unfortunately, the rule paved the way for Protestant scholasticism.

Later in the same century another attempt was made to establish a set of guidelines for interpreting the Bible. Matthias Flacius (also called Flacius Illyricus because he was born in Illyricum) wrote the first textbook on hermeneutics (1567). Regrettably, few historical methods are in it.

Doubts about the authorship of various biblical books continued to be raised. Erasmus and Cardinal Cajetan rejected the traditional authorship of some books. Luther had doubts about Hebrews, James, Jude, and Revelation and put them at the end of his Bible. Calvin questioned the authorship of Joshua, 1 and 2 Samuel, and Hebrews. Carlstadt, a German theologian and Reformer, rejected the Mosaic authorship of the Pentateuch.

The post-Reformation period (1550-1600) was generally a regressive time in biblical studies. The split between Catholicism and Protestantism was definite. The period was one of

intolerance, heresy-hunting, and witchcraft mania. Both sides
became inflexible and excluded direct examination of Scripture.
In Catholicism church tradition, ecclesiastical councils, and
the Bible were the authorities; in Protestantism the Protestant
councils, creeds, and the Bible were authoritative. The Protestants theoretically made the Bible their chief guide, but any
interpretation of it which disagreed with their councils and
creeds was attacked. The dogmatic exegesis intended to support the Protestant creeds has been called "confessional interpretation." The Dutch Reformed theologian Jakob Hermands-
zoon (Latinized as Jacobus Arminius), however, refused to
make the creeds the basis of interpretation. Protestant dog-
matists, in their dispute with Jesuit zealots, insisted on the
inerrancy of the Bible.

In summary, the sixteenth century established the principle that translation and interpretation should be made directly from the text in the original language. The Bible was
printed in the original languages and in the vernacular. A few
scholars carried forward the practice of grammatical, literal
interpretation. Textual criticism advanced with the work of
Erasmus. Luther and Flacius introduced into Christianity the
principle that a set of rules or guidelines are needed for interpretation of the Bible.

The Protestant Reformation hastened the appearance of
the historical approach in that, by making Scripture the main
authority (in theory) in Christianity, it aroused intense interest in studying the Bible. The effect of this stimulus was de-
creased, however, by the fact that the Catholic-Protestant controversy created such intolerant religious attitudes that biblical interpretation generally was forced to support the accepted
doctrines.

SEVENTEENTH CENTURY

While the Bible in the sixteenth century had been the accepted authority for Protestants, by the end of the seventeenth
many learned men were questioning its supreme worth. Conservative clergy and the laymen in general, however, contin-

ued to defend old views. In contrast to the succeeding centuries, Germans in the seventeenth century did not produce much
new biblical scholarship, apparently the result of the Thirty
Years War and its aftermath. At this time scholars began to
refer to careful study of the Bible as "biblical criticism."
"Criticism" does not imply an effort to find fault, but rather,
as in "literary criticism," close examination for the purpose
of understanding and evaluating the material.

Role of Philosophy and Science

The climate of the seventeenth century was more favor-
able than that of previous centuries for the rise of historical
methods of interpreting the Bible. Two fields of thought which
affected men's attitudes were largely responsible: philosophy
and science.

Philosophy in this century exalted reason above tradition,
and this view had its influence on theology and biblical interpretation. Several philosophers advocated questioning and investigation as a policy in those fields.

The Socinians, an anti-Trinitarian group in Poland, were
rationalists who believed that the Bible and reason agree. The
Socinians formulated a statement of their principles, the Raco-
vian Catechism, at Racow, Poland, in 1605. In it they asserted
that the Scriptures are the only source of truth and that "right
reason" is present in them, and therefore Socinians reject "every interpretation [of the Bible] which is repugnant to right
reason."

The French philosopher and mathematician René Descartes based philosophical reasoning upon mental experience;
he thought that anything that can be conceived as a logical,
coherent whole must be true (not a valid premise). Nevertheless, his emphasis on doubt as a method eventually encouraged
others to doubt, then to investigate, then to discover.

The English Political philosopher, Thomas Hobbes, in
his book entitled *Leviathan*, rejected both the authority of the
Catholic church and the bibliolatry of Protestantism. He believed that the Bible is not uniquely inspired. Another English
philosopher, John Locke, was a vigorous exponent of free inquiry and toleration; like other rationalists, he maintained that

Christianity and the Scriptures are consistent with reason
(1695).

The Dutch philosopher, Baruch Spinoza, held a panthe-
istic view of God as present in nature, and thus he rejected belief in a personal God and an immortal soul. He wanted to promote the rights of philosophy in a society dominated by theology. In his *Theological-Political Treatise* he maintained
that "in a free commonwealth it should be lawful for everyman
to think what he will and to speak what he thinks." To support his views he studied the Bible carefully. He maintained
that the Bible is imperfect and that the books of the Bible
should be treated the same as other ancient literature. He
recognized these historical methods of interpretation: know
the nature of the languages of the Bible, examine the contents
of each book, and learn the situation in which each book was
written. Spinoza's book aroused tremendous opposition in theological circles. He was expelled from the synagogue in 1656
at the age of twenty-four by Jewish authorities and forced to
leave Amsterdam.

Science, too, improved the intellectual climate. The scientific attitude gave scholars the courage to question and to investigate, and it suggested methods by which study could be
more systematic and effective. Leading scientists of the time
set the example of investigating and drawing new conclusions in
spite of opposition. In the preceding century Nicolaus Copernicus had advanced the startling theory that the sun is the center
of the planetary system; this was contrary to the biblical assumption that the earth is the center, and therefore was very
upsetting to the orthodox. In the seventeenth century his helio-
centric theory was endorsed and expanded by the astronomers
Kepler and Galileo. The Inquisition charged Galileo with heresy and forced him to recant. Nonetheless, the unorthodoxy of
the great scientists Kepler, Galileo, and Newton fostered a
spirit of freedom of thought. All three men believed that the
Bible should be understood in the light of scientific knowledge;
this attitude spread among the learned.

Linguistic and Textual Study

Soon after James I ascended the throne of England, he

held a conference (1604) to hear the complaints of the Puritans.
One complaint, among others, was that they could not in good
conscience subscribe to the Book of Common Prayer because
its biblical quotations were from a "corrupted translation," the
Geneva Bible. King James was a Bible student who had translated some Psalms, and he agreed that the Geneva Bible (1560;
first English version with verse numbers) was an inferior translation. Therefore he met the Puritan objection by authorizing
a new translation to be made by "the best learned" men in Oxford and Cambridge Universities; forty-seven biblical scholars
made the translation. This authorized Version was printed in
1611 and was the only version authorized by the king for use in
the religious services "in all Churches of England." It originally contained the Apocrypha, the late Jewish books now in
the Anglican and Catholic Bibles.

Some Christian sects today use only this version and denounce modern translations. They are unaware that the scholars who have made the best modern translations have precisely the same goal as the scholars who translated the Authorized
Version, namely, to produce an accurate translation of the
text based on the best manuscripts known, expressed in current language. Modern translators have important information
unknown in 1611, and if the translators of the Authorized Version were alive today, they would agree that the Bible should
be available in a modern translation incorporating the new
knowledge.

Louis Cappel (Latinized as Capellus), a Huguenot, was
a professor at the Protestant seminary at Saumur, France. He
wrote a book entitled *Sacred Criticism*, in which he observed
variant readings in the manuscripts of the Hebrew text of the
Old Testament and also differences between the Hebrew text and
the ancient versions. From patristic and Jewish literature he
compiled quotations from the Old Testament that demonstrated
the carelessness and ignorance of the scribes who produced the
manuscripts. This evidence showed that the claims of the divine preservation of the text were untenable. His book was finished in 1634, but there was so much theological opposition to
it that he was unable to publish it until 1650, with the aid of his
son Jacques, who had become a Catholic.

Lexicons, or language dictionaries, of Old Testament He-

brew had been written earlier, but comparable lexicons of New
Testament Greek did not appear until the seventeenth century.
The first scholarly lexicon of New Testament Greek was compiled by Georg Pasor and published at Herborn (north of Frank-
furt) in 1619. It was not strictly a dictionary, however, for
the arrangement was by word-roots. The first New Testament
Greek dictionary with the words arranged in alphabetic order
was the one compiled at Basel by Ludovicus Lucius (1640).

Richard Simon, a French Catholic priest, became especially interested in Greek and Near Eastern languages while
studying at the Sorbonne University in Paris. He became acquainted with Jewish scholars who introduced him to the Talmud. Simon entered the French Oratory, a congregation of
secular priests loyal to the decrees of the Council of Trent.
Nevertheless, he rejected the ecclesiastical basis of interpretation of Scripture and insisted on going to the source, the Bible itself. He remarked that the church fathers had "entirely
neglected the Hebrew text." He wrote a book entitled *Critical
History of the Old Testament* in which he interpreted the text
philologically and historically and concluded that Moses did not
write the Pentateuch. This and other unorthodox conclusions,
and his controversies with the Port Royalists and Benedictines,
led to his expulsion from the Oratory and to denunciation by
both Catholics and Protestants.

Background of the Bible

The background of the Bible—the history, ideas, and customs which influenced it—began to be discovered. One way of
learning the background is to find similar or parallel passages
in other literature written about the same time and in the same
or a nearby region. Hugo van Groot (surname Latinized as
Grotius), the founder of international law, was a Dutch lawyer
who had studied classical philology and therefore insisted that
the Bible be interpreted grammatically. Grotius collected
many parallel passages in the Greek and Latin classics and
published them beside the correponding biblical passages in his
Notes on the New Testament.[7a]

Soon afterwards John Lightfoot, a Christian biblical and
rabbinic scholar at Cambridge University, collected and organ-

ized literary parallels from the Talmud in an effort to show
the Jewish background of the New Testament. The parallels
were published in his six-volume work, *Hebraic and Talmudic
Studies*.   Unfortunately, most of his parallels are later than
the New Testament, so they do not necessarily reflect its background. Nevertheless, he took a vital step toward the histori-
ical approach: he recognized the principle that wide knowledge
of the Jewish background is required to understand the New
Testament.

A Hebrew-language scholar at Cambridge University,
John Spencer, has been called the founder of history-of-religions studies (the influence of religions on one another). In his
*Three Books on the Laws of the Hebrews, Their Rituals and
Doctrines*, he tried to trace the connections between Israelite
laws and those of other Semites. He was hindered by the fact
that he did not have access to the source materials which have
since been discovered through archaeology. He was castigated
for his unorthodox recognition that the Israelites might have
been influenced by the religion of their neighbors.

Jean Mabillon made a valuable advance in historical
methodology. He produced objective guidelines for dating ancient documents (1668); he was the first to put paleography
on a scientific basis. Accurate dating of documents is important in determining whether they were contemporary with the
writing of the Bible. He also aided biblical study in 1691 by
stoutly defending the right of men under monastic vows to engage in scholarship. Mabillon was one of the Maurists, a
French congregation of Benedictine monks who made outstanding historical and literary studies in the seventeenth and eighteenth centuries.

Thus in the seventeenth century the independent thinking
of a few philosophers and the investigations of a few scientists
began to create an atmosphere in which the historical approach
to the Bible could emerge. Moderate progress occurred in the
areas of translation, textual criticism, grammatical interpretation, and recognition of the necessity of knowing the historical background. Two new methods appeared in embryonic
form: the application of the Jewish and pagan backgrounds
to the study of the New Testament, and the equal importance

of applying the Semitic background to the study of the Old Testament. Recognition of this second method constitutes the birth
of the history-of-religions approach to the Old Testament. The
historical method of dating ancient documents emerged.

EIGHTEENTH CENTURY

The eighteenth century, the period of the secular Enlightenment, brought a wider acceptance in educated circles of the
scientific method and a fuller application of reason to religion
and philosophy, with much skepticism of traditional religious
beliefs. Deism, a philosophy of natural religion based on human reason instead of revelation, had a broad effect. Influenced by Deism, prominent philosophers of the Enlightenment—
Hume in Scotland, Paine in America and France, and two
Frenchmen, Diderot and Voltaire—exalted reason and discarded traditional views of the Bible. John Locke had done
this at the close of the seventeenth century. These philosophers, in their interpretation of the Bible, tended to be guided too much by Deism and philosophical rationalism, however.
They made a valuable contribution nevertheless, for they
opened the door a little wider for the entrance of new ideas.
Compared with their radical philosophy, historical interpretation of the Bible did not seem quite so unorthodox. The
Aufklärung, as the Enlightenment in Germany was called, aided by the patronage of the Prussian king, Frederick the Great,
prepared the way for the rapid advancement of "higher" biblical criticism in German lands in the next century.

Nevertheless, official opposition to biblical and theological unorthodoxy remained strong. When Semler rejected the
doctrine of divine inspiration of the Bible and attempted to determine which parts of it are of permanent value, he was sub-
jected to an outburst of personal criticism that he called "vio-
lent and utterly unfounded condemnation."[8] Frederick the
Great wrote a letter to the philosopher Kant, reprimanding
him for his unorthodox theological views. The king accused
him of writing in a derogatory manner about some basic teachings of Holy Scripture and Christianity.[9] Thomas Paine's book,
The Age of Reason, presented his disagreement with tradition-

al Christian doctrines, biblical and otherwise, and caused him to lose his friends in the United States, England, and France.

Linguistic and Textual Study

Philological exegesis, using both grammar and lexicology, was firmly established in the eighteenth century by two scholars. A Lutheran churchman, Johann Albrecht Bengel, applied the philological method in his famous exegesis of the New Testament published in 1742. Johann August Ernesti, a Lutheran professor of theology at Leipzig, emphasized that the task of the interpreter is to attach to the text the same meaning that the author himself attached. Ernesti combined historical and grammatical knowledge in his *Principles of Interpretation of the New Testament*.

Textual criticism developed rapidly and became alarming to the orthodox because it uncovered an increasing number of variations in the text, resulting in much uncertainty as to which are the original readings. It also raised questions such as these: Since John 5:4 is not in some manuscripts, is it really part of the Bible or not? If one thinks that he should "believe every word of the Bible," which manuscript should he believe?

Although the sixteenth century editions of the printed Greek text of the New Testament had been disturbing, the second Elzevir edition (1633) had been reassuring, because its preface stated that it is the "text received by all" (and therefore came to be known as the Textus Receptus, "Received Text"). The statement was misinterpreted as meaning that it was the divinely received, correct text; thus there seemed to be no doubt and no cause for alarm as to what was the original text.

The situation changed in the eighteenth century. John Mills (commonly written as "Mill") at Oxford Unversity spent thirty years collecting 30,000 variant readings of the Greek New Testament in nearly one hundred manuscripts, commentaries, and patristic writings. He listed this multitude of variants in the margins of his text (1707). Johannes Bengel pioneered in setting forth a set of rules for textual criticism in his printed edition of the Greek text (1734). These rules provided guidelines for determining which readings were probably in the original text. He observed that the older manuscripts tended to have better readings.

Johann Jakob Wettstein was a Protestant pastor in Basle. After he was twice removed from office because of his Socinian, anti-Trinitarian views, he became a professor at the College of Remonstrants in Amsterdam. His two-volume edition of the Greek New Testament (1751-52) included many variants previously unrecorded, and he devised a system of letters and numbers to designate the specific manuscripts. Caspar René Gregory improved these symbols in 1908. Wettstein's greatest accomplishment, however, was his commentary on the text, printed in his same edition; in it he listed parallels from classical and rabbinic literature. He recognized that the Bible was a product of its times and environment, and that the parallels aid readers to understand the Bible by illustrating its Jewish, Greek, and Roman backgrounds.

The first edition of the Greek text to depart from the Textus Receptus and to substitute other readings in the text itself was William Bowyer's, which he printed in England in 1763. The previous editions had printed the Textus Receptus as the text, and had merely listed variants in the margins or in a critical apparatus. Wettstein's edition, however, had been disturbing in that it indicated that certain variants were genuine instead of the corresponding readings in the text. Bowyer went a step farther: he dared to change the Textus Receptus text itself. Wettstein had planned to do this, but when authorities learned of his plans from sample pages, he was regarded as a heretic and was prevented from printing his revised text. Bowyer's procedure was soon followed in Germany by J. J. Griesbach in his edition of the text (1775-77).

Similar projects were conducted with the Old Testament text. Benjamin Kennicott, canon of Christ Church, Oxford, employed scholars to assist him and worked for twenty-five years collating the variant readings in manuscripts and printed editions of the Hebrew text. These variants were published by Oxford University Press in 1776-80. Giovanni de Rossi, professor of Oriental languages at Parma, Italy, also collated many manuscripts and printed editions of the Hebrew text; the results were published in Parma, 1784-98.

Two valuable linguistic tools were produced early in the century. Abraham Tromm (Latinized as Trommius) at the

Groningen university compiled a concordance to the Septuagint, listing the Greek words in the text and giving their Hebrew equivalents. Since the Septuagint is a translation of the Hebrew Scriptures into Hellenistic Greek, it reveals which Greek words at that time had the same or similar meaning as the Hebrew words in the Old Testament. Through the use of a concordance of this kind, a New Testament scholar can find various meanings that a certain Greek word or expression had in the Hellenistic world.

The second linguistic tool was a new type, a Bible dictionary. This term does not designate a lexicon, or language dictionary, but rather a concise encyclopedia of names and subjects in the Bible. Although Eusibius in the fourth century had compiled a descriptive list of geographic names in the Bible, the first dictionary describing the persons, places, and subjects mentioned in it was written by a French Benedictine monk, Augustin Calmet, in 1722.

Literary Study

In the eighteenth century literary criticism was called "higher criticism" by Johann G. Eichhorn, to distinguish it from textual, or "lower," criticism. Higher criticism included the efforts to determine the date, authorship, literary nature, and sources of the biblical books.

Two aspects of biblical interpretation—both of which are directly related to literary study—had appeared in the past, but received special attention early in the eighteenth century. John Locke, in his essay entitled *A Paraphrase and Notes on the Epistles of St. Paul*, published posthumously (1705-1707), emphasized the necessity of observing the contexts of passages. Also, the belief that Jesus' life fulfilled scriptural prophecy was clearly exposed as contrary to the historical setting of the Old Testament passages. The English Deist, Anthony Collins, demonstrated that the "prophecies" do not refer to Jesus and some are not even prophecies.

Source criticism developed slowly. In 1711 H. B. Witter noticed that there are two Creation stories in Genesis and that "Yahweh" is the name for God in one and "Elohim" is the name in the other. In 1753 the French Catholic Jean Astruc, physi-

cian to Louis XIV, concluded on the basis of those two names
that Moses must have used two main source documents in Genesis. He erred in thinking that Moses wrote Genesis— in fact,
his purpose was to defend that traditional view. In 1798 the
German scholar K. D. Ilgen was the first to recognize that
not just one, but two different strands, or sources, in Genesis
use the name Elohim.[9a]

Real source criticism of the gospels did not emerge until the next century, but the possibility of sources in these
books was recognized. In 1716 Jean Leclerc (Latinized as
Clericus), professor of church history at the Remonstrant College in Amsterdam, suggested that the evangelists who wrote
the canonical gospels may have used earlier sources. Johann
Gottfried Herder, general superintendent and court preacher
at Weimar, Prussia, concluded that Mark is the earliest gospel (1796). His conclusion was contrary to the church tradition that Matthew was the earliest.

Some vain efforts to blend all four gospels into one account were made. In the sixteenth century Andreas Osiander
had tried this in his *Greek and Latin Gospel Harmony*. In the
eighteenth century Johann Hess, in his book on the life of Jesus, attempted to fit the synoptic stories into the framework
of the Gospel of John. Herder strongly objected to such efforts
and rightly insisted that we should let each evangelist "retain
his special purpose, complexion, time, and locale."[10]

Comparing the gospels with each other to observe their
differences as well as their similarities is a prerequisite step
for understanding them. It leads to recognition of the distinc-
tiveness of each gospel; it provides evidence for source and
redaction (editorial) criticism; and it gives deep insights into
the nature of the early Christian community.

A valuable literary tool for comparing the gospels is a
"synopsis," which prints the whole text—not a summary—of
the gospels side by side in vertical columns. When the same
saying or story occurs in two or more gospels, the parallel accounts are printed opposite each other for easy comparison.
Usually only the synoptic gospels (Matthew, Mark, and Luke)
are printed in a synopsis, for John has so little material that
is in the other gospels. The first synopsis in English was *A
Harmonie upon the three Evangelists, Matthew, Mark and*

Luke, published in London in 1584. Apparently it had little impact upon biblical scholarship. The first to use the word synopsis as a name for the synoptic gospels in parallel format was Griesbach in his book of this type published in 1776. This type of tool was used increasingly thereafter.

Analytical comparison of the gospels began in the latter half of the eighteenth century. Hermann Reimarus, who was professor of Hebrew and oriental languages at Hamburg, described great differences between John and the other three gospels. Herder soon called attention to them too (1796-97). An English vicar, Edward Evanson, also observed them, and then went on to list differences among the synoptic gospels themselves and even between passages within the same gospel.

Important progress was made in recognizing the literary characteristics of the Old Testament. Robert Lowth, professor of poetry at Oxford University and later bishop of Oxford and of London, recognized parallelism as a characteristic of the Hebrew poetry in the Bible. The poetic parallelism usually consists of a couplet in which the second clause either repeats the same idea as, or states the opposite of, the thought in the first. In his book, *Academic Lectures on the Sacred Poetry of the Hebrews*, Lowth reported his discovery of the nature of Hebrew poetry.

J. G. Eichhorn wrote *Introduction to the Old Testament,* which was the first comprehensive description of the Old Testament as literature. He realized that the Pentateuch and Isaiah are composite and that some books were written later than their traditional dates. He treated the Hebrew Scriptures as Near Eastern literature, not as unique revelation. He has been called the father of Old Testament criticism. Later he wrote introductions to the Apocrypha and the New Testament.

Historical Situation

An essential ingredient of the scientific historical method is a genuine historical sense. In previous centuries biblical scholars had failed to recognize the great difference between their own day and biblical times, and they had no awareness of the different periods of time in the ancient world. The leaders

of the Reformation as well as the contemporary Catholic biblical interpreters lacked the necessary historical knowledge.

The Enlightenment introduced biblical scholars to a sense
of history in general and to the concept of historical time in
particular. Jean Turretini, professor of church history at Geneva, warned that the conditions of his day should not be read
into those of the scriptural writers, but instead we must "put
ourselves into those times and surroundings in which the prophets and apostles wrote" (1728). [11] Gabler, in his academic in-
augural address at Altdorf in 1787, appears to have been the
first to grasp the relevance for biblical study of different historical periods of time. [12]

Archaeology was especially useful in giving scholars a
sense of historical time, for it revealed great differences
among various periods of history. The first major archaeological expedition to the Near East was conducted by the French
in Egypt beginning in 1798. It bore little resemblance to modern expeditions, however, for it was part of a military invasion conducted without the consent of the local country and with
little excavation. Napoleon loaded an army of 38,000 men and
a group of 175 "learned civilians" into ships and invaded Egypt.
The Egyptians were soon conquered, and the scholars began to
survey and collect Egyptian antiquities. The artist Vivant Denon eagerly sketched everything in sight. Then Admiral Nelson destroyed the French ships, Napoleon fled to France, and
the English took to the British Museum the Egyptian antiquities the French had collected. The most important consequences of this unusual expedition were Denon's sketches, the
establishment of the Egyptian Institute in Cairo, and the antiquities placed in the British Museum, including the famous
Rosetta Stone. The inscription on the Rosetta Stone is repeated in three languages, a fact which enabled Thomas Young and
J. F. Champollion to find the key to deciphering Egyptian hi-
eroglyphics—a boon to archaeologists.

In the past the miracles in the Bible had appeared to be
the guarantee of the validity of the Christian faith. Jesus' miracles were regarded as proof of his divinity. In the eighteenth
century, however, the new philosophical and scientific attitudes caused some persons to conclude that the miracle stories
are only myths. Those attitudes, combined with knowledge of

myth in secular literature (especially from the studies of C. G.
Heyne, a classical philologist), produced the "myth school" of
biblical interpretation in the eighteenth and early nineteenth
centuries. Its leaders were Eichhorn, Gabler, Georg L. Bauer, Wilhelm De Wette, and David F. Strauss. They recognized the probability of influence from the gentile environment.
They searched for myths in Greek and Roman literature as a
guide to identifying similar myths in both the Old and New Testaments. Their recognition of myth in the Bible was an important advance, but sometimes they labeled too much material
as "myth," and they lacked sufficient knowledge of Near Eastern parallels to the mythology of the Old Testament. Nevertheless, they made an important contribution when they recognized
that the miracles were not historical events, but, like other
miracle stories in antiquity, were the products of a superstitious age.

The spirit of the Enlightenment stimulated interest in the
life of Jesus. The historical approach to his life was delayed,
however, by the rationalistic approach that was prominent in
the eighteenth and nineteenth centuries. Under the influence
of rational philosophy and Deism, efforts were made to describe the religion of Jesus as true, natural (deistic) religion,
which the early church had distorted or replaced. In the de-
cade 1730-40, three Englishmen, Matthew Tindal, Thomas
Chubb, and Thomas Morgan, interpreted Jesus' teaching along
these lines. Morgan's book in particular was a forerunner of
the nineteenth-century liberal lives of Jesus (see next chapter).
Morgan claimed that Jesus preached a true rational religion in
contrast to the narrow Jewish religion, and that Paul followed
Jesus, but Peter was devoted to traditional Judaism. Although
there were some grains of truth in them, the deistic interpretations of Jesus were unsound in their rationalization of Jesus'
teaching. They were founded on the assumption that Jesus
must have been perfect and therefore his teaching must have
been consistent with rationalism.

In the second half of the century, however, a historical approach to Jesus' life appeared in the work of Hermann
Reimarus. His view of Jesus was so unorthodox that it was a
tremendous shock to traditional Christianity. As Albert
Schweitzer expressed it: "Before Reimarus, no one had at-

tempted to form a historical conception of the life of Jesus.
. . . Thus there had been nothing to prepare the world for a
work of such power as that of Reimarus. "[13] In addition to
teaching languages at Hamburg, Reimarus studied the Bible
and deist philosophy. A few of his writings were published,
but his main work, a manuscript of four thousand pages, was
so unconventional that he dared only to circulate it among his
friends. After his death in 1768 his friend Gotthold Ephraim
Lessing began to publish the most important sections of it as
anonymous *Wolfenbüttel Fragments*, even though he disagreed
with most of it. In 1778 Lessing published the most unorthodox fragment under the title *On the Intentions of Jesus and
His Disciples*. In it Reimarus tried to place Jesus in his Jewish setting and put the gospels in the setting of the early church.
He observed that Jesus was Jewish in his thinking about the
Messiah and the coming kingdom of God and did not intend to
substitute a new religion for the Jewish religion. He also
pointed out many inconsistencies in the gospels. Some of Reimarus' conclusions were extreme and mistaken, but his great
contributions were that he studied the gospels carefully, examined Jesus' career historically, and recognized the possibility
that the experiences of the early church influenced the content
of the gospels. He combined many fields of knowledge in his
interpretation of the New Testament, and he was the first to try
to incorporate to any extent the Christian background in the
study of the gospels—two vital elements in the historical approach.

A necessary step in understanding the gospels is to realize that the evangelists' purpose in writing them was to promote the faith of the Christian community, not to write biographies of Jesus. After remarking that the Gospel of John
best demonstrated this fact, Herder wrote (1796), "it is also
true that one ought not to think of biography as the main concern even of the older Gospels. "[14]

Birth of the Historical Approach

Werner Kümmel has called Johann Semler "the founder
of the historical study of the New Testament. "[15] In his writings Semler tried to make New Testament interpretation a sci-

ence, based on historical principles. Semler, a Lutheran professor of theology in the university at Halle, Prussia, combined many fields of study in his work. He had a wide knowledge of classical and oriental languages and literature. He studied New Testament text and canon, rejected the doctrine of biblical inspiration, insisted on thorough grammatical interpretation, and maintained that Scripture is a product of its times and therefore must be studied in relation to the historical circumstances in which it was written. Like Reimarus, he recognized the importance of the Christian background of the New Testament; he anticipated F. C. Faur (19th c.) in observing the rivalry in the early church between Jewish Christians and gentile Christians.

Johann Michaelis, too, combined different fields of knowledge in scholarly fashion. He studied Arabic in addition to the biblical languages and conducted research on the Syriac version of the Bible. His six-volume work, *Mosaic Law*, treated the laws in the Pentateuch as human in origin. The fourth edition of his *Introduction to the New Testament* (1788) was the first modern introduction to the New Testament, combining study of the Greek language, textual criticism, and the origin of the individual books. Herbert Marsh's English translation of that edition was instrumental in introducing the historical approach and German scholarship to America, for it strongly influenced the eloquent preacher, Joseph Buckminster, at the beginning of the next century.

Although many predecessors had used a few historical methods in their interpretation of Scripture, it had remained for Semler, Michaelis, J. G. Eichhorn, Ernesti, and Reimarus to assemble many methods into a system and apply the combination to the task of understanding the Bible. The system included more than linguistics and textual criticism. The scientific spirit of the Enlightenment and the increase in fields of knowledge made a more comprehensive approach possible. The comprehensive approach, even in its primitive stage, was a great achievement. Nevertheless, additional relevant fields of knowledge remained to be discovered, and all the fields required further development.

An important feature of the Enlightenment that is not so

well known as its scientific and philosophical developments is
this remarkable progress in the understanding of the Bible. In
the eighteenth century, for the first time, the intellectual climate permitted scientific, historical study of the Scriptures.
Although professors and clergymen were punished for their unorthodoxy by being dismissed from their positions, they were
no longer burned at the stake. New secular knowledge furnished
materials and methods for significant progress in biblical study.
Major improvement of old fields of knowledge and especially
the discovery of many new fields of investigation effected a genuine intellectual revolution.

Among the old fields of study, textual criticism was the
most active. Many variants were collected; rules of textual
criticism were drawn up; the superiority of old manuscripts
was recognized; finally, better readings replaced some of those
in the Textus Receptus when the Greek New Testament text was
printed. Philological interpretation of the New Testament was
securely established. Moderate progress occurred in the field
of source criticism of Genesis.

The astonishing aspect of biblical study in the eighteenth
century, however, is the number of whole new fields discovered.
Four new types of tools were published: a concordance to the
Septuagint, a Bible dictionary, a synopsis of the synoptic gospels, and modern-type introductions to the Bible. For the first
time in history, the differences among and within the canonical
gospels were systematiclly recorded. The essential nature
of Hebrew poetry was discovered. In previous centuries biblical investigation had been mainly linguistic and literary, but
now historical fields of study emerged as a historical sense was
acquired. Archaeological interest in recovering the past arose.
At last, biblical miracle stories were recognized plainly as
myths. For the first time, the Christian background was acknowledged as a necessary field of knowledge for understanding
the New Testament. Not until the eighteenth century was Jesus' life examined historically.

Above all, that century was the period when biblical
scholars started to combine the various relevant fields of
knowledge into a systematic approach. They began to make a
synthesis of the disciplines then known. The historical approach to the Bible was born.

CHAPTER 6

THE NINETEENTH CENTURY

In the nineteenth century, especially the second half, the historical approach to the Bible grew rapidly. Theological attitudes were slightly more tolerant. More people were engaged in biblical research, and more pertinent factual information was uncovered by both secular and religious scholars. The methods which had been found in previous centuries were developed further, and new methods were discovered which expanded the scope of the historical approach.

The policy of letting the Bible speak for itself was emphasized by a few scholars. In his *Confessions of an Inquiring Spirit*, Samuel Taylor Coleridge, the English poet, laid down a simple but basic principle. He declared that people should form their estimate of the Bible directly from its contents, not from the opinions and theories of others. Benjamin Jowett, professor of Greek at Oxford, stressed that it is not necessary that Christian churches believe and teach the verbal inspiration of the Bible. He maintained that the main duty of the biblical scholar is to find what the original author meant; this saves the interpreter from the mistake of treating the literal as symbolic, and the symbolic as literal. Jowett also criticized the Calvinists for limiting their attention to a few proof texts and ignoring the rest of the Bible.

Religious conservatives continued to resist stoutly the growth of the historical approach, however. William Paley, English churchman, ably defended the traditional faith in his *A View of the Evidences of Christianity*, published in 1794. This book was very influential in the nineteenth century. Until 1900, the reading of this work of Christian apologetics was a prerequisite for admission to Cambridge University.

Linguistic and Textual Study

An archaeological discovery of tremendous importance for the understanding of the Greek language in the New Testa-

ment came at the close of the nineteenth century and beginning
of the twentieth. Previously the accepted view was that "New
Testament Greek" is unique, unlike secular Greek, because its
vocabulary and syntax differ somewhat from classical Greek.
Theologians regarded New Testament Greek as proof that the
Bible is divinely inspired; they said that God had even dictated
the New Testament in his own special form of Greek! But
Adolf Deissmann, while a privatdocent (unsalaried university
lecturer paid directly by students' fees) at Marburg and later
while professor of New Testament at Heidelberg, studied mis-
cellaneous Hellenistic papyri from Egypt purchased by the University of Berlin. He observed in the papyri some of the same
Greek terms and syntax which were generally believed to be
only in the Bible. Thus he discovered that New Testament
Greek is simply Hellenistic Greek. He next examined how the
terms were used in the papyri, thereby acquiring knowledge
of some of the precise meanings of the terms. Deissmann's
demonstration in his books (1895-1908) that New Testament
Greek is secular Greek aroused the ire of theologians and especially Friedrich W. Blass, a professor of classical philology at Halle-Wittenberg, who attacked his work because it dis-
credited the doctrine of the divine inspiration of the Bible. In
rebuttal Deissmann wrote: "For the investigation of the Greek
Bible it is important above all things to get rid of the methodological idea of the sacred uniqueness of its texts."[16]

In the nineteenth century the main development in the
field of the translation of the Bible into English was the increasing dissatisfaction with the Authorized Version (AV). As
a result of the demand for updating it, a committee of translators produced a revision of it in England, the Revised Version (RV; 1881-95). A few years later Americans produced the
American Revised Version (ARV; 1901), a slight revision of
the RV to bring the translation into harmony with American linguistic usage.

A different kind of translating occurred which also played
an important role in the growth of biblical scholarship. Biblical research performed on the Continent was translated into
English. The translations made the research known in England
and America, and stimulated new study in those countries. As
we have seen, Herbert Marsh translated Michaelis' *Introduc-*

tion to the New Testament into English at the close of the eighteenth century. Early in the nineteenth Connop Thirlwall, bishop of St. David's, Wales, translated Schleiermacher's *Essay on the Gospel of Luke* into English. Both translations fostered scholarship abroad, but the translators were denounced at home for making such unorthodox books available.

Further major advances in textual criticism were made. A principle which emerged in the preceding century now became a firm rule for establishing the Greek text of the New Testament: Obtain the earliest manuscripts possible and generally use them to construct the text. In the nineteenth century Karl Lachmann, professor of classical and German philology at Berlin, dared to carry the principle to its logical end; he discarded the Textus Receptus entirely and made ancient manuscripts the basis of his printed text (1831).

Constantin Tischendorf, professor of theology at Leipzig, also recognized the importance of early New Testament manuscripts written in Greek, and he searched zealously for them from 1840 to 1860. He traveled to many libraries in Europe and the Near East, and at Saint Catherine's monastery at Mount Sinai he discovered a very valuable early manuscript, Codex Sinaiticus.

In spite of the work of Lachmann and Tishchendorf, biblical scholars generally adhered to the Textus Receptus—until Westcott and Hort. Brooke F. Westcott and Fenton J. A. Hort were clergymen and professors at Cambridge University. After thirty years of work they produced a Greek text of the New Testament (1881-82) of such excellent quality that the inferiority of the Textus Receptus was very apparent. They applied Lachmann's principle of using the earliest manuscripts available, and therefore they relied primarily on Codex Vaticanus and secondly on Codex Sinaiticus. These fourth century manuscripts were the earliest Greek New Testament manuscripts then known. Because of its superiority Westcott and Hort's text was a dominant influence on the English translation, the Revised Version. John W. Burgon, Dean of Chichester, and some other conservatives stubbornly continued to advocate the Textus Receptus and vehemently denounced the Westcott and Hort text and the Revised Version.

Hort made another important contribution to progress.

In his introduction to the Greek text he described at length his rules for selecting the best of the variant readings, an improvement on the rules drawn up by Bengel about 150 years earlier. Hort's rules of textual criticism were the standard for many years.

The Jewish scribes who transmitted the Hebrew text of the Old Testament did not create quite as many variants as the Christian scribes who transmitted the New Testament text. A reason is that some Jewish scribes counted the letters after they copied a book, and if the number was more or less than the standard count for that book, they searched for the error. Nevertheless, variants crept into the text of the Old Testament too. In an effort to correct the situation, Christian D. Ginsburg collated 73 manuscripts and 19 printed texts, and then summarized the readings in the footnotes of his publication of the Hebrew text (1894). His work was more accurate than that in earlier printed editions.

Excellent tools for biblical linguistic studies were compiled in the nineteenth century; some of them are still very useful. Gesenius' Hebrew lexicons are examples. H. F. Wilhelm Gesenius, professor of theology at Halle, was the leading expert in his day on classical Hebrew. His Hebrew-German dictionary was a thorough lexicon of biblical Hebrew and Aramaic (parts of Ezra and Daniel are written in Aramaic). It was the foundation of his five-volume *Thesaurus* (1829-42), his most extensive lexicon. In 1892 Francis Brown, Samuel R. Driver, and C. A. Briggs revised and translated Gesenius' lexicon into English; this book passed through several editions and remains a standard work in the field. Brown and Briggs were professors at Union Theological Seminary in New York; Driver was professor of Hebrew at Oxford. Joseph Coppens has called Briggs "the founder of American scientific exegesis."[17] Gesenius' Hebrew grammar was outstanding too; the revision and English translation of it by Emil F. Kautzsch and A. E. Cowley (1909) excels in scholarship. William Rainey Harper at the University of Chicago devised a very effective method of teaching Hebrew, his famous "inductive method" (1885).

Outstanding grammars and lexicons of New Testament Greek were produced also. Two important grammars were the one by J. Georg Winer, who at the time was professor of theology at Erlangen, and the one by Alexander Buttmann, professor of public instruction in Potsdam. In contrast to his predecessors, Winer recognized that biblical Greek should not be forced to conform to either Hebrew syntax or classical Greek. His book was the first scientific grammar of New Testament Greek. Buttmann recognized the possible influence of the Septuagint upon the writing of the New Testament, and therefore he included Septuagint usage in his grammar.

A very valuable aid was the Greek lexicon by Henry George Liddell and Robert Scott, both of Oxford. It gave the meaning of Greek words in classical and Hellenistic literature. Since then it has gone through many revised, expanded editions and has become the standard work in its field. Perhaps the best New Testament Greek lexicon in English in the nineteenth century was Joseph H. Thayer's, which was a favorite in seminaries for many decades.

Several good concordances of the Hebrew text of the Old Testament were produced late in the nineteenth century, including one compiled by George V. Wigram with the assistance of Tregelles and Davidson, and one by Solomon Mandelkern. The best concordance of the Greek text of the New Testament produced in that century is the one by William F. Moulton and Alfred S. Geden; it is based mainly on the Westcott and Hort text. A Scotsman, Robert Young, wrote an analytical concordance which provides scholarly knowledge to the reader who does not know Greek and Hebrew. It lists in English translation all occurences of a particular Hebrew or Greek word in the Bible. An American, James Strong, produced a comprehensive concordance of the words in the Authorized Version. A concordance of special value for learning Hellenistic Greek usage is the *Concordance to the Septuagint* compiled by Edwin Hatch and Henry A. Redpath, which became a standard tool in biblical research. Even though it is more recent, it does not entirely supersede the concordance compiled by Trommius in the eighteenth century.

Sir John C. Hawkins of Oxford wrote *Horae Synopticae,* which is still a useful tool for the study of the linguistic traits and relationships of the synoptic gospels. In his book he compiled lists and statistics of the words and phrases characteristic of each of the gospels.

By the end of the century all the better introductions to and commentaries on the Bible incorporated the historical approach to some extent. H. A. W. Meyer, a Lutheran pastor in Hanover, edited the famous Meyer series of commentaries on the New Testament. In the first volume (1829) he stated emphatically that it is the duty of the biblical exegete to determine "impartially and historico-grammatically" the meaning intended by the author, and also to be unconcerned whether that meaning agrees with current philosophy, "the dogmas of the church or with the views of its theologians."[18] Leopold Rückert, a teacher in the secondary school in Zittau (near Dresden), in his commentary on Romans stressed the historico-grammatical method and the necessity for the exegete to ignore his own views and to maintain "freedom from prejudice."

Wilhelm De Wette's introduction to the Old Testament was the best one produced in the first half of the century. He was professor of theology at Berlin. Abraham Kuenen, professor of Old Testament at Leiden, wrote a three-volume introduction to the Hebrew Scriptures (1861-65), and Driver wrote an introduction in 1891 that was widely used for many years— both scholars used the historical approach. Bernard Duhm, who taught Old Testament exegesis at Göttingen and Basel, wrote commentaries on Isaiah, the Psalms, and Jeremiah that were genuine historical studies.

Winer published a Bible dictionary in 1820 which was much more comprehensive and scholarly than the one produced earlier by Calmet. Winer's dictionary was widely used in German lands through the nineteenth century.

The compilation of accurate lexicons, grammars, concordances, and commentaries is slow, tedious work. The scholars who produced them advanced the historical approach greatly by giving us these essential tools.

Literary Study

Doubts about the traditional dates and authorship of the Old Testament material continued to grow. De Wette concluded (1805) from its literary nature that Deuteronomy was written at the time of King Josiah (ca. 625 B.C.). In his commen-

tary on the Psalms he recognized that at least some of the
Psalms could not have been written by David. The German
Old Testament scholar, Wilhelm Vatke, demonstrated (1835)
that the Levitical laws, or Priestly Code, in the Pentateuch
originated after the Exile instead of before it. Three years
earlier a French professor at Strasbourg, Eduard Reuss, had
recognized this in his lectures, but was afraid to publish the
idea. Karl Graf (1866), a German scholar of the Hebrew language and pupil of Reuss, and Kuenen (1869-70) developed the
conclusion drawn by Vatke and Reuss. Julius Wellhausen, the
famous professor of Semitic languages, adopted and expanded
their view further, and caused a sharp revision of the history
of Israel's religion.

The traditions about the authorship of many New Testament books were recognized more widely as erroneous. Like
Reimarus and Evanson in the eighteenth century, Erhard F.
Vogel, Karl G. Bretschneider, and others in the nineteenth
concluded that the Gospel of John could not have been written
by the apostle John. Schleiermacher said that Paul did not
write 1 Timothy. By showing that the language in all three
pastoral epistles (1, 2 Timothy, Titus) is very unlike that of
Paul, J. G. Eichhorn (1812) and F. C. Baur (1835) demonstrated that those books are not Pauline. Hermann H. Cludius,
superintendent of Hildesheim, noticed the non-Jewish nature of
1 Peter and concluded that it was written, not by Peter, but by
a gentile Christian who was not an apostle. Eichhorn rejected
the traditional authorship of 2 Peter and had doubts about
James, Jude, and 1 Peter.

Throughout the nineteenth century conservative biblical
scholars zealously defended traditional authorship. A prominent exponent of the old view was Theodor Zahn, who taught
New Testament at several German universities near the close
of the century.

Literary study of the Bible led to source criticism and
redaction criticism. Close examination of the books disclosed
that sources were incorporated in some and that some have
been revised, or redacted. This aspect supported other characteristics of the books as evidence that they were not written
by the traditional authors. Redaction may consist of the changes and additions to the source material made by the author or

editor of a book, or it may take the form of changes and additions made by a redactor after the book was written.

Graf, Wellhausen, and Duhm made major contributions to source and redaction criticism of the Old Testament. The Graf-Wellhausen hypothesis of the origin of the Pentateuch is that these first six books of the Bible consist of four main documents (J, E, D, P) and later redactions of them, and that the four documents were rewritten and combined at different times. Wellhausen also realized that the author of 1 and 2 Chronicles reinterpreted the past in terms of his own day by "Judaizing the past" to support Israel's religion and nationalism (1878). Duhm recognized that the Hebrew prophets were in a state of ecstasy when they uttered prophecies. In his studies of Isaiah and Jeremiah he devised methods of distinguishing the words spoken by the prophets from the redactionary material added later (1892, 1901). He was the first to identify accurately the work of the third writer in Isaiah, referred to today as "Trito-Isaiah" (Isa. 56-66). He also commented that the value of the prophetic books is in their ethics and theology, not in their alleged prophecies of Jesus (1875).

Literary criticism of the New Testament progressed more than in any previous century, especially in respect to the gospels. Because Christian liberals made the life of Jesus, not the Bible, the basis of religion, they searched for the "historical Jesus" to determine what he actually said and did. Their search greatly stimulated detailed study of the gospels and the development of source and redaction criticism. The studies raise the question of the relationships among the synoptics and their sources; the question became known as "the synoptic problem." Lachmann was the first to establish on solid evidence the theory of the "priority of Mark" (1835), that is, the view that Mark is the earliest of the four gospels. The idea had been suggested by J. B. Koppe in 1782. Lachmann's theory rested on his observation that the narratives in Mark occur in the other two synoptic gospels and in the same order. Lachmann believed that all three gospel authors used a common written source, which accounts for the similarity among the three gospels.

The real literary relationship of Mark to Matthew and Luke was discovered simultaneously (1838) and independently

by Christian G. Wilke and Christian H. Weisse. Wilke was a
German Lutheran pastor who had been dismissed from his position. In a detailed study made independently of Lachmann,
he recognized that the presence of the Marcan narratives in
Matthew and Luke must be the result, not of an unknown source,
but of the use of Mark as a written source by the authors of the
other two synoptic gospels.

Weisse, professor of philosophy at Leipzig, not only
reached the same conclusion, but carried the solution of the
synoptic problem a step further. He discovered that the authors of Matthew and Luke used two sources. In addition to
Mark they used a collection of "sayings." Weisse regarded the
doublets (two occurrences in a gospel of the same story or saying) in Matthew and Luke as proof of two sources, each of
which contained the story or saying. His discovery was soon
labeled "the two-source hypothesis." He assumed that the apostle Matthew was the author of the sayings source, but that
groundless notion has been discarded. On the other hand, the
basic two-source theory is sound, as Heinrich J. Holtzmann,
in his careful linguistic and literary study of the synoptic gospels, demonstrated very convincingly. The second source (or
sources) is usually referred to as "Q," from the German word
Quelle, "source." The work of Lachmann, Wilke, and Holtzmann established the field of source criticism of the gospels.

Bruno Bauer had the insight to recognize that the evangelist who wrote Mark added to his source material the idea that
Jesus forbade the spirits and people to tell about his healings.
This is the evangelist's device to try to explain why so few
during Jesus' lifetime believed he was the Christ: most people
did not know about his miracles, so they did not believe. At
the beginning of the twentieth century Wrede expanded this "theory of the messianic secret," but concluded that the Christian
community, not the evengelist, created the notion. A few years
later Albert Schweitzer agreed with Bauer that the author of
Mark originated the idea.

Another kind of literary study of the New Testament is
the analysis of the Old Testament quotations in the New Testament. Crawford Howell Toy, while professor of oriental languages at Harvard, pioneered in this field by examining the
quotations in detail.

Although discrepancies in the Bible, especially the gospels, had been listed clearly in the eighteenth century, apologetic efforts to explain away the inconsistencies continued. Eusebius, Chrysostom, Theodoret, and Augustine had struggled with the problem of the discrepancies. From the sixteenth to the nineteenth centuries, inclusive, many books were written which attempted to explain the contradictions as only "apparent." A thorough, but futile, apologetic effort was John W. Haley's *An Examination of the Alleged Discrepancies of the Bible*, published in 1874.

Background of the Old Testament

The history of religions was established as a scientific field of study in the nineteenth century. A pioneer in this work was Godfrey Higgins, a British archaeologist. From about 1813 until his death in 1833, he devoted his life to a quest for information on the subject. He wrote a history of the Sabbath and a study of the Celtic Druids. His most important book, however, was *Anacalypsis*, published posthumously, which was an investigation of the origin of languages and religions.

In the nineteenth century the knowledge of the history of religions was applied to the Bible mainly in connection with the Old Testament. The culture of the Israelites was often similar to that of a neighbor, either because both cultures sprang from the same roots or because the Israelites adopted and modified features of the culture as a result of contact between the peoples. A weakness of Wellhausen's work was that he failed to recognize the influence of other cultures upon Israel.

An important study of the Semitic environment of the Old Testament was made by the Scottish scholar, W. Robertson Smith. Formerly he taught oriental languages and Old Testament exegesis at Free Church College in Aberdeen, but his writings cast doubt on the divine inspiration of the Bible, so he was tried for heresy and dismissed from his professorship. He next was elected a Fellow at Cambridge University, and in 1888-91 he presented at Aberdeen three series of lectures on the religion of the ancient Semites, including the Hebrews; only the first series was published. After John Spencer (17th c.), Eichhorn and Herder (18th c.) had compared Semitic writings.

Smith revived the field of the history of religions by examining
the culture of ancient Semitic nomadic tribes, particularly their
ideas of the "holy" and of sacrifice. His premise was that "the
natural basis of Israel's worship was very closely akin to that
of the neighboring cults."[19] Although some of his conclusions
should be modified, he corrected Wellhausen by recognizing
that in primitive tribes, including the Hebrews, religion was
not individual but social and tribal. Smith also showed that the
element in religion that is the slowest to change is ritual; therefore it is the best aspect to use for recovering the nature of ancient nomadic religions.

        To a large degree it was archaeology that made the his-
tory-of-religions studies of the Old Testament possible; the
general Semitic background was little known until archaeology
began to disclose it. In contrast to Napoleon's invasion, the
archaeological expeditions of the nineteenth century were peaceful expeditions which searched for Assyrian, Babylonian, Canaanite, and Hebrew antiquities. Early in the century standard
methods of excavation did not exist, and archaeologists were
careless in their work. Auguste Mariette in the 1850s and
Heinrich Schliemann in the 1870s, however, led the way in developing scientific methodology.

        In 1838 Edward Robinson of Union Theological Seminary
in New York and Eli Smith, an American missionary and Arabic scholar, crisscrossed Palestine systematically in search
of ancient sites. Their work introduced a scientific approach
to archaeological surface exploration of Palestine. Robinson's
report of their survey of Palestine laid the foundation for future
geographical and archaeological study of that country. In 1842
the Royal Geographical Society of London awarded Robinson a
gold medal for his work. He was the only American before the
Civil War to achieve international recognition as a biblical scholar. Another topographical survey of Palestine was made by
Selah Merrill for the American Palestine Exploration Society
in 1875-77. Archaeological topographical surveys in the nineteenth century aided archaeologists in selecting sites to excavate, and they recorded some remains which have since disappeared.

        While excavating the site of ancient Nineveh, Sir Austen
Henry Layard discovered in 1845 the library of Ashurbanipal,

king of Assyria in the seventh century B. C. The texts written on the thousands of clay tablets could not be translated at first. Another English archaeologist, Sir Henry C. Rawlinson, skillfully succeeded in deciphering the inscription of Darius the Great on the rock of Behistun. That inscription was written in three languages, Persian, Assyrian, and Babylonian. Rawlinson's discovery enabled scholars to translate the Assyrian library and many other tablets written in cuneiform script.

As the opportunity to translate ancient Egyptian and Mesopotamian inscriptions and literature arose, grammars and dictionaries of Near Eastern languages were compiled to aid translators. These tools benefited biblical study, for the resulting translations often disclosed previously unknown aspects of the Old Testament's environment.

The pioneer in applying knowledge of Assyrian archaeology to Old Testament study was the German professor Eberhard Schrader; he incorporated it in his revision of De Wette's *Introduction to the Old Testament*. In 1872 he effectively replied to Alfred von Gutschmidt's attack on Assyriology, and in 1875 he became the first professor of that subject in Germany (in Berlin). Soon Francis Brown at Union Theological Seminary in New York also became expert in observing the relations between Assyrian archaeology and the Old Testament. He wrote an outstanding discussion of the use and abuse of Assyriology in biblical study, and he was the first professor in the United States to teach Assyriology.

Tablets inscribed in Akkadian script were found in 1887 at Tell el-Amarna in Egypt. They include letters sent to the Egyptian kings Amen-hotep III and Amen-hotep IV (Akh-en-Aton) in the fourteenth century B. C. by vassal rulers and administrators in Syria, Phoenicia, and Palestine. Among the letters are some written by the governor of Jerusalem appealing for Egyptian military assistance to repel the "Hapiru" who were plundering the land and whose king was capturing the cities. These letters reveal the chaotic conditions at a time when the Egyptian rule over Palestine was weak.

Archaeology is now generally accepted as a necessary field of study for discovering information that aids our understanding of the Bible. But at first many biblical scholars ignored it or looked on it with suspicion, because it indicated

that biblical religion was not so unique as tradition had led them
to believe. Rudolf Kittel, however, applied the information
from the Amarna tablets in his two-volume account of Hebrew
history.

Knowledge of the geography of the lands involved is also
essential. George Adam Smith's *Historical Geography of the
Holy Land* was a landmark of this kind. Smith traveled extensively in Palestine, Syria, and Egypt. His book was widely
read and was used in courses in many colleges and seminaries;
twenty-five editions of it were printed.

What really happened in the past was often different from
the accounts in ancient sources, and reconstructing, or determining, actual history is an essential aspect of the historical
approach. A German secular historian, Barthold Georg Niebuhr, wrote a three-volume history of Rome that incorporated
source analysis. His methodology influenced some biblical
scholars, especially F. C. Baur. Secular methods of investigating history transformed the interpretation of the Bible.

Kuenen (1869-70) and Wellhausen (1878) were pioneers in
applying some of the new methods to the reconstruction of Israelite history. Nevertheless, influenced by the nineteenth century philosophy of cultural evolution, which maintained that society develops in a straight line from the lowest toward the
highest forms, they erred by postulating three successive
stages of development of Israel's religion: popular, prophetic,
and priestly. Actually, all these types often existed at the
same time.

Skepticism grew concerning the historical accuracy of
the Old Testament. Some Biblical scholars realized that its
books were written to promote certain beliefs and practices
and that this fact must be taken into account. John William
Colenso, Anglican bishop of Natal, Africa, questioned both the
traditional authorship of the Hexateuch and the historicity of
its accounts. He was deposed by his superior bishop in 1863,
partly because of such unorthodoxy and partly because he permitted the Christian natives to continue practicing polygamy.
Wellhausen and his followers, too, rejected the traditional view
that the Old Testament is a reliable record of Hebrew history;
they further denied that there has been divine intervention in
the affairs of human history.

The Israelites' hopes for the future of their nation played an important role in their history, and recognition of the nature and variety of those aspirations is necessary. The first to grasp this historically were the Italian Jew David Castelli (1874) and the American Christian Charles Briggs (1886).

Background of the New Testament

Gradually biblical scholars developed their understanding of the Jewish background of the New Testament and the influence of Judaism on early Christianity. Edward Everett, Unitarian minister in Boston and later president of Harvard, recognized in 1814 that when the apostolic writers applied Old Testament quotations to Jesus "in a reference other than their original and true one," they did so because as Jews they were using the same method of interpretation of Scripture that the rabbis used.

Emil Schürer, while professor of New Testament at Giessen, Germany, wrote the second edition (1886–87; much superior to the first edition) of his history of the Jewish people from 165 B.C. through the first century of the Christian era. Regrettably, he, and many others since, exaggerated the extent of Jewish legalism. Nevertheless, Schürer achieved his aim of providing a fuller view of the Jewish background and environment of primitive Christianity.

Adolf Hilgenfeld, professor of New Testament at Jena, was the first to recognize clearly that Christian apocalyptic writings (secret revelations about the future) grew out of Jewish apocalyptic thought. The influence of Jewish eschatology (beliefs about the end of this age or world) upon Paul's theology was pointed out by Richard Kabisch, professor of New Testament and systematic theology at Halle.

Otto Everling, a German Evangelical pastor, examined the Jewish literature current in Paul's day and observed that Paul's notion of angels and demons came from contemporary Judaism. The famous Old Testament scholar, Hermann Gunkel, commented that Paul's concept of the activities of the Holy Spirit was typical of popular Judaism in his day (1888).

For many years it was customary to divide the non-Christian religious background of the New Testament into Judaism

and Hellenism, without recognizing the existence and influence
of Hellenistic Judaism, which was Judaism mixed with the
thought of Greek and Near Eastern religions and philosophies.
However, Otto Pfleiderer, professor of systematic theology at
Berlin, realized that Paul's theology was a combination of early Christianity, Pharisaic Judaism, Hellenistic Judaism, and
Greek mystery religions. The discovery that Hellenistic Judaism was a strong influence on the New Testament was an important advance.

Knowledge of the Christian background of the New Testament grew too. Both the New Testament and the early Christian literature outside of the canon supply important information about the life and thought of the early Christians. The
canon made the Christian literature outside of it seem unimportant, but actually much of this literature comes out of the
same general church stream as the New Testament. Even the
early Christians found that their books were so similar in nature that they had great difficulty in deciding which belonged in
the canon. Franz Overbeck, while professor of early church
history at Basel, recognized the principle that all early Christian literature should be studied in order to reconstruct church
history (1873, 1875). In 1886 Albert Eichhorn, who was professor of church history at Halle, also insisted on this principle.[20]

An early Christian writing, previously unknown to the
modern world, was found in Constantinople in 1873 by P. Bryennios. It was the *Didache* (pronounced did-a-KAY), or *Teaching of the Twelve Apostles*, an early guide to morals and
church practices. Joseph B. Lightfoot, professor of divinity
at Cambridge and later bishop of Durham, was the first to study
intensively any of the Apostolic Fathers, namely, Clement of
Rome, Ignatius, and Polycarp (1869-85). He tried to determine their date and authenticity. Adolf von Harnack made the
first extensive survey of early Christian literature (1893-1904).
Whereas Lightfoot's works were intensive studies of a few writings, Harnack's work was a four-volume comprehensive survey
of Christian literature until Eusebius (ca. 350), with dates. In
a lecture (1897) Wilhelm Wrede agreed with scholars from
Eichhorn to Harnack that early Christian literature and history
should be studied as a whole, and not limited to the canon.

The growth in the knowledge of early Christian writings fostered the understanding of early church history, which is reflected in the writings. A major development in learning the Christian background was the recognition of the rivalry between the Judaizers (the Jewish Christians who believed that all Christians should continue to observe the Jewish law) and Paul (and the members of his churches), who believed that gentile Christians are free from that law. As early as 1718 John Toland, an Irish Protestant Deist, had realized that those two groups had existed, but his discovery was soon forgotten. Ferdinand Christian Baur, professor of church history and dogmatics at Tübingen, presented the idea anew very forcefully (1831, 1835, 1847). He drew attention to Paul's references to rivals who followed the leadership of James (Gal. 2:12) and Peter (1 Cor. 1:12) and insisted on Jewish circumcision of converts (Phil. 3:2; Gal. 2). Baur concluded that the Judaizing party originated in the Jerusalem church under the leadership of James, Jesus' brother, whereas Paul was the leader of the gentile Christian party opposed to circumcision. Various New Testament books reflect the fact that the conflict between the parties affected the church so deeply that many attempts were made at mediation and settlement. The author of Acts has altered history by setting aside the differences between Paul and Peter in an effort to bring harmony to the church; therefore, said Baur, Acts is not a reliable source of history. Although Baur went too far by seeing the Judaizing issue everywhere in the church (he thought that any New Testament book that does not refer to it must be late), the existence of the dispute and its influence on Acts is certain. Baur found that the gospels, too, were written primarily to promote ideas (1847). He also recognized that the Christian background of the gospels not only consists of the time of the life of Jesus, but extends up to the time that the authors wrote. This is a very important principle, applied less successfully in the previous century by Reimarus.

Edwin Hatch, Anglican churchman, delivered the Bampton Lectures at Oxford in 1880 on the subject of the organization of the early Christian churches. He discerned the change in organization from administration by presbyters, or elders, to administration by bishops. He recognized that the presbyter

system was inherited from Judaism and that the bishop system
was borrowed from the gentile world, for "bishop" was the
term for the financial administrators of Greek religious asso-
ciations.

Knowledge of the Christian background not only influenced biblical interpretation directly, but also affected the
writing of introductions to the Bible and histories of early
Christianity. Reuss wrote the first introduction to the New
Testament books that placed them within the setting of early
church history. Carl Weizsäcker, professor of church history
at Tubingen, assembled some of the new information and wrote
a history of Christianity in the apostolic age.

The gentile or pagan background of the New Testament
is very important, not only because Christianity early expanded into gentile lands, but especially because the Gentiles who
were converted to Christianity usually brought with them vocabulary, ideas, and practices from their former religions. Thus
gentile culture influenced the life of the Christian communities
and the writing of the New Testament. Recognition of the gentile background became specific in the nineteenth century. Grotius in the seventeenth and the myth school in the eighteenth
centuries had searched for parallels in classical literature,
but the relation was usually loose, such as some similarity of
a certain Greek myth to a certain biblical myth. At the close
of the nineteenth century, however, a few scholars of the history-of-religions school traced some direct cause-and-effect
relationships. Hatch not only discovered that the Christian office of bishop was adapted from the pagan world, but he pointed out other Greek influences, including philosophy, on early
Christianity (1900). Paul Wendland, a classical philologist,
suggested in 1895 that both Philo and New Testament writers
adopted some Cynic-Stoic philosophy and literary forms.[20a]

Two other German classical philologists, Hermann Usener (1889) and Albrecht Dieterich (1891) examined magic papyri from Egypt and noted possible influence from the Hellenistic religions popular in New Testament times. Dieterich remarked that Paul's mention of the "elements" ("spirits" is not
in the Greek text) in Galatians 4:3, 9 must be a reference to
the same physical elements (earth, air, fire, and water) that
are regarded as demons in the magic papyri. It was an im-

portant advance when scholars looked for possible influence from the religions actually current among the people in the environment of early Christianity.

Albert Eichhorn noticed that the idea of eating and drinking Jesus' body and blood is contrary to the Old Testament (eating blood is expressly forbidden in Lev. 7:26-27), and he commented that its origin is difficult to explain. He rightly discerned that the notion must have come from the gentile world, but he erred in connecting it with gnosticism.

Franz Cumont, curator of the royal museum at Brussels, produced a very thorough compilation of the literary matter and archaeological remains pertaining to the cult of Mithra, the mystery cult which was very popular with the Roman soldiers. His work (1896-99) was the first comprehensive study of a pagan mystery cult; it still provides contemporary source material for studying the gentile environment.

Lives of Jesus and Paul

Many "lives of Jesus" were written in the nineteenth century that were not accurate. Conservative Christians ignored historical methods in interpreting the gospels. Liberal Christians used the methods only when the results suited them. Influenced by the philosophy of rationalism, the liberals presented Jesus' life as entirely reasonable from the nineteenth-century standpoint. The gospel miracle stories were not recognized as myths, but were reinterpreted as natural events which could have happened. In an effort to reconcile belief in the accuracy of the Bible with disbelief in the supernaturalism of the miracle stories, Heinrich Paulus wrote an extremely rationalistic life of Jesus, published in 1828.

An aspect of most other rationalistic lives of Jesus was that they eliminated Jesus' acceptance of Jewish eschatology with its belief in the imminent coming of the kingdom of God, the resurrection, and the judgment day. Both Schleiermacher and Karl Hase eliminated the eschatology and rationalized the miracles in their accounts of Jesus. Both preferred John to the synoptic gospels because that gospel removes Jesus' preaching from its eschatological framework. Schleiermacher apparently was the first to give lectures on the life of Jesus (at the

Berlin university, 1819-32). They were not published until
1864, after his death, when they were reconstructed from students' notes of his lectures delivered in 1832. They profound-
ly influenced the views of Christian liberals. Holtzmann, too,
excluded eschatology from Jesus' thinking, and claimed that
Jesus expected to bring about the spiritual rule of God in the
hearts of men, a rational kingdom of goodwill (1863). The
nineteenth-century liberal interpretations of Jesus culminated
in Adolf von Harnack's presentation in his *Textbook of the
History of Dogma* (vol. 1, 1886).

    Two influential biblical scholars mixed a considerable
amount of the historical approach into their rationalistic interpretations of Jesus. David Strauss, in his famous *Life of Jesus* (1835-36), recognized that Jesus preached the coming of
the Jewish eschatological kingdom. Strauss rejected the Gospel of John as a source, and showed that though there are
myths in all four gospels, those in John are later and more developed than those in the synoptics. In 1839 Strauss was
called to the university at Zurich to be professor of dogmatic
theology, but his book so provoked the antagonism of conservative Christians that the university withdrew the appointment
and gave him a small pension instead. He spent the rest of his
life as a free-lance writer in various German cities. Regrettably, when he wrote the revised edition of his *Life of Jesus*
(1864), he eliminated the eschatology and portrayed Jesus completely in terms of rationalistic theology.

    The second scholar to mix the historical and rationalistic
approaches was F. C. Baur (1847). He came nearer to being a
historian than Strauss, however. He concluded that the differences between John and the other three gospels are not the result of more historical information in John, for such information is not there. Instead, he said, the differences are the result of the evangelists' tendencies, or views they wanted to promote; the Johannine author was dominated by the "overriding
idea" of the divine glory of Jesus. Baur stated that Jesus taught
a pure, moral religion, but Paul substituted for it faith in the
person of Jesus. Baur erred, however, by rationalizing Jesus'
teaching and in thinking that the Gospel of Matthew does not exhibit a tendency to foster the evangelist's point of view.

    How should we evaluate the liberal "lives" of Jesus? In

spite of their faults, these sketches made a contribution. Their boldness in being the first to make a sharp break with traditional views about Jesus opened the way for better work later. The fact that they were related to rationalist philosophy and to its offspring, deistic theology, both of which were popular in educated circles, increased their influence. A second positive value was the recognition of the humanity of Jesus. Also, these liberal writers rightly recognized that religion should be reasonable, but they erred in thinking that the life of Jesus necessarily was in harmony with rationalist philosophy. Finally, some of the authors were groping their way toward historical methods in that they recognized myths and tried to distinguish between historical and unhistorical material in the gospels.

On the subject of Jesus' life, liberal and conservative Christians shared three faults. First, both groups failed to make adequate use of historical methods. Second, their portraits of Jesus were very inaccurate. The third fault in common was that they were biased against recognizing the Jewishness of Jesus' religion.

A few scholars rejected rationalism and tried to write genuine historical biographies of Jesus. While the French orientalist, Ernest Renan, was on an archaeological expedition in Palestine, he wrote his classic *Life of Jesus*, which sold widely for many years in French, German, and English. The book caused his dismissal from the Collège de France in Paris. Like the liberals, he portrayed Jesus as entirely human, but unlike many of them, he maintained that Jesus believed in Jewish eschatology.

The typical liberal claim that Jesus' preaching was independent of Judaism was so contrary to the evidence that sooner or later it was bound to be exposed by historians. Reimarus had concluded in the eighteenth century that Jesus proclaimed the Jewish kingdom of God, but biblical scholars ignored his conclusion. Late in the nineteenth century Johannes Weiss, professor of New Testament at Göttingen, examined the apocalyptic writings prevalent in Judaism in Jesus' day, with their predictions of the coming of a new age, the Messiah, judgment day, and resurrection of the dead. Weiss demonstrated that it was this eschatological kingdom that Jesus proclaimed (1892).

Conservative and liberal Christians alike reacted against his interpretation, for it upset their respective theologies. Even the historical-minded biblical scholars Gunkel and Wilhelm Bousset opposed the idea. But Weiss soon received decisive support from Albert Schweitzer's two books on the subject at the beginning of the next century: *The Mystery of the Messiahship and the Passion* and *From Reimarus to Wrede*. The second book became famous in England and America under its English title, *The Quest for the Historical Jesus*. These books clearly established the Jewish eschatological and national character of Jesus' message.

The unorthodox speculative lives of Jesus written by liberals stirred up zealous opposition from Christian conservatives. Martin Kähler wrote a book, *The So-called Historical Jesus and the Historic Biblical Christ* (1892), which epitomizes the conservative stance against both the rationalists and the historians. He was professor of New Testament and systematic theology at Halle. He claimed that it is "the task of the dogmatic theologian" to fight against "historical scholars." "The real Christ," he claimed, is "the Christ who is preached"; the historical Jesus is irrelevant for Christian faith.[21] Several fallacies are inherent in his argument. One is that Kähler classified all the lives of Jesus in his day as "historical," a label the rationalist accounts do not deserve. Secondly, as W. G. Kümmel has expressed it, he failed "to appreciate the inescapability of historical research in the Gospels."[22] Thus he rejected historical methods that are now standard in biblical interpretation. The third fallacy is Kähler's claim that the Christ who is preached is the "real Christ." Actually, that Christ never existed; he is even more a product of human imagination than is the Jesus of the rationalists!

Several writers even charged that Jesus was only a fictional character. Bruno Bauer, a theologian at Bonn University, concluded that all the gospels are derived from an original gospel written by one person and that Jesus was not a historical person. (Early in the twentieth century Arthur Drews, a teacher at the Technical High School at Karlsruhe, Germany, wrote a two-volume work, *The Christ Myth*, in which he, too, asserted that Jesus never lived. A Frenchman, P.-L. Couchard, drew the same conclusion in 1924).

Is it possible that Jesus was only a myth? It is true that much has been assigned to him that never happened, and in the ancient world there were many stories, told as true, about people and deities who never lived. The fact that millions of people through the centuries have believed in Jesus does not prove his reality. Nevertheless, the "Christ-myth school" of thought was wrong. One feature in early Christian tradition shows plainly that Jesus was an actual person, not a myth. The central belief in very early Christianity was that Jesus is the Messiah, the Christ, and fulfills Old Testament prophecy. But Jews rightly objected that several basic features of his life did not agree with the prophetic expectation of the Messiah, and in the New Testament as well as in the early Christian literature outside of it, the authors frequently strain to answer the objection. One such feature is the death of Jesus at the hands of the gentile rulers, the Romans. Jewish predictions agreed that the Messiah would be a king who would overthrow the gentile rule over the Jews, but Jesus' career was just the opposite. Instead of defeating the Romans, he was killed by them! If Jesus were a mythical figure, deliberately created by Christians, they would not have invented the embarrassing feature of his crucifixion by the Romans, a feature that early Christian apologists found so difficult to explain.

Not only Jesus' life, but Paul's life and teaching were idealized too. F. C. Baur, in his *Paul, the Apostle of Jesus Christ*, claimed that as a result of his conversion experience Paul perfected Jesus' spiritual religion and interpreted baptism and the Lord's Supper as symbolic acts, not sacraments. In the first volume of his history of dogma, Harnack took a similar position and ignored Paul's eschatology and the influence on him of Hellenistic religions. Such erroneous interpretation of Paul was refuted at the beginning of the next century.

America and the Historical Approach

The historical approach to the Bible came to America very slowly. Early in the nineteenth century the influence of English Deism and German biblical scholarship reached the United States, mainly at Harvard and in Unitarianism. Harvard's Divinity School was established in 1819 and Yale's in

1822. Joseph Buckminster, pastor of Boston's Brattle Street
Church, purchased in Europe a library of 2300 books of biblical criticism that were scarce in America. But he died at the
age of twenty-eight in 1812 before he could put his books to use.
Edward Everett was the first American to earn a German doc-
torate (his was in the biblical field, at Göttingen, 1817); then
unfortunately, he changed to other fields, and his training and
brilliant intellect were lost to biblical studies. However, a
few other New England scholars—Moses Stuart, Theodore Parker, Edward Robinson—did contribute to biblical interpretation.
Nevertheless, their influence was not widespread, and when
they died, American biblical scholarship virtually died with
them. Anti-intellectualism prevailed in the United States
through most of the century. The churches tended to ignore
biblical scholarship, and they directed their attention to the
promotion of denominational and theological causes. Biblical
studies were mainly in seminaries rather than universities,
and the seminaries were expected to serve the promotional
interests of the churches.

Biblical scholarship returned to America in force only
at the close of the century, when the Old Testament scholars
Charles Briggs and Francis Brown joined Union Theological
Seminary in New York, and the new University of Chicago established (1890) its Divinity School, its New Testament Department in the Humanities Division, and its Oriental Institute.
Two enthusiastic biblical scholars were largely responsible for
this development at Chicago, William Rainey Harper, president of the university, and Edgar J. Goodspeed, founder of the
New Testament Department.

More Prejudice against Scholarship

Although by the end of the century the historical approach
to the Bible was widely accepted in educated circles in Europe
and America, religious conservatives continued to wage war
against it on both continents. There were other examples besides the ones we have mentioned.

In Europe Christian conservatives decided that Baur's
pupils had no right to be on the theological faculty at the Tübingen university, so they transferred them to other faculties or

dismissed them from the school. Orthodox opposition prevented Strauss from becoming professor of theology at Zurich.
These are early examples of a recurrent pattern: the unorthodox were forced out of theological faculties, so they had to take
positions on other faculties. Seven English scholars, in their
book *Essays and Reviews* (1860), advocated free inquiry in religion and the Bible. Samuel Wilberforce, Bishop of Oxford,
attacked them as "guilty of criminal levity," and Christian laymen demanded that they be expelled from the church. Two of
the seven authors received synodical condemnation, but the
verdict was reversed by the Privy Council. The book itself
was synodically condemned in 1864. For his pioneering work
on the history of Israel, Wellhausen was attacked so vehe -
mently by church authorities that in 1882 he resigned his professorship of Old Testament at Greifswald, Germany. He,
too, had to change to a non-theological position, that of professor of Semitic languages, first at Halle, and later at Marburg and Göttingen. In an effort to hold the line in Roman Catholicism, the church placed many liberal Christian works on
the Index of proscribed books. Papal infallibility was declared
in 1870, and several encyclicals were issued to inhibit the
growth of modernism in the church. For his unorthodoxy, A.
Loisy in 1893 was removed from his position as professor of
biblical exegesis at the Catholic Institute in Paris.

In the United States C. H. Toy's interpretation of Scripture while he was teaching at Southern Baptist Theological Seminary was so upsetting to the seminary's constituents that he resigned in 1879. The following year he became a professor at
Harvard. Briggs, the great scholar of Hebrew language at
Union Theological Seminary in New York, was convicted of heresy in 1893 by the General Assembly of the Presbyterian
Church, but he was ordained later by the Protestant Episcopal
Church. "Fundamentalism" as an organized movement in opposition to "modernism" in religion began with the Bible Conference of Conservative Christians, which was held at Niagara
in 1895. The conference declared the necessity of faith in the
"five points of fundamentalism," one of which was the verbal
inerrancy of Scripture.

Similar tension arose in Judaism. At the beginning of
the century laymen like Israel Jacobson, followed later by rab-

bis such as Abraham Geiger, established the Reform Judaism
movement in German territory. It spread to England and the
United States. A prominent leader in America was Rabbi
Isaac M. Wise, a leader in organizing the Union of American
Hebrew Congregations (1873) and Hebrew Union College (1875).
This liberal movement willingly accepted the historical approach to Scripture and held that only the moral law of the Hebrew Scriptures is binding on Jews. The leaders drew up the
Pittsburgh Platform of 1885, a statement of their theology and
principles. Reaction against Reform Judaism quickly arose,
however, and Samson R. Hirsch in Germany founded New Orthodox Judaism, devoted to the observance of the whole Torah,
with emphasis on the ritual law. Conservative Judaism, led by
Rabbi Zecharias Frankel in Germany, chose a middle course
between the Reform and the Orthodox movements.

        In summary, the nineteenth century—especially the sec-
ond half—brought tremendous progress. Modern English translations of the Bible appeared. English translations of German
biblical research aided the spread of the historical approach.
In New Testament textual criticism, Lachmann discarded the
Textus Receptus as the basis of the Greek text, and the principle was established that the earlier Greek manuscripts should
be the basis of the text. Textual criticism advanced in the Old
Testament field too.
        In linguistics Gesenius, Brown, Driver, and Briggs de-
veloped Hebrew lexicology and grammar. Liddell, Scott, and
Thayer advanced Greek lexicology, but Deissmann's discovery
that New Testament Greek is Hellenistic Greek was the greatest advance in this field. Excellent Hebrew, Greek, and English concordances were produced; introductions and commentaries finally incorporated the historical approach.
        Major developments in literary criticism of the Bible oc-
curred. By the close of the century the traditional authorship
of many books was generally rejected by scholars. Source and
redaction criticism, especially the Graf-Wellhausen hypothesis,
revolutionized Old Testament interpretation. Kuenen and Wellhausen, with their concepts of periods of time and development
in Hebrew history, changed biblical interpretation, though they
carried their ideas too far. In New Testament literary criti-

cism, the "synoptic problem" was recognized, and as solutions, the theory of the priority of Mark and the two-source hypothesis were established. Redaction criticism and detailed study of Old Testament quotations in the New Testament emerged.

The history-of-religions method of interpretation was established, and the Semitic background of the Old Testament was recognized as a necessary field of knowledge. Archaeology was discovered to be essential too, for it was through its aid that the Semitic background was found. Topographical surveys, archaeological expeditions, and decipherment of ancient scripts led to new understanding of the past. Palestinian geography was investigated scientifically.

The nature of the Jewish environment of early Christianity was more fully understood, and Jewish influence upon the New Testament became more apparent. New Testament writers' application of Old Testament passages to Jesus was found to be invalid, and the method of interpreting the passages was seen as Jewish. Recognition of the existence of Hellenistic Judaism and of its influence upon early Christianity was an important development.

The Christian background of the New Testament emerged as another essential field with the discovery of rival parties in the primitive church and with systematic study of contemporary non-canonical Christian literature. Weizsäcker began the modern effort to describe the history of the early church. As for the gentile background of the New Testament, more specific and more contemporary material was selected; Greek philosophy, magic papyri, and Hellenistic mystery cults were examined for possible influence on early Christianity.

Both rationalistic and historical lives of Jesus were written, which stimulated detailed study of the gospels. The rationalistic ones erred by modernizing Jesus, but they had the merit of calling attention to the ethics in the gospels and, like the historical lives, they helped to open the way for study of Jesus as a man. Weiss and Schweitzer restored Jesus to his Jewish setting by pointing out the eschatological nature of his preaching.

The discovery of reliable methods of investigating and reconstructing history was one of the great achievements of secularism in the nineteenth century. Biblical scholars adopted some of these methods and thereby caused a revolution in the interpretation of the Bible. Previously biblical study was largely linguistic and literary, but now it became more historical, with genuine concern for the historical situation and background.

CHAPTER 7

THE TWENTIETH CENTURY—A

The conflict between traditionalism and modernism in religion has continued in Judaism and Christianity in the twentieth century. To some extent it has spread to Hinduism, Buddhism, and Islam also. In Catholicism the tension came to a head in 1907 when Pius X formally condemned modernism in the church, and in 1908 when he excommunicated the French professor, Alfred Loisy. The struggle between the two forces has been especially intense in Protestantism, where it replaced the Protestant-Catholic clash and the Protestant denominational disputes as the primary battlefield. The fundamentalists exceeded all other Protestant evangelicals in denouncing the historical approach. Few of them had ever studied it. In 1919 the World's Christian Fundamentals Association was formed; it conducted rallies in American cities and split the Protestant churches into fundamentalist and modernist groups. The fundamentalists founded numerous "Bible schools," which carefully prevented their students from learning the historical approach. Evangelists, or revivalists, were invariably fundamentalists. The question of the acceptance of fundamentalism revived again after World War II, becoming a source of tension and division in the evangelical and even some mainline churches.

In spite of the opposition to it, the historical approach advanced, both in factual knowledge and in methodology. A larger number of scholars were engaged in this research than ever before. In Catholicism Pius XII's encyclical, *Divino Afflante Spiritu*, "By the Inspiration of the Holy Spirit" (1943), urged biblical scholars to study the text in its original languages (instead of the Latin Vulgate) and to follow the literal meaning whenever possible. Pope John XXIII encouraged Catholics to employ scholarship in the study of Scripture, and Vatican Council II promoted this policy. In Protestantism a document entitled *Guiding Principles for the Interpretation of the Bible* was adopted by the Ecumenical Study Conference held at Oxford in 1949. Many professors fostered biblical scholarship through their research and teaching.

So much research and publication has occurred in the twentieth century that only some of the most outstanding developments can be mentioned here. The historical approach has not merely expanded—it has exploded, in both volume and scope.

Linguistic and Textual Study

A linguistic issue in the first half of this century was whether or not the gospels and Acts were composed in Aramaic, later translated into Greek, and the Aramaic text subsequently lost (since no Aramaic text has survived). Two men were responsible for this conservative theory—conservative because it seemed to increase the probability that those books contain early, historically accurate material. In 1916 Charles C. Torrey, professor of Semitic languages at Yale, made this claim for Acts; a few years later both he and Charles F. Burney, professor of biblical interpretation at Oxford, said John was originally written in Aramaic. In 1933 Torrey applied the theory to all four canonical gospels. These men argued that Jesus probably spoke in Aramaic, so his words must have been written down first in Aramaic. Also, they said, there are "Semitisms" in the gospels, especially John. The Semitisms are Greek expressions and syntax similar to those in Aramaic and Hebrew; Burney and Torrey claimed that they were carried over into the Greek text by the translators.

Ernest C. Colwell, professor of New Testament at the University of Chicago, wrote a book, *The Greek of the Fourth Gospel*, which was a direct refutation of Burney's *The Aramaic Origin of the Fourth Gospel*. Colwell examined the text of Greek papyri of the Hellenistic and Roman eras, and he found that they, too, contain Semitisms, even though they were originally written in Greek. Thus Colwell discovered that, as the result of the influence of Semitic languages, Hellenistic Greek (in which both the New Testament and the papyri were written) had assimilated Semitic expressions and syntax. The presence of these features therefore does not necessarily indicate "translation Greek." Paul knew Aramaic and used a few Aramaic terms (e.g., *marana tha*, "Our Lord, come," 1 Cor. 16:22), but no one claims that his letters were originally written in Aramaic. Further evidence is the fact that the content of many gospel traditions indicates that they originated in the church in Greek-speaking communities. A further weakness of the Aramaic theory is that its basis was not evidence so much as it was conservative zeal to support the authority of the Bible.

The exciting aspect of textual criticism in this century has been the discovery of earlier manuscripts of the biblical text than have been known since antiquity. Considering that the earlier manuscripts tend to be closer to the original text, some of these discoveries aroused great interest among both scholars and the public.

The manuscripts which received the most publicity are the Dead Sea scrolls found at Qumran in 1947-56; they were written by Jews in Palestine from the second century B.C. to the middle of the first century A.D. A portion of these scrolls contain the Hebrew text of some of the Hebrew Scriptures, or Old Testament, and their content ranges from a fragment of a book to a whole book of the Bible. They are the earliest Old Testament manuscripts known (the oldest previously known was written in the ninth century A.D.). The text in these scrolls sometimes agrees with the Masoretic text, which has been standard among Jews and Christians for centuries, but sometimes it agrees with the Septuagint version and sometimes with the Samaritan text of the Pentateuch. These variations show that the text had not been standardized at Qumran. The effort to achieve uniformity of the text evidently began with the work of the Pharisees at the Council of Jamnia around A.D. 90. The second group of Dead Sea scrolls, those found at Wady Murabbat, were written A.D. 100-135, and in them the scriptural text is uniform and agrees with the Masoretic text. This indicates that the rabbis at the Council of Jamnia succeeded in standardizing the text and that the Masoretes transmitted essentially that same text. The scrolls found at Qumran--in contrast to those found at Murabbat--do not follow the pattern that the earliest manuscripts contain the form of the text nearest the original; apparently a reason is that sectarian interest altered the text at Qumran.

Rudolf Kittel's printed critical text of the Old Testament

is based on the manuscripts transmitted by the Masoretes. In
several successive editions, it has been predominant in seminaries in both Europe and America.

In the field of New Testament textual criticism, the most
significant events of the century have been the discovery of
older New Testament manuscripts in Greek. Previously the
two earliest and best that were known were the fourth century
manuscripts, Codex Vaticanus and Codex Sinaiticus. (The Romans were the first to use the codex, or book type of manuscript, and the early Christians adopted that form.)

In 1931 the Chester Beatty papyri were found and market-
ed by dealers in Egypt. One, P^{46}, was written around A.D. 200
and is very valuable as an early source of the text of Paul's letters. Some leaves are at the University of Michigan and some
are in the Chester Beatty Library in Dublin. Another papyrus,
P^{45}, is a third century codex of the gospels and Acts, in frag-
mentary condition. Its text varies so much from what appears
to be the original text, that it is an exception to the general
rule in New Testament textual criticism that the earliest manuscripts are to be preferred.

P^{52} is a tiny fragment from a papyrus codex of the Gospel of John. Written around A.D. 135, it is the earliest New
Testament manuscript known. It contains only a portion of a
few verses of John 18. Although purchased in Egypt for the
John Rylands Library by B. P. Grenfell in 1920, it remained
unknown until C. H. Roberts identified and published it in 1935.

A Bodmer papyrus, P^{66}, is a codex of the Gospel of John
written in Egypt around A.D. 200. Martin Bodmer purchased
it from a dealer, and it was first published in 1956-58 in transcription by Victor Martin at the University of Geneva. There
were errors in the transcription, however, and a corrected
edition, with facsimiles, was published in 1962.

P^{75}, another Bodmer papyrus from Egypt written about
the same time as P^{66}, originally contained Luke and John, but
only Luke 3-18, 22-24, and John 1-15 have survived. The text
in P^{75} is nearer to the original than that in P^{66}. P^{75} was
published in 1961 and, like P^{66}, is in the Bodmer Library near
Cologny, Switzerland.

These papyri, and a few fragments of others, bring us
closer in time and text to the original New Testament. The

fact that the earliest New Testament texts have been found so recently caused a student to remark, "It makes me feel like I want to grab a shovel and dig for more!"

At the close of the nineteenth century Eberhard Nestle, biblical professor at Tübingen, published his Greek text of the New Testament. Successive revised editions were produced first by him, later by his son Erwin Nestle and Kurt Aland. The twenty-fifth (1963) and the twenty-sixth (1979) editions incorporate the readings from the newly found manuscripts. It is the most widely used Greek text.

Today Greek New Testament manuscripts are identified by C. R. Gregory's system of notation (1907). He revised F. H. Scrivener's system (19th c.), which was an expansion of Wettstein's (18th c.). Now when additional manuscripts are found, Kurt Aland at Münster in Westfalen assigns numbers to them, using Gregory's system.

The discovery of earlier manuscripts stimulated interest in producing more new translations of the Bible. In 1939 the University of Chicago published an accurate translation made directly from the Hebrew and Greek texts, entitled *The Complete Bible: An American Translation*. The translation was called "complete" because it contained the Apocrypha. The translators, chiefly J. M. Powis Smith, Theophile J. Meek, and Edgar J. Goodspeed, were well qualified for the task. The translation most widely used in the mainline Protestant churches, however, is the Revised Standard Version (RSV). It is a revision of the ASV, and like it, preserves some of the expressions of the AV. The translators used textual knowledge from recently discovered manuscripts and philological information from the ancient Semitic and Hellenistic worlds.

Three other English versions are generally accurate. *The Jerusalem Bible* (JB) is an English translation of a French version produced by the Dominican Biblical School at Jerusalem. It incorporates knowledge of the environment of the Old Testament, but the notes and the introductions are weak on modern information. *The New American Bible* (NAB) is a translation produced by The Catholic Biblical Association of America and sponsored by The Confraternity of Christian doctrine. Catholic and Protestant scholars collaborated in this work. This version has been criticized for its concern with liturgical use and for the inconsistent quality of its notes. The Jewish Publication Society is producing *The New Jewish Version* (NJV) of the Hebrew Scriptures, under the editorship of a very capable scholar, Harry M. Orlinsky. Its translators have adhered to the Masoretic text.

More than one motive is responsible for making and publishing new translations. Usually biblical scholars are genuinely interested in making accurate English versions. Invariably they also want to translate into up-to-date English. The desire to translate into modern speech was behind James Moffatt's translation of the Bible in 1926 and Ronald Knox's translation of the New Testament in 1944. When the goal is to translate into modern speech, there is danger of overdoing it, sacrificing accuracy. In the opinion of some biblical scholars, this is the case with *The New English Bible*(NEB). Sometimes the primary motive is promotion of Christianity, especially conservative Christianity; this appears to be the case with *Today's English Version* (the New Testament section was published first as *Good News for Modern Man*) and *The Living Bible*, which in some passages are so interpretive that the reader finds not the Bible, but the opinion of the translators! The profit motive is primary with some publishers. The Bible has long been the world's best seller, and a publisher may be tempted to market a new translation, even though it is not an improvement.

In the twentieth century many superior reference tools have been published. New editions of the Brown-Driver-Briggs and Köhler-Baumgartner Hebrew lexicons have appeared or are in preparation. Excellent lexicons of New Testament Greek have also been produced. For their Greek lexicon, the English scholars James H. Moulton and George Milligan included papyri and non-literary documents among their sources. They began the project in 1908, but after Moulton was killed in World War I, Milligan completed it in 1929. Walter Bauer, professor of New Testament at Göttingen, revised and augmented Erwin Preuschen's lexicon of 1910. Bauer's fourth edition, however, was largely his own work and included the Greek words in early Christian literature outside the New Testament that he found by thorough search of those writings. The fourth and fifth editions have been revised and translated into English by William F. Arndt, F. Wilbur Gingrich, and Frederick W. Danker.

A remarkable lexicon of a special kind was compiled by Gerhard Kittel, professor of New Testament at Tübingen, with the assistance of thirty-nine other German scholars. They began in 1932 to produce a theological dictionary of the New Testament. Forty years in production, this multi-volume set is the fullest dictionary of its kind. The distinctive feature of the work is the comprehensive and detailed discussion of the philological and theological aspects of the Greek words, including the usage in the Septuagint, New Testament, and Jewish and Graeco-Roman backgrounds.

Great progress was made, too, in producing superior grammars of New Testament Greek. A. T. Robertson, professor of New Testament interpretation at Southern Baptist Theological Seminary in Louisville, wrote a thorough grammar of New Testament Greek "in the light of historical research"; like some of the lexicons, it passed through several revised editions. Friedrich Blass wrote a grammar of New Testament Greek in 1896; the fourth edition was revised in 1913 by Albert Debrunner at Bern. This, and successive editions of it, became the predominant reference on the subject. Robert W. Funk, while professor of New Testament at Drew University, translated and revised the 9th/10th German edition in 1961; his revision became the standard in America.

The pioneering work in the compilation of biblical concordances had already been done. In the twentieth century, however, a new technique was used to compile a concordance; the first concordance to the RSV was the first biblical concordance produced by a computer, compiled by John Ellison in 1957. An analytical concordance to the Revised Standard Version of the New Testament has been compiled since by Clinton Morrison. A complete concordance to the Greek text of the New Testament is one compiled under the direction of Kurt Aland. Whereas Moulton and Geden's concordance was based on the Westcott-Hort edition of the text, Aland's is a concordance to a modern Greek text which incorporates readings from the manuscripts discovered in this century. E. Camilo dos Santos has supplemented the Hatch-Redpath concordance to the Septuagint.

Numerous commentary series have been published in this century. "The International Critical Commentary" (ICC) was written for scholars and is famous for its detailed philological analysis of the text. Two other series in English published in the first half of the century are *The Moffatt New Testament Commentary*, written for readers who do not know Greek, and *The Interpreter's Bible*, written for clergymen. Both of these commentaries introduce non-scholars to the historical approach. In the same period the two leading German scholarly commentary series were H. A. W. Meyer's, begun in the nineteenth century, and Hans Lietzmann's, started in 1906. Currently "The Anchor Bible," "Hermeneia," and "The Old Testament Library" are the leading American commentary series. Even today, however, commentaries still tend to be too conservative and to omit much of the gentile and Christian backgrounds of the New Testament.

Many introductions to the Bible have been written, of varying quality. Most deal with either the Old Testament or the New Testament instead of the whole Bible, partly because it is almost impossible to describe adequately such a large subject in a single volume. Important Old Testament introductions have been those by Robert Pfeiffer, Julius Bewer, and Otto Eissfeldt. Good introductions to the Apocrypha are Bruce Metzger's and that in Pfeiffer's *History of New Testament Times*. Kee and Young's *Understanding the New Testament* has been widely used in college classrooms.

Other types of tools for biblical study have been improved also. *A New Standard Bible Dictionary* was compiled by fifty-five scholars, and the more recent, five-volume (including supplement) work, *The Interpreter's Dictionary of the Bible*, is superb. Excellent Bible atlases have been published, including *The Westminster Historical Atlas of the Bible* and *The Oxford Bible Atlas*. Denis Baly's description of the geography of the Bible is a standard guide.

Literary Study

Numerous traditions in the Old Testament went through stages of growth through the years, from oral, to written, to

expanded written form. In the 1930s Professor Johannes
Hempel of Berlin traced the history of Hebrew literature from
oral units through various stages of written forms to the present books of the Bible. He recognized, too, the tendency of
Hebrew writers to create history or retell it. He pointed out
the influence of the Hebrews' religious viewpoint on their literature in each of the literary stages. According to their
viewpoint, all that happened in Israel's history was in accor-
dance with the will of their god, Yahweh. Other Semites in
the ancient world also composed history and revised history
to promote their nation and their religious beliefs and rituals.
Myths were created for similar purposes. We have to be
aware of this motivation in order to understand the literature.
One of the most comprehensive general histories of Hebrew
literature was written by Adolphe Lods, professor of Hebrew
language and literature at the Sorbonne, Paris.

Religious poetry is a category of Hebrew literature with
remarkable beauty of expression. Many pronouncements of
the prophets, as well as the Psalms and Song of Solomon, are
poetry. Sigmund Mowinckel, professor of Old Testament at
Oslo, in his studies of the Psalms interpreted them as cultic
rather than individual in origin; that is, the Psalms were composed by the priests for use by the worshipers. The final
form of the Psalms, he remarked, was the result of centuries
of liturgical use. Although he apparently pressed some of his
theories too far, he stimulated many biblical scholars to investigate the possible influence of the religious life of the community on the poetry.

Literary parallelism, recognized in the eighteenth century as a characteristic of ancient Hebrew poetry, was found
in the twentieth century to have been a feature of the poetry of
the Israelites' neighbors also. In the 1930s the poetic Canaanite texts discovered at Ugarit were deciphered. H. L.
Ginsberg, professor of Bible at the Jewish Theological Seminary of America, examined them and found that Ugaritic as
well as Hebrew poems used conventionally fixed pairs of words
in the parallel relationship. He and Umberto Cassuto demonstrated that Canaanite and Hebrew poetry sprang from a common, Syro-Palestinian, literary tradition. While at the Oriental Institute Stanley Gevirtz made a detailed study and cited

many examples of pairs, such as "thousand(s) . . . ten thousands," and "cursed . . . blessed."

The dates of Hebrew poetry have often been debated. David Robertson has attempted to establish criteria for detecting poems written before the eighth century B.C.

Wisdom literature, which gives practical advice for daily living in this world, is another type of biblical writing. Similar writings were in the literature of other peoples of the ancient Near East, from which the Israelites borrowed some literary forms as well as some ideas. Wisdom books were composed in Egypt from the third to the first millenia B.C., and they were also written in Babylonia. It was discovered that Proverbs 22:17-23:11 is a quotation from the Egyptian wisdom book, *The Teaching of Amen-em-ope*, composed in the latter half of the second millenium. One of the first to study the Old Testament in the light of such knowledge was the English churchman and scholar, W. O. E. Oesterley at the University of London, in 1927. A good recent anthology of studies of Hebrew wisdom writings has been edited by James Crenshaw.

J. Coert Rylaarsdam, while professor of Old Testament at the University of Chicago, saw that the earliest Hebrew wisdom literature, like that in Egypt, originally was secular in nature, and lacked the Hebrew religious theses of Israel's destiny and election by Yahweh. In it wisdom is something that man can obtain for himself. In later traditions, wisdom is a gift from Yahweh and is identified with Hebrew law. G. von Rad contended in 1970 that even the earliest wisdom traditions in Israel were assimilated into Hebrew religion. His theory is not as plausible as Rylaarsdam's, for the "Judaizing" of wisdom was a cultural process which must have taken time.

A very significant development in the twentieth century is the large number of intensive studies of the literary structure of the Bible. Wellhausen's documentary theory of the Pentateuch was modified by his followers. They recognized more fully than he that the J and E documents were not each written by a single author, but are themselves composite. These scholars extended the documentary theory to the Book of Joshua. Conservative reaction against the theory was strong. Trying to save the old view that the Pentateuch was written by a single author, Cassuto and A. Bea contended that

the linguistic and stylistic differences in it are merely delib-
erate variations in the style of the author. This unsound argument has been used to deny the multiple authorship of other
composite books of the Bible too. Inconsistency in a biblical
book should alert us to the probability of composite authorship,
for invariably the combined work of several writers is more
inconsistent than the writing of a single author.

Opposition to the documentary method came also from a
new field, form criticism of the Old Testament. It originated
in Germany, and is generally known as *Formgeschichte* (lit.
"form history"). It is the study of units of biblical tradition by
analyzing their literary form in relation to the *Sitz im Leben,*
the "setting in life," that is, their role in the life and faith of
the contemporary religious community. The units (sometimes
called "pericopes") are presumed to have originated independently of each other in the oral tradition. The ultimate origin
of the idea is the work of secular scholars who formulated
rules of development that various types of popular literature
apparently followed; leaders in that research were Ferdinand
Brunetiere (1890) and Axel Olrik (1909). The oral tradition
theory was applied to Genesis (1901) and to the Psalms (1904)
by Hermann Gunkel (he called his method *Gattungsgeschichte*
("genre history," type criticism). He claimed that the literary type of the unit of oral tradition discloses the specific situation in the life of the people in which the tradition arose. His
classification of the psalms into five main types opened up a
whole new field of study of the origin and nature of individual
psalms. Mowinckel applied form criticism to the royal
psalms associated with the kings. Both Gunkel and Mowinckel
provided new insights into the role of the Israelite kings and
their relation to the god Yahweh. Hugo Gressmann, privatdocent for Old Testament exegesis at Kiel, applied the method
to Exodus (1913). Several German scholars, including the Old
Testament professors, Gerhard von Rad and Martin Noth, have
studied the Hebrew Scriptures extensively in the light of form
criticism. A current project to produce a twenty-four volume
commentary on the forms of Old Testament literature is co-
edited by Rolf Knierim of the Claremont Graduate School and
Gene M. Tucker of Emory University, with the cooperation of
the Institute for Antiquity and Christianity in Claremont.

The oral tradition theory can be carried too far, as when Ivan Engnell at Uppsala excluded the possible use of written sources in the first four books of the Bible. It is speculative to assume that all traditions must have gone through an oral stage. George Widengren, also at Uppsala, has reasoned logically that some Israelite prophecy may not have been transmitted orally before being set down in writing.   Evidence from the ancient Near East indicates that religious traditions were written down early, so oral transmission may not have been as large a factor in the literary history as some scholars have believed.

The recognition grew that the Israelites revised history and wrote stories as history to promote national and religious interests.   Leonard Rost analyzed 2 Samuel 9-20, and concluded that it is a Succession Narrative composed to support the Davidic dynasty. A study of the theology in the historical books of the Old Testament was made by G. von Rad. According to that theology, Yahweh is master of the universe and controls history; he has chosen the Israelites to be his people, and he uses history to reveal his will to them.

Literary criticism of the gospels has developed to an advanced stage as the result of many detailed studies. The arrangement of the synoptic gospels in parallel for easy comparison has been very helpful, and is used in most seminaries. The best such arrangement of the Greek text was edited by Aland (1964), and the best in English translation was compiled by Burton Throckmorton, Jr.

The analysis of the literary style of New Testament authors is a major aspect of literary criticism. Cadbury carefully examined the style and literary method of the author of Luke in 1920, while F. J. Foakes-Jackson and Kirsopp Lake studied the composition and authorship of Acts (1920-33). Two Scotsmen, A. Q. Morton and James McLeman, made a computer analysis of the text of the fourteen epistles traditionally ascribed to Paul, and they found that the style is similar in only five: Romans, 1 and 2 Corinthians, Galatians, and Philemon. Therefore they concluded that only these five were written by Paul. Many biblical scholars add two more, Philippians and 1 Thessalonians.

Source criticism of the New Testament has focused

mainly on the gospels, Acts, 1 John, and Paul's letters. Harnack's **The Sayings of Jesus** was a classic study of "Q" in Matthew and Luke. Harnack, William Sanday, and others tried to identify the Q material. Its contents are outlined by Frederick C. Grant in his book, **The Gospels: Their Origin and Their Growth** (pp. 59-60). Richard Edwards has compiled a concordance to Q and described its theology.

As early as 1796 Jacob Eckermann had presented a source theory on the composition of the Gospel of John, and various source theories on John appeared in the nineteenth century. None of these had a solid foundation which withstood critical examination. The first scientific efforts at source analysis of John appeared in the journal articles of two men: the English clergyman, James M. Thompson (1915, 1916), and the German biblical scholar, Alexander Faure, in 1922. Bultmann (1941) was the first to conclude that there are four main strands in John: a narrative source, a speech source, the composition of the author, and the work of the final redactor who added chapter 21. [22a] But Bultmann erred in some of his criteria for determining to which writer the passages belong, and he was mistaken in assuming that the speech source was originally written in Aramaic by disciples of John the Baptist. In 1970 Robert T. Fortna, professor of religion at Vassar College, was the first to put the theory of a narrative source, called "The Gospel of Signs," on a sound basis supported with linguistic evidence, but he did not recognize the speech source and the work of the redactor. H. M. Teeple found the same four main writers in John that Bultmann detected, but differed from Bultmann on some of the content of their work and some of the criteria for determining the composition of each writer. He discovered that the source in the Prologue (John 1:1-18) is itself composite; the source is a Christian gnostic hymn which contains a source, a Jewish poem.

Redaction criticism of the New Testament has made splendid progress in this century. The effect of the authors' views upon their writing and their treatment of sources has been examined especially in the gospels. The authors of Matthew and Luke definitely were redactors, for when they used Mark as a source, they made changes in the Marcan material. It is also apparent that Matthew, at least, made changes in the

Q material. Recent research indicates that the author of John restated passages in his speech source by repeating them in a modified form, and he made other insertions to advance his point of view.

The effect of the evangelists' beliefs upon their writing the gospels is the subject of the classic History and Interpretation in the Gospels, written by Robert H. Lightfoot (1935). Lightfoot, who was professor of biblical exegesis at Oxford, concentrated on the evangelists' interpretation of their material; he asked what ideas they were trying to promote when they selected and arranged it. A year later Ernst Lohmeyer, professor of New Testament at Greifswald, Germany, recognized that Luke had an apologetic motive for representing the disciples as remaining in Jerusalem after Jesus' death instead of returning home to Galilee. In mid-century several German scholars were very active in this field: Günther Bornkamm and others analyzed Matthew, Hans Conzelmann examined Luke, and Willi Marksen studied the redaction in Mark. American scholars have continued this important work; for example, Edward Blair and Jack Dean Kingsbury on Matthew, Theodore Weeden on Mark, and Charles Carlston on the synoptic gospels.

Redaction has been detected in other New Testament books also. Martin Dibelius, professor of New Testament at Heidelberg, concluded that the speeches in Acts were composed by the author of Luke-Acts to promote certain views (1951). Eric Titus, professor of New Testament at the University of Southern California, discovered that chapter 13 in 1 Corinthians is a later insertion by someone else to modify Paul's strong endorsement of prophesying in chapter 14.

Form criticism has been applied extensively to the synoptic gospels. Although form criticism was used earlier in Old Testament research, the term Formgeschichte was used first by Eduard Norden in 1913 in connection with his study of the origin of the Athens speech ascribed to Paul in Acts 17; Dibelius applied it to the gospels in 1919. The form-critical method was applied to the gospels as early as 1912 by Wendland. He concluded that the gospels contain units of oral tradition which the evangelists combined to form the gospels. The traditions were selected, not for their historical, but for their edificatory value. He stated that the passion story is dif-

ferent from the other traditions in the gospels and must have
been one continuous story from its beginning. Wendland's
theory was expanded by Karl Schmidt, Dibelius, and Bultmann.
Bultmann in 1921 analyzed the synoptic units in detail as oral
tradition and discussed their revision by the evangelists.

At first form criticism was disliked by all conservative
Christians because it upset the traditional view of the authorship of the books. Moderate conservatives later endorsed it,
however, as a way to hold on to the belief that at least some
of the material is authentic tradition. They assumed that if a
gospel pericope came from oral tradition, it must be authentic.

Form criticism of the gospels has been pushed too far,
even though some oral units from preaching must have circulated among the churches. To what extent this oral tradition
is incorporated in the synoptic gospels is an open question.
In the case of the Gospel of John the answer is clear; consistent patterns of vocabulary, syntax, and subject matter show
that the sources were written, not oral. Erich Fascher,
Maurice Goguel, and L. Köhler doubted from the beginning
that form criticism applies to the gospels. Recently Erhardt
Güttgemann aptly remarked that form criticism developed
without taking literary criticism sufficiently into consideration.
Dibelius (1919) erred by assuming that certain literary forms
(short sayings and short stories ending in a pronouncement by
Jesus) necessarily indicate authentic tradition of the words
and deeds of Jesus; actually, unauthentic traditions about him
could have been written in those forms too. Also, oral tradition did not necessarily originate in the life and teaching of
Jesus; oral tradition about him could and did originate later in
the Christian communities. Form critics also assume too
easily that by paring off the redactions they arrive at historical acts and sayings of Jesus; the situation was that unauthentic stories and sayings could be expanded later as readily as
authentic ones.

In summary, examination of Greek papyri demonstrated
that Semitisms had been incorporated in the Greek language in
the Hellenistic and Roman periods as the result of cultural contacts, and that therefore Semitisms in the gospels do not indicate that the gospels have been translated from Aramaic. Tex-

tual criticism of the Bible made great strides forward in the twentieth century with the discovery of earlier manuscripts of the text than had been known for many centuries, especially the scrolls from Qumran with the Hebrew text of some of the Old Testament, and the Bodmer and Chester Beatty papyri with the Greek text of some of the New Testament. The manuscripts stimulated interest in making new translations of the Bible. New and greatly improved tools for biblical study appeared. Study of ancient Near Eastern literature facilitated the understanding of the literary types in the Old Testament. The literary structure of the Hebrew Scriptures was studied from the standpoint of oral tradition as well as written documents as sources. The literary characteristics of the New Testament, too, were recognized, including the style of the authors and their use of written documents and possibly oral tradition as sources. Major research was conducted on authors' revision and later redactors' revision of biblical material. Moderation is replacing excesses in form criticism of the Bible.

CHAPTER 8

THE TWENTIETH CENTURY—B

Archaeological and historical information essential for understanding the Bible also mushroomed in this century. Numerous excavations were made by universities, seminaries, and archaeological societies in Europe and America. Tremendous contributions to the knowledge of the historical background of the Bible were made through the discovery of ancient texts and monuments, more careful study of previously known literature and inscriptions, and coordination of biblical and historical investigations.

Background of the Old Testament

Excavations in Palestine have provided much information about the life and culture of the Israelites. The results of this work have been summarized in books by Millar Burrows of Yale, W. F. Albright of Johns Hopkins, and G. E. Wright of Harvard. A comprehensive survey is the four-volume *The Encyclopedia of Archaeological Excavations in the Holy Land*. Archaeology has also given historians knowledge about Jews outside of Palestine. Jewish papyri, written in Aramaic in the fifth century B.C., were found at Elephantine Island in the upper Nile in 1904-1908. A Jewish military colony lived there, and its papyri reveal the life of the colony. The papyri display a surprising amount of assimilation of pagan culture by those Jews.

Archaeology has also disclosed the culture of surrounding countries and the exchange of ideas and customs in the ancient Near East. In 1906-12 the German archaeologist, Hugo Winckler, excavated the ancient capital of the Hittites and discovered clay tablets which gave the modern world its first knowledge of Hittite civilization in the second millenium B.C. Beginning in 1929, C. F. A. Schaeffer, a French archaeologist, excavated Ugarit (modern name: Ras Shamra), the Canaanite capital in northern Syria. The close parallels, or similarities, between the Ugaritic texts and the Old Testament indicate that Canaanite religion influenced the Israelite rituals of sacrifice, the myths, and the attributes ascribed to Yahweh; this process began when the Hebrews settled among the Canaanites, and it continued after the exodus. Important comparisons of the Canaanite and Israelite religions have been made by A. S. Kapelrud, F. M. Cross, L. B. Fisher, and others.

Albrecht Alt, later professor of Old Testament at Basel, found that ancient Israel had more contact with Egypt than had been realized. E. Wallis Budge of Cambridge and the British Museum, and James H. Breasted of the Oriental Institute, made significant studies of the nature of ancient Egyptian religion. Breasted demonstrated that the Egyptians developed a social conscience long before the Hebrew prophets did. By showing that similar religious and ethical ideas existed in Egypt before they did in Israel, Breasted's work helped to disprove the claim that the Hebrew religion was uniquely revealed.

While Assyria dominated Palestine, features of its religion were admitted into the Israelite sanctuaries. The Israelite kings Ahaz and Manasseh promoted the process in order to gain favor with the Assyrian kings, but the reform kings, Hezekiah and Josiah, and the Israelite prophets reasserted the worship of Yahweh only. During the exile, elements of the Babylonian religion were modified and assimilated into the Yahweh cult. Descriptions of the Babylonian and Assyrian religions were written by Morris Jastrow (1912) of the University of Pennsylvania and by Samuel H. Hooke (1962), professor of Old Testament at the University of London. Outstanding special studies of ancient Near Eastern religions include Henri Frankfort's *Kingship and the Gods*, T. H. Gaster's *Thespis*, and E. O. James' *Myth and Ritual in the Ancient Near East*. While the Persians ruled over them, the Jews borrowed from them many religious beliefs. During the Greek period strong tension existed among Jews over the assimilation of Greek thought and customs.

Historians soon compared the new knowledge of these religions with what was known of the Israelite religion. They searched for instances of borrowing and of modification by the Jews of features of the religion of their neighbors and their conquerors. Scholars also observed the Israelite rejection of many foreign beliefs and practices. Leaders in the field early in this century were Hugo Gressmann in Germany and Julian Morgenstern in the United States. In 1922 Gustav Hölscher used knowledge of the Near East environment to delve more deeply than his predecessors into the nature of early Israel's religion. This kind of study was continued by Hooke (1933) and later by Cyrus Gordon, who was professor of Old Testament at Brandeis University. James Pritchard of Princeton made a thorough compilation of Near Eastern pictures and texts relating to the Old Testament.

At the turn of the century Rudolf Kittel and Ernst Sellin achieved a historical sense that was a substantial improvement over the prevailing views. They rejected both the traditional view of no change having occurred in Israel's religion and the evolutionary view of the Wellhausen school that there were three successive stages. They recognized a middle position that, although there was development, it was not in a straight line, and various kinds of religion often existed side by side. Thus Kittel and Sellin reached a sound understanding of the processes of history. The new historical sense led to a more accurate understanding of the Old Testament and Israel's past. Outstanding histories of Israel have been written by Martin Noth (1956) and by John Bright (1959).

The role of the prophets and the relation between them and the priests has been the subject of much investigation. Adolphe Lods wrote an important treatise on the prophets and their influence in shaping Judaism. However, the old view that there was always a sharp distinction between the theology of the priests and that of the prophets has been disproved. This indicates that, in spite of some differences, prophetic religion was not necessarily hostile to priestly religion.

Whether or not the stories of Abraham and the patriarchs in Genesis are at least partly historical is a question to which much research has been devoted. T. L. Thompson has rejected the arguments for the historicity of the patriarch stories, and John Van Seters has concluded that the traditions in the Bible are too late to enable us to recover the "Abraham of history." Many persons would like to corroborate the existence of Abraham, but the mention of an Abraham in the Ebla tablets can hardly refer to the biblical Abraham. Other persons must have had that name too, and there is no evidence so far that it refers to the same Abraham. A similar situation is the name Jesus on an ossuary found in Jerusalem; it does not prove that the bones of Jesus of Nazareth have been found, for Jesus, or Joshua in Hebrew, was a common name.

Research on the nature and development of Israelite thought has produced numerous studies of special topics. Professor Coppens regards Johannes Pederson's detailed study of Israel's life and culture as the outstanding work on the psychology of the ancient Israelites. At Oxford, H. Wheeler Robinson investigated the role in the Old Testament of the belief in divine inspiration and revelation. The comparison of the idea of law and covenant in Israel and the ancient Near East, including Hittite laws, was carefully made by George Mendenhall, professor of Near Eastern languages and literature at the University of Michigan. Christopher R. North examined the "philosophy of history" of the Israelites as presented in the Old Testament, that is, their view of history, based on their experiences and their interpretation of them. Recognition of the writers view of the place of the Israelites in history is very important.

Many Jews aspired to be independent of foreign rule and to be under their own king. The hope for a national kingdom was expanded under the influence of Persian thought to include a supernatural, eternal kingdom on earth, introduced with a resurrection of the dead and a judgment day. Joseph Klausner, professor of Hebrew literature and history at Hebrew University, Jerusalem, traced the origin and development of this national hope (1950). Sigmund Mowinckel described at length the Jewish concepts of the Messiah, or Christ, who would be the king to establish the new kingdom or new age (1951).

Many biblical scholars tried to describe Hebrew thought as a whole by writing a theology of the Old Testament. Some tried to unify it and organize it into an entirely consistent system; others, more discerning, acknowledged the variety of thought and tried to explain it. Walther Eichrodt, professor of Old Testament at Basel, wrote one of the better works of the latter type.

Background of the New Testament

The archaeology of the New Testament has not been investigated so thoroughly as has the archaeology of the Old.
Jack Finegan, while teaching at Iowa State College, described
both fields in one book. Archaeology has thrown much light
on the Jewish background of the New Testament. An important
example is the discovery of the uncanonical books among the
Dead Sea scrolls, followed by excavation of the site of the
sect's communal building. For a few years after the scrolls
were found a dispute arose over the date of the manuscripts.
Were they written before the birth of Jesus, or early in the
Christian era, or—as Solomon Zeitlin stoutly argued—in the
Middle Ages? Uncertainty over the date led to a further issue:
Were they written by Jews or Christians? Neither the statements in the text nor the paleography of the letters produced
agreement among scholars. Two developments, however, settled the date. Carbon 14 tests on the linen wrappings around
the jars in which the scrolls had been stored indicated a date
in the first century A.D. More specific evidence came from
the coins discovered when Qumran was excavated. The oldest
coins were from the reign of Antiochus VII Sidetes (138-129
B.C.), and the latest were made in A.D. 68. Thus this Jewish
sect existed at Qumran from late second century B.C. until
A.D. 68, and the carbon 14 test was proved to be accurate, for
the linen was wrapped around the jars when the scrolls were
hidden from the Romans when the latter conquered Qumran in
A.D. 68.

A second controversy quickly arose over the scrolls.
The similarity of some ideas in them to some in the New Testament threatened traditional Christianity's claim to uniqueness. Like the early Christians, the Essenes at Qumran opposed the temple priests in Jerusalem, held their own goods
in common, were confident that God had made the new covenant with them, and expected that God would soon establish his
kingdom on earth by means of a Messiah descended from David. A few scholars jumped to the conclusion that the scrolls
must have been written by Christians. Edmund Wilson's famous article in *The New Yorker* magazine in 1955 called public attention to the controversy. Millar Burrows discussed

the evidence and the issues with balanced judgment in two books written in the 1950s, a period characterized by reactionary views on the one hand and wild theories on the other. Today it is agreed that the scrolls belonged to a Jewish sect, apparently the Essenes. The coins demonstrate the sect's pre-Christian existence, and the documents lack any reference to anything uniquely Christian.

We have observed the importance of the discovery of Greek New Testament manuscripts. The remains of Christian catacombs, sarcophagi, and churches, with the exception of the earliest frescoes, are too late in origin to supply background of the Bible, however. Knowledge of the excavations of cities which were important in the rise of Christianity up to A. D. 150 is useful, and sometimes is applied in biblical study. Archaeological discoveries pertaining to the imperial cult, the mystery religions, and other aspects of the gentile environment of early Christianity are often neglected in books on New Testament archaeology, but they should be included.

Jewish literature written in or shortly before the period of Christian beginnings is significant for New Testament study because it gives us insight into the background of Jesus, his disciples, and Christian converts from Judaism. It also helps us to understand the thinking of Jews who disagreed with the apostolic preaching. In the twentieth century more Jewish literature from that period has become available through discovery and translation.

The famous Oxford biblical scholar, Robert Henry Charles, translated and interpreted uncanonical Jewish documents, mostly apocalyptic literature written in the first centuries B. C. and A. D. They are called "pseudepigrapha" because they were written pseudonymously, in the name of some famous Jewish hero of the past, to give them authority. In recent years a seminar called the Pseudepigrapha Group has met at the annual meetings of the Society of Biblical Literature and fostered research on these Jewish writings. The seminar's English translation of the documents, edited by James H. Charlesworth, is to be published by Doubleday.

The outstanding twentieth-century discovery of ancient Jewish literature is the finding of the Dead Sea scrolls, which we have mentioned. An excellent translation of them has been

produced by Theodor H. Gaster, eminent Hebraist and professor of ancient cultures at Fairleigh Dickinson University.

Moritz Friedländer, Jewish scholar in Vienna, demonstrated in 1905 that there was more variety in Jewish beliefs
in the time of Jesus than had been generally believed. This
fact has become increasingly apparent as a result of subsequent study of the pseudepigrapha and the Qumran scrolls.
These writings exhibit the prevalence in contemporary Judaism of the expectation of the coming end of the present age or
world. David S. Russell has given a good description of this
Jewish apocalyptic thought. The rabbinic writings in the Talmud omit the apocalyptic and sectarian beliefs, and thus the
Talmud supplies an incomplete picture of the Jewish background of early Christianity. Even rabbinic Judaism was
not so standardized as G. F. Moore presented it in his extensive work, *Judaism*. Recently Moore's treatise has been superseded by Ephraim Urbach's two-volume work, *The Sages*.
Urbach recognizes variety among the rabbis, and he also includes the writings of sects such as the one at Qumran.

Jews in the Diaspora were greatly influenced by Hellenistic culture. Philo of Alexandria, a contemporary of Jesus,
is a famous example. Erwin R. Goodenough of Yale examined
in depth the mysticism in Hellenistic Judaism, especially Philo. He may have carried too far his theory that the idea of
mystery was the paramount aspect of Hellenistic Judaism, but
the prevalence of mystery religions and mystic philosophy at
the time should make us realize that they may have influenced
Hellenistic Judaism along with Hellenistic Christianity.

In the twentieth century new efforts have been made to
determine the extent of Jewish influence on early Christianity,
especially by searching for parallels between the New Testament (mainly the gospels and Paul's letters) and Jewish literature. Early in the century the Jewish writings used were
chiefly those of the rabbis. The famous four-volume commentary based on passages in the Talmud and Midrash (1922-28),
initiated by Hermann Strack and compiled by Paul Billerbeck,
has two serious faults: it contains many factual errors, and
it is biased. Billerbeck's Christian bias led him to describe
Jesus as superior to the rabbis; he claimed that Jesus' teaching was original, unlike their teaching. In 1930 Claude Monte-

fiore, a leader of English liberal Judaism, corrected the bias
in Billerbeck's work. He pointed out that Jesus' teaching in
the gospels is very similar to that of the rabbis and that the
parallelism between them is closer than Billerbeck and other
Christian theologians were willing to recognize. Montefiore
erroneously assumed, however, that Judaism did not change
during the first few Christian centuries, and therefore he included second, third, and fourth century rabbinic traditions
in his reconstruction of the Jewish background of the gospels.
C. H. Dodd, professor of divinity at Cambridge University,
observed that some pagan writers, too, were influenced by Judaism in general and the Septuagint version of the Old Testament in particular (1935).

Events in Jewish history strongly influenced some authors of the New Testament. One event was the capture of Jerusalem and the destruction of the Jewish temple by the Romans at the end of the Jewish revolt in A. D. 70. S. G. F.
Brandon (1951), professor of comparative religion at Man-
chester, studied the effects on the church of the fall of Jerusalem. Some Christians interpreted the event as the judgment
of God on Jews for not believing that Jesus was the Christ.
Another event was the Pharisees' "Council of Jamnia" around
A. D. 90, which made observance of the Jewish law the test of
one's loyalty to Judaism; this event intensified the tension between Jews and Christians.

Knowledge of the Christian background of the New Testament also grew rapidly in the twentieth century. Often the New
Testament writers were trying to solve some of the problems
in the church or to defend their position on some issues.

Understanding of early Christian literature outside the
New Testament continued to grow through the discovery of additional writings and through analysis of the literature already
known. The Apostolic Fathers were known, but not readily
available in English until Kirsopp Lake translated them in the
Loeb Classical Library series (1912-13). He was professor
of New Testament exegesis at Leiden. Later Edgar J. Goodspeed also translated them into English, and recently R. M.
Grant has done so. Most of the Apostolic Fathers were written in the first half of the second century, contemporary with

the writing of some of the New Testament.

Another body of early Christian writings is the so-called "New Testament Apocrypha," written in the second and third centuries. These Christian documents should not be confused with the Apocrypha in some Bibles, which are Jewish writings. Many of the books in the New Testament Apocrypha were written by gnostic heretics and were never in the canon. Some of these books do reflect issues in the Christian communities, however, and give us a broader understanding of the various positions taken on them. M. R. James, Provost of Eton College, made this literature available to the English-speaking world with his translation of them in 1924. The best edition now available in English is the two-volume translation by R. M. Wilson of the Hennecke-Schneemelcher German compilation.

When some peasants were digging for fertilizer in a cemetery at Nag Hammadi, Egypt, probably in 1946, they discovered some manuscripts which had been hidden in a jar, perhaps late in the fourth century A.D. Some of these codices are Christian, some are not; all are Coptic translations of of Greek texts that had been in the library of a Christian gnostic sect. The codices contain forty-seven different religious tractates. The discovery of these documents is important because they furnish the modern world with its first direct knowledge of Christian gnosticism. Previously our knowledge of it came from quotations and comments by church fathers who were hostile to it. An English translation of this gnostic library has appeared recently, edited by James M. Robinson, Director of the Institute for Antiquity and Christianity in Claremont, California. Some of these treatises are too late in origin to cast much light on the New Testament, but the earlier ones provide insight into the passages influenced by gnostic thought. The library also reveals the nature of the heresy that the church fathers were fighting.

Some newspaper accounts stooped to sensationalism, claiming that new, authentic sayings of Jesus are in the Nag Hammadi codices. The sayings cannot be words of Jesus, however, for there is no evidence of gnosticism in Jesus' environment, the sayings are late in origin, and much in the sayings is contrary to Jesus' basic concept of the eschatological nature of the kingdom of God.

The influence of early Christian history upon the New Testament has become better known in this century. The first event to have a profound effect upon Christian writers was Jesus' life and death. Some aspects of Jesus' life, and especially his death, did not correspond to the Jewish prophecies and expectations concerning the Messiah, and many New Testment writers attempted to solve the problem. The problem caused Jews generally, and even the disciples immediately after his death, to doubt that Jesus was the Christ. In their efforts to solve the problem, the early Christians revised the Jewish idea of the Messiah and reinterpreted the life of Jesus. Also, Hellenistic Jewish and gentile converts to Christianity changed the concept of the nature of the Christ along the lines of their own cultural backgrounds. They produced a radical shift in Christology from a solely human to a divine Christ. This change in the church was a powerful element in the Christian background of the New Testament, as Wrede, Wellhausen, and Bousset recognized at the turn of the century.

Many other doctrinal changes, too, occurred in the early church. Martin Werner, professor of theology and philosophy at the University of Bern, wrote a comprehensive description of the process. But how could Christianity make radical changes in its beliefs so soon after Jesus' death? The transformation was virtually inevitable in a rapidly expanding movement without a central organization in control, a movement in which new converts with different ideas soon outnumbered the earlier members. There was an added factor that facilitated change, however: the belief of Christian prophets that the spirit of God or of Jesus revealed new knowledge to them that superseded old beliefs . Convinced that they had received spiritual revelations, Christians who had not known Jesus during his lifetime were emboldened to oppose the views of those who had (e.g. Paul's opposition to Peter, Gal. 2). Many important studies have been made of the subject, including those by C. K. Barrett, G. Dautzenberg, and D. E. Aune.

The controversy over Christian observance of Jewish law was two-pronged; it was a dispute within the church, and it was also a dispute between the synagogue and the Hellenistic wing of the church. Donald W. Riddle (1928), while professor

of New Testament literature at the University of Chicago, recognized that the controversies with the Pharisees ascribed to
Jesus in the gospels were really the disputes later between the
church and the Pharisees. This book, with its deep insight,
has never received the recognition that it deserves.

The apostles in their missionary preaching in the primitive church were absorbed with trying to demonstrate that Jesus was really the Messiah. Dodd examined the nature of the
preaching of the apostles (1936). He saw that their central
message was not the story of Jesus' life nor was it ethical
teaching; instead, the apostles' main theme was that Jesus was
the Christ who had really been raised from the dead and
would soon return to establish the kingdom of God.

An important advance in this century was the discovery
that the early Christians and the sect of John the Baptist were
rivals. Apparently each group claimed that its master was
the Christ.   Martin Dibelius, while privatdocent in New Testament at Berlin, in a careful study of the subject (1911),
reached this conclusion and observed that passages in the Gospel of John are a polemic against the followers of the Baptist.
Wilhelm Baldensperger had perceived this less accurately in
1898.

An aspect of Christian history, which is a part of the pagan environment as well, is the Roman government's persecution of Christians and the latter's reaction to it. Some Roman
emperors persecuted Christians for not worshiping the state
and the emperor; such display of loyalty was not required of
long-established religions, including Judaism. Donald Riddle
analyzed the behavior of the Christian martyrs in the light of
psychology and sociology (1931). R. M. Grant examined the
causes and effects of the persecutions (1955).

Christian gnosticism appeared in Alexandria before A. D.
125, and was soon classified as a heresy. We have observed
that gnostic documents were found at Nag Hammadi. Gnostics
regarded the physical body and the material world as inherently evil, while matters of the spirit are inherently good. The
gnostic heresy became so powerful that it shook the church to
its foundations in the second century. Christian gnostic literature was excluded from the Bible, but semi-gnostic thought
appears in Colossians and the Gospel of John. Bousset made

the first study in depth of gnosticism in 1907. Two excellent
discussions of the relations between Christian gnosticism and
the less unorthodox churches have been written by R. M. Grant
and by R. M. Wilson. Grant also compiled an English translation of source material on gnosticism, mainly extracts from
the writings of the church fathers.

To grasp the Christian background of the New Testament,
it is necessary to reconstruct early church history as a whole.
A serious attempt of this kind was the history of primitive
Christianity written by Johannes Weiss (1914) while professor
of New Testament at Heidelberg. A superior history of primitive Christianity is that written by Maurice Goguel (1946), who
was professor of New Testament in the École Pratiques des
Hautes Études in Paris. Hans Lietzmann's four-volume work,
A History of the Early Church, also includes a perceptive
history of the church in the New Testament period. He was
professor of church history at Berlin.

In the twentieth century tremendous advances have been
made in our understanding of paganism in the environment of
the early churches. For increased general knowledge of the
gentile background of the New Testament we are indebted to
the discovery and publication of gentile literature, inscriptions,
and art of the Graeco-Roman period, often found through archaeological excavation. In 1903 Albrecht Dieterich published
an ancient pagan document which he believed was a liturgy of
the cult of Mithra. It contains the belief in the soul's ascension through the heavens, an idea also found in Gnosticism.
The next year Richard Reitzenstein, while professor of classical philology at Strasbourg, published the text of *Poimandres*,
a second century A. D. tractate of the gnostic Hermetic cult in
Egypt. Reitzenstein went too far in claiming Hermetic influence on Christianity; nevertheless, close parallels indicate
that a common element in their backgrounds influenced both
Poimandres and the Gospel of John.

F. C. Grant, professor of biblical theology at Union
Theological Seminary, compiled gentile source material in his
book, *Hellenistic Religions*. In 1956 C. K. Barrett, profes-
sor of divinity at Durham University, collected documents, both
Jewish and gentile, to illustrate the background of the New
Testament. Recently, David Dungan and David Cartlidge com-

piled sources, mostly gentile, for the comparative study of the
gospels.

Many descriptions and studies of ancient pagan religions
and philosophies have been published. At the turn of the century Lewis Farnell at Oxford wrote an outstanding five-volume
description of Greek religion. The Swedish scholar, Martin
Nilsson, who before his death in 1967 was the world's leading
authority on ancient Greek religion, wrote an excellent history of the subject (1925, later revised). Franz Cumont's
book, *Oriental Religions in Roman Paganism*, helped to make
scholars aware of the large number of Hellenistic religions
that were spread over the Roman world. G. F. Moore's two-
volume work, *History of Religions*, excelled in combining
comprehensive survey of the subject, scholarly judgment, and
concise description. Incidentally, both Judaism and Christianity have had such strong prejudices against paganism that they
made "pagan" a derogatory epithet. Actually, pagan religions
and philosophies contained both desirable and undesirable features, as, indeed, have both Judaism and Christianity.

Bousset concluded that gnosticism was pre-Christian and
pagan in origin, came from Hellenistic-oriental rather than
Greek religions, and was mystical, not philosophical, in nature. Although the view that gnosticism originated in Judaism
is popular, there is very strong evidence that it originated in
paganism, as Bousset thought.

As more and more facts about the gentile environment
became known, many historians found pagan parallels with early Christianity. Eduard Norden, Hans Lietzmann, and Paul
Wendland analyzed the literary forms and compared the types
of Christian literature with Hellenistic literature; often the
same types were found in both bodies of writings.

Many ideas and rituals in early Christianity have been
found to be similar to those in paganism. Adam Fox selected
passages in Plato's writings which are parallels to biblical—
mainly New Testament—passages. Hans Dieter Betz edited
anthologies which compare Plutarch's theological and ethical
writings with early Christian literature. Joseph Dölger made
a thorough study of the concept of a deity as a fish. He found
parallels between the early Christian notion of Jesus as a fish
and the pagan idea and symbolism of the Syrian goddess Atar-

gatis as a fish. In 1903 Wilhelm Heitmüller, while privatdocent in New Testament at Göttingen, studied the possible influence of mystery cult religions on Paul's concepts of Christian
baptism and the Lord's Supper. Harold R. Willoughby's mas-
sive (over 600 pages) doctoral dissertation at the University of
Chicago reported the doctrine of rebirth in the mystery cults
and, in the second half of the dissertation, compared that doctrine with the similar doctrine in early Christianity. It is unfortunate that only the first half was published.

Numerous general comparisons between early Christianity and contemporary paganism have been made also, including those by S. J. Case (1929) and F. C. Grant (1962).
These and other scholars have found many parallels that are
too similar to have arisen independently.

The Mandaeans, a gnostic sect still surviving south of
Baghdad, probably originated in the second century A. D.
Reitzenstein believed that their writings, even though composed centuries later than the New Testament, contain pre-
Christian traditions and provide background for the Gospel of
John. Bultmann and Walter Bauer adopted this theory. Nevertheless, Lietzmann demonstrated in 1930 that there is no
reliable evidence that these writings contain pre-Christian
traditions, and he pointed out that the mention of John the Baptist in them is only in the latest layer. It is now generally
recognized that the Mandaean literature is too late in origin
to be a reliable source of information about the background of
the New Testament.

The history-of-religions approach to the understanding
of the New Testament and early Christian history utilizes the
parallels with paganism to determine how the gentile world influenced Christianity and how Christianity, in turn, adapted
and reinterpreted pagan culture in the process of developing
and promoting the Christian religion. This approach, however, offended those Christians who were intent on viewing
Christianity as unique. The mere suggestion that the new religion may have borrowed and adapted from other religions
aroused the opposition of liberals and traditionalists alike.
Harnack rejected it (in an academic address in 1901), as did
Schweitzer in 1911. In 1927, in his book on the origin of
Christian theology, Harnack waged war against it and argued

that the Hellenistic mystery religions did not influence Christianity until after New Testament times. Opposition was engendered, too, by mistakes that some members of the history-of-religions school made. Edwin Hatch, a nineteenth-century Christian liberal, had seen in Christianity only the ethics of the Sermon on the Mount, and he regarded virtually all Greek ideas as elements that should be discarded because they were foreign. Thus he admitted that there was Greek influence, but he erred by assuming that the Greek elements are automatically undesirable. Some writers went too far and saw more pagan influence than existed.

Lives of Jesus and of Paul

Many authors in the twentieth century have attempted to write a biography of Jesus. Often the portraits are incompatible with one another. All are derived from the canonical gospels, so why do they disagree? There are several causes. First, the passages in the gospels contain great variety and even contradictions. Therefore the writers are forced to select the passages to use as the foundation for their "biographies," and the diversity of their selections produces some very diverse portraits. Second, different people, including different biblical scholars, can interpret the same passage in very different ways. Third, the basis of selection of passages may be unreliable. There is honest difference of opinion even among historians on how to determine if a saying or incident is authentic. Fourth, both religious liberals and religious conservatives have been guilty of bias. Both have either ignored or misinterpreted biblical passages they disliked. Both have decided in advance what they wanted to find. Both have omitted historical knowledge when they interpreted the gospels.

Some lives of Jesus written in the twentieth century, however, reflect genuine historical research. Joseph Klausner, professor of Hebrew language and literature at Hebrew University, Jerusalem, in 1925 objectively described Jesus in relation to his Jewish background. Biblical studies by non-Christians were needed to correct the Christian bias (just as investigation of the Old Testament by non-Jews was needed to correct Jewish bias). An objective Christian reconstruction of Jesus' life was made by Sherman Johnson, New Testament scholar at the Church Divinity School of the Pacific in Berkeley.

Several issues concerning Jesus' life have been much debated. One often discussed at the beginning of this century was the problem of his "messianic consciousness"; that is, did Jesus believe that he was the Christ? Wilhelm Wrede (1901) was convinced that Jesus did not think of himself as the Messiah and that the faith in his messiahship originated as a result of the disciples' belief in his resurrection. This view has generally prevailed among New Testament scholars in this century, especially among Christian liberals. The traditional view, of course, is that Jesus believed himself to be the Messiah (Luke 4:41). In this case the traditional view may be right. The resurrection of the Messiah was not in the messianic prophecies, so belief in Jesus' resurrection was hardly enough to produce the faith in his messiahship. That faith is much more intelligible if Jesus and the disciples believed it before his death.

A related problem is whether Jesus was a political rebel. If he believed that he was the Christ, it is quite possible that he did expect to overthrow Roman rule, for the Jewish expectation in Jesus' environment was that the Christ would be a king who with God's help would do exactly that. According to Mark 15:7, a rebellion preceded Jesus' crucifixion, and in all four gospels Pilate regards Jesus as "the king of the Jews." The peaceful statements in the gospels are readily explained as the evangelists' efforts to convince the Romans, after the Jewish revolt against Rome failed in A.D. 70, that Christians were loyal to the state. Although this interpretation is unpopular, several scholars have concluded that Jesus did start a revolt. In a thorough study, Professor Brandon drew that conclusion (1967). Martin Hengel argued briefly against it (1970).

Another issue is whether Jesus expected the kingdom of God to come in the future or whether he thought it had arrived. The latter theory is called "realized eschatology." At first glance, two verses in Luke suggest that the kingdom had arrived. "If I cast out demons by the finger of God, then the kingdom of God has come upon you" (11:20 = Matt. 12:28); "the

kingdom of God is in the midst of you" (17:21). But there are
other verses in the gospels in which the kingdom is definitely
future. In Luke 22:18 we read, "from now on I will not drink
of the fruit of the vine until the kingdom of God comes." And
in Mark 9:1, "there are some standing here who will not taste
death until they see the kingdom of God come with power." C.
H. Dodd was the chief exponent of realized eschatology. Cadbury once wrote: "But the futuristic outlook of Jesus' teaching
cannot be eliminated. Realized eschatology is for many [per-
sons] unrealized and unrecognized wishful thinking."[23] Historians are now convinced that realized eschatology originated,
not with Jesus, but with Luke or his community to explain the
fact that the kingdom did not come.

A controversial issue is the relation between the religion
of Jesus and the religion of the early church. Did the church
preach the same religion that Jesus preached, or did it change
his message? One of the major works of research on this subject is Wilhelm Bousset's *Kyrios Christos* (1913). Bousset,
who three years later became professor of New Testament exegesis at Giessen, traced the modifications of the early
church's belief in Jesus as the Christ. Basic changes in the
belief did occur and investigating what the changes were and
why they were made is a fascinating project.

Many New Testament scholars lost interest in trying to
write a life of Jesus for reasons which C. T. Craig pointed
out in his survey in 1938. One reason is that modern study of
the gospels has made it clear that "Jesus cannot honestly be
made into a modern figure."[24] The liberal lives had been
written because the authors were confident they would find that
Jesus was modern in his thinking; more careful studies, however, showed that Jesus was a product of his age. A second
reason is that scholars have concluded that the amount of authentic material in the gospels is far too limited to enable anyone to write a real biography of Jesus.

Consequently, some Christian theologians turned to
Heilsgeschichte, "salvation history," and to existentialism,
which are not dependent upon Jesus' career. Oscar Cullmann,
professor of New Testament at Basel, introduced the theory of
Heilsgeschichte. According to this theology, it is not the
teaching of Jesus that matters, but the "Christ-event," the

revelation of God through Christ in history. The salvation of mankind, it is said, depends on the Christ-event, and that event was the theme of the apostolic preaching. Bultmann combined this idea with existentialist theology. According to him, our concern should be with self-understanding, that is, the self's understanding of the nature of its existence, which is related to the Christ-event.

Ernst Käsemann, while professor of New Testament at Göttingen, called for a "new quest" for the historical Jesus, on the grounds that early Christian preaching and the gospels did have some concern for the earthly Jesus, and thus there are some points in common between Jesus' teaching and the kerygma, or preaching.[25] Several New Testament scholars followed Käsemann's lead. The "new quest" was not really a search for the historical Jesus, however, but rather a search for the Christ of faith in a philosophical guise. The late Norman Perrin, professor of New Testament at the University of Chicago, in his discussion of the problem of recovering the teaching of Jesus,[26] calls attention to a basic weakness of the new quest, namely, its assumption that the Christ the apostles preached after crucifixion was the same as the Jesus who lived on earth. Another mistaken assumption of the new quest is its presupposition that the kerygma was uniform in its view of Jesus; actually, the apostolic preaching exhibited considerable variety in the concepts of Jesus.

Research and debate continues on the life of Jesus. The basic questions are still discussed, What did Jesus actually say and do? How much, or how little, of the gospel material is authentic, that is, reports history?

"Biographies" of Paul have been almost as varied as the reconstructions of the life of Jesus. At the beginning of this century Paul Wernle, Carl Clemen, and Adolf Deissmann idealized Paul's teaching along the liberal lines that F. C. Baur and Harnack had constructed in the nineteenth century. It was a psychological interpretation: Paul's conversion experience on the road to Damascus led him to a spiritual religion, which was therefore unlike Judaism, gnosticism, and Hellenistic mystery religions.

In 1902 Loisy attacked abstract idealization of Paul by Christian liberals, along with their idealization of Jesus. In

1904 Wilhelm Wrede, professor of New Testament at Breslau,
expertly opposed the liberals' spiritualistic and moralistic interpretation of Paul's theology. He perceived that Paul's doctrine of the Christ was not founded on the teaching of Jesus.
In the nineteenth century Otto Pfleiderer had recognized Hellenistic mystery cult influence on Paul, which was contrary to
the idealized, psychological interpretation. An earnest effort
to place Paul in his environment was Klausner's *From Jesus
to Paul* (1943), which presented Paul in the setting of Hellenistic Judaism. Samuel Sandmel wrote a historical study in which
he examined Paul's genius in making a road for the transition
from Palestinian Jewish Christianity to Hellenistic Christianity. Although Paul departed far from the religion of Jesus,
Sandmel remarked that Paul contributed the positive, permanent value of personal freedom, a value essential later in
the transition of religion to modern times. Recently F. O.
Francis and J. P. Sampley compiled *Pauline Parallels*, a
tool for comparing similar passages in ten letters written by
Paul or ascribed to him.

Determining Paul's life and thought has been a difficult
problem, partly because of the difference between his letters
and the account in Acts. When they differ, which should the
historian follow? The prevailing view in this century is that
the letters are more to be trusted because they are primary
sources (Paul wrote them), while Acts is secondary, with the
possible exception of the "we-sections" written in the first
person plural, which implies that the writer accompanied
Paul—but this could be a literary device patterned after Hellenistic journey-stories. Deciding which ideas are Paul's has
been a problem also because of uncertainty as to how many of
the letters ascribed to him are really authentic. It is virtually
certain that no more than seven—and perhaps only five—were
written by him, and even in them some passages apparently
are later insertions by others.

Editors of Scholarly Journals

In closing this survey of the twentieth century, we should
acknowledge the vital contributions made by the editors of the
scholarly journals devoted to ancient history and the interpre-

tation of the Bible. Some of the journals were founded in the nineteenth century, some in the twentieth; some are still being published, but others have ceased. The editors presented works of scholarship which might not otherwise have been published, and their standards for the acceptance of manuscripts raised the level of biblical scholarship. The editors are too numerous to name, but an eminent example is J. M. Powis Smith, professor of Old Testament and Semitic languages at the University of Chicago, who was editor of the *American Journal of Semitic Languages* from 1915 to 1932.

Some progressive clergymen have played an important role in making known to laymen and the public the results of biblical scholarship. An example is Harry Emerson Fosdick, the popular minister of Riverside Church in New York City from 1926 to 1946. He accomplished that goal through radio broadcasts of his sermons and especially through his book, *A Guide to Understanding the Bible*.

In summary, new knowledge of the history of religions, derived both from archaeology and from intensive study of previously known documents, contributed to the understanding of the Hebrew and early Christian environments. Improved reconstructions of Hebrew history and thought were produced. Knowledge of the Jewish background of the New Testament advanced through the translation and study of the pseudepigrapha, Qumran scrolls, Philo, and Josephus, and through comparison of the ideas in them and in rabbinic writings with those in the New Testament. Translations of the Apostolic Fathers, New Testament Apocrypha, and—to a lesser extent—gnostic documents enlarged the scope of the Christian background of the New Testament. Fuller knowledge of Christian history, especially of the issues within the church and between the church and the outside world, afforded a new grasp of the meaning of the New Testament. Historians arrived at a far better understanding of the gentile environment of Christianity through enlarged general knowledge of the pagan world and through the search for similar beliefs and practices in Christianity and pagan religions. Questions concerning Jesus' life and teaching continued to be investigated and debated. A few sensible "lives of Jesus" were written, but the conviction grew that reliable information is too limited to write a biography of Jesus. Accounts of Paul's life and teaching varied greatly too, but much progress was made in placing Paul in the framework of his environment.

Although tremendous progress was made in the nineteenth and twentieth centuries, the development of the historical approach to the Bible is far from complete. The historical approach is still in the process of becoming a mature science. The fact that so much more can be and should be learned makes the field fascinating and challenging.

CHAPTER 9

PRINCIPLES OF THE HISTORICAL APPROACH

The foundation of the historical approach to the Bible is a set of principles which underlie the specific methods we will explore in the following chapters. Historians accept similar principles as the basis for their examination of other ancient writings, and they have learned from experience that they are also essential for understanding Scripture. When viewed as a unified group, the principles constitute, in effect, a philosophy of biblical study. What are the principles?

1. The Bible must be studied historically if it is to be understood correctly. This is the only valid way to achieve the primary goal of the historical approach, which is to try to find the meaning the writers tried to convey to their readers. Therefore, as much as possible, we should know what has really happened in the past. We should also know, as much as possible, the purpose of each writer, and the cultural background, setting, linguistic characteristics, and literary nature of the books and their sources. The circumstances and cultures in biblical times were very different from ours. Ignoring this historical information invariably results in misconceptions, as the record of biblical interpretation abundantly demonstrates. We should recognize that our predecessors lacked this essential knowledge, but, by using it, we can interpret the Bible more accurately than they did.

2. The historical approach must be consistent with scientific methodology. Historians reject the pastime popular with theologians, that of belittling scientific methods. Historians do not accept the view that "secular" knowledge is inherently inferior to "religious" knowledge. The historical approach applies the basic method of scholarhip and scientific investigation, which includes four major steps.

a. Be objective. We should give all the evidence a fair hearing. We should be willing to follow the evidence, even if it makes us change our opinions and beliefs about things that seem very important.

b. Collect all available relevant evidence. In other words, we should gather all the information we can find which pertains to the passage we are studying. This step may necessitate active search for more evidence than we have known. The attempt to draw conclusions from only part of the evidence is a risky matter.

c. Analyze the evidence. We should examine the material closely to determine the nature of the evidence; we should ask what is its origin, type, and meaning. Next we should evaluate the evidence by asking if it is valid and if it really applies to the passage or question. Is it accurate?

d. Synthesize the evidence. We should determine the relationships among the pieces of evidence, and then draw our conclusions accordingly.

3. Biblical study should be unbiased, for contrary to a notion popular with theologians, it IS possible to be objective. Students and researchers may begin their investigations with presuppositions, but that does not mean that they cannot be objective. When, after investigation, they draw conclusions different from or contrary to the presuppositions with which they began, they have demonstrated that they can be objective. Objectivity consists not in lack of opinions or presuppositions, but in willingness to change them in the light of evidence.

Readers may have acquired prejudices and mistaken opinions about the Bible that make it difficult for them to be objective. If they will realize that religion does not necessarily stand or fall with traditional interpretation of the Bible, they will be more likely to develop a fair-minded attitude in biblical study.

4. The Bible should be allowed to speak for itself. Thus we should not ignore what the Bible does say, nor should we ascribe to it what it does not say. This simple principle seems to be especially difficult for humanity to follow. Of it we may state that narrow is the gate and hard is the road, and few there be who find this way of life!

Causes for failure of readers to recognize what the Bible really says include lack of information about a passage, mediocre translations, careless reading of the passage, and blind acceptance of what other persons claim it says. Yet another cause is eagerness to find in the Bible only what we want

to find; this is a case of lack of objectivity, which is contrary
to the first step in the basic method of scholarship we have
mentioned. A result of the error of not allowing the Bible to
speak for itself is that the error prevents us from performing
adequately the last three steps of principle number 2. That is,
the error keeps us from collecting all the essential evidence,
for what a passage really says is surely vital evidence of what
a passage really means. And if we have not collected all the
evidence, we certainly cannot expect to analyze and synthesize
a passage correctly.

The fallacy of not letting the Bible speak for itself is not
new. In the second century A. D. Rabbi Ishmael ben Elisha objected to some eisegesis by Rabbi Eliezer ben Hyrcanus and
remarked, "You say to Scripture, 'Be silent, while I expound' "
(Talmud, *Sifre on Lev.* 13:49). Let us take two examples.

 a. And he said to them, "Truly, I say to you, there are
    some standing here who will not taste death before
    they see the kingdom of God come with power" (Mark
    9:1).

The passage plainly states that the kingdom of God will
come before the death of "some standing here" in Jesus time.
Yet some people who sincerely "believe in the Bible" think that
the Bible teaches that the kingdom of God and Jesus will come
in the twentieth century A. D. or later! They clearly are not
recognizing what the Bible says.

 b. even the Spirit of truth, whom the world cannot re-
    ceive, because it neither sees him nor knows him;
    you know him, for he dwells with you, and will be in
    you (John 14:17. RSV, quoted here, errs by follow-
    ing the old AV in translating the pronoun referring to
    Spirit as "him"; Goodspeed, in *The Complete Bible,*
    translated it correctly as "it," for the Greek word
    for Spirit—*pneuma*—is neuter gender).

A Pentecostal tract on repentance states that one cannot
receive the "Holy Ghost" before he repents. The tract refers
to John 14:17 and adds that in this verse Jesus meant that

those who were unwilling to give up the carnal things of the world, "through repentance," cannot receive the Holy Spirit. The verse in John, however, does not mention repentance; in fact, neither the noun "repentance" nor the verb "repent" occur at all in the Gospel of John! The verse gives a reason why the world cannot receive the Spirit, but the reason has nothing to do with repentance. The reason given is that the world neither sees nor knows the Spirit of Truth. The tract claims that the verse supports an idea which, however, is neither there nor in the whole Gospel of John.

The authority given to the Bible in the past, we might expect, would have made its readers exercise great care in allowing the Bible to speak for itself. Often the effect was just the opposite. Eagerness to make the Bible support favorite beliefs and notions led people to find in the book things that it does not say. Recognition of what the Bible actually says seems like an obvious requirement, but the obvious has been often overlooked.

5. The context of a biblical passage should be taken into consideration, for it often contributes to the understanding of it. This is both a principle and a method. The surrounding verses usually provide information about the situation and the author's point of view. When a phrase, clause, or verse is lifted out of its literary setting and interpreted without reference to context, the information which should accompany it is stripped away. Without that information, all sorts of meaning can be ascribed to the isolated passage. When the practice of lifting material out of context is combined—as it often is—with zeal to support one's beliefs or ideas, misunderstanding of the passage is almost guaranteed.

Those who insist on the inerrancy of the Bible tend to ignore the principle of the necessity of observing the context. This enables them to use the "proof-text" technique. Clergymen of all types of faith are also especially prone to ignore the context, chiefly to support a sermon's theme. The theme is often a good one which deserves to be promoted, but its connection with the Bible is liable to be purely imaginary. Someone has remarked, "If preachers ever stop lifting verses out of context, it will ruin a lot of sermons!"

Nevertheless, there is danger of going to the other extreme by attempting to make the context broader than it is. This mistake occurs when a passage is interpreted as necessarily agreeing with material which actually comes from the pen of a different writer. The genuine context of a passage, however, consists only of the writing by the same author. The error is caused by either of two conditions. (1) When the Bible is assumed to be a unity, the reader may attempt to force a passage to fit another biblical book which has ideas quite foreign to those of the author of the passage. (2) When a reader is unaware that the author of a biblical book has used written sources or that a redactor has revised the book later, he interprets the book as though it were all written by one writer. The various writers, however, may have written under different conditions and with very different views.

Here are some examples which demonstrate the importance of the principle that the Bible should be interpreted contextually.

a. You shall not add to the word which I command you, nor take from it;. . . (Deut. 4:2a).
   I warn every one who hears the words of the prophecy of this book: if any one adds to them, God will add to him the plagues described in this book, and if any one takes away from the words of the book of this prophecy, God will take away his share in the tree of life and in the holy city, which are described in this book (Rev. 22: 18-19).

The Second Helvetic Confession of 1566, a Protestant document, lifted these two passages out of their contexts in an effort to prove that no more books, including the Apocrypha, should be added to the canon of the Bible. Actually, the context of each of these passages shows that a canon of books is not involved in either case. Deuteronomy 4:1 explicitly states that the matter in which no additions or subtractions are to be made consists of the statutes and ordinances which the Lord is giving to the Israelites at the time they take possession of the land of Canaan. As for Revelation, both the context and the two verses themselves show that it is the addition to and subtrac-from the words of that particular book which are prohibited, not the addition of whole books to the Bible. In fact, some New Testament books were written after Revelation was written and admitted into the canon. The passage in Deuteronomy was a bad choice as a proof text, because many Jewish books were written and added to the canon after Deuteronomy was written, and Christians wrote and added the whole New Testament after that time!

b. And in the days of those kings the God of heaven will set up a kingdom which shall never be destroyed, nor shall its sovereignty be left to another people. It shall break in pieces all these kingdoms and bring them to an end, and it shall stand for ever (Dan. 2:44).

The surrounding verses show that the kingdoms of "those kings" were Babylonia, Media, Persia, and the Greek rule established by Alexander the Great. The "divided kingdom" in verse 41 is a reference to the division of Alexander's kingdom among his generals after his death. The verse was written after these events had occurred; the author lived in the time of the divided Greek kingdom—specifically, about 165 B.C. in the reign of the Greek Seleucid king of Syria and Palestine, Antiochus IV Epiphanes. That king's persecution of the Jews is described in Daniel 11:21-39. The author wrote pseudonymously, presenting his own writing as a prophecy by Daniel centuries earlier.

Awake, a magazine published by Jehovah's Witnesses, gave this interpretation of Daniel 2:44 in its October 8, 1970, issue (p. 24): "And the Bible shows that very soon now God's kingdom will crush out of existence and replace all systems of man that now cause such grief. (Dan. 2:44)." It should be obvious to any reader that the magazine has utterly ignored the context and even some elements within the verse. That interpretation overlooks the fact that the context shows that the "days of those kings" was two millenia ago. The biblical author did not foresee the Christian era, nor did he attempt to predict events in it. Only by ignoring its setting can anyone imagine that Daniel 2:44 refers to the twentieth century of the Christian era.

c. Ernest C. Colwell, in his excellent little book, *The*

Study of the Bible, (p. 108), pointed out the ridiculousness of modernizing interpretations of passages removed from context and applied to the twentieth century by ignoring their reference to the time in which they were written. He observed that, according to the Schofield Reference Bible, Rosh, Meshek, and Tubal in Exekiel 38:2-3 mean Russia, Moscow and Tbolsk, "in the opinion of all interpreters" (!). He rightly remarked that the Schofield Reference Bible is asking us to believe that the first readers of Ezekiel could not possibly have understood what he was talking about. Colwell commented: "One wonders why God was so concerned about the generation which was to read the Schofield Bible and so little concerned with Ezekiel's contemporaries."

6. Study of the Bible must take into account the special characteristics of some ancient writings. One characteristic is especially liable to lead to misinterpretation if it is not recognized. It is the promotional, or propagandist, motivation behind many writings, a motivation which at times found expression in the form of a "history." The writers' philosophy of history tended to be very different from ours. Sometimes they revised actual events, and sometimes they created fictional narratives; in either case their purpose was to promote a certain point of view. If in such cases, we assume that the author was simply reporting actual history, we will misunderstand both the Bible and history.

7. Historical, objective study of the Bible should precede the efforts to make the book relevant for today, and in those efforts the interpretation of the Bible should be in harmony with the results of historical study. This principle is ignored in many of the attempts to make the book relevant. Zeal to make Scripture teach useful lessons for the modern world usually produces misconceptions. "Modernizing" the Bible results in assigning to it current ideas that it does not contain. We must remember that the biblical writers wrote for their readers, in their own time, and not for the readers in the twentieth century A.D.

Readers of the Bible today are often impatient to get to the essential lessons quickly without "wasting time" on studying biblical literature, history, and background, which seem to them unimportant. Actually, this information is not only important, but vital; there is no shortcut to the discovery of the relevance of the Bible. In order to determine the book's value now, we have to know what contributions it made in its own day. And in order to learn its contributions, we have to know the situations in which it was written. If we want to learn what contributions to religious and ethical development were made by Amos, Isaiah, Jesus, and Paul, for example, we must know with what problems they were concerned and how they tried to solve them. Only then can we decide the value of their teaching for us.

From this brief survey of some principles of the historical approach to the Bible, we move on to the application of specific methods in the approach.

CHAPTER 10

THE ORIGINAL LANGUAGES

A rule of the historical approach is, know the languages in which the Bible was written. This is an essential rule for historians, because when the text is translated into another language, some of the original meaning is liable to be lost or distorted. Sometimes the second language does not contain a word which has precisely the same meaning as one in the original text, and often the syntax, the construction of phrases and sentences, differs among languages and affects the meaning of a sentence. Those who study the text only in translation are at a disadvantage. Therefore scholars use the Bible in its original languages as the basis for modern translations and interpretation.

Most readers do not have the time and facilities to learn Hebrew and Greek. Nevertheless, they can readily acquire a knowledge of the major characteristics of those languages. With a general knowledge of Hebrew and Greek, readers are in a better position to understand some of the linguistic information in commentaries. Explanations of the text often refer to grammar of the original language and the meaning of particular words. And a general knowledge of the languages, combined with access to good lexicons, assists readers in evaluating translations of the Bible. Readers are handicapped if they use only an inferior translation of the Bible, and some linguistic knowledge helps them to select a good translation.

Characteristics of Hebrew

In general, the earlier in history a language originated, the more difficult it is to learn. The earlier languages are liable to be quite unlike modern European languages, with more complexity of verb forms, more irregularity, and a different system of grammar as the basis. Some of the Hebrew and Greek letters are in our alphabet, and some are not. All Hebrew letters and the majority of Greek letters are written in a manner different from the letters to which we are accustomed.

The Old Testament was written in Hebrew, except Ezra 4:8-6:18 and 7:12-26, Jeremiah 10:11, and Daniel 2:4b-7:28, which are in Aramaic. Hebrew belongs to the Northwest group of Semitic languages. The Semitic tongues include also the Babylonian, Assyrian, Ugaritic (Canaanite), Aramaic, and Arabic. They read from right to left, the opposite direction from Western languages. This is the reason that the pages of books printed in Hebrew run from "back" to "front," the opposite direction of the pages printed in European languages.

The Hebrew alphabet consists of 22 consonants and, strictly speaking, no vowels. Hebrew letters appear very different from Roman letters. Hebrew originally was written without vocalization, or vowels, and usually is printed that way today. The Hebrew text of the Old Testament, however, is often printed with the vowels added, especially as an aid for students. Because dots, or points, are added to the consonants to indicate some of the vowel sounds, a text containing them is called a "pointed" text. The Hebrew alphabet may be found in general encyclopedias and large dictionaries, usually listed under "alphabet."

The root of a native Hebrew word generally consists of three consonants; for example, a word for "go" is *hlk*, which is vocalized as *halak*. When there are more than three consonants in the root, the word invariably is a loanword, borrowed from another language. For example, *prds, pardes*, which means "park," is a Persian word assimilated into Hebrew.

The familiar word *kosher* is often seen in Hebrew on the windows of Jewish delicatessens. The three consonants, reading from right to left, transliterated into the Roman alphabet, are *r sh k* (the sh sound is one letter in Hebrew).

The omission of vowels in the original Hebrew text of the Old Testament can cause a problem. If the reader supplies the vowels of a different word with the same consonants, he is liable to change the meaning of the sentence. An example is in Deuteronomy 28:22, where the choice of vowels supplied determines whether a particular word there means "drought" or "sword." Thus we are not certain whether this verse states that Yahweh, "the Lord," will smite the Hebrews with a sword or with a drought. The danger can readily be seen in English. If we had only the consonants TP and then vocalized them, we might read the word as "tap," "tape," "tip," or "top." Usually we can tell which is the proper word by choosing the one that makes sense in the sentence, but sometimes two different words seem to fit, and it is difficult to decide which is correct.

The absence of word divisions in many ancient manuscripts creates difficulties too, especially when there are no vowels. Sir Frederic Kenyon gave this example in English: The consonants BSTRNG can be divided after B and vocalized as "be strong," or they can be divided after T and vocalized as "best ring." When copyists and translators differed on the word separation and/or vocalization of the Hebrew text, they created textual variants. The early Greek New Testament manuscripts usually lack word division too, but at least they have vowels.

A characteristic of classical Hebrew grammar is the frequent use of simple coordinate clauses instead of relative clauses. Frequently the clauses are connected by "and"; many sentences even begin with "and." Judges 3:7 is typical: "And the people of Israel did what was evil in the sight of Yahweh, and forgot Yahweh their god, and served the Baals and Asherahs" (Canaanite deities). This sentence structure has been obscured in some modern translations, but it is preserved in the Authorized Version.

The construct state is typical of Hebrew syntax. In it, one noun immediately follows another. The second noun is in the genitive case, and the phrase is translated by supplying "of" between the two nouns. Thus *ben asher*, "son Asher," is translated as "son of Asher," and *b^enim yisrael* means "sons of Israel." The construct often appears in the names of synagogues, as in Beth El, "House of God," and Beth Shalom, "House of Peace."

A pronoun subject of a verb is indicated by the verb ending, and a pronoun object of a verb is attached as a final suffix to the verb. Another characteristic of Hebrew is that certain letters can serve as prepositions by being prefixed directly to a noun or pronoun; "in the town," for example, becomes one word.

Classical Hebrew tends to express intellectual ideas in physical terms. This trait gives it an interesting, distinctive flavor when compared with Hellenistic Greek or modern languages. In the Pentateuch the people of Israel are described as "stiffnecked" (e.g., Exod. 34:9); this is a Hebrew way of saying that the people were stubborn in not obeying Yahweh. Thus a term which literally describes a human physical condition was used to express a mental attitude.

Ancient Hebrew contains many picturesque figures of speech, usually drawn from nature or from human daily life. It has many metaphors, such as "And who is a rock, except our God?" (Ps. 18:31), and it abounds in similes, for example, "the sun, . . . like a strong man runs its course with joy" (Ps. 19:4-5). Nature is often personified, as in "the morning stars sang together" (Job 38:7).

Characteristics of Hellenistic Greek

During the classical period (6th-4th centuries B.C.) the Greek language was divided into several dialects, of which there were three main groups, or families: the Doric, the Aeolic, and the Ionic. Geographic location was the source of the dialects. The vocabulary, grammar, and pronunciation varied not only among the Greek colonies in the islands, Asia Minor, southern Italy, Sicily, and southern Gaul, but even among the city-states in mainland Greece. One branch of the Ionic group, the Attic dialect of Athens, became dominant in the Greek world.

Contacts among Greeks from different regions resulted in some mixture of the dialects. In the Attic Greek of classical Athens, for example, a verb could have the Attic form in the present tense, but in a past tense have a form from some other dialect. The result is that there are many irregular verbs in Greek. This situation makes it difficult for beginning students to recognize a verb when they encounter it in an irregular form. Since words are listed in standard lexicons only in their regular form, an analytical lexicon has been compiled which lists all grammatical forms found in the New Testament; each form is identified, and the regular form is given under which the word is found in standard lexicons. A similar tool exists for biblical Hebrew.

Greek language underwent further change. In the middle of the fourth century B.C., Philip, king of Macedonia, conquered Greece, and Macedonia adopted the civilization of Athens. His son, Alexander the Great, swiftly conquered the Near East and actively spread Greek language and culture, with the intention of using Greek civilization to unite his empire into one world. These events accelerated the modification of Attic Greek, a process already begun. The result was Hellenistic Greek, simpler than the Attic; it became the international language used in commerce throughout the Mediterranean world. Greek, not Latin, was the language of the early church, even in Rome. Clement, bishop of Rome around A.D. 95, wrote in Hellenistic Greek, and the whole New Testament, including Paul's Letter to the Romans, is in that language.

Greek has an alphabet of 24 letters, of which seven are vowels. All Greek words which begin with a vowel have either a smooth or a rough breathing mark above the vowel. Smooth breathing has no effect on the pronunciation, but rough breathing has the effect of placing an h in front of the word—thus *Ellas* is pronounced as *Hellas*. Accent marks appear on all Greek words, except a few which are called "enclitics." In French, accent marks affect the pronunciation of the vowels under them, but have no effect on the stressing of syllables. In Greek the situation is the opposite: the vowel sound is unaffected, but the syllable under the accent mark is stressed when the word is pronounced.

The Greek vocabulary can convey many shades of meaning. Whereas classical Hebrew tends to be simple and concrete in its vocabulary, Hellenistic Greek contains many abstract and philosophical terms along with concrete words. Like most languages, Hellenistic Greek contains some loan words, especially those from Aramaic, Hebrew, and Latin; this resulted from acquaintance with literature in those languages and especially from contact with people who spoke those languages. Greek sometimes became "Semitized" through the adoption of Semitic syntax as well as vocabulary. The Septuagint version of the Old Testament is an example. Its translators tried to translate the Hebrew literally, and the result was Greek which contained many Semitic constructions.

Semitisms occur the least in the original writing of the more sophisticated authors. The Epistle to the Hebrews is written in the most sophisticated Greek in the New Testament and displays little Semitic influence. The Book of Revelation, in contrast, is written in relatively unpolished Greek, and contains many Semitisms. Modern Greek differs considerably from classical and Hellenistic Greek in grammar, vocabulary, and pronunciation.

Concordances

The use of concordances to locate verses which contain a certain word or phrase is well known, and needs no explanation. The concordance should be to the particular translation of the Bible we are studying, however, for otherwise some occurrences may be omitted because of differences in the translations.

Readers who have no knowledge of Hebrew and Greek can easily use Robert Young's *Analytical Concordance to the Bible*. This reference work is in many libraries. It combines features of a concordance and a lexicon. With this book, readers can find out what Hebrew or Greek term is in a verse, and whether their Bible translates it literally and accurately. This reference tool provides another service also. Often two words in the Hebrew or Greek text are translated into the same English word, even when the two original terms differ from each other in meaning. The English word "blessed" is an example. It occurs repeatedly in the Beatitudes in Matthew 5, and it is found in Luke 1:68, "Blessed be the Lord God of Israel." We might easily assume that "blessed" means the same thing in both passages. If we look up the word "blessed" in Young's concordance, however, we find that the Greek word in Matthew 5 is *makarios*, which means "happy." The Greek word in Luke 1:68 is *eulogētos* which means "praised." We understand the passages better when we realize that Matthew 5:5, for example, is saying, "Happy are the meek, for they shall inherit the earth," and Luke 1:68 means, "May the Lord God of Israel be praised."

Lexicology

Knowing the precise meaning of each word in the text is of vital importance. If translators do not know it, they cannot translate the Bible accurately, and if the Bible is not translated accurately, how can anyone who is dependent on the translation know the real meaning of a passage? Even if we know the original languages and can translate the text ourselves, we are dependent on the accuracy of the lexicons to supply the correct meaning of the words. Discovering and recording the possible meanings of the words at the time that they were written is the function of lexicology.

To find the meaning of the biblical words, lexicologists examine the meanings given a word not only in various passages in the Bible, but also in the mass of other ancient literature, papyri, and inscriptions contemporary with the Bible. Our knowledge of the meaning of the words has been built up gradually through the work of many scholars. As a conse‐ quence, modern translators can render the text more accu‐ rately than the best of translators could several centuries ago. Perhaps this fact can best be seen through some examples.

a. Burning lips and a wicked heart are like a potsherd covered with silver dross (Prov. 26:23, AV).

Like the glaze covering an earthen vessel are smooth lips with an evil heart (Prov. 26:23, RSV).

The Revised Standard Version translates as "glaze" the Hebrew term which the Authorized Version renders as "silver dross." Why? Silver dross is the scum that forms on top of molten silver, and is not something that is put on clay vessels or potsherds. The verse in the Authorized Version does not make good sense. Thanks to archaeological discoveries, the word has been found in ancient Canaanite and Hittite writings, where it means "glaze." This information was not available in the seventeenth century when the King James Version was produced.

b. For the hurt of the daughter of my people am I hurt;

I am black; astonishment hath taken hold of me (Jer.
8:21, AV).

For the wound of the daughter of my people is my heart
wounded, I mourn, and dismay has taken hold on me
(Jer. 8:21, RSV).

This verse is a clear example of mistranslation in the
seventeenth century causing misinterpretation in the twentieth
century. "I am black" in the King James Version should have
been translated as "I mourn." "I am black" quite under-
standably led to the opinion that Jeremiah was a Black man, a
conclusion drawn in a 1976 brochure of the House of Judah-
Congregation of Black Hebrew Israelite Jews, Chicago.

  c. And commanded them that they should take nothing for
their journey, save a staff only; no scrip, no bread,
no money in their purse (Mark 6:8, AV).

He charged them to take nothing for their journey except a staff; no bread, no bag, no money in their
belts (Mark 6:8, RSV).

The Greek word *pēra*, rendered as "scrip" in the Authorized Version, is translated as "bag" in the Revised Standard Version. Why? The injunction not to take scrip is virtually a repetition of the command to take no money. The explanation is that King James' translators were only guessing;
since their day, Hellenistic documents have been found which
reveal that *pēra* was the term for a bag used for begging money. This kind of pouch was carried by itinerant Cynic philosophers, traveling apostles of the Syrian goddess (Atargatis),
and others. Therefore we now know that the command not to
take a *pēra* does not refer to scrip, but rather prohibits begging.

  d. For yourselves know how ye ought to follow us: for
we behaved not ourselves disorderly among you (2
Thess. 3:7, AV).

> For you yourselves know how yo[u]
> we were not idle when we were w[ith you]
> 7, RSV).

The translators of the Authorize[d Version translated the]
Greek verb *atakteo* as "behave disor[derly." Since the time]
of King James I, however, many occu[rrences of this verb in]
classical and Hellenistic Greek have b[een studied by scholars.]
In these occurrences the meaning is "[to be idle," and that]
translation fits the context in 2 Thessalonians 3. Thanks to
lexicology, we now know that the reference is not to disorderly conduct by the Thessalonians. The problem at Thessalonica
was that Christians there had heard rumors that "the Day of
the Lord" (Jesus' return) had come (2 Thess. 2), and consequently they had stopped working. Paul, in urging them to go
to work, reminds them that he has set the example.

Readers, especially those who use commentaries, will
profit from learning the Hebrew and Greek alphabets. That
knowledge will enable them to find the words in lexicons of
biblical Hebrew and Greek. A commentary or other discussion of a passage may mention a word in the text of the Bible,
and readers who know the alphabet can look in a good lexicon
to determine for themselves the possible meanings of the term.
A fine lexicon, in English, of New Testament Greek is the revision by F. W. Gingrich and F. W. Danker of Walter Bauer's
fifth German edition. Langenscheidt's pocket dictionaries of
Hebrew and Greek are concise and inexpensive for beginners.
When using a Hebrew lexicon, it is necessary to remember
that the letters in the word run from right to left.

Those readers who wish to become really serious students of the Bible should take at least the introductory courses
in Hellenistic Greek and classical Hebrew.

Grammar and Syntax

The cases of nouns, the tenses of verbs, and the construction of sentences are very important in the interpretation
of the Bible. In general, this information is not available to
readers who do not know the languages of the original text, and
they must rely on the commentators. Nevertheless, one im-

pect of grammar is available to everyone who is us-
ccurate translation of the Bible; this is the tense of
rbs, whether past, present, or future. In Chapter 2 we
ntioned some instances of the error of the zeal to find in
the Old Testament "prophecy" of Christian events. From
New Testament times to the present day, the zeal has caused
Christians to misinterpret statements referring to past and
contemporary situations as though they referred to the future.
The practice is one way of ignoring what the Bible says.

The author of the Gospel of Matthew was quite prone to
interpret as future tense various verbs in the Old Testament
which are in the past and present tenses. Here is his interpretation of Jeremiah 31:15.

> Then Herod, . . . sent and killed all the male chil-
> dren in Bethlehem and in all that region who were two
> years old or under, according to the time which he
> had ascertained from the wise men. Then was ful-
> filled what was spoken by the prophet Jeremiah:
> "A voice was heard in Ramah,
> wailing and loud lamentation,
> Rachel weeping for her children;
> she refused to be consoled,
> because they were no more" (Matt. 2:16-18).

In Jeremiah the reference is to the mourning when many families of the conquered kingdom of Judah were carried into cap-
tivity in Babylonia, an event which had already occurred in
Jeremiah's day. The verbs are in the past, not future, tense;
therefore the verse could not be "fulfilled" by any event six
hundred years later. (Incidentally, there is no valid evidence
that Herod ever ordered a wholesale slaughter of male children.)

Translations

Some modern translators of the Bible intentionally produce a free, or loose, translation instead of a literal one.
They are trying to make the Bible more meaningful to the modern world. Loose translations, however, have an inherent

weakness: they deprive the reader of some of the flavor and
meaning of the Bible.   The simplifying translations tend to
lift the Bible out of its original setting, leaving out customs
and attitudes of the authors and their communities.   Such translations hinder our understanding of the Bible and our comprehension of history.   For example, 1 Samuel 17:26b reads as
follows in the Revised Standard Version: "For who is this uncircumcised Philistine, that he should defy the armies of the
living God ?" The Good News Bible, however, substitutes
"heathen" for "uncircumcised." The substitution hides the
fact that the Israelites took very seriously their religious
law requiring the circumcision of their male children, and
that the lack of the practice among some of their neighbors
was a source of prejudice against them (cf. Judges 14:3).

Mistranslating the Bible to make it agree with current
doctrines, philosophy, or fads is a serious mistake, often
made.   One of the motives for changing the text by means of
changing the translation is the desire to eliminate "sexism,"
real and alleged, in the Bible.   Examples are changing "Son"
to "Child," and "God the Father" to "God the Parent." It is
true that the Bible reflects the male dominance prevalent in
the ancient world, but eliminating the sexism distorts what
the authors wrote.   The underlying cause of this type of mistranslation is the erroneous belief that the Bible has to be
THE guide in religion and therefore must be perfect.

Translations should be reasonably literal, and readers
should have access to historical notes which explain the unfamiliar terms.   Only thus can readers grasp the down-to-
earth Hebrew diction and the mode of thought in ancient Judaism and early Christianity.

Although few readers can be expected to take the time
to master biblical languages, some knowledge of the characteristics of the languages is essential.   Linguistic information not only aids us in understanding the text, but also helps
us to get the "feel" of the ancient world.

CHAPTER 11

ESTABLISHING THE TEXT

What are the sources of the text of the Bible? When translators make a new translation, what do they translate?

Although translators use printed editions of the biblical texts in the original languages, their ultimate sources are the ancient manuscripts on which the printed texts are based. A difficult problem exists, however. The manuscripts do not always agree with each other. This raises the question, What is the original text? We cannot obtain it from the original manuscripts, because they were soon lost or worn out. Only copies of copies have been transmitted to us. As scribes copied the manuscripts through the centuries, they made changes in the text, sometimes accidentally, sometimes intentionally. When a scribe made a change, other scribes copied it, and still later, others copied their copies, and thus the corruption of the text spread. In addition, "correctors" made further alterations in the copies after they had been written. In the Middle Ages the text was somewhat standardized, but by then it was too late—the text was already corrupted. Although the Old Testament text fared a little better, no two manuscripts of the Bible read exactly alike; identical multiple copies were not produced until printing was invented. The problem of finding out how the text read when it was first written has created this basic rule in the historical approach: Establish the text. The importance of solving the textual problem is clear. We are liable to misunderstand the Bible if the text we use contains readings which were created later. A variant reading consists of words and/or constructions that are different from those in the same passage in another document.

Establishing the text, as well as learning the original languages, is a task for experts in the field. These experts, who are called textual critics, must acquire many years of training and experience. Although most readers of the Bible cannot be expected to acquire the necessary skills, they should know the principles the textual critics employ. In this chapter we will focus on the New Testament text, but most of the methods apply to the Old Testament too.

Obtain Early Manuscripts

How do scholars determine the original text of the Bible? With the New Testament, they begin by finding and using the earlier manuscripts. That procedure eliminates the latest of the alterations of the text. The text cannot be established on the basis of the date alone, however, for in some passages a manuscript written a century later may preserve an earlier reading than the earliest known manuscript. Nevertheless, the earliest manuscripts are generally the best, and those in the original language are usually superior to those in translation. In the Greek New Testament manuscripts known to date, any reading which first appears after the fifth century can hardly be original. In the case of the Old Testament, however, the earliest are not the most reliable. The earliest are among the Dead Sea scrolls, but the text in them has been altered considerably.

In chapter 7 we listed New Testament Greek papyri which were written around A. D. 200. There are also early vellum (skin) New Testament Greek codices written in uncial, or separate, letters. The date of these manuscripts ranges from the fourth to the ninth or tenth centuries. The earlier ones are Codex Vaticanus, or B (4th c.); Codex Sinaiticus, or S (4th c.); Codex Alexandrinus, or A (5th c.); Codex Ephraemi, or C (5th c.); Codex Washington, or W (4th or 5th c.); and Codex Bezae, or D (5th or 6th c.). Later New Testament Greek texts are the minuscule codices, produced from the ninth to the sixteenth centuries and written in a cursive hand, that is, with the letters connected. They are vellum manuscripts, except some of the latest which are paper.

New Testament papyri are designated with a capital P and a raised number, while the vellum uncial manuscripts are designated by an Arabic number preceded by a zero. Arabic numbers without an initial zero indicate the minuscule manuscripts. These international numbers are assigned according to the system devised by C. R. Gregory at the beginning of this century. A manuscript is given the lowest unassigned number

in its category. Thus P^{45} was the forty-fifth New Testament
manuscript to be catalogued that is written in Greek on papyrus. Capital Roman letters are used also as symbols for the
vellum uncial manuscripts. When manuscripts are cited in a
critical apparatus, the vellum uncials are usually cited by
their Roman letters, while the other manuscripts are designated by the Gregory system. Some modern English translations, however, cite variant readings merely as "some ancient authorities read"; the "authorities" include church fathers as well as manuscripts of the text. That is not a good
method of citation, for it is vague, and the church fathers are
of dubious value in establishing the text. The Fathers often
changed the text to support certain ideas, and the authenticity
of any textual variant that occurs only in their writings is very
questionable.

By modern standards, ancient manuscripts are usually
difficult to read. Often there is no space between words; sometimes parts of a page are missing; sometimes a manuscript is
in fragments, which is the case with some Dead Sea scrolls.
Therefore, after a manuscript is found, the exact letters,
words, and punctuation are determined by scholars, and the
text transcribed in modern form to facilitate study of the document.

Apply the Rules of Textual Criticism

The second step in determining the original reading of
the text is to discover and apply the rules of textual criticism.
Textual critics first collate the manuscripts; that is, they
carefully compare the manuscripts with each other and record
the variant readings of the passages in which the text varies
in different manuscripts. Next they observe the kinds of readings that first appear in the late manuscripts. They next analyze the variants to find the causes of the changes. They ask,
"Why did the scribe of a manuscript or a later corrector of it
make the change?" After the probable causes of the changes
have been found, criteria for judging the variants can be constructed. These criteria enable the textual experts to decide
which is probably the earliest among the variants of a passage,
even if the manuscripts are of the same date. Thus by study-

ing the history of the transmission of the text, scholars can
see how and why the text was changed, and they can establish
rules of textual criticism to use as guides in screening out the
alterations.

The original or at least the earliest-known reading cannot be determined on the basis of the number of manuscripts
that contain it. A very large majority of the manuscripts are
late in origin. Therefore, if the readings in the majority of
the manuscripts were the guide, the result would be only a late
form of the text, and many original readings would be lost.
One good third or fourth-century New Testament manuscript
is a better source than a thousand twelfth-century ones.

Textual variants are in two broad categories: accidental
and intentional. Accidental variants, in turn, may be "errors
of the eye" or "errors of the ear." First we will examine two
types of errors of the eye, which were the result of a scribe's
carelessness when he looked at the exemplar, the manuscript
he was copying.

a. Homoioteleuton

Which of these two variants of John 17:15 is the earlier?

Codex B*: I do not ask that you take them from evil.

Codex B^c, S: I do not ask that you take them from the
world, but that you keep them from evil.

An asterisk attached to a symbol for a particular manuscript indicates the original reading in the manuscript, while
a raised "c" attached to the symbol designates the reading as
it was changed by a corrector. Thus the first reading above is
the reading of the passage in Codex Vaticanus as it was written
by the "first hand." The second reading above is the reading
in Codex Vaticanus after a corrector changed it; the same reading is in Codex Sinaiticus (and virtually all other manuscripts).
It is apparent that a corrector inserted the additional words to
make Codex Vaticanus agree with the reading in other manuscripts. In this case the corrector really did correct the
manuscript by making it conform to the original text; in many

cases, however, the so-called "corrector" changed the text away from the original, which from the textual critic's point of view, made the text incorrect.

The key to understanding the origin of this variant in Codex B is to recognize that this is an example of that type of accidental omission known as homoioteleuton (pronounced ho-MOI-oh-te-LOO-ton). This type of omission could occur when there were two words in the passage that were either identical or at least had the same ending. The scribe read in his exemplar as far as the first occurrence of "them" (autous in Greek). Then he wrote down that much in the copy he was making. Next he looked back at the exemplar and happened to see the second occurrence of "them." He assumed, however, that the second "them" was the word he had just written down, so he went on from there, omitting the material in between. Thus he accidentally omitted "from the world, but that you keep them," and created a variant reading. Although homoioteleuton literally means "same ending," in most instances in Greek New Testament manuscripts the two key words are not merely alike in ending, but are identical.

RULE. When a shorter reading appears to be the result of accidental omission, choose the longer reading.

b. Dittography

Another kind of error of the eye is dittography, the repetition of a word or words. The scribe copied some words, and then, looking back at the exemplar, forgot how much he had copied, and repeated the last he had written. This type of error did not occur often, and it is easily recognized as a mistake.

RULE. Reject the reading that contains a senseless repetition of a word or words.

c. Errors of the Ear

Misspellings occurred also, and they are usually easily recognized as errors. Although they could be caused by carelessness in looking at an exemplar, most misspellings are clearly "errors of the ear." Sometimes to increase the rate of production in monasteries, one monk read aloud from the exemplar, while a group of other monks wrote down his dictation. Some illuminations (paintings) in the manuscripts show the monks making copies by that method. If the scribes misunderstood what they heard, they were liable to misspell a word. This occurred in Greek particularly with vowels having a similar sound. Scribes were liable to confuse the sound of the Greek short o (omicron) with the sound of the long o (omega), and to interchange the i (iota), the u (upsilon), and long e (eta) because of their similarity of sound. This kind of misspelling could even change the word. An example is in Luke 24:32 in minuscule 126, where confusion of vowel sounds caused a scribe to write "you" instead of "us," resulting in the senseless reading, "Were not our hearts burning in you?"

RULE. Reject spellings that apparently are errors resulting from dictation.

The second broad category of textual variants are those made deliberately, the variants created intentionally by the scribes. Usually intentional variants added to the text rather than subtracted from it. This fact leads to the following criterion:

RULE. Generally, prefer the shorter reading.
We turn now to the main types of intentional variants.

d. Stylistic Changes

Codex 126*: They gave him a piece of broiled fish (Luke 24:42).

Codex 126^C: They gave to him a piece of broiled fish (Luke 24:42).

In English we can say, "We gave him something," or we can say, "We gave something to him." Similar possibilities exist in the Greek language. Judging from the early manuscripts, the original reading in Luke 24:42 was: "They gave to him a piece of broiled fish." The scribe who wrote minuscule 126, however, wrote: "They gave him a piece of broiled fish." Later a corrector changed the text to read "to him," making it agree with other manuscripts. But the scribe of 126, or the scribe of his exemplar, preferred the other way of expressing the idea. The difference is merely a matter of style. The tendency of scribes and correctors to improve the style in manuscripts has led to another guide for determining the original text:

RULE. Prefer the reading with the rougher, less polished, style.

e. Assimilation from Other Passages

You are good, and you do good; . . . (Ps. 119:68, Masoretic text).

You are good, Lord, and you do good; . . . (Ps. 119:68, Septuagint and Qumran Psalms Scroll).

Assimilation of matter from another passage in the Bible occurs frequently in the work of scribes. In this example the word "Lord" apparently has been inserted later, suggested by the context. The Lord is addressed repeatedly by name in this psalm; two instances are nearby in verses 64 and 65. Some copyists and translators assumed that another occurrence of the sacred name was appropriate. The same variant occurs in both the Septuagint and the Psalms Scroll. The agreement cannot be accidental. Either both the Septuagint translators and the scribes at Qumran derived the reading from a common Hebrew tradition, or the Essenes at Qumran were influenced by the Septuagint tradition.

Here is an example from the New Testament of assimilation from another book of the Bible:

Codices B, D, W: Some said, "John the baptizer has been raised from the dead; . . . (Mark 6:14).

Codices S, A, C: He [Herod] said, "John the baptizer has been raised from the dead; . . ." (Mark 6:14).

In the parallel account in Matthew 14:1-2 it is Herod, not

"some," who made the statement. Apparently the original reading in Mark was "some said," but codices S, A, and C have adopted a scribal change in their exemplars which made Mark agree with Matthew, "he said." This kind of change is known as "harmonization," a process which occurred often in manuscripts of the gospels.

RULE. Reject the reading that apparently results from assimilation from another biblical passage.

f. Addition of Details

> In these lay a multitude of invalids, blind, lame, paralyzed (John 5:3-4, RSV).

> In these lay a great multitude of impotent folk, of blind, halt, withered, waiting for the moving of the water. For an angel went down at a certain season into the pool, and troubled the water: whosoever then first after the troubling of the water stepped in was made whole of whatsoever disease he had (John 5:3-4, AV).

Why is the text of the King James Version longer in this passage than the text in the Revised Standard Version?

In the ancient world storytellers tended to expand stories by adding imaginary details. The practice was common both in oral tradition and in written transmission of accounts. Sayings, too, were often expanded. Scribes and correctors often added details.

In the passage above, the text in the third and fourth century manuscripts had the short reading as in the Revised Standard Version. By the fifth and sixth centuries, however, a few manuscripts had part or all of the expansion. Correctors soon added it to Codex C. Codex A had part of it originally, and later a corrector added the rest. The insertion became universal in the Byzantine manuscripts, which were written by the Greek Eastern church in the Middle Ages. The mythological feature of an angel stirring the water apparently was added to explain the "troubling," or stirring, of the water mentioned in verse 7; it also enhances the miraculous aspect of the story.

A common, simple form of adding details was the prac-

tice of adding personal names. In the earliest manuscripts
Mark 1:41 reads "he stretched out his hand," but in nearly all
the late manuscripts it reads "Jesus stretched out his hand."
In this verse the context indicates that "he" refers to Jesus,
but sometimes names were inserted later for persons who are
unnamed and unknown in the original story.

RULE. Reject the readings that add details or otherwise
expand the story or saying. Another form of this rule is: Prefer the shorter reading.

g. Ideological Variants

Codices B, S, A : . . . the boy Jesus stayed behind in
Jerusalem, and his parents did not know (it). (Luke 2:43).

Codex C and Byzantine manuscripts: . . . the boy Jesus
stayed behind in Jerusalem, and Joseph and his mother
did not know (it). (Luke 2:43)

This verse in the fourth-century Codices Vaticanus and
Sinaiticus and in the fifth-century Codex A refers to Mary and
Joseph as "his parents," while the fifth-century Codex C and
the late manuscripts read "Joseph and his mother." This is
an example of an ideological variant, an alteration of the text
for the sake of certain ideas. Many of the ideological variants in biblical manuscripts are theological in nature, which is
the case in this example. Knowledge of the history of Christianity helps us to recognize this type of variant. A theological concern of the scribes was the protection and promotion of
the doctrine of the virgin birth of Jesus. The reading in this
verse was changed to eliminate the word "parents," because
the term indicates that Joseph was the father of Jesus.

RULE. Beware of variant readings that apparently were
created for ideological reasons.

h. Addition of New Stories or Sayings

The story of the woman accused of adultery and defended
by Jesus, in John 8:2-11, is in the Authorized Version, but absent in the Revised Standard Version. Why is this story not in

the modern version ?

Copyists and correctors not only frequently expanded the stories and sayings in the text, but occasionally even added new ones. The new material could be composed by the scribe of the manuscript, or it could be borrowed from oral or written tradition that was pagan, Christian, or Jewish. Often the material came from a different religion or culture and was revised to fit its new setting. This material is not authentic, for usually it first appears centuries after the writing of the biblical book to which it was added.

The story of the woman accused of adultery appears first in some Old Latin New Testament manuscripts written in the fifth century or later, and in Codex D (5th or 6th c.). In these documents it is placed in the Gospel of John at the beginning of chapter 8. In the Ferrar group of Greek minuscule manuscripts, which were written from the eleventh to the fifteenth centuries, the story is in a different location, immediately following Luke 21:38. The fact that this story teaches the ideal of tolerance does not necessarily make it a part of the original Bible. Stories and sayings that teach desirable moral ideals could be and were added later as well as those founded on superstition, polemics, or dogma. The authenticity of material cannot be judged on the basis of our admiration for it.

Another late story is in Luke 22:43-44. This is the concise story of an angel from heaven appearing and strengthening Jesus in Gethsemane, while Jesus in agony sweats great drops like blood. This legend is not in the third-century papyrus P^{75} nor in Codex B, written in the middle of the fourth century. It is in Codex Sinaiticus which was written in the latter half of the fourth century, but even there a corrector has removed it with deletion marks. Of the codices written in the fifth and sixth centuries, some contain the story and some do not. Thereafter it was generally accepted, along with other late insertions. This mythological story apparently was added to make the Gethsemane scene more dramatic. Unfortunately, it is included even in the Revised Standard Version.

How do textual critics establish the text in its original language ? They use the following procedure: (1) obtain the earliest and best manuscripts available, or at least facsim-

iles of them; (2) make accurate, readable transcriptions of
them in modern print; (3) collate the manuscripts to make a
record of the variants for easy comparison of them, verse by
verse; (4) analyze the history of the transmission of the text
to determine the cause of the variants; (5) with the causes as
a guide, establish rules of textual criticism for use in deciding
which variant in a passage is probably the original, or at least
the earliest reading known; (6) apply the rules and construct a
"critical edition" of the text, in an effort to establish the original text as nearly as possible, considering the current state of
knowledge.

The role of textual critics of the Bible has often been
misunderstood. The critics are not trying to destroy the text,
but to restore it. They seek the real Bible, the original.
Their goal is to peel off the accretions of the ages in order to
find that original.

The process of developing and applying the rules of textual criticism is not yet completed. We are still learning. An
expert can find questionable readings in even the best editions
of the Hebrew text of the Old Testament and the Greek text of
the New Testament, readings which probably were not in the
original text.

Two areas of textual study offer the possibility of considerable improvement. The rules learned from knowledge of the
history of the transmission of the text can be applied more
carefully and thoroughly in some passages. The second area
of research is a relatively new field, and probably has more
potential for increasing our present knowledge. This area is
that of determining the style of each writer or writers in each
book, and of using that information as a guide in recovering
the original text. When there are two variants of a passage,
and only one is consistent with the style and thought of the
writer of that passage, that reading is more likely to be the
original. Source criticism and redaction criticism are necessary allies of this kind of investigation. Important future
developments in this area are anticipated.

CHAPTER 12

TYPES OF LITERATURE—O. T.

The Hebrew Scriptures, or Old Testament, is a collection of writings by different authors produced over a period of about a millennium. Many of the books are composite, containing source materials and later insertions. The Song of Deborah (Judges 5), the Song of Miriam (Exod. 15:21), and a few other short poems in the Pentateuch may have originated as early as the twelfth century B. C. The latest book outside of the Apocrypha is the Book of Daniel, written 164 B. C. The latest in the Apocrypha are The Wisdom of Solomon and 2 Maccabees (1st c. B. C.). A wide variety of types of literature is to be found in the Hebrew Scriptures; the main types are laws, narratives, prophetic oracles, poetry, wisdom literature, drama, and apocalypse.

Laws

Some of the Hebrews who entered Canaan before the exodus were desert people with nomadic, tribal customs. After they and the Israelites of the exodus settled in the new land, they changed many of their customs as they adopted the agricultural and city life of the native population. The Israelites adopted laws, some of which they borrowed from their neighbors and modified, and some were new laws they formulated to defend their religion from the influence of their neighbors' religion. The latter laws emphasized that their people should worship only Yahweh, the god the Israelites brought with them from the desert; for example, "You shall serve Yahweh your god" (Exod. 23:25a). At the beginning of this book (example A) a verse from Exodus is quoted in which any Israelite who sacrifices to a different god is to be punished by death. The substitution of "the Lord" in English translations for the name Yahweh in the Hebrew text is an unfortunate practice; it obscures the fact that the situation was the struggle between the worship of the Israelite god Yahweh and the gods of other peoples.

You shall make no covenant with them or with their
gods. They shall not dwell in your land, lest they
make you sin against me; for if you serve their gods,
it will surely be a snare to you (Exod. 23:32-33).

You shall not boil a kid in its mother's milk
(Exod. 23:19b).

In the first passage above, Gentiles are not allowed to
live among the Israelites because the latter might be led into
worship of foreign gods. The first commandment in the Decalogue is a law against pagan deities. The second passage cited
above is a prohibition against a sacrificial meal in the Canaanite religion: eating the flesh of a young goat boiled in milk.

The earliest body of laws in the Bible is the Covenant
Code (Exod. 20:23-23:19). It contains civil and criminal law
(21:1-23:12) that is similar to some neighbors' laws, but displays a more humane development. The Ten Commandments
were eventually regarded as the core of the Torah, the written
law. The Torah included cultic laws on religious feasts (e.g.,
Exod. 23:14-19) and ceremonies (Exod. 25-31, from P, the
Priestly Code). The Torah grew through the centuries until it
included the present Pentateuch, which was canonized around
400 B.C. Later (approximately 100 B.C. to A.D. 200) the
oral Torah was produced by the Pharisees and their rabbis; it
consisted of interpretations and expansions of the written Torah.

As Colwell once observed,[27] a strain results when ancient laws are applied in later periods of history. A few laws
are timeless, but the majority are so closely related to the
contemporary culture that they simply do not fit a later time
with a different culture. For example, injunctions against
adopting Canaanite sacrifices are unnecessary today, because
the Canaanites no longer exist. Further, although there is
much variety in the Jews' concept of God, even the most orthodox concept today is not identical with that in Exodus.

Narratives

Jonah, Daniel, and the first eighteen books of the Old

Testament are in narrative form. Job is clearly drama, and Ruth, Esther, Daniel, and Jonah are generally regarded as fiction. The other fifteen narrative books range in content from actual history to miracle stories. Many stories were created to promote certain beliefs and attitudes.

Nevertheless, 1 and 2 Samuel and 1 and 2 Kings incorporate written sources which report many historical facts. Evidence of this includes the reports of incidents that are contrary to a later point of view. Although the Israelites believed that they would defeat the Philistines when they carried the ark of Yahweh with them, they lost the battle anyway, and the Philistines captured the ark (1 Sam. 4). (The stories of the disastrous effects of the ark on the Philistines while they possessed it, however, apparently is propaganda.) Although King David was a national hero, his sinful affair with Bathsheba and his plot against her husband are reported (2 Sam. 11).

The Israelites believed that the Lord had chosen them and that he controlled history. This theology of history led them to write stories in which Yahweh intervened in behalf of his chosen people. According to these narratives, he led them through the wilderness from Egypt to Canaan; he made covenants with them; he gave them laws; he helped them kill their enemies; he performed miracles for them and helped them perform miracles.

The Old Testament contains many miracle stories. We should not be surprised at this, for ancient literature abounds in such stories. After all, the ancient world was a superstitious one. The power to perform miracles was regarded as a necessary attribute of a deity. Miraculous deeds were esteemed as "signs," or proof, that the deity was, indeed, a powerful god who could aid and protect his worshipers. It was also believed that a deity could bestow on a chosen human, such as Moses, Aaron, and Elijah, the power to be a miracle worker. The performance of a miracle by a human was a "sign" that he was "a man of god," a man whose god had given him supernatural power.

In ancient art and literature the human miracle worker was often portrayed as using a rod to accomplish his feats, as Aaron did in Exodus 7-10 and Moses in Numbers 20. "And

Moses lifted up his hand and struck the rock with his rod twice; and water came forth abundantly, and the congregation drank, and their cattle" (Num. 20:11).

What mankind did not understand, it tended to attribute to supernatural causes. Strange phenomena in nature were regarded as miraculous acts of God. Examples are thunder and lightning and volcanoes (Exod. 19:16-18), earthquakes (Judg. 5:4-5), and eclipses (Joel 2:31).

An aspect of many Old Testament narratives is the expansion and revision of earlier accounts. This was often done by making insertions into the stories. Sometimes, however, a new document was written which retold the story or history to suit the interests of the writer. 1 and 2 Chronicles retells the story of the history from the reign of David to the exile of Jews in Babylon (from about 1000 to 587 B.C.). An account of that period had been written earlier in 2 Samuel and 1 and 2 Kings. Between 350 and 250 B.C. the Chronicler retold the story and constructed genealogies to give more prestige to the lower order of priests, the Levites. He ascribed to David's time some conditions that did not exist then, but were current in the Chronicler's own day. An example is the division of the Levites into four groups: overseers, officers and judges, gatekeepers, and singers (1 Chron. 23:2-5). The Chronicler was fond of exaggerating the size of the armies in ancient times. He even claimed that Asa, the king of Judah, had an army of 580,000 men who, with the Lord's help, killed the whole army of one million Ethiopians (2 Chron. 14:8-13)! The Chronicler apparently invented this story, for there is no mention of any battle with the Ethiopians in the account of Asa's reign in 1 Kings 15-16.

Although the "historical books" of the Old Testament contain some history, generally they were not written to provide accurate reports of specific events. Like many other ancient writings, they were produced and revised to promote certain beliefs, attitudes, and customs.

Prophetic Oracles

Although Israelite prophecy included predictions of the future, that was not the basic aspect of prophecy. The ancient view of prophecy was that it was essentially a declaration of God's will for individuals and/or the nation. The Lord had revealed his will by speaking to the prophet, who then proclaimed it to others. This belief is expressed with such phrases as "thus says the Lord" (Isa. 65:8), "the word of the Lord came to me" (Ezek. 6:1), and "hear the word of the Lord" (Isa. 1:10). Sometimes the prophet explicitly attributed his oracle to "the Spirit of the Lord God" (Isa. 61:1). Sometimes the revelation took the form of a vision: "I saw visions of God" (Ezek. 1:1) and "I saw the Lord sitting upon a throne" (Isa. 6:1).

Some prophecies or oracles were uttered orally, before they were written down; others probably originated in written form. In the period of the Judges (twelfth century B.C.) there were bands of prophets who prophesied (1 Sam. 10:10; 19:20), but left no writings. In the days of the major prophets, there were "schools" of prophets who transmitted and expanded in writing the oracles of their founders. Some of the prophecies are forecasts of the future; others were clearly written after the event. An example of the latter is the prediction of the fate of Zedekiah, king of Judah, after the Babylonians captured Jerusalem; it gives accurate details which reveal that it is a later insertion composed by someone who knew what had happened (Jer. 34:1-7).

Some of the prophetic oracles are poetry; others are written in prose. A characteristic of Hebrew poetry, as we have seen, is parallelism. In the synonymous form of parallelism, a statement is made, then repeated immediately in different words. An example occurs in the oracle in Zechariah:

> Lo, your king comes to you;
> triumphant and victorious is he,
> humble and riding on an ass,
> on a colt the foal of an ass (Zech. 9:9).

The fourth line expands the thought in the third line. The author of Matthew, although a Jewish Christian raised in the Jewish tradition, did not understand poetic parallelism. Consequently he misinterpreted the scriptural passage as a reference to two animals, and ass and its colt, and he created the surprising story of Jesus riding on both of them (Matt. 21:7)! The author of Mark, however, understood the verse correctly (Mark 11:7).

Here are some important principles that should be applied in interpreting the prophetic writings.

1. The prophets were concerned with the situations in their own day, and therefore we need to know as much as possible about those situations.

2. Because the prophets were writing about their own times, their predictions were concerned with the near future, not with the remote future. Thus it is a serious mistake to interpret the prophecies as intended for the twentieth century.

3. Because many of the prophecies are in poetic form, we need to be aware of the fact that they may contain synonymous parallelism, in which a phrase or clause repeats the thought in the preceding phrase or clause. Failure to recognize this literary feature can lead to misunderstanding of the prophecy.

Poetry

> And Miriam sang to them:
> "Sing to the Lord, for he has triumphed gloriously;
> the horse and his rider he has thrown into the sea"
> (Exod. 15:21).

Including the two in the Apocrypha, there are eight books of poetry in the Old Testament: Psalms, Song of Solomon, Lamentations, Job, Proverbs, Ecclesiastes, and in the Apocrypha, Wisdom of Solomon and Ecclesiasticus or the Wisdom of Jesus the Son of Sirach. The last four are also wisdom literature and will be discussed in the next section. In addition to these poetic works, some prose biblical books have poems in them. The Song of Miriam, quoted above, is an example of a poem in a prose setting.

Many ancient peoples, including Israelites, apparently produced songs before they wrote prose. At first, the songs probably were transmitted orally, and later some were incorporated in prose and some were written down as a collection. A few early songs are scattered through the narrative books of

the Old Testament, including the Song of Deborah (Judg. 5),
Song of Moses (Exod. 15:1-18), Song of Miriam (Exod. 15:21),
Song of Lamech (Gen. 4:23-24), Blessing of Jacob (Gen. 49),
and the Blessing of Moses (Deut. 33). Synonymous parallelism abounds even in these early songs, as it does in Canaanite
and other ancient Semitic literature; here is an example from
the Song of Deborah (Seir was a mountain range in Edom, so
the two lines have essentially the same meaning):

> Lord, when thou didst go forth from Seir
> when thou didst march from the region of Edom
> (Judg. 5:4; RSV).

The Psalms is a collection of songs that were used in
worship services in the temple in Jerusalem. Many of these
hymns were written by priests and Levites. The songs consist of four main types: hymns of praise to the Lord, prayers,
exhortations (including poems of warning and poems of encour-
ment), and songs of thanksgiving for victory over an enemy.
Although tradition later assigned some of the psalms to David
and others, the actual authorship is unknown. The contents of
some show clearly that they were composed much later than
David's time. After the hymns were collected, they were divided into five sections or books, with a doxology at the end of
each division (Pss. 1-41, 42-72, 73-89, 90-106, 107-150).
Apparently this was done to imitate the pattern of the Torah in
five books, the Pentateuch. The Hebrew word for God in
Psalms 42-83 is *Elohim*, whereas in all the other Psalms it
is *Yahweh*. This evidence suggests that chapters 42-83 originated independently and once formed a separate collection or
book. Some of the hymns contain later expansions. The date
of the present form of the Psalms is judged to be between 400
and 100 B.C. The Psalms were influenced by Egyptian, Babylonian, and Canaanite poetry.

Another category of poetry is the dirge or lamentation.
This type occurs in the Book of Lamentations and in the la-
ments of David (2 Sam. 1:19-27; 3:33-34).

Job is a special type of poetry in that it is also drama.
The characters in it engage in discussion of the ways of God;
they debate theological issues that have plagued mankind for

millenia. The discussion format and the poetic content clearly indicate that the book was written as a dramatic poem, not
as a biography or historical report.

Wisdom Literature

> That men may know wisdom and instruction,
> understand words of insight,
> receive instruction in wise dealing,
> righteousness, justice, and equity;
> that prudence may be given to the simple,
> knowledge and discretion to the youth —
> the wise man also may hear and increase in learning,
> and the man of understanding acquire skill,
> to understand a proverb and a figure,
> the words of the wise and their riddles
> (Prov. 1:2-6).

The wisdom literature consists primarily of collections
of rules for practical living, produced and transmitted by "the
wise." The passage above, quoted from Proverbs, is a summary of the purposes of wisdom literature. Jeremiah 18:18
lists the priest, the wise, and the prophet as the three classes
of intellectual leaders in Israel. The function of the wise was
to give counsel. In 2 Samuel 14 and 20 wise women are mentioned; later there were wisdom circles, or schools, which
produced and compiled proverbs, parables, and stories to
teach moral and practical lessons. Many historians believe
that the proverbs of the Israelites and other peoples of the
Near East originated in the courts of the kings.

As its name implies, the Book of Proverbs consists of
short, pithy aphorisms intended as guides for daily living.
Tradition has ascribed Proverbs to Solomon, but generally the
background reflected in the book belongs to a later age. Although some individual sayings probably are earlier, Proverbs as a book was formed sometime between 400 and 250
B.C. The fundamental unit in a proverb is a couplet, often
in the form of antithetical parallelism in which the second part
is the opposite, or antithesis, of the first part.

A slack hand causes poverty,
but the hand of the diligent makes rich (Prov. 10:4).

Ecclesiastes is not typical wisdom literature. Although the writer paid lip service to wisdom, it was not his real concern. He was disillusioned with life, because the wicked man prospers while the industrious laborer is poor. The author makes many pessimistic comments on life. "All is vanity" (Eccl. 1:2).

The author of Ecclesiasticus, on the other hand, had a more optimistic attitude. He tried to combine the wisdom of Proverbs with the study of the Jewish law. He wrote in Jerusalem around 180 B.C.

The Wisdom of Solomon praises righteous men and denounces the wicked rich who oppress the upright poor (1-5). Under the influence of Hellenistic philosophy, it personifies wisdom and identifies it with God's word by which he created all things (6-10). Wisdom 12:2 to the end of the book apparently was originally a separate work, for it differs from the rest in language, style, and substance. This section addresses the Lord in the second person, praises him as superior to other gods, and uses the history of Israel to support the theme. The dominant purpose of the Jewish writers throughout the book is to combat the tendency of some Jews to adopt Greek culture and abandon the worship of the Lord.

Apocalypse

An apocalypse is a Jewish or Christian writing, usually pseudonymous, which purports to be a divinely revealed, secret prediction of the eschatological future. This future generally consists of features such as the imminent end of the current age, the resurrection of the dead, the divine judgment, and the coming of a permanent righteous world established by God, either directly, or indirectly with the aid of a Messiah. The secret knowledge was hidden in symbolic imagery which was understandable to the readers for whom it was intended, but mysterious and unintelligible to outsiders. The term apocalypse is derived from a Greek word, *apokalupsis*, "revelation." In English, however, there is a distinction between

"apocalypse" and "revelation"; the latter is a broader term
and does not necessarily refer to a document. The typical
apocalypse is in the form of a vision, or series of visions; the
seer "saw" things. In the Jewish apocalypse the seer usually
is represented as a prominent Hebrew of the ancient past, such
as Enoch, Noah, Moses, and Daniel. Birds, animals, and
various things symbolize persons and kingdoms. The numbers
3, 4, 7, 10, and 12 occur frequently.

The apocalypse was prevalent in Judaism from 200 B.C.
to A.D. 150. It was born out of Jewish despair over political
conditions. Jews knew from their Scriptures that their ancestors had conquered the Canaanites and occupied their land.
They knew that in the reigns of Saul, David, and Solomon, the
tribes became a united nation with national pride. But the
nation became divided into Israel in the north and Judah in the
south. Then came the conquerors and foreign rule. Assyria
ruled over Israel, and in succession, Babylonia, Persia, the
Greeks, and in 63 B.C. the Romans ruled over Palestine.
Between the Greek and Roman rules there was a century of
Jewish independence, which revived nationalistic fervor. To
Jews, the periods of foreign rule, however, were times of
utter discouragement, intensified by the disparity between
the actual conditions and the belief that they were protected
by Yahweh as his chosen people. Some prophets had offered
hope by predicting better days in the future. The apocalyptic
writings furthered the prophetic hope by drawing grandiose
pictures of the collapse of their oppressors and, with God's
intervention, the triumph of Israel. Many of the apocalypses
incorporated eschatological beliefs. According to them, the
change would be accompanied by a cosmic cataclysm, and
conditions will become worse before they become better.
Iranian religion is probably the source of some eschatology.

The Book of Daniel is an apocalypse, and numerous
other Jewish books of this type were written which are outside
the canon.

> Daniel said, "I saw in my vision by night, and behold,
> the four winds of heaven were stirring up the great sea.
> And four great beasts came up out of the sea, different
> from one another" (Dan. 7:2-3).

> At that time shall arise Michael, the great prince who
> has charge of your people. And there shall be a time
> of trouble, such as never has been since there was a
> nation till that time; but at that time your people shall
> be delivered, every one whose name shall be found
> written in the book. And many of those who sleep in
> the dust of the earth shall awake, some to everlast-
> ing life, and some to shame and everlasting contempt
> (Dan. 12:1-2).

The first passage quoted from Daniel is the start of a "vision" in which four beasts symbolize four nations: Babylonia,
Media, Persia, and the Greek Seleucid kingdom. Chapter 7 of
Daniel continues by stating that the beasts will lose their dominion and that "the saints of the Most High" (i.e., the Jews)
will "possess the kingdom for ever." The second passage
above mentions briefly the eschatological ideas of the resurrection of the dead and the judgment. It is the judgment that
will decide whether the dead awake to eternal blessed life on
earth or to eternal shame and punishment.

Within the seven types of literature we have listed,
prayers and tracts are sometimes embedded. When we read
them, we should approach each type in terms of its own traditions and characteristics.

CHAPTER 13

TYPES OF LITERATURE—N. T.

The New Testament, as well as the Old, contains a variety of types of literature, including letters, formal epistles, narratives, and apocalypses. Miracle stories and parables are within the narratives. The dates of composition of the books range from mid-first century (Paul's letters) to mid-second century (2 Peter).

Letters

Adolf Deissmann, in his *Light from the Ancient East,* made a distinction between a letter and an epistle. Although the word "epistle" is sometimes applied to a letter, in this book we observe the distinction between the two terms. A genuine letter is an informal, personal message written directly to a specific person or group of persons, while an epistle is intended for wider circulation.

Deissmann examined many pagan papyri from Egypt, written in Greek during Hellenistic and Roman times. Among them were letters with formulas similar to those of the letters in the New Testament. The customary formula in the papyri was a salutation at the beginning consisting of the name of the sender followed by the name of the recipient, as in "Thaeius to her mother Syras." In many letters this was followed immediately by "greeting" or "many greetings." The closing sometimes expressed good wishes to the recipient and others; for example, "Before all else you have my good wishes for unbroken health and prosperity," and "Take care of yourself and all your household." Sometimes the closing ended with greetings *to* others besides the recipient, such as "Salute Ammonas my brother." Also, greetings *from* others were frequently included, for example, "Marcellus salutes you." The typical ending was "Farewell," followed by the date. Joseph Fitzmyer (1974) analyzed ancient letters written in Aramaic and found that the majority have five parts: a *praescriptio* (the names of the sender and the addressee), the initial greeting (such as "peace" or "bless"), secondary greetings (to others than the addressee), the body of the letter, and a concluding formula such as "Be at peace." In a few the date was added.

Here is a sample letter written in Greek on papyrus in the first century A. D., as quoted in Deissmann's *Bible Studies* (p. 24).

Indike to Thaeius, greeting. I sent you the breadbasket by Taurinus the camel-man; please send me an answer that you have received it. Salute my friend Theon and Nikobulos and Dioskoros and Theon [accidental repetition?] and Hermokles, who have my best wishes. Longinus salutes you. Goodbye. Month Germanikos 2.

The salutation and closing below are rather characteristic of Paul's letters.

Salutation

Paul, an apostle of Christ Jesus by the will of God, and Timothy our brother. To the church of God which is at Corinth, with all the saints who are in the whole of Achaia: Grace to you and peace from God our Father and the Lord Jesus Christ (2 Cor. 1:1-2).

Closing

Greet every saint in Christ Jesus. The brethren who are with me greet you. All the saints greet you, especially those of Caesar's household. The grace of the Lord Jesus be with your spirit (Phil. 4:21-23).

The similarity between Paul's letters and the pagan one is quite evident. In Paul's letters "farewell" occurs only in the closing of 2 Corinthians, and the date is never given. Pagan letters generally dealt with purely personal matters; this is the case with issues or problems in the local church to which Paul was writing. For example his discussion of resurrection is in direct response to the fact that some persons in the Corinthian

church did not believe that there would be a resurrection of
the dead (1 Cor. 15:12).

Copies of Paul's letters were made and circulated among
other Christian communities besides the one to which each was
addressed. By the middle of the second century his letters
were regularly read aloud in worship services in many churches. As a result of this practice, additions were made in some
of Paul's salutations and closings to adapt the letters to liturgical use. These additions are difficult to identify precisely,
but they certainly include the word "Amen" (inherited from
Jewish liturgy) in closings, and the doctrinal statement (verses 4-5) in the salutation in Galatians.

The question of which letters were written by Paul is still
debated. Of the letters attributed to him, Philemon, 1 and 2
Corinthians, Galatians, and 1 Thessalonians are certainly authentic. Some other material was inserted in them later, however. All of Philemon was written by Paul, except verse 9b.
Philemon, therefore, is the best letter with which to start a
study of Paul's style. Romans, 2 Thessalonians, Philippians,
and Colossians may have been written by him. The other letters traditionally assigned to him are certainly non-Pauline.

More research should be done to separate the genuine
Pauline passages within a letter from the non-Pauline material
which was inserted later by redactors and copyists. When non-
Pauline material is believed to have been written by Paul, we
are given a mistaken impression of his thought and style.

2 and 3 John apparently are letters, both written by the
same writer, although he refers to himself as "the elder" instead of by name. He asserts his authority over the church
and its members ("the elect lady and her children") to whom
he writes in 2 John, urging them not to receive into their house
any docetic missionaries who preach that Jesus Christ did not
come in the flesh. In 3 John he writes to commend the loyal
Gaius in that church and to threaten to come and to deal with
the insubordinate Diotrephes.

Epistles

An epistle is a short tractate in the form of a letter, written to promote or defend a point of view. The New Testament

epistles (except 1 John) have at least part of the letter format. They include Ephesians, the pastoral epistles, Hebrews, James, 1 and 2 Peter, 1 John, and Jude.

After the death of the first generation of apostles, many Christian writings were ascribed to those early leaders. This practice gave the writings prestige and authority. The authority was especially needed in the controversy with the gnostic heretics, who falsely claimed that their own documents were written by apostles. In catholic, or non-gnostic, churches the author of a work was sometimes unknown, so some scribe or church assigned an apostolic author to it. One method was to add a title at the beginning or end attributing the writing to an apostle. This technique was applied to the canonical gospels. Another method was to change the document to a letter format, with a salutation at the beginning that included the name of an alleged author. In other cases, however, the original author wrote pseudonymously and used the letter format to ascribe his work to an apostle.

The salutation in the New Testament epistles usually reveals that they were intended for the church at large. It is addressed to many churches instead of a single church or person. Ephesians is addressed "to the saints who are also faithful in Christ Jesus" ("who are at Ephesus" is not in the earliest manuscripts). 1 Peter is addressed to "the exiles of the Dispersion" in five Roman provinces in Asia Minor.

Internal evidence in the epistles demonstrates that they were not written by apostles. The date of Ephesians is later than the days of the apostles, for the church has already been built on the foundation of the apostles and the prophets (Eph. 2:20), an idea contrary to Paul's belief that the only foundation of the church was Jesus Christ (1 Cor. 3:11). The language, style, and thought of Hebrews is very unlike Paul's, but similar to contemporary documents produced in Alexandria, where Hebrews probably was written, Two facts show that 1 Timothy was not written to Timothy. First, in 1 Timothy the leader of the local church is called a bishop (3:1), a later office and title which did not exist in Paul's day (1 Cor. 12:28). Second, the content of the epistle is a matter of concern to churches generally, not just a particular individual (especially not an individual who was already familiar with the author and his teach-

ing, which would have been the case if Paul had written this to
Timothy). 1 Peter clearly was not written by Peter. Its content reveals a later date, the style of the Greek is too polished
to have been written by Peter (who probably did not even speak
Greek), and the quotations from the Old Testament are from
the Septuagint, which could hardly have been Peter's Bible.
2 Peter certainly was not composed by Peter, for (1) it alludes
to 1 Peter, a late epistle; (2) it incorporates most of Jude,
which was written late in the first century or early in the second; (3) by the time it was written, Paul's letters had been collected and accepted as part of the "Scriptures" (3:16).

The themes of the epistles dealt with problems facing
Christians generally at the time (A.D. 90-150). The author
of Ephesians wrote to gentile Christians to alleviate tensions
between them and Jewish Christians, so he emphasized unity.
He assured them that, though formerly as non-Jews they were
outside God's covenants, alienated from Jews and their God,
now Christ Jesus has united believing Jews and believing Gentiles in the church (2:12-14). 1 Peter was written to exhort
Christians to suffer persecution and honor the emperor. The
theme of submission is extended to slaves and wives, who
should be submissive to their masters and husbands, respec-
tively—and husbands should be considerate and honor their
wives. 1 Timothy was written to oppose heretical teachers in
the churches, teachers who probably were ascetic gnostics.
1 John was written to counteract docetic heretics who, believing that the flesh is evil, denied that the Christ was Jesus who
had come in the flesh. The author of 2 Peter wrote to denounce libertine-gnostic heretics, "false teachers," who
scoffed at the belief in Jesus' imminent second advent. James
was written by a Jewish Christian to emphasize that the ethical
ideals of proper attitudes in the heart and good deeds ("works")
are more important (Jas. 2:14-26) than Paul's emphasis on
faith (Gal. 3:2, 23-27).

Narratives

Two types of narrative books are in the New Testament: the
the Acts of the Apostles and the gospels.

a. Acts

Acts was written by the author of Luke; in fact, he wrote Luke-Acts as a two-volume work. The evidence for this con-clusion is that both books are addressed to the same man, The-ophilus; both, except for the sections incorporating source materials, are similar in style, vocabulary, and point of view; and at the beginning of Acts the author refers back to Luke as his "first book."

Acts presents an account of the first few decades of the history of the church, from soon after Jesus' crucifixion to Paul's trip to Rome. The book is a mixture of fact and fiction, and separating the two is a necessary but difficult task. Acts supplies insight into Christian beginnings that we cannot obtain elsewhere. Only Acts informs us of the split between the more orthodox members of the Jerusalem church, including the orig-inal disciples, and the "Hellenist" members.

> And they went through the region of Phrygia and Galatia, having been forbidden by the Holy Spirit to speak the word in Asia. And when they had come opposite Mysia, they attempted to go into Bithynia, but the Spirit of Je-sus did not allow them; so, passing by Mysia, they went down to Troas. And a vision appeared to Paul in the night: a man of Macedonia was standing beseeching him and saying, "Come over to Macedonia and help us." And when he had seen the vision, immediately we sought to go on into Macedonia, concluding that God had called us to preach the gospel to them (Acts 16:6-10).

Some passages are written in the first person plural (16:10-17; 20:5-21:18; 27:1-28:18); whether these "we" passages come from an early source, or were composed by the author of Acts, is a debated question. The passage from Acts quoted above illustrates the beginning of a "we" passage (at verse 9); observe the sudden shift from "they" to "we" and "us."

Although the second half of Acts relates the story of Paul, the author apparently did not know and use Paul's letters. He never mentions the letters nor even indicates that Paul wrote any. Further evidence of his unfamiliarity with the letters is the difference between the account in Acts 15 of the apostolic conference in Jerusalem and Paul's own report in Galatians 2. According to Paul, the decision reached at the meeting was that he should "remember the poor" and that he and Barnabas should preach to the Gentiles, while the Jerusalem apostles should preach to "the circumcised" (i.e., the Jews; Gal. 2: 9-10). According to Acts 15, however, the decision was that gentile Christians should abstain from unchastity and from eating meat that did not conform to Jewish law (15:28-29). Also, Paul took a strong stand against circumcising gentile converts, regardless of pressure from opponents (Gal. 2: 1-5), whereas Acts 16:3 represents Paul as circumcising Timothy out of respect for the feelings of Jews on the matter. When Acts and Paul disagree, Paul's letters should be preferred as the source, because they supply first-hand information and because Acts reflects the author's desire to minimize disagreements in the church.

The "speeches" in Acts are not the words delivered on the occasions in which they are set, for they do not fit the situation in which they are placed. Stephen's speech in chapter 7, for example, does not even mention the main charges against him (that he had spoken against the temple and the Mosaic law); instead, its theme is that Jews throughout history have persecuted prophets and not obeyed the Mosaic law.

The author of Acts wrote to promote certain points of view. One notion was that the Holy Spirit had possessed and guided the apostles, and that this force was responsible for the rapid growth of the church (1:4, 8; 2:4; 4:31). He also wanted to foster the belief that Christianity should accept Gentiles into membership. Peter (10:24) and James (15:13-20) are represented as becoming convinced that Gentiles should be admitted to the church. Non-Christian Jews and the conservative wing of Jewish Christians criticized the gentile churches, including those founded by Paul, for not observing the Jewish law. The author of Acts tried to meet the criticism by portraying Christians as continuing to obey the Torah. He depicts Paul as complying with the law and paying the expenses of four others under a vow of the law (21:20-26), actions that are not consistent with Paul's attitude in Galatians. The author also sought to minimize the conflicts with Roman authorities. According to Acts, the Roman authorities at Philippi, Corinth, and Jerusalem released Paul after arresting him, and King Agrippa and the Roman governor Festus agreed that Paul had done "nothing to deserve death or imprisonment" (26:31)—yet they sent him as a prisoner to Rome! If the Roman magistrates had declared Paul innocent, there would have been no need for him to continue his appeal to Caesar, nor would they have sent him to Rome as a prisoner. Acts provides examples of the importance of recognizing an author's motives and views in order to understand ancient narratives.

b. Gospels

The word "gospel" in Greek means literally "good news," and in the New Testament the term refers to the early Christian message, or preaching (e.g., Mark 1:14-15). Even in Mark 1:1 the word has this meaning: "the beginning of the gospel of Jesus Christ" refers to the beginning of the message about him. Later the term was applied to certain books, including some outside the canon. The canonical gospels are essentially narratives, although they contain sayings and—in form, at least—speeches. Of the uncanonical gospels written in the second century, some are narratives (e.g., *Gospel of Peter*), some consist of sayings (e.g., *Gospel of Thomas*), and some are tractates (e.g., *Gospel of Truth*).

Although the gospels appear to be historical biographies, they are really promotional literature in narrative form ("written that you may believe," John 20:31). The authors were not trying to write accurate biographies—that is clear from the freedom with which they changed their source material to agree with their own view or that of their Christian community. This explains why Jesus is very Jewish in Matthew (whose author was a Jewish Christian) and very anti-Jewish in John (whose author was a gentile Christian). The literary type or genre of the gospels is similar to that of ancient pagan "biographies," as Charles Talbert has shown. [28] This does not make them genuine biographies, however, for both historical and unhistorical accounts, as well as mixtures of both, were written.

The lateness of the composition of the gospels had a tremendous influence upon their content, a fact which must be recognized in order to understand them. Mark was written about A. D. 75, Luke 80-85, Matthew 90-95, and John 95-110. Thus their background ends, not with the death of Jesus (ca. A. D. 30), but with the time of their composition.

The similarities among the synoptic gospels reveal a direct literary relationship among them; Mark was used as a source by the authors of the other two. One indication is that almost all of Mark's stories and sayings are reproduced in Matthew and Luke, and generally in the same order. If the Marcan material in the other two gospels varies from the order in Mark, the variant order usually is only in one of them—the other gospel follows the Marcan arrangement. A second indication is the fact that Matthew and Luke tend to follow Mark's wording too. One or the other of those two may vary from Mark, but their statements seldom agree with each other against Mark. A third indication of dependence upon Mark is the nature of the variations from Mark. Those in Matthew are usually consistent with its author's point of view, and Luke's variations reflect its author's views. All this evidence leads to the conclusion that the authors of Matthew and Luke used Mark as a source and, acting independently of the other, each made some changes and insertions of his own.

And behold, one came up to him, saying, "Teacher, what good deed must I do, to have eternal life?" And he said to him, "Why do you ask me about what is good? One there is who is good. If you would enter life, keep the commandments" (Matt. 19: 16-17).

And as he was setting out on his journey, a man ran up and knelt before him, and asked him, "Good Teacher, what must I do to inherit eternal life?" And Jesus said to him, "Why do you call me good? No one is good but God alone. You know the commandments: . . ." (Mark 10: 17-19).

And a ruler asked him, "Good Teacher, what shall I do to inherit eternal life?" And Jesus said to him, "Why do you call me good? No one is good but God alone. You know the commandments: . . ." (Luke 18:18-20).

The passages above, presented in a synopsis format, illustrate the occurrence of Marcan material in the other two
synoptic gospels. The story is the same one in all three gospels. The wording varies, but Matthew and Luke each agree
with Mark considerably, but do not agree with each other
against Mark. The story also demonstrates that Matthew and
Luke reproduce the Marcan material in Mark's order. In all
the synoptics the story which precedes the one above is that of
Jesus blessing the children. In all three a prediction of Jesus'
death and resurrection follows the story in our passages, except that in Matthew a non-Marcan parable has been inserted
between them.

O Jerusalem, Jerusalem,
killing the prophets and stoning those who are sent to
you! How often would I have
gathered your children together as a hen gathers her
brood under her wings, and
you would not! Behold, your
house is forsaken and deso-
late. For I tell you, you
will not see me again, until
you say, "Blessed be he who
comes in the name of the
Lord" (Matt. 23:37-39).

O Jerusalem, Jerusalem,
killing the prophets and stoning those who are sent to
you! How often would I have
gathered your children together as a hen gathers her
brood under her wings, and
you would not! Behold, your
house is forsaken! And I tell
you, you will not see me until
you say, "Blessed be he who
comes in the name of the
Lord" (Luke 13:34-35)

These two parallel passages illustrate the Q material,
the sayings and a few stories which are in both Matthew and
Luke, but not Mark. The similarities in vocabulary, syntax, and thought indicate that the two gospel authors obtained
the material from a common source or sources. Formerly a
single source, Quelle, or Document Q, was advanced as the
explanation, but now several sources seem more probable—
at least a narrative source and a sayings source. Some material that is only in Luke probably was originally in Q also,
but the author of Matthew did not happen to use it. In addition,
a very few units in all three synoptic gospels apparently were
in Q as well as in Mark, for in them Matthew and Luke have

important agreements against Mark. An example is a parable
of the mustard seed (Mark 4:30-32). In the parallel accounts
in Matthew (13:31-32) and Luke (13:18-19), but not in Mark,
are the following expressions: "a man took"; "becomes/be-
came a tree"; "branches." It is very unlikely that both writers
would have independently made the same three changes in the
Marcan parable; both writers must have used a written source
which had these features.

The Q sayings in Matthew are more scattered and in different order in Matthew than in Luke. There are two probable
causes. The sayings probably lacked a narrative framework
in Q, and therefore writers felt completely free to rearrange
them when they used them. Also, the author of Matthew was
prone to rearrange material according to subject.

Matthew and Luke each contain additional material not
found in any of the other three canonical gospels. Some in
Luke appears to be from a source or sources, but that in Matthew apparently was composed by the author of that gospel, for
it exhibits his views and stylistic traits.

The origin of the Gospel of John, as well as that of the
synoptic gospels, has been misunderstood through the centuries. Alexandria, rather than Ephesus, probably was its place
of origin, indicated both by its contents and the fact that it was
used in Alexandria by a gnostic teacher, Basilides, early in
the second century, soon after it was written. The non-Pal-
estinian nature of its contents shows that the book was not
written by John, the disciple of Jesus, and the vocabulary,
style, and content show that it was not written by the author of
Revelation. Recent research shows that it was not written by
a single author, but is a composite work (see our chapter 7).

In the narrative source, which has been called the "Gospel of Signs," Jesus is a miracle worker whose miracles are
signs that he is the Christ. In the speech source the theology
is that of Hellenistic mysticism, which has some affinity with
gnosticism. Semi-gnostic features in the speech source include ideas such as the Father sent Jesus (8:18), who has come
from God (8:42c); it is essential to know whence Jesus came
and whither he is going (8:14); Jesus speaks what the Father
has taught him (8:28). But only the hymn source in the Prologue is fully gnostic. Both the author of the gospel and the

later redactor were very concerned about the problems and
issues in the early Christian communities.

The portrait of Jesus in the Gospel of John is extremely
different from that in the synoptic gospels. In John Jesus was
not born on earth, but has come down from heaven; he is boast-
ful instead of humble; only in John does Jesus denounce all non-
Christian Jews (8:44); only in John does he speak with the vocabulary and thought of Hellenistic mysticism, which cannot
possibly be historical. The explanation of the variety in the
four canonical gospels is to be found, not in the notion that different people report the same events differently, but rather in
the historical fact that the gospels reflect the variety of beliefs among the early Christian communities and writers.

c. Miracle Stories

The gospels and Acts contain miracle stories of various
types. The Semitic world believed that diseases could be
caused by demons, or unclean spirits, which entered a person
and took possession of him. The cure for the diseases was believed to be exorcism, casting the demons out of the person.
Stories were told of exorcisms performed by Jesus (Mark 1,
5, 9), by Paul (Acts 16:16-18), and by the disciples (Mark 6:13).
Healing might also be accomplished by the laying on of hands,
with no demons involved (Mark 6:5), or the sick person might
merely touch Jesus' garment (Mark 6:56). Sometimes "power," or strength, from the healer passed into the ill person,
effecting the cure (Mark 5:30). Putting the healer's spittle on
the eyes was believed to cure blindness (Mark 8:22-26; John
9:6-11). At times the invalid's faith that he could be healed,
followed by a command from the healer, sufficed (Acts 14:
8-10). One Jewish explanation for illness was that it was God's
punishment of the individual for his or her sins; this is reflected in John 9:2 and in the story of Jesus' healing a paralytic
by telling him that his sins are forgiven (Mark 2). The supreme kind of "healing" is that of restoring the dead to life
(John 11).

Other miracle stories have nothing to do with healing.
They include Jesus' feeding the multitutdes, walking on the
sea, and changing water into wine. The healing miracles and

the nature miracles in the New Testament had their parallels
in the Jewish and pagan worlds; all reflect the credulity of the
age.

Parables and Allegories

A parable is a brief, simple story to which something is
compared in order to teach a lesson. Only two genuine parables occur in the Old Testament: Nathan's story of the rich
man's theft of the poor man's lamb (2 Sam. 12:1-14) and Isaiah's parable of the unproductive vineyard (Isa. 5:1-2). In contrast, many parables are in the synoptic gospels. Parables
are used to make a point or lesson clearer and more emphat-
ic. Mark 4:11-12 (and parallel verses in Matthew and Luke)
represents Jesus as using parables to conceal knowledge from
outsiders who are not his disciples. Such a purpose is the opposite of the customary use of parables! Clergymen and biblical exegetes have labored to explain why Jesus would try to
prevent his listeners from understanding his teaching. Thanks
to historical scholarship, we now know that the tradition is unhistorical. It is only a later Christian attempt to explain why
so few people in Palestine believed the apostolic preaching
about Jesus. The rationale is that people did not believe because they did not understand, and that Jesus deliberately
spoke in parables so that they would not understand.

An allegory, too, is a story intended to convey a lesson;
it may be long or short. It has the added feature that details
in it represent other things or people. Whereas a parable requires only a general interpretation of its main theme, an allegory requires a detailed interpretation of its symbolic elements. Jesus as the True Vine is an allegory in John 15:1-8.
Two parables in the synoptic tradition are each followed by an
allegorical interpretation: the Parable of the Sower (Mark 4:
3-9, 13-20) and the Parable of the Tares (Matt. 13:24-30, 36-
43).

Apocalypse

The Book of Revelation is an apocalypse in the form of an
epistle addressed to "the seven churches that are in Asia, "

which are named. It is also called "the Apocalypse" because
it is the only New Testament book of that literary type. It
purports to be a spiritual revelation to John on the Lord's day
on the island of Patmos. Revelation, the most enigmatic work
in the Bible, can be understood if we know its composite nature, the circumstances which caused it to be written, and the
meaning of its symbolic imagery.

The author incorporated Jewish, and perhaps Christian,
sources in his book. Revelation 7:1-8, for example, apparently is from a Jewish apocalyptic source. The use of source
material explains some of the repetition, contradictions, and
poor connections in the text. An additional feature of Revelation is the presence of hymn-like passages, as in 4:8, 11, and
7:10, 12.

Revelation was written to encourage Christians in Asia
Minor when they were being persecuted by the emperor Domitian, and to try to stop them from committing apostasy, that
is, abandoning the Christian faith to avoid persecution. Con-
sumed with hatred for Rome, the author was more belligerent
and uncompromising in his attitude toward it than were the authors of 1 Peter and Hebrews. He sees Rome as a "beast"
which will soon be destroyed in connection with the coming
cosmic war between Satan and God. The details of the war and
the coming of the messianic kingdom of Jesus are cloaked in
figurative language which has always been a problem for interpreters. Satan is a dragon, the church is a woman, and the
ten horns (13:1) are the ten Roman emperors who have ruled
up to the writer's day.

Some New Testament authors were Jewish Christians,
like the author of Revelation, and some were gentile Christians. This difference in background of the writers influenced
their specific ideas and their general view of Christianity. The
ability to recognize an author's background is valuable for understanding his writing. A list of the characteristics of Jewish and Jewish-Christian writings in the New Testament period
has been compiled as an aid for recognizing Jewish-Christian
documents.[29]

CHAPTER 14

LITERARY METHODS

We have seen that many biblical books are composite and that recognition of this fact was long delayed by the belief in their traditional authorship. Some of those erroneous traditions were created when certain books were written pseudonymously; other traditions arose after the books were written when someone assigned authorship to them. In either case the alleged author was invariably some famous person who had lived in the past and whose words could be accepted as authoritative. Consequently it seemed quite heretical to suggest later that several writers produced a book instead of the traditional author.

How Composite Books Were Written

As evidence of the composite nature of various books became known, biblical scholars raised questions concerning the literary origin of each. How many writers were involved in the composition of a particular book? Precisely which words or verses were written by each person? What was each writer's point of view and motives for writing? What was his characteristic literary style? In what situation and environment did each write?

Scholars also wanted to know by what process composite biblical books were written. Did a writer use either oral tradition or written documents as source material? If so, how did he treat his sources? And after the book was written, did a redactor make his own insertions in it?

There were various ways that an author could treat a source. He might use all of it or only part of it. He could leave all of it together as a block, or he might split it up, inserting other material between the sections. He might use two or more sources and interweave, or conflate, them. Both the author of the Gospel of Matthew and the author of the Gospel of Luke conflated their sources, blending the Gospel of

Mark with the source material "Q."

Redaction was a literary technique widely employed in the ancient world. An author could revise, or redact, his source material. Also, after a book was written, a different person, often referred to as a "redactor," might revise the book. Redaction could consist of changes in the matter someone else had written, or, more frequently, simply of the insertion of more material. The motive for redaction often was to foster certain views held by the redactor. For example, the author of Matthew added a saying to the Mark and Q materials which reflects his bias against the Gentiles and Samaritans:

> These twelve Jesus sent out, charging them, "Go nowhere among the Gentiles, and enter no town of the Samaritans, but go rather to the lost sheep of the house of Israel" (Matt. 10:5-6).

The author of Matthew was a Jewish Christian who, unlike Paul, another Jewish Christian, still held the traditional Jewish attitude toward non-Jews. He made this addition to his sources to support his point of view.

In chapter 9 we quoted the injunction in Deuteronomy 4:2 against adding to the word which the Lord had commanded, and the curse in Revelation 22:18-19 upon anyone who adds or subtracts from that book. Such laws and threats would not have been necessary if the practice of later redaction had not been prevalent in both Old and New Testament times.

Source Criticism and Redaction Criticism

The terms "source criticism" and "redaction criticism" are used increasingly by historians to refer to the efforts to discover how composite writings were produced and to identify the work of each writer. Source criticism is the systematic attempt to find and interpret in a book the material in a source or sources which the author incorporated in it. After the source material is detected, the critic tries to understand both what it meant in the original work and what it meant to the writer who reused it. The source critic wants to know

why the author of the biblical book used the source material.
He asks what ideas in the source appealed to the biblical author.

Redaction criticism is the systematic effort to determine
what changes a writer made in another person's writing, and
why. In the case of an author incorporating source material,
the redaction critic examines the changes and insertions the
author made in his source material. In the case of a redactor
revising the book after it has left the author's hands, the critic examines the redactor's changes and insertions. The critic is especially interested in the motivation, theological or
otherwise, behind the changes and insertions.

Source criticism and redaction criticism are very closely related, and essentially the same methods are used in each.
They are necessary elements in the broader field of literary
criticism, which includes also the style and literary type of
the book.

How can we tell if a biblical book is composite? The answer is, by using the clues in the book itself. When a book includes sources or has been revised, some telltale traits of the
procedure usually remain. The traits are clues which enable
us to establish criteria for detecting composite writing. The
clues consist of seven types of evidence.

1. Inconsistencies. If some aspects of a writing are not
in harmony with one another, they should alert us to the possibility that more than one hand may have been involved. Although it is possible for one writer to be inconsistent, in actual
practice inconsistencies are far more liable to occur when
there are two or more writers. Several persons are almost
certain to differ among themselves in their style and thought.

According to the Bible, how many pairs of each kind of
bird and animal did Noah take into the ark?

> And of every living thing of all flesh, you shall bring two
> of every sort into the ark, to keep them alive with you;
> they shall be male and female. . . . Noah did this; he
> did all that God [*Elohim*] had commanded him. (Gen.
> 6:19, 22; P).

> Then the Lord [*Yahweh*] said to Noah, ". . . Take with

you seven pairs of all clean animals, the male and his mate; and a pair of the animals that are not clean, the male and his mate; and seven pairs of the birds of the air also, male and female, to keep their kind alive upon the face of all the earth" (Gen. 7:1-3; J).

Of clean animals, and of animals that are not clean, and of birds, and of everything that creeps on the ground, two and two, male and female, went into the ark with Noah, as God [*Elohim*] had commanded Noah (Gen. 7: 8-9; P). ("Two and two" is a Hebrew expression meaning by twos, or pairs.)

The inconsistency between one pair and seven pairs of birds and clean animals is easily explained. Two separate accounts of the Flood story have been conflated, or blended together. In one, from a source which modern scholars call "P" and in which the Hebrew word for God is *Elohim*, only one pair goes aboard, but in the other, from a source which moderns refer to as "J" and in which the Hebrew term for the deity is *Yahweh*, seven pairs of birds and desirable animals are saved. When the two accounts were combined, the inconsistency was allowed to remain, out of respect for the texts.

Inconsistencies can occur, too, from later insertions, either by a redactor who revised the book or by a scribe who copied the text. Often the person making the addition was intent on making a point of special interest to him, and either did not notice or else ignored the resulting discrepancy. Example E in the first chapter of this book illustrates this phenomenon. In that passage (John 4:1-2), the statement that "Jesus was making and baptizing more disciples than John" is contradicted by the addition, "although Jesus himself did not baptize, but only his disciples." Someone later thus changed the text to try to bring it into harmony with the synoptic gospels. In this case, a scribe, not the redactor, probably made the insertion, for its style differs from that of the redactor who added chapter 21. Why did he not simply delete the offending statement? The reason is that some redactors and most scribes respected the text enough not to delete matter in it-- but not enough to prevent them from adding to it.

2. Literary Difficulties. When more than one hand has been at work on a book, some "rough spots" may be created. Scholars refer to a rough spot as an "aporia," a Greek term which literally means "difficulty." Sometimes there are rough connections—two passages do not fit together very well. Sometimes a statement is not reasonable when compared with another passage in the book. At the end of chapter 5 in the Gospel of John, Jesus is still in Jerusalem, but in the next verse he "went to the other side of the Sea of Galilee." But Jerusalem is not on one side of the Sea of Galilee; in fact, it is many miles away. In John 14:31 Jesus says to his disciples, "Rise, let us go hence." But they do not go anywhere until three chapters later, after Jesus has preached a very long sermon. These are examples of rough spots occurring in composite literature.

3. Duplicate Stories. If a story is repeated in a book, the repetition usually indicates the work of a second writer. A single author has little or no reason for composing the same story twice in the same document. If there are two versions of the story in his sources, however, he may reproduce both accounts. Or, as in the case of the two Creation stories, someone later may decide to add a second account for the sake of promoting an idea not in the earlier one. In our first chapter (example B) we asked why the story of the origin of life is retold. The answer is that the two accounts were written by different writers, centuries apart, and that priests added the later account to foster Sabbath observance by representing God as having set the example of resting on the seventh day.

4. Vocabulary. Differences in vocabulary between two sections of a book also indicate that at least two persons have been at work. This evidence is especially strong when each section uses a different term for the same thing. This is the case with the two Creation stories. One account consistently uses the Hebrew word for "God," while the other consistently uses the Hebrew expression "Lord God." Also, in one account the Hebrew word translated as "create" occurs frequently, but it never appears in the other, even though the acts of creation are mentioned frequently. The two stories also show that inconsistency of thought can indicate two different writers. In the earlier account the Creation occurred in one

day, but in the later one it required six days (so that God could
rest on the seventh day).

Genesis 37 supplies another example of two different
names for the same person:

> Now Israel loved Joseph more than any other of his chil-
> dren, because he was the son of his old age (v. 3).

> Then Jacob rent his garments, . . . and mourned for
> his son [Joseph] many days (v. 34).

It was not carelessness on the part of a writer that was responsible for the use of the different names, Israel and Jacob.
Instead, the cause was the conflation, or combining, of two
different accounts.

5. Style. Another clue which indicates composite writing is variation in style (grammar, syntax, literary technique).
The possible contrasts in style between two writers include poetic versus prose style, terse versus expansive, rudimentary
versus sophisticated, and simple versus complex. Many ancient writers did not change the style of the source material
when they copied it, because the style usually did not affect the
meaning, and stylistic unity in the final document was not an
important concern to them. Consequently, style can be a very
valuable guide in detecting the work of various writers.

To use stylistic criteria, a scholar must, of course,
work with the text in its original language. In Greek, for
example, two different words mean "send," and one writer
might always use one term, but a second writer in the same
document might consistently use the other. Anyone reading
the Bible only in English translation is unaware of this. The
text used should conform to the original text as closely as possible, for later alterations can lead a scholar astray.

The stylistic traits of each writer are easily recognized
when the work of each remains in a solid block. For example,
Isaiah's style in his own composition (in Isaiah 1-39) contrasts
with that of Deutero-Isaiah. As Professor Pfeiffer once remarked, "the conciseness, variety, and concreteness of Isaiah's poetry contrast sharply with the eloquent verbosity, re-
petitiousness, and vagueness of Is. 40-55."[30] An example of

a composition in poetic style inserted into a prose work is
"Hannah's prayer" in 1 Samuel 2:1b-10. Its style is not that
of an impromptu prayer, such as Hannah would have given on
the occasion; it is the style of a special kind of poetry, a formal hymn. The content, too, does not fit the context. The
"prayer" makes no reference whatever to Hannah's situation;
it clearly is a hymn for group singing, a hymn in praise of
"the Lord" (God) and "his king" (verse 10). According to the
setting of the "prayer," Hannah pledges her son Samuel to
the Lord, but the prayer or hymn itself is concerned instead
with a king—and Samuel was not a king.

Separation of the work of different writers is more difficult when their writing is broken up into many pieces and
interwoven. Here stylistic criteria are especially needed.
This is the situation in the Pentateuch and in the Gospels of
Matthew, Luke, and John.

6. Thought. The several writers in a composite book
may have had different attitudes and ideas. This type of evidence provides ideological criteria for determining the work
of each writer. One writer could have been quite concerned
about a topic which was of no interest to another writer. Or
two of them may have had very different views on the same
subject. The writers may have written in very different situations, and consequently the statements made by one do not fit
the circumstances in which the other wrote. Sometimes two
writers lived in separate cultural environments and at different times.

The Book of Amos supplies us with an example of the
contrasting points of view of two writers. The outlook is
gloomy in the prophet Amos' own writing, for he predicted dis-
aster and divine punishment on the people of Israel because of
their sins against the Lord. Later, another writer tried to
change the tone of the book by making a few insertions and by
adding the last five verses. In these verses the outlook is optimistic. According to them, the Lord promises that "all the
hills shall flow" with sweet wine, and he says, "I will restore
the fortunes of my people Israel." Thus a redactor tried to
change Amos from a book of despair to a book of hope.

Sources used in the J and E documents in the Pentateuch
demonstrate the use of material from a different cultural envi-

ronment from that in which the authors of J and E lived. J and
E were written by Hebrews in a Hebrew environment, but they
contain a few stories which reflect the laws and customs of the
Hurrian society from which some Hebrews had emigrated.
The Hurrian laws and customs were not continued in Hebrew
society, and therefore do not fit the environment of the J and E
authors. Martin Noth and E. A. Speiser concluded that the
Hurrian features were in oral tradition incorporated in J and
E, oral tradition formed before the Hebrews migrated to Pal-
estine.

A New Testament example of a later addition which reflects a different point of view and a different environment is
John 21. That last chapter was added later by a redactor after
the author had finished the gospel. This conclusion is indicated by the syntax and the more orthodox views in chapter 21,
and by the fact that the original gospel clearly comes to an end
at the close of chapter 20. The last chapter lacks the Hellenistic mysticism of the gospel proper, for it was written in a
Christian community which was more traditional in its background.

7. Pattern. Evidence is cumulative. One type of evidence may not be convincing, but several types of evidence,
all pointing in the same direction, can establish a case. The
case for composite writing is quite decisive when different
types of evidence form a consistent pattern. This is the situation, for example, when particular vocabulary, stylistic features, and ideas occur only in combination with each other and
only in certain parts of the work. This pattern, or combination, reveals the traits of a particular writer. Patterns of the
writers' characteristics occur frequently in composite biblical
books.

Importance of Source Criticism and Redaction Criticism

Research on the literary origin of biblical books is developing rapidly among historians, although some conservative biblical scholars still ignore or oppose it. Even those who
recognize that some books are composite are liable to insist
that the fact is unimportant. A book should be interpreted as
it now stands, they claim, without reference to the prehistory

of its present form.

However, the practice of ignoring the composite nature
of books in the Bible leads to some very undesirable results.
When readers assume that a single author wrote a whole book,
they freely use one passage as a guide for the interpretation
of another passage in it.   But if the passages were written by
two different writers, readers are transferring the thought of
one writer to the other writer.   Writer A, however, may not
have shared all the ideas expressed by writer B.   Thrusting
upon an author statements made by someone else is liable to
cause readers to attribute to him thoughts he never had.   Thus
one error that results is the assignment to the book as a whole
some ideas which actually are in only part of it.   Also, readers may make a false synthesis and ascribe to the book ideas
which are not even in part of it.   Assuming that the whole book
was written by one author, and that therefore all passages in
it are in harmony with each other, readers may try to inter-
relate statements which really are quite unrelated.   The result is an artificial synthesis of the book's contents; readers
generate ideas and imagine that they are in the book.

Thus a positive value of the examination of sources and
redaction in the Bible is that it can save us from assigning to
an author thoughts that were never his.   It prevents some types
of misinterpretation of the text.

A second important result of source and redaction criticism is that it discloses ideas in the Bible which have remained hidden under the single authorship tradition.   The internationalism of Deutero-Isaiah was not clearly apparent until
scholars recognized that the author was not the prophet Isaiah,
who held nationalistic attitudes.   The distinctive views of the
authors of Matthew and Luke were not evident until redaction
criticism separated their own writing from their source materials.   The contrast between the Christology of the Gospel of
Signs source and the Christology of the author of John was not
recognized until the composite nature of the fourth gospel became known.

A third, and very important, positive result of the analysis of composite biblical books is a more comprehensive picture of what has happened in the past.   It contributes to our understanding of history by revealing more variety of thought than

was previously recognized. Especially significant is the discovery of the intensive struggle for men's minds, the intellectual contests within religious movements.

Although we may be disappointed to learn that a favorite
passage was not written by Paul, for example, it is enlighten-
ing to find that other early Christians were creative writers
too. Source and redaction criticism provides a better understanding of the Bible and a broader view of history.

The basic theory of form criticism has been that the recurrent settings, or situations, in the life of communities in
the ancient world produced small units of oral tradition. The
settings included births, deaths, marriages, worship, and military victories. Each kind of setting, it was said, produced a
corresponding, group-created form (genre, type) of tradition.
Each genre had characteristic length, structure, and tendency—
for example, hymns and laws. Consequently, scholars who
applied form criticism to the interpretation of the Bible assumed that by identifying the genre of a unit of tradition, they
learned the kind of setting in which the tradition originated.

Recently some form critics have recognized that the
theory of form criticism needs to be revised. They no longer
maintain that the traditions were necessarily oral in their
earliest stage. Douglas A. Knight at Vanderbilt Divinity
School and Rolf Knierim have recognized that the setting of Old
Testament traditions, at least, were more varied in nature
and scope, more flexible, and more complex than formerly
believed. [31] Also, the setting did not necessarily determine
the genre. For example, a hymn could have originated in a
royal court or in a temple, in a group situation or in the mind
of an individual poet. A law could emanate either from a king
or from a group of priests. The importance of genres and
structures has certainly been exaggerated. In the case of the
synoptic gospels, the fact that a pericope, or unit of tradition,
was altered later is not proof that the earlier form was authentic or historical; traditions about Jesus which originated in the
Christian communities could be changed later just as readily
as tradition which originated with Jesus. Further, written traditions could be changed later as readily as oral traditions, so
later change is not proof that the original form of the pericope
was oral.

Form criticism, however, has made some positive contributions to biblical study. 1. It disclosed that there are units of tradition, originally independent of their present context, in both the Hebrew Scriptures and the New Testament. 2. While the history-of-religions approach pointed out the general environment, the cultural milieu, of the Bible, form criticism searched for the specific situation in which a tradition arose. Form criticism aroused intense interest in the situation in the religious community responsible for the formation and transmission of tradition. 3. Form critics tried to find the purpose behind the tradition. If we can discover why a tradition originated, we can understand it better.

Structuralism

Structuralism, or structural exegesis, is a linguistic attempt to interpret the Bible by assuming that beneath the surface of the text there are "deep structures" which express in coded form the realities greater than those stated in the text. The deep structures are alleged to exist in the human unconscious, and therefore underlie linguistic expression. Structuralists try to discover deep structures in a text, and then find meaning by relating them to each other and to "cultural structures" and "structures of enunciation." The basic fallacy of the method is that it sets up a scheme of artificial structures, then forces the text into its schematization, allowing the structuralist to find meanings which the text never had. Structuralism is very subjective, and historians generally reject it as a valid method of biblical interpretation.

Source and redaction criticism are vital elements of the historical approach. Some aspects of form criticism are important too; the literary aspects can be grouped with source and redaction criticism, while the setting and purpose of tradition can be classified as aspects of the background of the Bible. Structuralism is acknowledged to be outside the historical approach.

CHAPTER 15

ARCHAEOLOGY

Strictly speaking, archaeology is not a separate method
in the historical approach. Instead, it provides information
which is essential in several of the methods, including the study
of languages, text, literature, and historical background. Nevertheless, archaeology is a complex field with its own characteristics, and therefore deserves separate treatment in a survey of historical methods.

Scientific archaeology was preceded by the unscientific
quest for holy relics—for example, the Holy Grail—and the
attempt to identify sacred sites. Although these efforts were
expressions of interest in the past, the motivation behind them
differed greatly from that of modern historians. Relics were
sought because miraculous power was believed to be attached
to them. Sacred sites were found or claimed to be found because they were thought to be holy. In Christianity these practices go back at least to the fourth century, when Constantine
dispatched a team to Palestine to locate holy places. His mother, Helena, made a pilgrimage to the Holy Land in search of
Jesus' cross. (To this day tourists gaze in awe at "the very
spot" where biblical events are alleged to have occurred. Often the actual location is unknown, and some of the "events"
never occurred in the first place! The interest in sacred
sites, however, is very profitable for the local peoples, the
tour guides, and the travel agencies.)

Nature of Archaeology

Archaeology is the scientific discovery, collection, and
study of the material remains of human life and culture in the
past. The material remains are in two basic categories: written and unwritten. The written evidence ranges from inscriptions of one or more words to documents containing whole
books. The writing may be on stone, clay tablets, papyrus,

parchment, or on walls. The unwritten material can consist
of almost anything pertaining to human activity: tools, weapons,
jewelry, art, architecture, and other remains.

Some remains have survived above ground and have required only exploration to be discovered. Other remains were
covered with debris and earth for centuries and have been found
by excavation. Occasionally material has been hidden for years,
but is discovered without excavation; for example, the first
Dead Sea scrolls were found when Bedouin boys entered a cave
in an isolated region.

We are concerned here with archaeology which contributes to our understanding of the Bible and its environment.
Originally biblical scholars believed that such archaeology was
limited largely to Palestine. Later the geographical scope of
archaeology related to the Old Testament was enlarged to include other regions in the Near East, particularly Egypt, Mesopotamia, and Syria. As interest in the environment of the
New Testament arose, the archaeology of the rest of the Mediterranean world, especially Greece and Rome, was included
by historians. "Biblical archaeologists" however, still tend to
limit the area to Israel and Jordan. The weakness of that policy is that it omits some of the most important information.

One type of location that requires excavation consists of
the sites of ancient cemeteries. Ancient graveyards often furnish more than bones of the dead; at times artifacts were bur-
ied with the deceased for their use in the afterlife, and sometimes the interior of tombs and catacombs were painted. The
gnostic codices found at Nag Hammadi were in a single grave.

The sites of ancient cities also require excavation, and
they are the most important archaeological source. Even the
site of a single city can yield a lot of information, but often—
especially in Palestine—the remains of several cities, one
above the other, are found at the same site. When an ancient
town was destroyed by fire, war, or earthquake, it could be
rebuilt by the inhabitants, or a completely new town could be
constructed years later by people with a different culture. It
was customary to rebuild on top of the old debris instead of
removing it—fortunately for modern archaeologists! This process could be repeated many times at the same site, resulting
in the formation of a mound, which in Arabic is called a "tell."

Each occupation of the site left its own layer, or stratum, of debris, floors, and building foundations. The strata are therefore invaluable for tracing the history of a site and dating each layer; there can be no doubt that a particular stratum is earlier than the strata above it.

Perhaps the best way to become acquainted with the nature of archaeology is to know how archaeologists proceed. They have learned to operate scientifically, in contrast to the work before 1870.

Before remains of the past can be studied, they obviously have to be found. Topographical surveys have located the sites of some towns by observing where sherds (broken pieces of pottery) are emerging from the soil. Tells usually have a characteristic shape, and many have been located through the use of aerial photography.

After a site has been selected, permission to excavate must be obtained from the governmental department which has jurisdiction over archaeological sites. In the early days of archaeology, excavators took away whatever they wanted; the excavators were usually from a foreign country, and thus the local country lost all the valuable remains which could be transported. Today that unfair practice has been generally corrected, and the local country retains a fair share of the artifacts, selecting its share first. After the proper arrangements have been made, the site is surveyed, and a section of it is chosen for digging. Often preliminary test trenches are dug to determine the best areas to excavate. The area on which to dump the earth and useless debris is decided upon, usually at the side of the tell.

A mound is excavated, stratum by stratum, and the contents of each layer carefully examined and recorded. If walls, floors, or prominent artifacts are encountered, they are photographed *in situ* and drawn to scale before the excavation proceeds to lower levels. Recognition of the fact that the layers represent successive occupations of a site was an essential development in archaeology. Pioneers in the science of stratigraphy were two Germans, Heinrich Schliemann, who excavated Troy and Mycenae in the 1870s, and Wilhelm Dörpfeld, who conducted many excavations in Greece in the following decades. Today American and British excavations generally follow the

modern stratigraphic methods practiced by the British archaeologist, Kathleen Kenyon, at Jericho in the 1950s.

Dating the material is a vital step in the archaeological
process. Inscriptions can disclose the time that a site was occupied or a layer constructed. A coin usually has some indication of its date, such as the name and portrait of the contemporary ruler. The style or characteristics of art, tools, and
weapons changed through the centuries, and this fact is very
useful for dating artifacts.

In Palestine, pottery is especially valuable for determining dates, for virtually every site abounds with sherds. By recording the characteristics of the pottery found in each stratum,
a system of dating based on those characteristics has been developed. The features noted include shape, decoration, finish,
and method of manufacture. If evidence is found in a stratum
which provides a certain date, then strata with the same pottery
characteristics at other sites in the region can be assigned the
same date. The English archaeologist, Sir W. M. Flinders
Petrie, introduced a scientific system, based on pottery, of
dating strata and their contents. While excavating in Egypt,
he arranged the pottery he found in pre-Dynastic graves into
chronological order, thus producing the method which he called
"sequence-dating." Later, in 1890, he made the first scientific excavation in Palestine when he dug the mound of Tell el-
Hesi. His system of dating was developed further by an American, F. J. Bliss.

Other methods of dating have also been devised. If inscriptions are found, paleography can be very helpful, for
styles of writing, as well as styles of pottery, changed with the
times. A method of dating ancient organic material is the car-
bon-14 test, which has been refined; its accuracy has settled
many disputes over the age of artifacts.

"Stone Age," "Bronze Age," and "Iron Age" are standard terms used in descriptions of the chronology of the ancient past. Those ages differed in time in various parts of
the world. In 1836 Christian Thomsen, in the National Museum of Denmark, was the first to separate antiquities into stone,
bronze, and iron implements, and then use those groups as the
basis of a chronological scheme. He proposed that human culture could be divided into three stages. First, the period when

human tools and weapons were made of non-metallic materials such as wood and stone. Second, the era when humans had learned to smelt copper and to alloy it with tin, so that tools, weapons, and other articles were made of bronze. In the third stage, mankind knew how to make various articles from iron. In Palestinian archaeology the following scale is used for the historical period:

Early Bronze (EB)	ca. 3000-2100 B.C.
Middle Bronze (MB)	ca. 2100-1550 B.C.
Late Bronze (LB)	ca. 1550-1200 B.C.
Iron I, or Early Iron (EI)	ca. 1200-900 B.C.
Iron II, or Middle Iron (MI)	ca. 900-600 B.C.
Iron III, or Late Iron (LI)	ca. 600-300 B.C.

Each of these ages is subdivided into shorter periods.

It is vital that excavations be conducted carefully and thoroughly. The operation cannot be repeated after the evidence is dug up and moved, so the work must be done correctly the first—and only—time. A pioneer in applying this scientific principle was the American archaeologist, George Andrew Reisner. After performing archaeological work in Egypt, he excavated the city of Samaria. He combined the best of the British and German methods with his own genius; the results were accurate surveying and improved analysis of stratigraphy and architecture. His recording of his excavations was thorough, with full use of photography and filing cabinets. He was a master of large-scale operation.

After a season of excavation is finished, archaeologists produce detailed reports, with drawings and photographs, for publication. This task is less interesting than excavating, and a final report of some excavations is never completed. When final reports are not made, the effect is a loss to human knowledge, a loss which cannot be replaced.

Recently old archaeological techniques have been improved, and many new ones have been employed. Underwater exploration of shipwrecks is a relatively new type of archaeology. Aerial photography is a new method of locating a site and of visualizing the relationships among its various structures. Electronic devices and techniques, geological analysis, chemical analysis, and archaeomagnetic analysis (of ceramics) are now being incorporated in the work. Intensive knowledge of ancient art and society is essential. Archaeology is increasingly becoming a multidisciplinary science.

The significant remains which are portable are transported to museums for preservation, future study, and the education of the public. Finally, archaeologists, historians, and subject specialists interpret the materials to gain new insight into mankind's past.

Use of Archaeology

One function of archaeology is the identification of the sites of ancient towns and buildings mentioned in the Bible. The location of some biblical cities is unknown today. The sites of others are indicated by the continuance into modern times of their ancient names or some form of them, for example, Jerusalem. The sites of some cities were unknown until archaeology established them. Formerly, the site of Lachish (Josh. 10:31) was not known. Archaeologists looked for it first at Umm Lakis, then at Tell el-Hesi, and finally found it at Tell ed-Duweir. The location of the ancient town of Gezer (2 Sam. 5:25) was made certain by the discovery of an inscription carved in the rock just outside the city. The Aramaic inscription, made in the first century B.C., reads: "Boundary of Gezer." The site of the ancient town of Gibeon is indicated by its modern Arabic name, El-Jib, or Al-Jib. The identification is made certain by archaeology. In the debris in the town's pool excavators found three jar handles surviving from the eighth century B.C. The handles have the name "Gibeon" inscribed on them, in Hebrew.

The foundations of many ancient buildings have survived, supplying valuable information. From them we learn the number and size of the buildings (and therefore an indication of the extent of the city and the size of its population), the location and construction of outstanding buildings such as palaces and temples, and some of the distinctive features of the town. Excavations also reveal approximately how early and how late a site was occupied.

Archaeology provides philological information useful for understanding the Bible. Inscriptions and documents reveal the grammar, syntax, and spelling characteristic of a period.

After this information has been collected and organized, it, too, serves as a guideline for dating strata and artifacts. It can also indicate the probable era in which a literary tradition originated. Further, it gives us insight into the history of language. Inscriptions show that the Hebrew language in Palestine varied in different localities and different periods of time. The ostraca (inscribed fragments of pottery or stone) from Samaria (8th c. B.C.), the inscription in the Siloam tunnel (ca. 700 B.C.), and the Lachish letters (588 B.C.), demonstrate linguistic changes. There are philological differences among the books of the Old Testament simply because the books were written at different times and places.

As we have seen, archaeology has made significant contributions to lexicology. The discovery of the usage of terms in other writings has enabled historians to translate and to interpret the text of the Bible more accurately. Sometimes the term which is found is exactly the same word, in the same language, as the term in the Bible. The only very ancient Hebrew literature which has been preserved, however, is that in the Bible, and therefore we often lack parallel usage in other Hebrew writings. Some Hebrew words occur only once or twice in the Bible, and their meaning was not certain until parallels were found in related languages.

Clay tablets written in the Akkadian (Babylonian and Assyrian) language have been helpful in this regard. The Hebrews adopted some Akkadian words (e.g., "shekel" and "cubit"). Also, both Akkadian and Hebrew retained some terms from the proto-Semitic language, from which both emerged. Consequently, the occurrence of these words on cuneiform tablets reveals the meanings and shades of meaning of the same words in the Bible. Various inscriptions reveal that ancient Hebrew was closely related to the Canaanite (Ugaritic) and Phoenician languages. The Israelites lived among the Canaanites and adopted aspects of their culture, and the linguistic influence upon Hebrew is not at all surprising. Ugaritic clay tablets have cast new light on some biblical terms. An example is the expression translated in the Authorized Version of Psalm 68:4 as "him that rideth upon the heavens." Essentially the same expression occurs in Canaanite myths where it refers to the mode of travel of the storm-god Baal. Thus

the correct translation of the expression is "him who rides upon the clouds." The biblical passage also illustrates Canaanite
influence upon Hebrew theology, for in this psalm Yahweh, too,
travels through the skies. A few Egyptian, Persian, and Greek
words entered the Hebrew language as a result of trade, migration, and foreign rule over Palestine. Archaeology affords
fuller understanding of the meaning of those words by finding
occurrences outside the Bible.

Another function of archaeology is to supply additional
historical information related to the Bible. One type of such
information is that which confirms the existence of some place,
person or thing mentioned in Scripture, or the occurrence of
some event recorded in it. When the site of a biblical town is
definitely identified, we know that the biblical author was referring to a real place, not an imaginary one. Similarly, when
something mentioned in the Bible is found, its existence in the
past is confirmed. When David captured Jerusalem from the
Jebusites, he told his men to go up the "water shaft" (2 Sam.
5:8). This vertical shaft has been found. Also, Hezekiah,
king of Judah in the eighth century, secured easier access to
the water supply by constructing a pool and a conduit (2 Kings
20:20); these, too, have been found in the form of a tunnel
leading to the Pool of Siloam.

Archaeology also attests to some biblical events. For
example, a Hebrew inscription was discovered in 1880 in the
Siloam tunnel; it describes how the tunnel was cut through the
rock. Contemporaneous with Hezekiah, the inscription com-
memorates his achievement, and verifies the biblical statement that the king brought water into the city by making a pool
and conduit. Another event reported in the Bible is the invasion of Palestine and the plundering of Jerusalem by Shishak
(Sheshonk I), king of Egypt (1 Kings 14:25-26). That invasion
is listed in the record of his exploits inscribed at Karnak, and
a fragment of a stele (a carved stone pillar) of his has been
found at Megiddo.

Archaeology aids in fixing the date of some biblical
events. For instance, Acts 18:12 states that Jews brought
Paul before the tribunal of Gallio, the proconsul of Achaia.
An inscription at Delphi shows that Gallio was proconsul in
Achaia in A.D. 52. The preceding verse in Acts states that

Paul had preached to the Corinthians for a year and six months. Thus the combined evidence from the Bible and archaeology indicates that Paul probably came to Corinth in A.D. 50.

Information about ancient customs including those in the Bible, is another benefit furnished by archaeological science. Covenants between the Hebrews and their god Yahweh are prominent in the Hebrew Scriptures. Covenants between peoples and their gods were prevalent in other Near Eastern religions too. George E. Mendenhall discovered that the ultimate source of the religious covenants consisted of the Near Eastern treaties between the dominant or suzerain state and the vassal state. He recognized that both the idea and the legal form of the Old Testament covenants grew out of the suzerainty treaties, which extend back to the second millennium B.C. The covenant is only one of many manifestations of the Near Eastern practice of transferring to gods the concepts and practices applied to kings.

The eighth-century sherds found in Samaria demonstrate that at that time many Israelites in the northern kingdom practiced the custom of incorporating the basic part of the name Yahweh in their personal names. Various archaeological remains reveal that other Near Eastern peoples did the same with the names of their deities. In the postexilic era, however, the practice was discouraged among the Jews, for the priests became convinced that the divine name was too sacred to bestow on humans or even to pronounce.

A custom of Israelite writers was to give Yahweh the credit when their nation prospered or won military victories (e.g., 2 Kings 3:18). When Israel did not fare well, the prophets usually explained the condition as the punishment of the Lord upon the people for sinning against him. Much the same theological perspective was prevalent in other Near Eastern lands, as archaeology discloses. On the Moabite Stone, for example, Mesha, the King of Moab, ascribes his victory over Israel to the Moabite god, Chemosh ("Sun"). Earlier, the situation was the opposite: the Israelites defeated the Moabites. On the same stele Mesha stated that the cause of that defeat was that "Chemosh was angry at his land."

Archaeology contributes to the understanding of the Bible as literature. In addition to supplying insight into the nature of

the parallelism in Hebrew poetry, this science aids us in determining the approximate dates of some early Hebrew poems.
For example, the spelling in 2 Samuel 22 and the earliest of
the Oracles of Balaam (Num. 24:3-9, 15-19) is so similar to
that in the tenth century Phoenician inscriptions and the Gezer
Calendar that all these writings probably came from the same
century.

The discovery of Near Eastern myths has enabled historians to see how the Israelites used and revised them for their
own purposes, changing names and part of the content. According to the Babylonian creation myth, the god Marduk made
the universe by defeating and splitting apart the primordial
sea serpent, or dragon, Tiamat. From its upper half he created the sky and all that is in it; from its lower half he created
the earth and all that is on it. Some Israelites adapted the
story to their own culture and brought it into harmony with
monotheism. Allusions to Yahweh's conquest of the primordial serpent, Leviathan, are in Job 26:13, Psalm 74:14, and
Isaiah 27:1. In the two creation stories in Genesis, however,
the method of creation is very unlike that of the Babylonian
story. But in Genesis 1 the method is rather similar to an
Egyptian creation myth. The Egyptian god, Ptah, created all
things by uttering their names; the Hebrew god, Elohim, created all things by commanding that they come into existence.
In both cases speech was the means of creation.

As the ancient Sumerian myth of a universal flood moved
northward and westward through the centuries, each country
adapted the story to its own culture. Enough original features
are in all versions to demonstrate their common source.

Laws constitute a major portion of the Pentateuch, and
archaeology reveals the Israelite use and development of the
laws of their neighbors. Hammurabi, king of Babylonia
in the eighteenth century B.C., produced a lengthy law code,
which had a wide influence for many centuries. A copy of it
was found at the site of ancient Susa in 1901. Some laws in the
Pentateuch are the same as those in the Hammurabi Code.
Both include the principle of "an eye for an eye," and in both
theft is punishable by death. In the Babylonian law both men
and women could divorce their spouses, but in the Israelite
law only men had that right (Deut. 24:1). In respect to slaves,

however, Israelite law was more humanitarian than the Babylonian, and it did not continue the Babylonian practice of more lenient laws for aristocracy than for commoners.

Knowledge of the Palestinian setting of Judaism and the primitive church has been enlarged by archaeology. Excavations at Jerusalem, Sebaste, Masada, Qumran, and Caesarea were especially important. Two important Greek inscriptions found in Jerusalem are the one warning Gentiles not to enter the inner court of the Jewish temple under penalty of death, and the other a first-century record of the construction of a synagogue by Theodotos. The latter inscription confirms the traditions that the main purpose of synagogues was the reading and teaching of the (Jewish) law and that synagogues had "rulers" (cf. Mark 5:36; 6:2; Luke 4:16).

Excavations in the Mediterranean lands supply concrete evidence of the prevalence of pagan religions in New Testament times. Images of at least eight pagan deities have been found in Paul's home town, Tarsus, for example. Temples, inscriptions, and representations of mystery-religion deities have appeared throughout the Graeco-Roman world. Many remains have been found of the Roman imperial cult, a major cause of the Roman persecution of the early Christians.

Occasionally archaeological discoveries serve to correct statements in the Bible. When the archaeological evidence and the biblical evidence disagree, both obviously cannot be correct. Professor Burrows once made this comment on the problem: "In some cases there can be no question as to which testimony must be rejected. The evidence is so clear and indisputable that a fair judge must regard it as definitely refuting and correcting statements in the Bible."[32] Examples are not difficult to find. The Book of Daniel (5:31; 9:1; 11:1) errs by making "Darius the Mede" the conqueror of Babylonia. Actually, the conqueror was Cyrus the Persian, as archaeology demonstrates. His successor was Darius, who was a Persian, not a Mede. Two passages in Genesis (21:22-32; 26:1-33) represent the Philistines as living in Palestine in the days of Abraham and Isaac. The Philistines, however, did not occupy that land until later. But they did live there in the writer's day, and he assumed, erroneously, that they were there in the patriarchal age also.

Misuse of Archaeology

Although archaeology is an essential aid to biblical interpretation, we must beware of its misuse. One kind of misapplication is the assumption that if archaeological or other indisputable evidence has not been found for a thing or an idea, it did not exist. Much of ancient thought and activity was never recorded, and many of the records that were made have been lost or destroyed. Other records may exist, but remain to be discovered. For example, some biblical scholars used to deny that certain eschatological ideas existed in Judaism in Jesus' day; nevertheless those ideas were documented in the Dead Sea scrolls discovered several decades ago. On the other hand, it is also a mistake to assume that something did exist in the past when there is no historical reason or evidence for it.

The wrong motivation leads to misuse of the archaeological data. The data may be selected on a biased basis; only that which supports the interpreter's view, or at least is neutral is considered. One-sided selection of the information is characteristic of many books, articles, films, and radio and television programs dealing with biblical themes. Consequently the public receives a distorted picture of archaeology, the Bible, and history.

In reaction against the scientific discrediting of many traditional views, defenders of the authority of the Bible have tried to undermine the public's confidences in the sciences. One scientific discipline, however, has generally escaped their attacks, namely archaeology. This situation is the result of the hope that archaeology, especially that of Palestine, will "confirm the biblical record." The zeal to "defend" the Bible is the main cause of the misuse of archaeology. That zeal is not a valid motive for archaeological research, for it produces a biased approach. Those who proceed from that motive are not interested in finding any evidence contrary to their view of the Bible. As we have remarked, although archaeological discoveries often agree with Scripture, sometimes they do not.

Archaeology is misused when erroneous conclusions are drawn from it in order to "authenticate Scripture." That commonly occurs when the ancient evidence confirms the existence of some person, place, or thing mentioned in the Bible. Some individuals have jumped to the conclusion that such evidence proves that the whole Bible is true. Others make the more modest claim that archaeology has demonstrated that the particular event occurred. Neither conclusion is necessarily valid. The verification of something mentioned in an account does not confirm all the details in the story, much less the entire Bible. Ancient writers, like modern ones, often incorporated some facts into accounts that were essentially fictional. The archaeological discovery of a personal name which occurs in the Bible is not necessarily a reference to the same person, for often several or even many people in ancient times had the same name.

Burrows called attention to additional ways that archaeology has been misused in relation to the Bible. [33] He remarked that "it is taken for granted that if the historical record is accurate, the spiritual teaching [in the Bible] also is reliable." The historical accuracy of the Bible, even where established, does not prove the validity of its theology in either the Old Testament or the New Testament. Confirming the Babylonian conquest of Israel does not prove the validity of the interpretation of the event by Hebrew prophets. Nor does an inscription from a city Paul visited establish the correctness of his view of Jesus as the Christ. The same principle applies to interpretations of the Bible today. That is, we must beware of assuming that establishing the historical accuracy of a biblical account automatically verifies current interpretations of the event—including our own.

Excessive claims of archaeological support for the Bible are a disservice to religion. Temporarily the claims arouse enthusiasm, but after the facts are more fully known, the public tends to associate the false claims with religion generally. In the long run such claims diminish respect for religion.

CHAPTER 16

THE BACKGROUND OF THE OLD TESTAMENT

Knowledge of the background of the Hebrew Scriptures and familiarity with the environment in which they were written are essential for understanding them. The background and environment consist of the events, political situation, social conditions, psychology, and religious practices in the lives of the Israelites and their neighbors. Especially important in the cultural milieu was the thought of the people. What ideas did they have, and why? How much did their point of view affect the Bible?

Origin of the Israelites

The origins and early history of the Israelites are not clear, for too little is known, and the problem of separating history from interpretation in the Pentateuch and "historical" biblical books is difficult. Nevertheless, some important facts are known.

During the first half of the second millennium B.C. Arameans, who were Semites, migrated northward in Mesopotamia to Haran, the Hurrian capital. Some of them, as well as Hurrians, moved on to Palestine and Syria. This movement is reflected in the story of the migration of Terah from Ur to Haran and of Abraham from Haran to Canaan (Gen. 11:31-12:4). The Hurrian connection is indicated also by the Hurrian customs carried over into the patriarchal stories; some of these customs were revealed by the excavation of clay tablets at Nuzi in Mesopotamia. The "patriarchs" in the Bible are not historical persons, but personifications of tribal beginnings. This may be the case even with Abraham.

The possible connection between the Hebrews and the "Hapiru" (mentioned in the Amarna tablets and elsewhere) is debated. The Hapiru were descendants of nomadic tribes who wandered in the fringe areas of Palestine, Syria, Mesopotamia, and Egypt. They clung to tribal customs and were reluctant to

settle down and adjust to either agricultural or urban life.
Usually they were mercenary soldiers or, to obtain security,
voluntary slaves; sometimes they were robbers. Eventually
they took over a large area around Shechem in central Palestine. Egyptian texts of the thirteenth century often mention
the Hapiru as the pharoah's slaves working on his projects.
The Hapiru settled down and merged with the local population,
for they are not mentioned as a separate group after 1150
B.C. [34]

Hebrews wandered into Egypt at various times. Some
probably came from the desert on the east, while others probably came from Palestine, as the story of Joseph indicates.
Some came voluntarily; some were prisoners forced into slav-
ery. In the thirteenth century, in the exodus, a considerable
number migrated to southern and central Palestine. In the resulting conquest, the invaders must have been assisted by Hebrews within the country. Thereafter the combined group is
known as the Israelites. In 1220 B.C. they were thus known,
for the pharaoh Marniptah listed "Israel" on his stele as one
of the groups he defeated in Palestine.

The Israelites were a mixed race, whose ancestors included the Semitic Arameans, Amorites, Hittites, Canaanites,
and Hapiru, together with the Israelites from Egypt. They
also included some non-Semitic Hurrians. After the Israelite
conquest of Canaan, the Israelites and the Canaanites had to
unite in their wars against their neighbors (Midianites, Moabites, Ammonites, and Philistines). This forced cooperation must have aided the integration of the two groups of
peoples.

Political Factors

In the fifteenth century Thut-mose III established Egyptian
rule over Palestine and Syria.   Sometime in either the fourteenth or thirteenth century the Hittites invaded Palestine and
some settled there. Ramses II reasserted Egyptian authority
around 1250 B.C., but it soon became weak again. The Philistines, a people from the Aegean, settled on the coast around
1200 B.C., and about fifty years later they ended all effective
Egyptian control over Palestine.

The biblical accounts of Moses and the exodus present problems to historians. The accounts were written long after the events, and the details cannot be trusted. It is virtually certain that there was an Israelite migration, or migrations, from Egypt to Canaan, and it is probable that there was a Moses who introduced Yahwism among the Israelites. The latter view is supported by archaeology, for no trace of the name and worship of Yahweh before the exodus has been found in Palestine. The exodus is dated around 1250-1200 B.C.

The hero Joshua is represented in the Book of Joshua as a leader of a united Israel, a warrior who led all the tribes in a bloody conquest of all Canaan. Chapter 1 of the Book of Judges is probably correct, however, in reporting that the Israelites were not yet united and that the conquest of Canaanite city-states was accomplished at different times by different tribes acting separately or in small groups of tribes. The conquest of the Canaanite cities was incomplete, and the coastlands were not acquired. The tribes of Gad, Manasseh, and Reuben took territory east of the Jordan River; Manasseh occupied land west of it also.

The Israelites were convinced that it was Yahweh who had given them their victory over the Canaanites, enabling them to possess the land (Josh. 23:3). Therefore both the invaders and their Hebrew allies who were already in the land joined in a covenant at Shechem that henceforth they would serve only Yahweh, and not foreign gods (Josh. 24:20-26).

During the period of the Judges (ca. 1200-1020 B.C.) Israel was a loose confederation of twelve tribes. This sacral league was weak as a political organization and failed to unite all the tribes when one was attacked. The Philistines were the most serious threat, as they advanced inward and northward. The fall of the town of Shiloh in the eleventh century established the supremacy of the Philistines over the Israelites.

The Philistine victories induced the Israelites to demand a king to govern them in order to achieve more unity and military strength. Before the Israelite conquest, each typical Canaanite city-state had had a king to rule over it, but when the Hebrews settled in the land, they did not adopt the practice because it was not according to their custom in the past. Saul

was chosen as the first king of Israel, but the new political
arrangement stirred objections (summarized in 1 Samuel 8:11-
18). Saul's kingdom was not highly organized, and eventually the Philistines killed him and defeated his army at Mount
Gilboa. Unlike David later, Saul failed to be a capable admin-
istrator, but his kingship prepared the way for David's success.

After David became king of Israel (1000 B.C.), he captured Jerusalem, fortified it, had his palace built there, and
obtained the sacred ark of Yahweh, housing it in a tent in Jerusalem. (Solomon later moved the ark into the holy of holies,
the inner sanctum of the temple.) David's actions, together
with his own connections with Judah, enabled him to unite
northern and southern Israel into a nation, with its religious
center in neutral territory, Jerusalem. Next he conquered
(first) the Philistines, then the neighboring states, one by one.
As a result, the extent of the kingdom of Israel was larger
under him than under any other king. There were two causes:
the military skill of David and his general Joab, and the contemporary weakness of the foreign nations in the Near East.
The tribal democratic spirit had stood opposed to the concen-
tration of power in a monarchy, but David's popular reign
dispelled much of the opposition. Even before he became king,
his popularity with the people aroused Saul's jealousy. In later
tradition David was viewed as the ideal king, although he certainly had his faults. To obtain the beautiful Bathsheba as his
wife, he had her husband killed; he waged unprovoked wars on
neighboring countries, and his general Joab waged a six-month
campaign to exterminate the male population of Edom.

Solomon was the next king of Israel (962-922 B.C.).
Adonijah, David's eldest surviving son, expected to succeed
his father, but the prophet Nathan induced David before he died
to proclaim Solomon, David's son by Bathsheba, as king. Solomon enlarged the city of Jerusalem and constructed palatial
buildings, including the magnificent temple. He obtained the
materials and the skilled craftsmen from Phoenicia, and the
common labor by forced levies on Israel. Solomon's wealth
flowed from his oppressive taxation of his subjects, his taxes
on the international trade routes which passed through his kingdom, his merchant fleet, his iron and copper mining and re-
fining, and his horse and chariot trade. While he acquired

great wealth, his people became impoverished. He strengthened the chariot forces and the fortifications of several Israelite border towns. Nevertheless, in contrast to David, he did
not expand Israel's territory. Solomon later had an undeserved
reputation as the wisest man of his time, and later some Hebrew wisdom literature was erroneously assigned to him. That
reputation, however, contrasts with his actual character, for
as reported in the Bible, he was selfish, extravagant, and ty-
rannical. He had many foreign wives and concubines (1 Kings
1:1-3; the number given is surely an exaggeration), partly as a
result of his foreign alliances sealed by marriage. These women induced him in his later years to worship their gods instead of Yahweh (1 Kings 11:4-8).

Solomon's reign sowed the seeds of rebellion against the
united monarchy. His labor levies and high taxes caused deep
resentment, especially among the northern tribes. Jeroboam,
an officer of the king, had once fled to Egypt, probably after
starting an unsuccessful revolt; soon after Solomon's death he
returned. After Solomon's son, Rehoboam, refused to de-
crease the levies and taxes, the northern tribes chose Jeroboam as their king instead of Rehoboam. The result was a division into two kingdoms, Israel in the north, and Judah in the
south with Jerusalem as its capital and Rehoboam its king. In
opposition to the Davidic religious center, the Jerusalem temple, Jeroboam transformed the northern tribal sanctuaries at
Dan and Bethel into national shrines for the worship of Yahweh,
where he was represented by bull images. Yahweh continued
to be worshiped also in the temple.

The division into two Hebrew kingdoms lasted from 922-
721 B.C. Throughout its history the kingdom of Judah continued to be governed by descendants of David, with the exception
of Athaliah's six-year reign in the ninth century. Israel, on
the other hand, had many changes of dynasty. About 870 B.C.
its king, Omri, constructed the city of Samaria as Israel's new
capital, replacing Tirzah.

At times tension, even wars, arose between Israel and
Judah, caused by political rivalry and religious differences,
especially Yahwism opposed to Baalism. Fear caused Judah
to urge the Syrian kingdom, Aram (capital: Damascus), to in-
vade Israel. By the middle of the ninth century both Israel

and Judah were sufficiently weak that Moab, under its king
Mesha, succeeded in freeing itself from Israel's rule, and
Edom soon revolted from Judah's domination. As both Aram
and Assyria grew in power, the southern and northern Hebrew
kingdoms turned to Assyria for protection from Aram. Israel
and Judah would have fared better if they had united against
those countries instead of relying on foreign alliances. They
did stand together in 850 B.C, when Ahab, king of Israel, and
Jehoshaphat, king of Judah, fought Aram. The eighth century
brought peace between Judah and Israel.

The threat of Assyria to its western neighbors was manifest as early as 853 B.C. A coalition of those neighbors, including Israel, stopped the invasion by Shalmanezer III at the
battle of Qarqar on the Orantes River. Assyria threatened
again in 734 B.C., and Israel and Syria formed an alliance
against Assyria. Israel had already been weakened by internal
dissension and revolutions. Refusing to join the alliance, Ahaz,
king of Judah, asked Assyria for help. Assyria responded by
conquering Israel and deporting many of its people (721 B.C.).
Thus ended the northern kingdom of Israel.

Hezekiah, king of Judah, continued to remain submissive
to Assyria until Sennacherib ascended its throne in 705 B.C.
Then, in spite of Isaiah's objections, Hezekiah joined in the
general revolt which the king of Babylon organized throughout
the Assyrian empire. Hezekiah prepared for it by improving
Jerusalem's defenses, including the construction of the Siloam
tunnel to ensure the city's water supply in time of siege. As
part of his revolt, he sought to eliminate the Assyrian religion
which Assyria had ordered be substituted for Yahwism. He removed the "high places," as the local sanctuaries were called,
and he tried to centralize Yahweh worship in the Jerusalem
temple. Sennacherib attacked, and Hezekiah had to pay enormous tribute to him, Manasseh, the next king of Judah, restored the old sanctuaries and the worship of foreign deities;
he added astralism, the worship of the dead, and human sacrifices.

When the Assyrian king Ashurbanipal died in 626 B.C.,
the Babylonian king revolted. With the aid of the Medes to the
east, he completely destroyed the Assyrian empire by 610,
even though Egypt fought against him. The Assyrian weakness

permitted the contemporary king of Judah, Josiah, to carry
out a new religious reform in 621 B.C. The reform was based
on a book found in the temple; historians generally believe it
was an earlier, shorter form of the Book of Deuteronomy.
Josiah, like Hezekiah before him, sought to restore Yahwism
and centralize it in Jerusalem. He, too, abolished the local
sanctuaries; he repaired the temple and summoned all Israel
to celebrate the Passover in it. Babylonia defeated the Assyrians (610 B.C.), then Egypt (605 B.C.). Then Jehoiakim, king
of Judah, pledged loyalty to Babylonia, but he soon revolted unsuccessfully. Later another king of Judah, Zedekiah, revolted, but the result was the destruction of Jerusalem, the
deportation of the intellectual, political, and religious leaders
to Babylon, and the end of the kingdom of Judah (587 B.C.).

In 550 B.C. the king of Persia, Cyrus II (often called
"Cyrus the Great"), began the process of establishing the
Persian empire. He threw off the Medes' yoke, mastered the
country of Lydia, and conquered and annexed the Babylonian
empire. In 538 B.C. he decreed that the Jews who had been
captive in Babylon could return to their homeland and rebuild
the temple. Unlike the Assyrians, the Persian rulers permitted freedom of religion.

Alexander the Great defeated the Persians at the battle
of Issus in 333 B.C., and he soon conquered Egypt also. After
his untimely death, his generals (called "the Successors")
fought each other, and eventually his kingdom was divided
among three of them and their descendants. The resulting
three dynasties were the Ptolemaic (ruled Egypt), the Seleucid
(generally ruled Syria and Asia Minor), and the Antigonid
(ruled Macedonia and sometimes Greece). Until the battle of
Paneion (198 B.C.), Palestine was under the dominance of
the Ptolemies, however. During this Greek period Jews were
divided in their attitude toward Greek culture. The wealthy
classes readily adopted it, while the masses, following Ezra's
precedent, maintained separatism. The Maccabean family in-
stigated a Jewish revolt (168 B.C.) when the Seleucid king,
Antiochus (IV) Epiphanes, angered orthodox Jews by imposing
heavy taxes, prohibiting the practice of the Jewish religion,
and ordering sacrifices to idols. Eventually the Maccabeans
and their descendants (known as the Hasmonean dynasty)

gained both political and religious freedom. The Hasmonean
rulers assumed the high priesthood, and beginning with Judas
Aristobulus I (104 B.C.), took the title of king, thus combining
in one person the offices of high priest and king.

Religious Factors

Religion strongly influenced the whole cultural life of all
peoples in the ancient Near East. For the understanding of the
Bible, this field of knowledge is equal in importance to the political history.

In the patriarchal period (2000-1500 B.C.) ancestors of
the Israelites worshiped Canaanite deities. Later many Israelites, too, worshiped Canaanite deities at Canaanite shrines (1
Kings 14:22-24). Judges 8:33 reports a time when Israelites
made Baal of the Covenant *(Baalberith)* their god. El (pronounced āl) was the chief of the Canaanite pantheon and sat
higher in the heavens than the other gods; accordingly he was
sometimes called Elyon ("Most High"), an attribute ascribed
later to Yahweh (Ps. 97:9). Melchizedek, Canaanite king of
Jerusalem, was a priest of El Elyon (Gen. 14:18). Hebrew
names compounded with "El" in Genesis show the influence of
the worship of El (e.g., Gen. 4:18).

Another term for God in the Hebrew Scriptures is Elohim; it occurs in the P source and is characteristic of the E
source. Literally, it is plural and means "gods," as in Judges 9:13. Elohim could also be used to refer to a single god,
which is the typical usage in the Old Testament, for example,
Genesis 20:3. This usage is not original with the Israelites,
for it occurs in the Canaanite Amarna letters and in Phoenician
inscriptions. In the singular sense it could imply the power of
all gods combined in one god. Later the term was used in a
monotheistic context.

According to biblical tradition, Yahweh revealed his name
to Moses while the latter was working for his father-in-law, a
Midianite priest. Then Moses led the Israelites out of Egypt,
with Yahweh as their God, who made a covenant with them at
Mount Sinai (Mount Horeb in E and D). The Mosaic traditions
have raised may unsettled questions among historians about
the religious aspects, including these: (1) Was Yahweh a Mid-

ianite god whom Moses began to worship while he was living among the Midianites (in Exod. 3:15 Yahweh reveals his name to Moses at that time)? (2) Was Yahweh originally one of the mountain and weather gods of the Near East (thunder and lightning are connected with his descent to Mount Sinai, Exod. 19)? (3) When did the Hebrews or Israelites begin to worship Yahweh? In Exodus 3 Yahweh tells Moses that he is "the God of your fathers, the God of Abraham, the God of Isaac, and the God of Jacob," but this is an example of biblical authors' efforts to support Yahwism by claiming that the Hebrews had always worshiped Yahweh. There is biblical evidence that the Hebrews did not worship him in the patriarchal period. For example, in some traditions their god is El or Elohim, not Yahweh, and in Exodus 6:3 we find the admission that "by my name Yahweh I did not make myself known to them" (Abraham, Isaac, and Jacob). There is also significant archaeological evidence: the name Yahweh has not been found in Palestine in any inscription written before the exodus. If Moses and the exodus gave the Israelites a new god, one whom they believed had chosen them as his own people, made a covenant with them, led them from Egypt to Canaan, and had enabled them to conquer the land, then their subsequent zeal for him is quite understandable. That zeal was fostered also by the struggle against foreign gods.

David and Solomon (in his earlier years) actively supported Yahwism. At that time or later, the J document was compiled to foster it. As we have seen, some of the suc - ceeding kings served other gods, but with strong support from the prophets, Yahweh triumphed. Yahweh was believed to be present in the ark of the covenant, a box which the Israelites could carry into battle (Num. 10:35-36) and which was finally lodged in the temple.

In the history of Israel a variety of religious faith occurred. Before the exodus the Hebrews worshiped Canaanite deities, and until the post-exilic period some Israelites at times worshiped them as a result of close association with Canaanite neighbors and spouses. Another form of faith was the belief that other gods existed, but "Yahweh is greater than all gods" (Exod. 18:11) and is "exalted far above all gods" (Ps. 97:9). The shift away from the Canaanite religion was facilitated by the identification of El with Yahweh; the Hebrews eventually regarded them not as two gods, but as one with two different names. These names are in parallel in Balaam's poem (Num. 23:8); "El Yahweh" occurs in Psalm 85:8. The process of combining deities occurred in many ancient religions.

The eighth century prophets, Amos and Isaiah, took a preliminary step in the direction of monotheism. They believed that, although Yahweh might not be the only god, he-- and not the gods of other nations--controlled the destinies of other peoples besides the Hebrews (Amos 9:7; Isa. 10:5-6). In the Deuteronomic Code genuine monotheism appears ("Yahweh is God; there is no other besides him," Deut. 4:35). Second Isaiah in the exile agreed with this theology quite fully (Isa. 43:10-11).

The struggle between the worship of Yahweh and the worship of foreign gods continued throughout the Old Testament period. From time to time Hebrew kings opposed the pagan religions. Late in the tenth century Asa, king of Judah, removed Canaanite idols and male prostitutes (1 Kings 15:12-14); in the ninth century Jehu, king of Israel, killed all the Baal worshipers (2 Kings 10:15-28); in the eighth century Hezekiah, king of Judah, removed Canaanite sanctuaries and idols (2 Kings 18:4); in the seventh century the Judean king, Josiah, removed the Baalism and astralism brought in by Manasseh and restored Yahweh worship in the temple (2 Kings 21:3-9). The sexual license of Baalism, with prostitutes in the sanctuaries, contrasted sharply with the sexual standards of Yahwism. During the exile some Jews in Babylon, fearing the pagan influence of their environment, became very zealous for Yahweh: they insisted strictly on observance of the Sabbath and the practice of circumcision. When he returned to his homeland, Ezra forced the Jews there to divorce their non-Jewish wives, to observe the Sabbath, and to support the temple. In the second century the Hasmoneans fought against the influence of Greek religion. They were also hostile to the rival religion of the Samaritans, even though it was based on the Pentateuch; John Hyrcanus destroyed their temple on Mount Gerizim.

Foreign religious influence aroused the opposition of the Hebrew prophets as early as Elijah (9th c.), who resisted Jezebel's attempt to impose the worship of a Phoenician god, Baal Melkart, on all Israel. The work of the prophets Zephaniah and Jeremiah gave support to Josiah's reform. Prophetism and nationalism combined to promote Yahwism. The prophets often fostered personal and social ethics. The prophet Amos, with his denunciation of those who oppressed the poor, and Second Isaiah, with his internationalism, have inspired fair-minded persons through the centuries.

During the Hasmonean period three religious parties arose in Judaism: the Pharisees, Sadducees, and Essenes. The Sadducees were in charge of the temple in Jerusalem and disappeared after the Romans destroyed it in A. D. 70. The Essenes, who produced the Dead Sea scrolls and had headquarters at Qumran, also disappeared after the revolt in the first Christian century. The Pharisees, associated with the synagogues and the instruction of the Jewish people, survived as rabbis; their interpretations of the Torah are preserved in the Talmud.

Ideological and Psychological Factors

The political and religious factors produced attitudes and points of view which determined the nature of many Old Testament traditions. One of the attitudes was the zeal to promote certain beliefs and practices. Actual history was often interpreted to support them. In other cases biblical narratives and statements were created to support them. A similar process operated in other cultures also. If we are to understand the Bible and the history of civilization, we must recognize that this process occurred; otherwise we are liable to accept "apologetics" as history.

One method of using "history" for that purpose was the use of anachronisms, the placing of later ideas in an earlier setting. The desire to promote the worship of Yahweh in opposition to the worship of other gods caused writers and some of their sources to try to trace Yahwism back to primitive times. According to J, men began to call upon the name of Yahweh in the time of Seth, Adam's son (Gen. 4:26)! We have seen the claim in Exodus that Yahweh was the God of Abraham, Isaac, and Jacob. Similarly, the beginnings of various reli-

gious beliefs and practices were assigned to earlier periods.
The origin of the prophetic movement was thrust back into
patriarchal times in E by declaring that Abraham was a "prophet" (Exod. 20:7).

In Genesis the patriarchal stories are often efforts to
explain the origin and history of peoples. A yearning to know
how things began is characteristic of the human mind. Biblical
scholars call the patriarchs "eponymous ancestors" because
they symbolize a tribe or a nation and represent its unknown
ancestors. Esau represents Edom; Jacob represents Israel,
and his sons are the tribes of Israel. Often the experiences
of a son of Jacob represent tribal history.

The theme that the Lord controls history is prominent in
many Old Testament books, and Hebrew history was interpreted and reconstructed to agree with it. The misfortunes which
befell the Israelites conflicted with their faith in Yahweh. The
problem was acute when a foreign power defeated them in battle or conquered the nation. The prophets, like Mesha and the
Moabites, concluded that their god was angry with his people
and was using the foreign power as his instrument to punish
them. "And the people of Israel did what was evil in the sight
of Yahweh, . . . Therefore the anger of Yahweh was kindled
against Israel and he sold them into the hand of Cushanrisha-
thaim king of Mesopotamia" (Judges 3:7-8; cf. 2 Kings 21:10-
15). The fall of the kingdoms of Israel and Judah, followed by
the exile, was a severe strain on Israel's faith (cf. Lam. 5:
20-22). Some Jews turned to other gods (Jer. 44:15-19; Ezek.
20:32). Israel survived by adopting the theological explanation
that the defeat was God's way of punishing and purifying his
people and afterwards the nation will be restored. Thus there
was hope for the future.

The repeated domination of Jews by foreign rulers contrasted sharply with the power and extent of their kingdom
under David. After the exile a psychological response of Jews
to their history was the messianic hope, the expectation that
a king would come and with God's help would overthrow foreign
rule and permanently establish the Jewish kingdom. A forerunner of the hope was the conviction that the next Davidic king
in Judah would be better than the last one. In Isaiah 9, which
was quoted at the beginning of this book, the prophet predicts

that a child, already born, will establish David's kingdom forever and govern it with peace, justice and righteousness. The
prophecy in Isaiah 11 is also preexilic. The prophet expects
that a righteous descendant of Jesse (David's father) will have
the spirit of Yahweh, the spirit of wisdom and knowledge; he
will slay the wicked and establish a peaceable kingdom, to
which Yahweh will return the Jews dispersed abroad. The
exile brought the messianic hope that a future ideal king, the
Messiah, would restore the Jewish kingdom.

A motive which affected biblical tradition was the desire
to exalt writings by assigning them to heroes of an earlier age.
Thus the Psalms were assigned to David, and Solomon was giv-
en credit for the Proverbs. It is very doubtful that these books
contain any material that was composed by those two men; certainly most of the contents originated at a much later date.

Sometimes history was retold to promote certain causes,
beliefs, or practices. The Chronicler retold the history of Israel to elevate the Levites. Outside the Bible, the Book of
Jubilees revises Jewish history to foster calendar reform and
the observance of traditional rites; Josephus rewrote Jewish
history to raise Roman opinion of Jews after their revolt.

The Foreign Environment

As we saw in chapters 6 and 8, various scholars have led
the way in relating Israel's culture to that of its neighbors.
Some of the foreign influence was only temporary, which was
the case to a large degree with Canaanite Baalism and Assyrian astralism. Other foreign aspects had a more permanent
effect; they were borrowed and adapted to the Hebrew religion,
and continued in Judaism in the modified form. An example is
the Canaanite harvest festival which became the Hebrew Feast
of Booths, or Feast of Tabernacles, a festival of thanksgiving
not only for the autumn harvest (a Canaanite feature), but also
for the Exodus (a feature added by the Israelites).

The Persian religion had a strong impact on Jews, partly because the lenient policy of the Persian rulers created a
friendly atmosphere with less resistance to foreign ideas and
practices. Judaism acquired from Zoroastrianism the belief
in the future resurrection of the dead, followed by a judgment

day and a physical immortality on a new rejuvenated earth.
This type of thinking occurs in Isaiah 65:17 and Daniel 12:2.

Canonization

The books of the Old Testament were not regarded as
sacred scripture until long after they were written. The
Jewish basis for canonizing books was the belief that their
contents had been divinely revealed, usually as inspired prophecy (which was not necessarily a prediction of the future).
The first writing to be accepted as Scripture was the Deuteronomic Code. Erroneously it was believed to have been written by Moses, who in that code is referred to as a prophet
(Deut. 18:15,18); thus its contents were assumed to be inspired, even though it was viewed as "the book of the law"
(2 Kings 22:8; note that in the Sinaitic traditions law is divinely revealed directly). Gradually this code was enlarged
to become the Book of Deuteronomy and combined with J, E,
and P to form the Pentateuch, which became known in Judaism
as "the law of Moses." The Pentateuch was canonized sometime around 400 B.C. The books called "the Prophets" were
canonized around 200 B.C., and "the Writings," which are
the remaining books in the Palestinian canon of the Bible, were
added gradually, a process completed in the first century A.D.
When Jews in Alexandria translated their Scriptures into Greek,
producing the Septuagint, they included the Apocrypha; this
process, too, was completed in the first century of the Christian era. This difference between the Palestinian canon and
the Alexandrian canon of the Jews is responsible for the presence of the Apocrypha in the Bible of the Roman Catholic, Anglican, and Episcopal churches, and its absence generally in
the Bible of the Protestant churches. In Judaism the official
canonization of the books was an approval of the contemporary
practice; a similar process took place later in the churches
in respect to early Christian literature.

CHAPTER 17

THE JEWISH BACKGROUND OF THE NEW TESTAMENT

The Jewish, Christian and pagan backgrounds of the New Testament are unfolding as more documents and artifacts are found and as previously known materials are better understood. All are fascinating fields of investigation, which can best be appreciated by reading the contemporary literature of those cultures.

Jesus was a Jew, trained in the Jewish synagogues. His disciples and the earliest converts after his crucifixion were Jews. Christianity began, not as a new religion, but as a movement within Judaism. Therefore, in order to understand Jesus, early Christianity, and the literature of the New Testament, we must know the Jewish background. That background has been loosely divided into "Palestinian" Judaism and Hellenistic Judaism; the latter was Judaism strongly influenced by Greek culture. "Palestinian" Judaism was not confined to Palestine, however, and there apparently was Greek influence on some Jews in Jerusalem, as the reference to the "Hellenists" in Acts 6:1 indicates. Nevertheless, Hellenistic Judaism flourished mainly in the Diaspora, especially among the Jews in Alexandria.

Contemporary Jewish History

Certain events in contemporary Jewish history had an important impact on the writing of the New Testament. Pompey in 63 B.C. established Roman control over the Jews. Herod the Great, who was not a Jew, persuaded the Romans to make him the king of Palestine, subject to Rome (37-4 B.C.). He persecuted many of his subjects, including members of his own family. He rebuilt the Jerusalem temple and constructed many other magnificent buildings, leaving his government with a huge debt. After his death, his kingdom was divided among his three sons, who served as puppet rulers for Rome: Archelaus governed Judea, Samaria, and Idumea; Herod Antipas ad-

ministered Galilee and Perea; Herod Philip governed the area
northeast of the Sea of Galilee. Archelaus' harsh treatment of
Jews and Samaritans caused each group to send a delegation to
Rome to complain. The emperor Augustus deposed him and
made his territory a province, governed by a procurator. Pon-
tius Pilate was the procurator A.D. 26-36. The heavy taxation
caused intense resentment of the Roman rule, a fact which explains the seriousness of the question in the synoptic gospels
about paying taxes to Caesar. Numerous would-be Messiahs
attempted to start revolts against Rome; they are referred to
in Mark 13:22 as "false Christs and false prophets." Therefore the Romans were wary of any Jewish popular leaders who
were regarded as Messiahs and/or prophets; these leaders
were either rebels or potential rebels, and the penalty for rebellion was crucifixion. Jesus was viewed as such, as the
title "Christ," the manner of his death, and the title, "King
of the Jews," on his cross indicate. The wealthy Sadducees,
fearing a rebellion, cooperated with the Romans in securing
Jesus' arrest. Afterwards, Jewish zealots continued to agi-
tate against Rome, refusing to pay taxes to it and robbing
those who did. Thus rebels could be called "robbers" (cf.
Matt. 27:44). In A.D. 66 rebels succeeded in arousing the
people to revolt, but four years later the Roman general Titus crushed the rebellion when he destroyed Jerusalem and
its temple. The tension continued and flared up again in Bar
Kochba's unsuccessful revolt against the Romans in A.D. 132-
135.

        The destruction of the temple in A.D. 70 put an end to
what had been an essential element in Judaism. This event
was a great shock to the Jewish people. In the controversy
between Jews and Christians, some Christian writers interpreted the event as God's punishment of Jews in general who
did not believe that Jesus was the Messiah. The Pharisaic
rabbis saved Judaism by elevating the position of Torah and
the synagogue, so that the temple no longer seemed necessary. The Sadducees, who had been in charge of the temple,
ceased to exist as a separate group.

        At first Christianity was a sect within Judaism, and its
members were all Jews who had no intention of breaking away
from their faith. The vast majority of Jews did not join the

new sect. The issues which served as causes of the eventual break between the two religions are listed in the next chapter. Tensions rose to a point at which each side was unfair to the other. Certain events after the crucifixion added to the tensions. Jews persecuted Jewish Christians in the first century[34a] (in later centuries, Christians persecuted Jews). The Zealots resented the Christian refusal to join the Jewish revolts against Rome. The gentile converts, who grew rapidly in numbers, brought in from their pagan background some features repugnant to Jews (see chapter 19). Proclamation, oral or written, that Jews were God's chosen people offended Gentiles, both Christian and non-Christian. In contrast, the Christian community in Jerusalem remained loyal to Judaism, but when Jews first revolted against Rome, it fled to Pella across the Jordan River, then disappeared. The authors of the Gospel of Matthew and the Epistle of James were Jewish Christians who still regarded Christianity as within the Jewish fold.

Eschatology

Originally the future kingdom which Jews expected to come was simply a political one. Although Yahweh would assist a Jewish king in establishing it, the kingdom would come in natural ways. It would be independent of foreign rule, and everyone in it, including the king, would be completely righteous and faithful to the Lord. Beginning in the Persian period, however, supernatural features were added which increased the differences between the present age and future ideal age, features which included the resurrection of the dead, the judgment, and immortality of the righteous on a new purified earth. "Eschatology" is the term for the Jewish and Christian (adapted from the Jewish) beliefs concerning the end of the present age and the beginning of the new.

Jewish apocalypses appeared in the first two centuries B. C. and the first two centuries A. D. that predicted what the writers expected to happen when the new age came. Early Christians also wrote books of this type. This literature is called "apocalyptic" because it purports to be divine revelations, usually in the form of visions or dreams, of what God had previously kept secret or hidden. "Apocalypse" and "apocalyptic" are from the Greek word meaning "an uncovering," "a revelation."

The expectations about the future were far from standardized. Some Jewish writers thought the new age would be a single, everlasting period under an immortal king; others divided the future into a temporary messianic age under the king whom God would send, followed by an eternal age under the direct rule of God; others foresaw no messianic kingdom but only an eternal age ruled directly by God. The new age could be called "the kingdom of God," or as the rabbis labeled it, "the age (or "world") to come."

In the New Testament the customary term for the future kingdom is "kingdom of God." This expression is not in the Hebrew Scriptures, but the idea is in Daniel 6:26. The actual expression, "kingdom of God," does occur in the Apocrypha (Wisdom of Solomon 10:10) and the Pseudepigrapha (Psalms of Solomon 17:4).

Jews expected that the future kingdom would be preceded by miraculous events as "signs" that it was about to appear. [35] In Acts 2:19 and the synoptic gospels we find expressions of this expectation. In both Judaism and Christianity, however, "signs" did not necessarily refer to miracles announcing the end; they could be simply signs of the miracle worker's power.

The belief that the advent of the kingdom would be accompanied by the bodily resurrection of the dead and a judgment day apparently entered Judaism from Zoroastrianism. It appears in Daniel 12:2. Statements of Jewish eschatology are in 2 Esdras 7:26-44 and 2 Baruch 49-51. In the typical Jewish statements only Jews and converts to Judaism will be raised from the dead. God will restore the physical body and raise it from the grave; the soul will be brought down from the "chambers," or storehouses, in the heavens and reunited with the body; then the body will be transformed into an incorruptible, or imperishable, body. Paul described the new body in Hellenistic terms as an "imperishable," "spiritual body" (1 Cor. 15:42-54). A tension existed in both Judaism and early Christianity between two different concepts of immortality: an imperishable body on earth versus the immortality of only the soul in heaven. The Palestinian Jewish view of immortality

was that a person would be incomplete without both body and
soul and therefore in the immortal state they will be together
again. Some Diaspora Jews, influenced by astralism and Greek
thought, changed to belief in the immortality of the soul in
heaven. The early Christian belief in the resurrection of the
physical body is clearly expressed in 2 Clement 9:1, which
states: "And let none of you say that this flesh is not judged
and does not rise again." In contrast, in 1 Peter 1:9 the out-
come of Christian faith is "the salvation of your souls." Today many Christians believe that immortality consists of the
soul dwelling in heaven, and they are unaware that the affirma-
tion of "the resurrection of the body" in the Apostles' Creed
refers to immortality on earth.

A common mistake is to assume that the disciples' belief in Jesus' resurrection indicates that they therefore thought
he was divine. Rather, the disciples shared the Jewish belief
that all righteous dead Jews would be raised. At first the faith
that God had raised Jesus must have simply indicated that the
general resurrection had begun. After a few days or weeks,
it became apparent that others had not been raised, and therefore the disciples believed that God had conferred a special
distinction on Jesus by raising him first. In Paul's words, he
was "the first fruits of those who have fallen asleep" [i.e.
died] (1 Cor. 15:20, 23). This special honor accorded Jesus
lent support to the belief that he must be the Christ, even
though in Judaism resurrection from the dead was not a special
attribute of the Messiah.

According to Matthew 3:2, John the Baptist preached to
his listeners that they should repent because the kingdom of
heaven was at hand (in Matthew "heaven" is a Jewish metonym,
or related substitute term, for God). This was also Jesus'
basic message (Mark 1:15), which we cited in D in chapter 1.
In that passage "gospel" means the "good news" that the kingdom of God was coming very soon. The Dead Sea scrolls demonstrate that the Essenes, too, expected the new age to arrive
rather soon. After John's arrest, Jesus took up his mission
of calling people to repentance. The connection between repentance and the coming of the kingdom was that the judgment
would occur when the kingdom came, but if Jews would repent
of their sins beforehand, God would forgive them and they

would pass safely through the judgment. Belief in repentance as a means of securing God's forgiveness of one's sins was characteristic of Judaism (e. g. , Ezek. 18:30-31). Forgiveness of sins is associated with the new age in Jeremiah 31:34.

The baptism of the Essenes at Qumran was a repeated purification routine, whereas the baptism performed by John and Jesus apparently occurred only once. Nevertheless, the underlying philosophy was the same: repentance should accompany baptism, as in the *Manual of Discipline* 5:14. Baptism purified the body, while repentance purified the heart and soul. In Christianity, however, baptism soon became an initiation ritual. In Jewish Christianity it conferred the gift of the Holy Spirit (Acts 2:38). Although in Judaism baptism was associated ritual. In Jewish Christianity it conferred the gift of the Holy Spirit (Acts 2:38). Although in Judaism baptism was associated with the Spirit, it did not bestow it. In the New Testament the connection with repentance disappeared; Paul omits it. [35a] ther for Jews in general or for righteous Jews. The Essenes claimed that they were God's elect, and Christians made the same claim for themselves; both groups applied to themselves the prophecy in Jeremiah that Yahweh will make a new covenant with his people (31:31-33). The Essenes believed that after purifying them with the Holy Spirit, "God has chosen them to be the partners of his eternal covenant" (1QS 4:22). Paul regarded himself as a minister of the new covenant (2 Cor. 3:6), and the author of Hebrews asserted that Christ is "the mediator of a new covenant" (9:15), a belief he developed in chapter 8. A related idea in ancient Judaism was the belief that, although many Jews had been taken captive to other lands and many had forsaken Yahweh, a righteous remnant would survive to form the nucleus of a new Israel (Isa. 10:21). Christians were convinced that they themselves were the righteous remnant whom God had chosen (Rom. 11:5).

The parallels between the Essenes' and the Christians' use of the Old Testament ideas is not surprising when we remember that at its earliest stage Christianity, too, was a sect within Judaism. Both evolved from the same background. Although the Pharisees accepted these biblical concepts, they did not confine them to their own group as closely as did the Essenes and Christians.

The Messiah

In Jesus' day the Pharisees and the Essenes generally believed that God would soon send the Messiah to establish the new kingdom. The main function of the Messiah would be to free Israel from foreign rule by overthrowing its enemies. After ruling for 400 years (2 Esdras 2:28) or 1,000 years (Rev. 20:4), he will turn the kingdom over to God to rule. Where no Messiah was expected, God himself would destroy the enemies.

The term "Messiah" has its origin in the ancient practice of anointing kings when they took office by pouring oil on their heads. Saul, the first Israelite king, is called Yahweh's "anointed one" in 1 Samuel 12:3, 5. The Hebrew word which means "anointed one" is <u>mashiah</u>, which is loosely transliterated into English as "Messiah." The Greek word which means "Anointed One" is <u>christos</u>, which appears in English as "Christ." Jesus' name was simply "Jesus" or "Jesus of Nazareth," but later "the Christ" was added as a title, and finally Gentiles who did not know the meaning of the title interpreted it as a proper name--thus his name was changed in Christian tradition to "Jesus Christ" or even "Christ."

Almost from the first the future king was thought of as an ideal figure. Although he would be ruthless in waging war against all enemies when he established the kingdom, afterwards peace, justice, and righteousness would prevail. In Isaiah 11 we read that "the Spirit of Yahweh shall rest upon him, the spirit of wisdom and understanding, . . . his delight shall be in the fear of Yahweh, . . . with righteousness he shall judge the poor, and with the breath of his lips he shall slay the wicked" (vv. 2-4). The belief that the Spirit of the Lord would rest upon the Messiah influenced the gospel account of Jesus' baptism. Jewish emphasis on the righteousness of the Messiah also influenced early Christian interpretations of Jesus.

a. The Davidic Messiah

Several types of Messiah existed in Jewish messianism. By far the most prominent kind in New Testament times was

the descendant of David. This "Son of David" is described at
length in Psalms of Solomon 17-18 (ca. 50 B.C.).

Behold, O Lord, and raise up unto them their king, the
son of David,

At the time in which Thou seest, O God, that he may
reign over Israel Thy servant.

And gird him with strength, that he may shatter unrighteous rulers,

And that he may purge Jerusalem from nations that
trample (her) down to destruction.

Wisely, righteously he shall thrust out sinners from
(the) inheritance,

. . .

And he shall gather together a holy people, whom he
shall lead in righteousness,

And he shall judge the tribes of the people that has been
sanctified by the Lord his God.

And he shall not suffer [i.e., permit] unrighteousness
to lodge any more in their midst,

Nor shall there dwell with them any man that knoweth
wickedness,

For he shall know them, that they are all sons of their
God.

And he shall divide them according to their tribes upon
the land,

And neither sojourner nor alien shall sojourn with them
any more.

He shall judge peoples and nations in the wisdom of his
righteousness.

And he shall have the heathen nations to serve him under
his yoke;

. . .

And he (shall be) a righteous king, taught of God, over
them,

And there shall be no unrighteousness in his days in
their midst,

For all shall be holy and their king the anointed [i.e.,
the "Christ] of the Lord.

. . .

He will rebuke rulers, and remove sinners by the might
    of his word;
And (relying) upon his God, throughout his days he will
    not stumble;
For God will make him mighty by means of (His) holy
    spirit,
And wise by means of the spirit of understanding, with
    strength and righteousness [based on Isa. 11:2]
    (Ps. of Sol. 17:23-42, R. H. Charles' tr.).

The Son of David was the type of Messiah expected by the
Essenes and many other Palestinian Jews, as well as some in
the Diaspora. Jesus is regarded as the Son-of-David Messiah
in Romans 1:3-4, the synoptic gospels, 2 Timothy 2:8, and
Revelation 22:16.

    b.   The Preexistent Messiah

The preexistent Messiah was another type. Unlike the
human Son of David, he was a supernatural Messiah. He appears in the Parables section of 1 Enoch (chapters 37-71,
written in the first century B.C.). In some passages he is
called the "Righteous One" or the "Anointed One." The title
"Elect One" simply means that he is the personage chosen, or
elected, by God to be the Messiah. The title "Son of Man" is
more complex in origin. It apparently originated as the result
of Jewish reinterpretation of Daniel 7. There we read that in
one of Daniel's visions he saw that "with the clouds of heaven
there came one like a son of man and he came to the Ancient
of Days," who gave him everlasting dominion and kingdom (vv.
13-14). "Son of man" is a Semitic expression which means
"man," as in Ezekiel (e.g., 2:1), and "like a son of man"
means "like a human being," usually in form or appearance.
The passage in Daniel probably is based on a Near Eastern
myth of the conferring of the kingship upon a god by the supreme deity of the assembly of the gods. Baal and Ashur each
traveled in a cloud. The author of Daniel, attracted to the
idea of everlasting dominion, reinterpreted the "one like a
son of man" as a symbolic representation of the Jews, "the
saints of the Most High." In the Parables section of 1 Enoch,

Daniel 7:13-14 is again reinterpreted, this time as a reference to the Messiah.

Considering that "son of man" literally means "man," one would expect that the title "Son of Man" would designate a human Messiah. But that is not the case--he is a supernatural being. The origin of this usage is probably to be found in the concept of a primordial Man. [36] On the other hand, "Son of God" in primitive Christianity indicated a human Messiah. This usage was the result of labeling Israelite kings as God's sons (e.g., 2 Sam. 7:14; Ps. 2:7). Before the end of the first century, however, gentile Christians, influenced by their pagan background, used the title Son of God in the sense of a divine being.

The Son of Man in the Son-of-Man passages in the Parables section of 1 Enoch[37] will perform the main function of the Messiah, casting kings from their thrones and reigning over the earth. In addition, he will have characteristics arising from his supernatural nature. He and his name are preexistent; he was chosen as the Elect One and hidden by the "Lord of Spirits" (God) before the creation of the world. The Lord of Spirits has revealed him to the holy and righteous, whose lot he has preserved because they have hated all the works and ways of this unrighteous world. At the appointed time the Son of Man will come down to earth, overthrow the kings and the mighty because they did not praise him, and punish the wicked who have denied the name of the Lord of Spirits and persecuted the houses of his congregations (righteous Jews). The Lord of Spirits will seat the Son of Man on his throne of glory and pour the spirit of righteousness (the Holy Spirit) upon him. The Son of Man (instead of God) will conduct the judgment. The word of his mouth will slay all the sinners. The holy and righteous will rejoice in the punishment of the mighty who opposed God's chosen people. The righteous, elect dead will rise from the earth and be clothed with garments of glory, which make them immortal. Thereafter the Lord of Spirits will abide over the righteous, who will live with the righteous Son of Man on earth forever. The righteous people will have peace and "an upright way" forever in the name of the Lord of Spirits.

A supernatural, preexistent Messiah appears also in 2 Esdras (13), a Jewish apocalypse, written probably in the first century A.D. In it the seer sees "a man come up out of the sea," who (a feature from Daniel 7) "flew with the clouds of heaven." A multitude tried to fight him, but from a great mountain he burned them up with a stream of fire from his mouth. Then he came down from the mountain and met a peaceable multitude. After the apocalyptist awoke, the Most High explained to him the dream, a symbolic preview of "what shall happen in the last days." The man from the sea is God's "Son," whom he has been keeping for many ages. After certain "signs" occur, the Son will be revealed. He will stand on Mount Zion, "reprove the assembled nations for their ungodliness," and destroy them "by the law" [the Torah]. The peaceable multitude in the vision represents the ten Israelite tribes which the Assyrians took captive and the Jews "found within my [God's] holy borders" [Palestine]; they "shall be saved." Only the seer has been enlightened with this knowledge, for he has studied God's law, which has given him wisdom and understanding.

A preexistent Messiah occurs also in a Jewish section of the Sibylline Oracles, in book 5 which probably was written in the first quarter of the second Christian century (5:414-433). "A blessed man from the plains of heaven" will come with a sceptre in his hand. He will win dominion over all, destroy cities and the wicked with fire, and restore to the good the wealth which the wicked took from them. He will make a radiant new Jerusalem with a large, beautiful temple in it--an appealing hope after the Roman destruction of Jerusalem and the temple in A.D. 70.

The idea of a supernatural Messiah may have originated in Hellenistic Judaism. The concept was encouraged by the failure of human Jewish kings and Messiahs: the dwindling and eventual end of the Hasmonean kingdom, the various Messiahs in the first century A.D., and the revolts against Rome in A.D. 66-70 and 132-135. Jesus is viewed as the Son of Man in some passages in the four gospels and in Acts 7:56. In those passages Jesus has some of the same features which are associated with the Son of Man in the Parables section of 1 Enoch (preexistence, descent from heaven, and the conduct of the judgment). In both the Parables and Matthew, the Son of Man will sit on the throne of his glory (1 Enoch 62:5; Matt. 19:28). This evidence indicates the influence of the Parables or a similar writing upon early Christianity.

c. The Prophet-Messiah

The prophet-Messiah was yet another type. This concept
of the Messiah was a development from the role of Hebrew
prophets in the past. The basic role of all prophets in ancient cultures was the public proclamation of a message received from a deity. The preaching of Hebrew prophets often
determined the nature of biblical laws. Consequently it was
generally expected that the future prophet in Judaism would be
a lawgiver.

In New Testament times some Jews thought that a prophet would come in "the last days"; such a prophet can be labeled "the eschatological prophet." He could be a forerunner
of the Messiah, or he could accompany him, or he could be the
Messiah himself. When the same person is both prophet and
Messiah, he combines the teaching and lawgiving function of
the prophet with the king's function of waging war to establish
his kingdom and then judging and ruling it in peace. Kings,
too, had the function of lawgiver, as in Isaiah 42:4, and Saul
was both prophet and king. The eschatological prophet could
be conceived of as an unnamed prophet and could be referred to
simply as "the Prophet," as at Qumran (1QS 9:11) and in John
1:21. Or he could be a famous prophet of the ancient past
whom some believed had been transported alive to heaven and
would return: Elijah, Moses, or Jeremiah. Yet another concept was that he would be "a prophet like Moses," based on
Deuteronomy 18:15-19. The belief that Elijah was still alive
made it possible to expect him to return to earth alive before
the resurrection, when the deceased prophets would appear.
In Malachi 3:1 the Lord will send his messenger of the covenant before he, the Lord, comes. In chapter 4, a later addition to the text, this anonymous forerunner of the Lord is interpreted as Elijah, whose function will be to reconcile parents and children. John the Baptist is interpreted as Elijah
in Mark 1:2; 11:13 and Matthew 11:14; 17:10-13. The idea is
rejected in John 1:21. Some people thought Jesus was Elijah
(Mark 6:15; 8:28).

Although the belief existed in Judaism that Moses him-

self would return in the last days of the present age, the belief
in the coming of a prophet like Moses was more prevalent. In
Deuteronomy this prophet is not connected with eschatology,
but the connection was made by the beginning of the Christian
era. Philo believed that this prophet would "suddenly appear,"[38] and the Samaritans expected a prophet like Moses
who might even be Moses himself. Josephus reported that in
the first Christian century several Messiahs led their followers into the desert, even as Moses had once done. Jesus is
represented as the Prophet-like-Moses type of Messiah in Acts
3:22-23 (cf. 7:37) and in the Pseudo-Clementine literature.
Jesus is portrayed as the new Moses, the new lawgiver, in the
Gospel of Matthew. [39]

d. The Priest-Messiah

From Simon Maccabeus (141 B.C.) on, the Hasmonean
rulers held the office of high priest, and Judas Aristobulus I,
as we have seen, was the first Hasmonean to proclaim himself "King of the Jews." Stirred by that family's achievements,
a Jewish writer in the Testament of Levi regards the Messiah
as the priestly type. Thus the overthrow of foreign rule by
the priestly family created a new concept of the Messiah.

> Then shall the Lord raise up a new priest,
> And to him all the words of the Lord shall be revealed;
> And he shall execute a righteous judgment upon the earth
>   for a multitude of days.
> And his star shall arise in heaven as of a king,
> Lighting up the light of knowledge as the sun the day,
> And he shall be magnified in the world.
> . . .
> And there shall be peace in all the earth.
> . . .
> The heavens shall be opened,
> And from the temple of glory shall come upon him
>   sanctification,
> With the Father's voice as from Abraham to Isaac.
> And the glory of the Most High shall be uttered over him,
> And the spirit of understanding and sanctification shall

rest upon him.

. . .

And in his priesthood the Gentiles shall be multi-
    plied in knowledge upon the earth,
And enlightened through the grace of the Lord;
In his priesthood shall sin come to an end,
And the lawless shall cease to do evil (Test.
    Levi 18:2-9).

The statement in verse 6, "the heavens shall be opened," evidently influenced the account of Jesus' baptism in Matthew 3:
16, for there, too, the heavens are opened when the Messiah
receives the Spirit. The general idea that the Messiah will be
a priest is reflected in the Epistle to the Hebrews, where it is
applied to Jesus (Heb. 5). In the Testament of Levi one person is prophet, priest, and king. The Essenes, however, expected an eschatological person of each of those types. Their
Manual of Discipline tells us that the men of their Community
must not depart from their law until the coming of the Prophet,
the Anointed Priest, and the Anointed King (1QS 9:11).

The Law

The Torah was generally accepted in ancient Judaism as
the very core of religion, and observance of it was vital. The
Essenes believed this just as ardently as the Pharisees, for
each member of their sect should "return to the law of Moses
with all his heart and all his soul" (CD 15:12). They believed
that complete observance of the law was essential for entrance
into the messianic age. By the second century B.C. the law
was identified with divine Wisdom.

Nevertheless, Jews varied in their opinions of the status
of the Torah in the future. Many believed that it would endure
forever; it is "the eternal law" (1 Enoch 99:2). Many believed
that in the messianic age there would be new interpretations
of the law that would clarify the obscurities in it. The Essenes
felt compelled to make a new interpretation of the Torah whenever the Holy Spirit revealed it. They thought that by with-
drawing to the wilderness, as they had done, and interpreting
the law, they were preparing the way of the Lord in the wilder-

ness and thus fulfilling Isaiah 40:3 (1QS 8:12-16; in the synoptic gospels the Baptist's preaching is interpreted as the fulfillment of the same passage). The Essenes viewed their interpretations of the Torah as temporary, for they would be ruled by them only until the coming of the messianic age. In effect, though not in theory, the new interpretations could make important changes in the law.

Some Jewish writers and rabbis expected new knowledge and new laws in the future, which were not necessarily interpretations of Torah, but would be expansions of it. In other Jewish traditions, however, a new law was anticipated that would replace the old. This idea is in a Hellenistic Jewish section of the Sibylline Oracles in the second century B.C.: "A common law for men throughout all the earth shall the Eternal [God] perfect in the starry heaven" (3:757-758). The expectation of a new law occurred among some of the rabbis too, though mostly later than New Testament times. That expectation is in the *Targum of Isaiah* 12:3, which rests on first century A.D. traditions: "and you shall receive a new law with joy from the chosen ones of righteousness."

Knowledge of Jewish thinking about the law helps us to explain the variety of attitudes toward it in the New Testament. A major issue arose in Christianity: Should Christians obey the Jewish Torah? The disciples, who were Jews, did. But what about the gentile converts? In Judaism, gentile converts obeyed the Torah. But Paul, a Hellenistic Jewish Christian, maintained that because the Christ (and thus the messianic age) had come, the law has been supplanted by faith and by the Spirit (Gal. 3 and 5). In those chapters nothing is said about a new law to replace the old, but that is strongly implied by the mention of "the law of Christ" in Galatians 6:2 and 1 Corinthians 9:21. Considering that Jesus did not actually proclaim a new law, the idea that the old law is nullified and that there now exists a new law, the law of the Messiah, or Christ, must have been suggested by the Jewish background.

A different view of the Torah is taken in Matthew 5:18: "till heaven and earth pass away, not an iota, not a dot, will pass from the law until all is accomplished." Although this passage may possibly imply that the law is eternal, the phrase "until all is accomplished" suggests that the law endures throughout the messianic age, but will not in the age to come when a new heaven and earth are created and all things prophesied are accomplished.

A developing attitude toward the Torah in early Judaism was the insistence on doing "works of the law." "Works" included performing certain rituals, but the trend was toward emphasis on doing good deeds required by the law, both the written (Hebrew Scripture) and the oral (interpretations by the Pharisees) law. That development explains the contradiction between certain passages in Galatians and the Epistle of James. Deeply involved in the controversy over the observance of the law, Paul as a Hellenistic Jewish Christian zealously argued that man is "justified by faith in Christ, not by works of the law" (Gal. 2:16). Shocked by such a point of view, the more orthodox Jewish-Christian author of James stoutly defended the doctrine that "man is justified by works and not by faith alone" (Jas. 2:24). Actually, both writers regarded ethics, good works, as essential, but their foundations were different. Paul's basis was the Spirit, for "the fruit of the Spirit is love, joy, peace, patience, kindness, goodness, . . ." (Gal. 5:22).

Stephen and other Hellenists in Jerusalem, rather than Paul, may have been the first to break away from the Jewish law (Acts 6:11,13; the charge that the witnesses were "false" is consistent with the Christian defence of Jesus and the apostles). Considering the great importance attached to the law in Judaism, the non-observance of the Torah by some Christians was certain to lead to the break between Jews and Christians. Jesus himself, as well as his disciples, did not break with the Torah as a whole, although, like some rabbis, he disagreed with certain features of it, according to Matthew 5:31-41. When the Jewish persecution of Christians in Jerusalem occurred, only the Hellenists were persecuted and had to leave town (Acts 8:1). The disciples believed that Jesus was the Christ, but that did not make them unorthodox enough to be persecuted. Rejection of the authority of the Torah, however, amounted in conservative Jewish sight to apostasy, a rejection of Judaism. Thus the Hellenists' unorthodoxy in their attitude toward the Jewish law is indicated by the stoning of their leader, Stephen, by the officials. Gentile Christians later enlarged the split still farther when they regarded Jesus as divine. After those two decisive steps, Christianity was definitely a separate religion.

Even those early Christians who rejected the observance of the Jewish law still accepted the law as Scripture, and it became a part of the Christian Bible. Why? The main reason is that Christians inherited from Judaism the belief in the fulfillment of the Hebrew Scriptures to support their claim that Jesus was the Messiah. Christians misinterpreted the Old Testament in order to make it support the claim, but as we observed in chapter 2, both Jews and Christians misinterpreted the Scriptures because they lacked essential information and methodology.

The temple in Jerusalem, administered by the Sadducees, was a powerful influence in Judaism until its destruction in A.D. 70. Faithful Jews endeavored to celebrate the Passover there at least once in their lifetime, which is why there was a large crowd in Jerusalem at the time of Jesus' arrest. When the temple was destroyed, the event was a tremendous shock to Jews because of the temple's role in religion and the belief that it was God's house. After its destruction, some Christians, writing in the heat of the controversy between Jews and Christians, interpreted the destruction of the temple and Jerusalem as God's punishment upon Jews for not believing that Jesus was the Christ.

Jewish ethics left an indelible mark on the New Testament. According to Mark 10:17-19, when a man asked Jesus what he must do to inherit eternal life, Jesus directed him to the Ten Commandments. According to Mark 12:28-31, Jesus declared that the two greatest commandments are the Jewish Shema (Deut. 6:4) and the Old Testament command to love your neighbor (Lev. 19:18). The Jewish Testament of the Twelve Patriarchs (2d half of 2d c. B.C.) had already combined the substance of these two commandments. Rabbi Akiba (early 2d c. A.D.) regarded the injunction to love your neighbor as the most comprehensive rule in the Torah (*Sifre* on Lev. 19:18). Paul stated that that rule fulfills the whole law (Gal. 5:14), and the Jewish-Christian Epistle of James calls it "the royal law" (2:8). Rabbi Hillel regarded the Jewish form of the Golden Rule as the essence of "the whole law" (*Sabbath*

31a); in Matthew 7:12 the Christian form of it is "the law and the prophets." Many parallels exist between the Sermon on the Mount and rabbinic literature; Romans 12:14-21 is similar.

A characteristic form of Jewish ethical teaching consisted of lists of vices and virtues. Sexual sins were usually included. Jewish Christians continued the same kind of teaching; an example is Paul's list in Galatians 5:19-23.

Hellenistic Judaism was the Judaism into which gentile, especially Greek, culture had penetrated. The extent of the foreign influence varied; Philo in Alexandria carried Hellenistic interpretation of Torah to surprising lengths. Hellenistic-Jewish thought in the New Testament is most evident in the letters of Paul and the Epistle to the Hebrews.

By recognizing that certain features in early Christianity were derived from Jewish sources, we can study their nature in Judaism and thus obtain a fuller understanding of their significance in the New Testament.

CHAPTER 18

THE CHRISTIAN BACKGROUND OF THE NEW TESTAMENT

The situation in the various Christian communities had an enormous impact on the writing of the New Testament. Biblical scholars did not realize this until Hermann Reimarus (18th c.) and F.C. Baur (19th c.) began to discover its influence. Of the three types of environment (Jewish, Christian, and pagan) of the New Testament authors, the Christian was the most influential. Nevertheless, its role is still insufficiently recognized, even among scholars. The Christian setting consisted of (1) the events which occurred in the Christian communities and (2) the issues and disputes, both internal and external, with which the early Christians had to deal in their preaching, teaching, and writing.

Early Christian History

Throughout history, the events which occur in the life of a community influence and shape the thinking of the group, and the early Christians were no exception. Therefore we need to know what happened in the early church up to the middle of the second century when the last biblical book was written. The New Testament itself is our main source for Christian history in that period, although--especially in the second century--considerable information comes from uncanonical Christian literature and from other sources.

A problem in reconstructing the history of the early Christian communities is that of separating historical facts from the accounts and statements that originated in efforts to explain events, to promote beliefs, and to deal with issues. We have seen that there is a similar problem in the interpretation of the Old Testament. Often allusions to events tell us more about what really happened than do narrative accounts. The following sketch is a reconstruction of events which are significant for the understanding of the New Testament.

According to Josephus (Ant. 18.5.2), Herod Antipas put
John the Baptist to death because he feared that John, or his
followers, might start a rebellion. After John's death, Jesus
preached John's basic message, a call to repentance because
the kingdom of God was imminent (Matt. 3:2; 4:12, 17). How
much, or how little, of the other teachings in the synoptic gospels represents authentic teaching of Jesus is a debated question. Religious and ethical teaching could be added to tradition later just as easily as miracle stories. The Gospel of
John is not a reliable source of Jesus' words, for its Hellenistic thought does not fit Jesus' Palestinian environment and
synagogue training, but it does fit the situation later in some
Hellenistic churches, especially in Alexandria.

Faithful Jews tried to make at least one pilgrimage in
their lifetime to the temple in Jerusalem to celebrate the Passover. When Jesus came to the city for that purpose, the Sadducees feared that he might start a revolt against the Romans.
The Sadducees were opposed to Jewish revolts, because they
did not want to jeopardize their own prosperity, and because
they recognized that a revolt could not succeed against the
powerful Romans. Two aspects of Jesus' death definitely indicate that Pilate believed that he intended to overthrow Roman rule and become king: (1) the title, "King of the Jews,"
nailed to Jesus' cross, and (2) the crucifixion, which was the
customary way the Romans dealt with rebels. It is clear, too,
that the disciples believed that Jesus was the Christ who would
"restore the kingdom to Israel" (Luke 24:21; Acts 1:6). That
belief would, of course, be strong evidence as far as the authorities were concerned.

The origin of the belief that God had raised Jesus from
the dead apparently was Peter's vision of Jesus after the disciples had fled home to Galilee (Mark 14:27-28; 16:7; 1 Cor.
15:5; Luke 24:34). The earliest tradition of the resurrection
faith (1 Cor. 15:3-7), a tradition Paul had learned before he
wrote to the Corinthians, bases the faith entirely on visions.
An empty tomb is not mentioned either in that tradition or in
Paul's own defence of the resurrection faith (1 Cor. 15). The
fact that an empty tomb is not mentioned until the gospels were
written several decades later indicates that the tomb stories
arose after Paul's time. Paul surely would have mentioned an

empty tomb if he had known of such a tradition. At first the other disciples doubted Jesus' resurrection (Matt. 28:17; Luke 24:11; John 20:25), but Peter convinced them (Luke 22:32). Then they returned to Jerusalem, the capital of the coming kingdom of God, which they believed had begun to arrive with the resurrection of the dead, including Jesus. When they found that the general resurrection was not occurring, however, they soon concluded that Jesus, like some Old Testament prophets, must have ascended to heaven. Surely he would return soon, they thought, when the kingdom appeared. Then he would complete the task of the Christ. The author of Luke/Acts tried to counteract the embarrassing flight of the disciples to Galilee by portraying them as remaining in Jerusalem. In spite of his denial of Jesus, Simon (Peter's real name) became a hero in the church, for he was the foundation stone of the faith in Jesus' resurrection. Because the faith began with him and he persuaded the other disciples, Simon became known as "the Rock" ("Cephas" in Aramaic and "Petros" [Peter] in Greek).

While the followers of Jesus awaited his return, they met in a house for prayer (Acts 1:13-14). They preached to others and their numbers grew. The members of the young Christian community held all their possessions in common (Acts 4:32). A dispute arose between the "Hellenists," the Greek-speaking Jewish Christians, and the "Hebrews," the Aramaic-speaking Jewish Christians, in that church (Acts 6). According to Acts, the Hellenists complained that the Hebrews neglected their widows in the daily distribution of food. To settle the dispute, the twelve disciples asked the Hellenists to select seven of their group as leaders to serve tables while the disciples attended to preaching. The dispute must have involved more than food, however, for Stephen, one of the seven, became very active in preaching (instead of leaving it to the twelve). A major difference in religious beliefs must have existed between the two groups, for Stephen's preaching caused the non-Christian Jewish authorities to stone him to death and to persecute the other Hellenists so that they fled to other parts of Judea and to Samaria (Acts 8:1). The disciples, on the other hand, apparently were not so unorthodox, for they were not persecuted and remained in Jerusalem.

The persecution produced a significant development; it

caused the Hellenists to spread the Christian movement outside of Jerusalem. The apostles preached to Jews only, but converts from Cyprus and Cyrene preached to Greeks in Antioch (Acts 11:19-20), which was the beginning of the mission to the Gentiles. In the first few decades of the church, however, most of the gentile converts were men "who fear God" (Acts 13:16), Gentiles who worshiped Yahweh and attended the synagogue services, but never actually joined Judaism (probably largely because of the circumcision requirement). Jewish eschatological beliefs and arguments from the Hebrew Scriptures appealed to them more than to those Gentiles who lacked knowledge of Judaism. Paul began his mission by preaching to Jews and God-fearers in the synagogues, but Jewish hostility to his preaching forced him to go outside the synagogues, speaking to Gentiles in general (Acts 18:6).

Saul of Tarsus had joined in the orthodox Jewish persecution of the Hellenist Christians in Jerusalem. Some of them fled to Damascus. He followed, intent on taking them back to Jerusalem as prisoners, but his conversion experience transformed him from a zealous persecutor to a zealous promoter of Christianity. Paul (Greek name), as Saul (Hebrew name) was called later, and Barnabas became very active in the Antioch church, which sent them to Jerusalem with funds for the church there, and later sent them on missionary journeys.

The division between the orthodox Jewish Christians and the Hellenistic Jewish Christians, which had begun in Jerusalem, continued. Paul aggravated it with his insistence that gentile converts were free from the Jewish Torah, and therefore they could eat with gentile Christians and need not be circumcised (Gal. 2-3). After returning from their first missionary journey, Paul and Barnabas, taking with them an uncircumcised Greek convert, Titus, went to Jerusalem to defend their acceptance of Gentiles into the faith without requiring them to obey the Torah. Although other brethren in Jerusalem strongly objected, James, John, and Peter agreed at this "Jerusalem Council" that Paul and Barnabas could continue their policy, although the Jerusalem Church would continue to preach only to Jews.

Several factors could have convinced Paul that the Jewish law was no longer necessary. (1) Some rabbis thought that

the Torah would be replaced when the new age came. [40] (2)
Paul believed that the Spirit was now the guide and authority
for believers. (3) Paul and other early Christians believed
that Jesus' death had atoned for sin, hence repentance was no
longer required (therefore Paul did not teach the necessity of
repentance, or even mention it).

Paul's insistence that gentile converts need not obey the
Torah had two significant results. First, it fostered the rapid
expansion of the new movement among Gentiles. Secondly, it
prepared the way for the break between Judaism and Christianity, after which the latter became a separate religion.
Others, too, aided these developments, but their influence did
not equal that of Paul's dynamic personality. Conservative
Jewish Christianity did not suddenly disappear, however, for
near the end of the first century the authors of the Gospel of
Matthew and the Epistle of James defended the Jewish law.

The leaders of the Jerusalem church fell out of favor
with the non-Christian Jews, and to please them king Herod
Agrippa I killed James the son of Zebedee (and probably his
brother John too, for Christians later regarded both as martyrs), and imprisoned Peter (Acts 12). Acts erroneously
places this event before the Jerusalem Council. The Jerusalem church soon ceased to be a factor in Christianity, for at
the outbreak of the Jewish rebellion in 66, it fled to the gentile
city of Pella in the Decapolis, presumably to escape Jewish
persecution for not joining the revolt.

The misunderstanding which arose between Jews and
Christians was one of the great tragedies of history. As we
have seen, friction began with Jewish leaders persecuting
Stephen and the other Hellenists in Jerusalem. According to
Acts, Paul on his missionary journeys was persecuted by orthodox Jews (13:50; 14:19; 20:3; 23:12), as well as by Gentiles.
In his own writing Paul refers to his persecution by both groups
along with other hardships (2 Cor. 11:23-27). Jewish persecution of churches in Judea is alluded to in 1 Thessalonians 2:
14, and Matthew 10:17 mentions the flogging in the synagogues.
(For Roman persecution, see next chapter.) The controversy
between Jews and Christians reached a climax late in the first
century when Jews excluded Christians from the synagogues,
which is referred to in John 16:2. Christians responded with

propaganda against Jews. One tactic was to quote Scripture against them and to charge that God had hardened their hearts against believing that Jesus was the Christ and that they had killed the prophets (e.g., the speech ascribed to Stephen in Acts 7). The synoptic gospels report that it was the "chief priests" (Sadducees) who bribed Judas to betray Jesus. But by the time the gospels were written, Christians had begun to shift the blame for Jesus' death to Jews in general. "Scribes and elders" (Pharisees) and the Jewish multitude share in the responsibility in the accounts of Jesus' arrest and trial. Moreover, Pilate is portrayed as reluctant to execute Jesus, a feature recognized by historians as very improbable. A Roman governor would not make a judicial decision on the basis of mob pressure, especially if rebellion, or potential rebellion, was involved. In the descriptions given by Philo and Josephus, Pilate is far from a kindly, lenient man. The historical fact cannot be denied that Pilate ordered Jesus to be crucified. The worst anti-Semitism in the Bible is in John 8:17, 44; 10:34.

Several causes were responsible for the misunderstanding between Jews and Christians. The nonobservance of Torah in churches at a time when Christianity was regarded as a Jewish sect, angered Jews because it was flagrant heresy. The resulting Jewish persecution and excommunication of Christians from the synagogues created strong Christian resentment. Much antagonism existed in the Roman world between Gentiles and Jews, and converts to Christianity were liable to bring their prejudices with them when they joined. As gentile Christians placed increasing emphasis upon their belief in Jesus' divinity, Jews were further offended. Monotheism was even more vital in Judaism than the Torah, and the divine attributes assigned to Jesus were contrary to the doctrine that there is only one God. Examples of this trend away from monotheism are the practice of calling Jesus "Lord" (a title Jews reserved for Yahweh, God); praying to Jesus; and such statements as "at the name of Jesus every knee should bow, in heaven and on earth and under the earth" (Phil. 2:10). These features were also contrary to some pagan philosophies. In response to the criticism that they were not monotheists, Christians eventually formulated the doctrine of the Trinity: God, Jesus Christ, and the Holy Spirit are not three gods, but one God.

The rapid spread of Christianity into major cities of the Mediterranean world was an important factor in determining the nature of early Christian literature. The variety of thought in the New Testament is the result not only of the fact that different authors were involved, but also that they lived in widely scattered cities with different cultural environments which affected the life of the Christian communities.

The organization of the early churches went through several changes. In the Jerusalem church, Jesus' disciples were the leaders; they and their followers held their meetings in their homes. Although the gospels and some passages in Acts depict twelve disciples as the leaders, Paul states that James and John (the sons of Zebedee) and Peter "were reputed to be pillars" there (Gal. 2:9), and it was with them that Paul and Barnabas made an agreement. Even the gospels and Acts reflect this, for of the disciples of Jesus they mention by name, those three predominate. After Herod Agrippa I killed James and John and imprisoned Peter, however, Jesus' brother James became the leader of the Jerusalem church. Thus the basis of leadership there changed from discipleship to blood relationship to Jesus. Jewish-Christian churches, and perhaps some gentile-Christian churches too, had a council of elders, or presbyters, derived from a similar practice in Judaism.

In early gentile churches, the leaders were of various types. Paul listed them in this order: "And God has appointed in the church first apostles, second prophets, third teachers, then workers of miracles, then healers, helpers, administrators, speakers in various kinds of tongues" (1 Cor. 12:28). These apostles were not disciples who had traveled with Jesus, but preachers, or evangelists, who proclaimed the gospel and won converts. The teachers trained those who were already members. The "speakers in tongues," ranked at the bottom of the list, were those who ecstatically babbled unintelligible sounds, believing that they were inspired by the Spirit.

Christian prophets believed that the new age had come and God had poured out his Spirit on them. This belief had its roots in the Jewish background, although there were prophets in paganism too. The Christian prophets played an important

role in the early church. As problems and issues arose, they
produced some of the answers. They were especially influential in creating changes in Christian thought and tradition.
Paul described his own "abundance of revelations" (2 Cor. 12:
1-7). Paul's gospel was not the same as that of some other
apostles, and he admitted that no man had taught it to him; he
stoutly defended it, however, on the basis that he had received it as revelation from Jesus Christ (Gal. 1:12). Thus in
early Christianity a tradition transmitted by the apostles could
be, and often was, superseded on the basis that a revelation
was more recent and was received directly from the Spirit of
the Lord, which could be viewed as either the Spirit of the
Lord God or the Spirit of the Lord Jesus. As a result of the
spiritual revelations, a large variety of Christian beliefs and
practices arose, and many of them were not in agreement with
each other. The author of 1 John warned that there were many
false prophets in the world and the spirit which inspires them
is not the Spirit of God (4:1).

By the beginning of the second century many gentile
churches had a bishop. Originally he was an overseer who
supervised the administration of the local church, including
the work of deacons, who ministered to the widows and the
poor. As the diversity of beliefs increased, and especially
after Christian gnosticism became prevalent, the need for
some standardization was painfully apparent. To solve the
problem, the bishops acquired the authority to declare what is
the true faith, and members were required to accept his de-
cisions. Ignatius, the bishop of Antioch, repeatedly insisted
in his letters that the bishop is to be obeyed even as Christ is
to be obeyed. In New Testament times no bishop yet had authority over all the churches in a region.

The Christian prophecy which departed the farthest from
the original gospel was that of the gnostics. Saturninus, Basilides, Marcion, Valentinus, and other gnostic leaders appeared in the first half of the second century, each with his
own form of speculative theology. A wide variety of thought
existed in gnosticism, but the foundation invariably was dualis-
tic: the material world is inherently evil, in contrast to the
spiritual, which is good. Souls originated in the highest level
of the heavens, but unfortunately they became imprisoned in

human bodies, which are automatically bad because they are physical. Salvation consists of acquiring this secret knowledge, gnosis, which will enable the soul to escape from the wicked flesh and return to the heavenly, spiritual realm, its proper home. This type of thought originated in paganism, not Judaism or Christianity. [41] When some converts introduced this type of thought into Christianity, it soon was regarded as heresy for several reasons: (1) Because of their doctrine that the physical world is inherently evil, gnostics could not accept the Jewish and Christian monotheistic belief in one God who created the universe. A good god, they maintained, could not have created a material world. Therefore the Jewish god of the Old Testament was an evil, or at best an inferior, god. The good, supreme God, the Father, is spirit (cf. John 4:24) and belongs to the heavenly, spiritual realm. Marcion, a gnostic at Rome near the middle of the second century, was a leader in expressing this view. (2) Gnostics rejected the Old Testament for essentially the same reason; it was the Scripture of the wicked creator-god. (3) The gnostic view that the physical body is evil produced a problem in respect to Jesus' life. Since flesh is bad, how could the savior, Christ, have had a physical body ? The docetics, who constituted a school of thought in gnosticism, had an answer. They decided that Christ must have been a spirit who descended from the heavens and entered the body of the physical, human Jesus at his baptism (after all, Christian tradition already claimed that the Spirit had entered Jesus at that time, Mark 1:10). Thus the human Jesus only appeared to be the Christ (hence the term "docetic," from the Greek word meaning "seem" or "appear"). It was only the human Jesus who died on the cross; at the crucifixion the spirit Christ left him and returned to the heavens. Although a wide variety of beliefs existed in the early church, the gnostics were the only early Christians who thoroughly undermined the theological and christological foundations of the church. They did this by rejecting monotheism, the Old Testament, the belief that Jesus was the Christ, and the doctrine (generally accepted by Christians by the second century) that Jesus' death atoned for the sins of believers.

Although some semi-gnostic thought and expressions appear in Colossians 1:19 ("fullness" dwelt in Christ), the Gospel

of John, and later in the writings of Clement of Alexandria, the
New Testament generally is free of it. In fact, the authors of
1 Timothy and 1 John definitely opposed gnostics and their
teaching. In 1 Timothy there is only one God (2:5) and everything he created is good (4:4); non-gnostic Christians are the
ones who know the truth (4:3). Christians should not believe
the myths and genealogies some were preaching (1 Tim. 1:4;
4:7; 2 Tim. 4:4), which were characteristic of gnosticism.
In our chapter 1 (F) we asked what kind of knowledge the reader is warned against in 1 Timothy 6. The word translated as
"knowledge" is the gnostic Greek term *gnosis*. Both this
word and the ideas opposed in 1 and 2 Timothy indicate that
the false teachers (1 Tim. 1:6-7) were propagating gnosticism, not ordinary knowledge. The docetic separation of
Christ from Jesus is also opposed in 1 John: Jesus is the
Christ (2:22), who came in the flesh (4:2-3; 1 Tim. 3:16),
and whose blood cleanses from sin (1:7; 5:6); Christians
must believe that Jesus is God's Son (1:7; 2:23; 3:23). We
cannot expect to evaluate these passages accurately if we
fail to realize the reasons for the extreme emphasis on
these particular beliefs about Jesus.

Ideological and Psychological Factors

As Christianity grew, many problems developed. Arguments and issues arose in the church, both between individuals and between Christian communities. Issues arose also
between Christians and Jews, and between Christians and Gentiles. The subject matter of the New Testament deals largely
with those issues and problems. Not only did authors write to
present a solution or to advance arguments, but often redactors made later insertions for similar purposes.

We have already observed some of those issues and problems. They included the questions of gentile Christians' obedience of the Jewish law, Jesus' resurrection and messiahship,
the coming of Elijah, and the nature of the body the dead will
have when raised from their graves. We have seen the growing misunderstanding between Jews and Christians, which culminated in the division into separate religions. The diversity
created by Christian prophets and especially by gnostics pro-

duced very serious problems. Other issues and problems
arose also, to which we now turn our attention.

The very first problem in Christian faith was the doubt
that God had raised Jesus from the dead. The doubt was soon
dispelled among the disciples but remained among non-Christians. Eventually Jews charged that the disciples perpetrated
a hoax by stealing Jesus' body from his grave. Christians responded by claiming that Pilate authorized a Jewish guard to
watch the tomb (and thus Christians could not have stolen the
body; Matt. 27:62-66). The Jewish charge and the Christian
counter-claim are not historical events, but fictional products of the dispute.

But even if Jesus was alive again, many ideological
problems remained. How could he be the Messiah, or Christ,
when he had not performed the Messiah's main task of overthrowing foreign rule of Palestine ? The answer seemed obvious. God must have taken him to heaven temporarily, but Jesus will return to finish his work. This return (Parousia--
from Greek--, or Second Advent) will occur when the kingdom
of God comes, in the lifetime of the disciples (Mark 9:1; 13:
30); they will not have gone through the cities of Israel before
the Son of Man comes (Matt. 10:23). The members of the
church at Thessalonica were idly waiting for it, and Paul had
to urge them to go to work (2 Thess. 3). Some Christians even
reported that the day of the Lord had already come (2 Thess.
2:1-2).

As the days went by without the Second Coming of Jesus,
Christians found various explanations. One, borrowed from
Jewish apocalyptic, was that conditions must yet become worse
just before the new age comes (Mark 13:17-19); some thought
an anti-Christ would come first. A rationale which had al -
ready been used in Judaism was: Yes, the end of this age is
coming, but it has been delayed. "The gospel must first be
preached to all nations" (Mark 13:10) was one answer; another
was to quote Psalm 110:1 as the reason for the delay (Heb. 1:
13). A different answer was that the kingdom of God has
started to arrive, beginning with Jesus' ministry. This explanation, which has been called "realized eschatology," is
in Luke 17:21. The passage has often been mistranslated as

"in you," as though it were a spiritual condition; the correct translation is "among you" or "in your midst." The idea in Luke is that the process of the coming of the kingdom of God began with Jesus' life, but the process is not yet completed. The gnostics, who rejected eschatology entirely, solved the problem by saying that Jesus is not coming back nor will there ever be a kingdom of God on this earth. Instead, Christ, God, and the kingdom are spiritual. Although the Gospel of John opposes docetism ("the Word became flesh," 1:14), it has some gnostic-like ideas. It spiritualizes the Second Advent by depicting Jesus as promising that God will send the Spirit of Truth, which apparently takes the place of Jesus' return (14:16-17; 16:13-14). The same gospel, like gnosticism, rejects the coming of a kingdom of God on earth, for in it Jesus proclaims that his kingdom is not of this world (18:36); whether the Greek text is translated as "kingdom" or "kingship," the verse rejects an earthly kingdom.

The belief that Jesus had ascended to heaven and would soon return to establish the kingdom was one of the problems in the early Christian communities. Contrary to their claim that Jesus fulfilled prophecy, the expectation that the Messiah will ascend to heaven and return to earth is nowhere in the Scriptures or other Jewish writings. The second half of the belief, however, was found in the Jewish idea of the preexistent Son-of-Man Messiah, who will come down to earth from heaven. As we saw in chapter 17, the close parallelism in words and thought between the Son of Man sayings in the gospels and in the Parables of 1 Enoch indicates that some form of the Parables was the source for both Christians and the author of 1 Enoch. The Son-of-Man sayings in the gospels originated in a Jewish-Christian effort to prove that a descending-from-heaven Jesus could be the prophesied Messiah. [42]

Eschatology presented other problems for the early church. If the kingdom of God is about to arrive, where are the signs of its coming? Such signs are predicted in Joel 2: 30-31 and referred to in Acts 2:19-20 (cf. 1 Cor. 1:22). One Christian answer was: there will not be any (Mark 8:11). The Q material presents other views. In one passage people are denounced for not having recognized the signs of the times (Matt. 16:1-3=Luke 12:54-56), which presumably have occurred. In another Q passage, only one sign will be given, the sign of Jonah (Matt. 12:38-39=Luke 11:29-30), that is, the sign is that preaching to the Gentiles is occurring.

The demand for signs is also directed against Jesus. What signs or miracles did he do to indicate that he was really the Christ? The Jewish expectation that the Messiah would perform miracles must have put pressure on the Christian communities to portray Jesus as a miracle worker. This is reflected in Acts 2:22, which emphasizes that Jesus' qualifications were attested to by miracles and signs which God did through him. The Gospel of John gives much prominence to stories of Jesus' miracles which are "signs" which should cause readers to believe that he was the Christ (20:30-31).

A further problem which confronted the early church was that of explaining Jesus' death if he was the Christ. Why did he die before establishing the new kingdom? That was not in accord with Old Testament prophecy and Jewish expectations. Two main kinds of Christian answers are presented in the New Testament: (1) Jesus' death was according to divine plan (Acts 2:23; 4:28). To support that premise, early Christians erroneously claimed that the Scriptures prophesied the death of the Messiah (Luke 18:31; "even as it is written of him," Mark 14:2), and gospel authors portrayed Jesus as accepting and predicting his fate (Mark 10:32b-34). (2) A second solution proposed was the atonement doctrine: Jesus' death ("blood") atoned for the sins of believers (Mark 10:45; Rom. 5:9-10). How could Jesus' death atone for people's sins? The background of the idea was in Judaism. In the Old Testament animal sacrifices could atone for sins (e.g., Lev. 4:20), and in Isaiah 53 the death of the Suffering Servant (which had already occurred) is a sacrificial offering for the iniquity of the people. In 4 Maccabees the author regards the martyrdom of the Maccabean leaders as a ransom for the sin of the whole Jewish nation (6:28; 17:21-22).

Other aspects of Jesus' life also did not fit that of the expected Messiah. The most popular type of Messiah whom Jews expected was the "son of David." Consequently several Christian efforts were made to try to prove that Jesus was a descendant of the famous king. The authors of Matthew and Luke each have a genealogy tracing Jesus' ancestry back

retain the Jewish Bible. The fact that it circu-
k translation (the Septuagint) definitely aided the
new religion among Gentiles.

f Gentile Christianity

id influx of gentile converts transformed the na-
urch. Some Hellenistic influence came from Hel-
sh converts, but generally the most radical chang-
gentile members. Before examining the types
at occurred, we may well ask, How could these
major alterations in the beliefs and practices
y? Was not church tradition established by then?
seen that there was already variety and even
within the church, especially between Hellenis-
llenistic converts. The same factors that per-
ndition in Jewish Christianity, continued to oper-
gentile converts. No authority, whether an in-
rganized group of individuals, or a written docu-
to control the churches as a whole.
f that the divine Spirit made new and more au-
elations to Christians was an idea readily accep-
le churches. It promoted change, because new
d supplant older tradition. In Judaism "the
rd" was the Spirit of God, the Holy Spirit. Gen-
, and apparently some Hellenistic Jewish Chris-
sus "Lord." Thus a reference to the Spirit of
Septuagint or in Christian writings was easily
a reference to the Spirit of the Lord Jesus.
eason that gentile converts could easily alter
and beliefs was that they soon joined in such
that they overwhelmed Jewish Christianity,
dy weakened by the loss of the original Chris-
in Jerusalem and by controversies between
ns and Jews. In 1 Corinthians Paul is strug-
tile converts from bringing pagan customs into
modern times, even though Christianity has
authority to maintain the traditions, changes
hen new converts from a different background
er of the old members. In Latin America, Ro-

through David, but they do not agree—in fact, they do not
agree even on the identity of Jesus' grandfather. The two genealogies were written independently of the virgin birth stories, for they trace Jesus' ancestry through his father Joseph,
not through Mary. Either the author of Luke or a later scribe
tried to reconcile the Lucan genealogy with the virgin birth by
inserting "as was supposed" (Luke 3:23).

The fact that Jesus' home town was Nazareth in Galilee
instead of Bethlehem in Judea was a source of skepticism that
he was the Davidic Messiah (John 7:41b-42, 52; cf. 1 Sam.
20:6). The authors of Matthew and Luke tried to solve the
problem with stories that Jesus was born in Bethlehem. A
difficulty with the stories is the improbability of their ways of
getting Jesus' parents from Nazareth to Bethlehem (for his
birth) and home to Nazareth. For example, when the Romans
took a census, they wanted people to be at home to be counted,
as a Roman edict of A.D. 104, found among Egyptian papyri,
plainly states. [43] To have people travel to the town of their
ancestors, as Luke 2:4 represents Joseph as doing, would be a
very confusing way of taking a census!

Another problem with Jesus' career was the fact that he
was baptized for his sins by John the Baptist. The Messiah
was expected to be a completely righteous, sinless person.
But Jesus' baptism by John implied that he was not sinless;
therefore, how could he be the Messiah? The author of Matthew tried to meet the objection by adding 3:14-15. [44]

Not only the New Testament writers, but early church
fathers tried to reconcile Jesus' life to the Jewish expectations
of the nature of the Messiah. In the second century Justin and
Tertullian, and later Cyprian of Carthage and Ambrosiaster
diligently searched the Old Testament for passages which
seemed to fit Jesus.

Other Christian problems and ideological factors, too
numerous to describe here, influenced the writing of the New
Testament. They include the claim that Christianity is the
new Judaism, replacing the old Judaism; the problem of the
rival claims of John the Baptist's followers; the problem of a
Christian with a non-Christian spouse; and the relations among
different Christian communities.

CHAPTER 19

THE GENTILE BACKGROUND OF THE NEW TESTAMENT

Of the three types of background of the New Testament, the gentile background has received the least attention. This is partly because it has not been investigated as much as the others, and partly because of bias against anything "pagan." Yet it had important effects on the New Testament and Christianity, as new converts turned away from some of the Jewish roots. Sometimes it is difficult to distinguish between gentile influence and the influence of Hellenistic Judaism, which had already adopted some Hellenistic ideas.

The Growth of Gentile Christianity

At first the apostles preached only to Jews. The earliest gentile converts to Christianity were proselytes, Gentiles converted to Judaism (Acts 6:5, Nicholaus; 13:43). More numerous were the "God-fearers," Gentiles who attended synagogue services and worshiped Yahweh, but who had not actually joined Judaism. The first mention in Acts (chapter 10) of gentile converts is that of the Roman centurion, Cornelius, "a devout man who feared God," who was baptized together with his family and friends in Caesarea. Whether this story is history, or whether it was created to portray Peter as won over to the mission to the Gentiles, is a debated question. It does reflect the fact that God-fearers were early converts. In Acts 11 the earliest gentile converts, at least in Antioch, were "Greeks" —whether they "feared God" is not stated. According to Acts, Paul and Barnabas conducted their mission by preaching in synagogues to "men of Israel and you that fear God" (13:16). Later, after being driven out of synagogues and persecuted, Paul declared: "From now on I will go to the Gentiles" (18:6). When Paul and others preached outside the synagogues, the Gentiles in the audience would not be limited to God-fearers, unlike the situation in the synagogues. The God-fearers were already familiar with Jewish messianic hopes

and eschatology, so the ear
would be far more meaningf
The God-fearers were the b
and the mission to Gentiles

Not all Jewish Christ
should be preached to Gent
party" opposed Paul for ac
with the Jewish law requir
2:12). The Jerusalem chu
Jewish-Christian author of
adhered to the original vie
be only to Jews, not Genti

Nevertheless, from
membership grew rapidly
gentile Christians must h
tians.

Several factors cau
a fast rate. The sense o
must act at once to be re
judgment day, frightened
ogy has operated in evan
tury, too.) Both pagan
mised eternal salvation,
threat of an imminent ju
after death, but not a g
ment.)

We have seen tha
of obeying the Jewish T
pealing to Gentiles. C
movement was the new
replacing the old Judai
ism and Christianity s
and more, in effect, C
new religion. The se
tiles, because Jews a
with them for several
emptions that the Ror
munities in some lar
Rome. Nevertheless
Judaism and that Jes

Christians t
lated in Gre
growth of the

The Effects

The ra
ture of the cl
lenistic-Jewi
es came from
of changes th
converts mak
of Christianit

We hav
sharp division
tic and non-H
mitted that cc
ate among the
dividual, an o
ment was able

The beli
thoritative rev
ted in the gent
revelation cou
Spirit of the L
tile Christians
tians, called J
the Lord in the
interpreted as

A third r
church custom
large numbers
which was alre
tian community
Jewish Christi
gling to stop ge
Christianity. I
several types o
have occurred v
exceed the numi

man Catholic religion has been modified by the former religion of native Indian converts. During World War II many Blacks migrated to Chicago, Detroit, and Los Angeles; neighborhoods and churches that had been all white suddenly became predominantly or even entirely Black. The new members introduced into the worship services Southern customs that previously were absent in the churches they joined.

Just what effects did the gentile converts have on the Christian movement? One type of result was the reinterpretation of features that already were in Jewish Christianity.

a. Influence of Pagan Religions

Although the faith in Jesus' resurrection arose from the combination of Christian experience and the Jewish background, Gentile converts attached a different significance to the faith. To them, Jesus' resurrection indicated that Jesus was a god, for the gods Osiris, Attis, and Adonis had died and been restored to life. A deified Christ was a new concept in Christology, although the preexistent Son of Man was midway between that view and the human, Son-of-David Christ.

Baptism has an interesting history. As we have seen, Jewish Christianity enlarged its effects by regarding it as conferring the Holy Spirit upon the new converts. As the new religion spread into the Hellenistic world, a new dimension was added to Christian baptism. As a result of his baptism, the convert immediately became a new person. He was "reborn," or "regenerated," pure and sinless, like a new-born baby. In the ancient world water was widely used in purification rituals, either by sprinkling or by bathing. In addition, in the cults of Isis, Osiris, and Mithra, at least, water baptism was part of the ceremony by which devotees were initiated into those mystery religions. Although we do not know many de-tails because of the secrecy attached to the initiation, we do have a little information from both archaeology and ancient pagan and Christian writings. For example, a baptismal chamber was found in the Isis temple at Eretria, Greece. In some Mithraic chapels a water basin was built into the front edge of a podium, and centered between its ends, connected to inlet and outlet troughs so that fresh water could flow through them continuously. The regional museum in Ptuj, Yugoslavia, has reconstructed the interior of a Mithraic chapel, using materials found in archaeological excavations of nearby Mithraea. In the reconstruction, as in the original site, a water tank, about two feet square and about three feet high, made of marble slabs, stood at the edge of the right-hand podium midway down the length of the podium. The Carnuntum Museum, in Bad Deutsch Altenburg, Austria, and the Roman camp at Saalburg, Germany, each has a font on a pedestal, about three feet high, found at the entrance to Mithraic chapels; some Christian baptismal fonts are similar.

We are not sure how early or late the mysteries influenced the form of Christian baptism (such as sprinkling and the use of fonts), but we do find in the New Testament two passages which interpret Christian baptism in a manner similar to some mystery cults' interpretation of their baptismal rites. In Mithraism and the cults of Isis and Osiris baptism was viewed as the death of the old sinful self, which was reborn, or regenerated, as a new sinless self which was in mystical union with the deity. [45] Consequently, the new self, like the deity, has become immortal and will continue to live after death.

Why was baptism connected with the death of the old self? Apparently the key is that baptism by immersion was regarded as death of the old self by drowning; the doctrine carried over into baptism by sprinkling. Paul, in Romans 6: 1-14, insists that by baptism Christians are united with Christ Jesus in a death like his, and therefore "we shall certainly be united with him in a resurrection like his. We know that our old self was crucified with him so that the sinful body might be destroyed, and we might no longer be enslaved to sin." Thus, as in certain mystery religions, baptism made the person pure and sinless, assured of blessed immortality. A century later Justin agreed with the doctrine and asserted that after baptism the Christian "should live without sin henceforth" (*Dialogue with Trypho* 44.4). The belief that Christians received the Spirit at the same time naturally strengthened the conviction that henceforth they should be sinless (cf. Gal. 5: 16-26). As in the mysteries, baptism causes "regeneration" in Titus 3:5.

Gentile Christians reinterpreted some of the religious terms used in Jewish Christianity. To some, "Son of God" must not refer to a human Messiah, for in their background the term was used literally and therefore referred to a god or a demigod. The Jewish Septuagint, used by Gentile Christians, substituted Kurios, the Greek word for Lord, for the Hebrew name for Yahweh. "Lord" was applied to various pagan gods (Lord Sarapis; the name of the god Adonis means "Lord"). Some Roman emperors attached the title to their names as a sign of their divinity. Gentile converts applied the word "Lord" to Jesus, not just as a respectful form of address meaning "Master," but as a title for a divine person. The phrases "my Lord and my God" (John 20:28) and "our Lord and Savior" (2 Peter 2:20), applied to Jesus in the New Testament, are expressions applied to gods in paganism. Justin even argued that the Lord who spoke to Moses from the bush was not God the Father, but Christ, who is Lord and God (Dialogue with Trypho 55-63); thus Jesus, in effect, is a second god. We have observed the threat to monotheism in Philippians 2:10-11 and some passages in the Gospel of John.

Gentile Christians not only reinterpreted Jewish-Christian traditions, but also introduced some new ideas and practices from their background. The idea that Jesus was divine in nature but had a human birth easily suggested that, like some of the pagan demigods, his father was divine even though his mother was human. But why should his mother be a virgin? The virgin birth stories in Matthew and Luke were intended to insure that Joseph was not Jesus' father and to elevate Jesus' qualifications. Some pagans believed that women who had never experienced sex were purer than other women and therefore better qualified to be the mother of a god's son. In paganism a virgin birth was ascribed to some mythological and to some historical persons—the latter included Plato, Alexander, and Augustus. Plutarch (ca. A.D. 100) stated that the Egyptians believed that a divine spirit could cause pregnancy: "it is not impossible for the spirit of God . . . to engender certain beginnings of birth" (Numa 4).

At first glance we are surprised to find Jewish elements in the biblical virgin birth story, considering its parallels in paganism. The Jewish elements include an angel, the Holy

Spirit, and the statements that Mary will give birth to the Messiah. All of these elements, however, were generally adopted by gentile Christians as a result of their use of the Septuagint and their early contacts with Jewish Christians. The claim that Jesus' birth fulfilled prophecy is a typical addition by the author of Matthew. The main purpose of the story evidently is to make Jesus literally the son of God, thus reinterpreting the original Jewish-Christian concept of a Davidic "Son of God," who is entirely human. The total evidence indicates that the story began in a very Hellenistic Christian community, either of Gentiles influenced by the Septuagint, or a mixed Jewish-Christian and gentile-Christian community.

The virgin birth is contrary to many other traditions in the New Testament. Joseph is plainly regarded as Jesus' father in Luke 2:27, 33, 41, 43, 48, and John 1:45; 6:42. The genealogies in Matthew and Luke were written to try to show that Jesus was a descendant of David and therefore is the Christ; both genealogies trace the descent through Joseph, not Mary, so the writers who originally composed them obviously believed that Joseph was Jesus' father. And, of course, the virgin birth doctrine is incompatible with the doctrine of a pre-existent, incarnated Christ. Later the church fathers struggled in vain to reconcile the various Christologies.[46]

In even the earliest traditions of the last supper (1 Cor. 11:23-26; Mark 14:22-24), Jesus is represented as identifying the bread and wine with his body and blood, which the disciples should eat and drink. Considering Jesus' training in Judaism, in which consuming blood is strictly forbidden in the Torah (Lev. 17:14) because blood is the very life of the animal (or human), it is scarcely credible that Jesus would ask his disciples to eat his flesh and drink his blood, even symbolically. The belief in the ancient Near East, including the Torah, that the blood is the life, was the result of the observation that when animals and humans were wounded and lost their blood supply, they died. It is very probable that the Lord's Supper, or Eucharist, rite was introduced by gentile converts who had already practiced a similar ritual before joining. Justin quoted the last supper tradition in which Jesus identified the bread and wine with his body and blood and commanded the disciples to eat and drink them. Then Justin admitted that a similar rit-

ual was practiced in the initiation into the mysteries of Mithra;
he attributed the similarity to imitation by wicked demons in
Mithraism *(1 Apology* 66). The ultimate origin of the rite was
the ancient identification of a deity with an animal; by eating
the flesh and drinking the blood of the animal, the worshiper
assimilated enough of the deity to live after death. Later this
crude ritual was refined by substituting bread and wine (or
wine mixed with water). Immortality is clearly the result of
the Eucharist in John 6:48-58 and in the writing of Irenaeus
(Against Heresies 5. 2).

The shift from Sabbath to Sunday as the holy day of the
week is another contribution from gentile Christianity. The
Sabbath (from sunset Friday to sunset Saturday) was the sacred day, "the seventh day," in Jewish Christianity. Gentile
converts, however, celebrated Sunday, "the first day," of the
week (midnight Saturday to midnight Sunday). The main reason probably was the fact that Sunday was the holy day in the
Roman culture from which they came; it was the day of the sun
god on which he should particularly be worshiped. Contribut-
ing factors may have been the desire to break away from Jewish customs, as well as the reason Christian writers gave,
namely, the tradition that Jesus rose at dawn on the first day
of the week (the day and the hour sacred to the sun god).

Papyri, written in Greek and found in Egypt, reveal the
prevalence of the belief in magic, exorcisms, and divine healing. In the story in John 9:1-12 Jesus heals a blind man by a-
nointing the man's eyes with clay mixed with Jesus' spittal. A
similar miracle is ascribed to the healing god Asklepios in a
papyrus: "To Valerius Aper, a blind soldier, the god Aescula-
pius [Latin form of Asklepios] revealed that he should go and
take blood of a white cock, together with honey, and anoint his
eyes three days. And he received his sight, and came and
gave thanks publicly to the god." [47]

b. Influence of Pagan Philosophy and Ethics

Pagan philosophy affected the writing of the New Testament in some respects, but it had more influence on the patristic writers. Whereas the mystery religion aspects were
brought into the church mainly by gentiles, philosophy came

through Hellenistic Jews just as readily as through Gentiles. Greek and Roman philosophy was generally monotheistic, and therefore blended easily with Judaism, in contrast to the polytheism and cultic rituals of the mystery religions.

Four Greek philosophies of the classical period—Platonism, Cynicism, Stoicism, and Epicureanism—were still quite influential in New Testament times. Many educated Romans had studied at least one of these, and Cynics traveled around, begging and preaching to all who would listen. Justin acknowledged that he was a Platonist before becoming a Christian. The Stoics taught that the universe is guided by an impersonal force, reason, which they also called nature, or God, which is manifest in human reason. Nearly all Greek philosophies were deeply concerned with promoting ethics, including the four basic virtues taught by Plato: temperance, courage, wisdom, and justice. Stoics taught that the goal of a person's life should be to become a wise man, that is, to live a virtuous life guided by reason. They stressed the importance of "conscience," a term which occurs often in the New Testament (e.g., Acts 23:1; Rom. 9:1; 1 Tim. 1:5). The Cynics opposed superficiality in culture, and envy, hatred, and strife. Although the Epicureans advocated pleasure as the greatest good, they rated pleasure of the soul higher than pleasure of the body. They believed that pleasure of the soul is acquired through the knowledge that there are no gods, Fate, or life after death, which therefore need not be feared. Some ethics were taught in certain mystery religions (Orphism, Mithraism, and the cult of Isis), but the goal of life in the mysteries is salvation of the soul. Generally in Greek philosophy, virtue is the goal. Roman philosophers built upon the Greek foundation; much syncretism of philosophies occurred, especially a Cynic-Stoic combination.

Various New Testament ethics are paralleled in Greco-Roman philosophy and, in many cases, in ancient Jewish literature also. The thought of committing adultery is as bad as the deed itself in Matthew 5:28 and in the Jewish Pseudepigrapha (T. Benj. 8:2). The general principle that it is wrong to even wish to do evil was expressed around 460 B.C. by the Greek philosopher, Democritus. Around 300 B.C. Zeno, the founder of Stoicism, stated that the intention to do evil is equiv-

alent to doing it. In Romans 12:17-21 and the Sermon on the
Mount we find the mandate not to return evil for evil. This
principle appeared centuries earlier in Proverbs 20: 22 (contrary to "an eye for an eye" in Exod. 21:24) and in Socrates'
teaching (Plato, *Crito* 10). Mutuality in marriage (1 Cor. 7:
3-4) was taught by the Stoics.

   c. Pagan Literary Influence

     The canonical gospels are paralleled to a considerable
degree by Hellenistic narratives which portray a "divine man,"
or "man of God," a miracle worker to whom a god had given
supernatural power. The literary form of these "biographies"
of miracle workers was a development from the short story of
a particular miracle. Sometimes the hero was a historical
teacher to whom miracles were later ascribed—Pythagoras
and Apollonius of Tyana, for example.[50]

     Another literary form was the diatribe, a moral address
in conversational style. The listener or reader was usually
addressed directly in the second person. Both Cynics and
Stoics used it. The speech ascribed to Paul in Athens (Acts
17) is this type of address. The pagan literary background is
made explicit here, for a Greek saying is quoted as from
"your poets" (17:28b), and a line from a hymn to Zeus in Ara-
tus is quoted (17:28a).

     The Stoics composed statements of the responsibilities
to each other of the members of a household, that is, of husbands, wives, parents, children, and slaves. Statements of
this type are called *Haustafeln*, a German term. An example
is in the *Epistles* of Seneca (94). Similar lists are in 1 Corinthians 7 and Colossians 3:18-25. Stoics, as well as Jews
and Christians, compiled lists of vices and virtues. Long ago,
Wettstein, in his commentary on Matthew 9:12, observed that
the saying, "They who are whole have no need of a physician,"
occurs in the works of many Greek classical writers.

     Differences between a belief, custom, or literary fea-
ture in paganism and a parallel in Christianity does not disprove gentile influence. Christians naturally made modifications in what they borrowed from paganism, just as they did in

what they inherited from Judaism, in order to adapt those features to their religion.

Relations with the Romans

Jesus was crucified as a rebel, and the Roman authorities continued to be suspicious of the loyalty of the apostles
and their converts. The apostles did not remain hostile to Roman soldiers, however, for Roman soldiers were soon admitted to membership in the Christian community (Acts 10), and
friendly allusions to them occur in the New Testament. Incidentally, the conversion of Roman soldiers may explain the
apparent early influence of Mithraism on Christianity, for the
worship of Mithra was prevalent in the Roman army.

Christians did not join the Jewish revolts against Rome
in 66-70 and 132-135, for they were waiting for Jesus to return and end the Roman rule. The growing tension between
them and Jews was also a reason, especially in the second revolt, led by Simon "bar Kochba" (see note 34a).

Nevertheless, Christian relations with the Roman government gradually worsened, changing from occasional individual or local persecutions to empire-wide persecution by the
emperors Decius and Valerian in mid-third century. Peter
and Paul evidently were martyrs (John 21:18-19; 1 Clement 5),
and according to a tradition in Eusebius (2.25), both died in
Rome at the same time.

The first persecution of Christians by the Roman government was conducted by Nero. When a fire swept through
Rome in 64, Nero was blamed for it. According to Tacitus
(*Annals* 15.44), Nero blamed it on the Christians in Rome and
tortured them cruelly. Tacitus states that Christians are
"criminals," "a class hated for their abominations," and that
Nero arrested those in Rome and convicted them "of hatred of
the human race." Why did Romans, including Tacitus, hate
the Christians? One clue is that both Tacitus and Suetonius
refer to Christianity as a "superstition." The belief in the
resurrection of the dead was mocked by some Greeks (Acts
17:32), and the beliefs in Jesus' resurrection and second coming would be viewed as superstition by educated Romans. Another clue may be the fact that the controversies between Jews

and Jewish-Christians created public disturbances which could
become so numerous that the emperor Claudius (41-54) expelled Jews (and Jewish-Christians) from Rome. But what
was the basis of the charge that Christians hated the human
race? Their denunciation of the immorality and idolatry of
many of their neighbors probably made them unpopular. Also,
Tacitus charged the Jews, too, with hating the human race,
and he connected it with their attitude toward Gentiles (Hist.
5.3-5). We know that Jewish exclusiveness created resentment in the Roman world, and Christian exclusiveness (the
teaching that only persons baptized in the name of Jesus Christ
are saved for eternity) may have offended the unpersuaded.

The original doubt of Christian loyalty to the state was
soon augmented by another cause: the refusal of Christians to
worship the goddess Roma, who personified the Roman nation,
and the emperors. That worship was not required of Jews,
for the Roman government's policy of religious tolerance ex-
empted them because of their monotheism. Christianity lost
that advantage after it began to separate from Judaism. Romans accused the Christians of being "atheists" because they
did not believe in the Roman gods.

Deification of emperors developed slowly. Hellenistic
kings in the regions which became Roman provices had long
been honored as gods, so it is not surprising that emperor
worship began there. While Octavian, or Augustus, was emperor (27 B.C.-A.D. 14), cities in all the provinces of the
empire voluntarily erected temples and altars for the worship
of Roma and Augustus. Octavian apparently did not seek the
honor and was not worshiped in Italy. Augustus was a title
conferred on him by the Senate; subsequent emperors kept the
title, and consequently were automatically deified in the provinces when Roma and Augustus were worshiped.

Gaius Caligula (37-41) eagerly claimed divinity for himself and sisters. He prescribed sacrifices to be offered to
himself, and asked that he be hailed as "Lord."

The title "Lord and God" was applied to the emperor
Domitian (81-96) by contemporary writers, and he seems to
have required the members of his official household to accord
him that title. The same title is given to Jesus in John 20:28.
Octavian, after his death, had been worshiped in Rome at the
Augustales established for the purpose. Domitian set up a

similar priestly college of the Flaviales for the worship of the
Flavian emperors, namely, his own deceased father, Vespa-
sian, and his deceased brother, Titus. Domitian's autocratic
policies led to a conspiracy in 89 to overthrow his rule. From
then on he persecuted all whom he suspected of disloyalty.
Pagan philosophers objected to emperor worshp, and Domitian
twice banished them from Rome. He persecuted the nobility
and evidently Christians too. In 96 Clement of Rome referred
to recent calamities which had befallen the church there. The
Epistle to the Hebrews probably was written by the church in
Alexandria to urge the church in Rome at the time to stand
firm and not commit apostasy to escape persecution. Hebrews
10:32-34 refers to an earlier persecution the church had suffered, which presumably was Nero's. Domitian was worshiped in Asia Minor, for a temple was built in Ephesus to
house his statue. Christians evidently were persecuted in
Asia Minor for not worshiping him, for Revelation was written
at this time to encourage churches there which were under attack.

While Trajan was emperor (98-117), Pliny the Younger,
his legate in the province of Bithynia and Pontus, wrote to him
to inquire how to treat the Christians there. Pliny reported
that he had asked them if they were Christians, and that if they
said they were, he asked twice more, threatening them with
punishment. If they persisted in affirming that they were
Christians, he ordered them to be executed, unless they were
Roman citizens, in which case he sent them to Rome to be
judged. (Paul, too, had been sent to Rome after he, as a Roman citizen, appealed to Caesar; see Acts 25). If they denied
that they were Christians, Pliny tested them by ordering them
to recite a prayer to the gods, make supplication with incense
and wine to Trajan's statue and images of the gods, and to
curse Christ—"things which (so it is said) those who are really
Christians cannot be made to do." In his reply, Trajan com-
mended Pliny and stated that, though Christians should not be
sought out, they should be punished if accused and convicted,
unless they denied they were Christians and proved it by "worshiping our gods." (Pliny, Epistles 10. 96,97). "Our gods"
undoubtedly were the state gods, Roma and the deified emperors, past and present. 1 Peter, written to encourage perse-

cuted Christians in Asia Minor, was probably written at this time, for Bithynia and Pontus are among the regions to which it is addressed, and as in Pliny, Christians are persecuted for the name of Christ (4:14). It was during Trajan's reign that Ignatius, bishop of Antioch, suffered martyrdom in Rome.

Christians responded to Roman persecution in two very different ways. One way was to comply, at least temporarily, with Roman demands. That situation is reflected in the references to those who have committed apostasy in times of tribulation (Heb. 6:6; Hermas, Parable 9.19, 21). Some writers urge their brethren to be submissive to rulers, including the emperor and his governors (1 Peter 2:13-14; Titus 3:1); they are even asked to "Honor the emperor" (1 Peter 2:17).

The opposite response was to stand firm, to remain faithful unto death. The author of Revelation commends various churches for their "patient endurance" and for not denying Jesus' name (1-3). The author of Hebrews urges his readers to "hold fast the confession of our hope without wavering" (10:23). Christians should endure the fiery ordeal because they will be rewarded (1 Pet. 4:12-14) when Jesus returns (Rev. 1:7; Heb. 10:25; 1 Pet. 5:10). Ignatius and some others even sought martyrdom because they believed that it insured their eternal salvation[51]. On the other hand, Christians are threatened with eternal punishment if they commit apostasy, for afterwards they cannot be restored to repentance (Heb. 6: 4-6). In the Shepherd of Hermas, however, repentance is allowed once—and only once—after baptism (Mandate 4.3).

Although Roman persecution caused Christianity to lose some members through apostasy and martyrdom, it also helped the church to grow. The courage with which some Christians endured pain and death attracted attention and aroused the admiration of many, as Tacitus admitted. Confident that they would soon be rewarded, martyrs faced death with calmness and joy, to the amazement of the gentile world. The church gained far more members than it lost.

CHAPTER 20

THE VALUE OF THE HISTORICAL APPROACH

The historical approach is now standard in all major colleges and universities which have courses pertaining to the Bible. It is virtually universal in mainline Jewish and Christian seminaries.

Nevertheless, the historical methods of studying the Bible are not generally known. One cause is that, unlike some ultra-conservative forms of Christian religion, this new knowledge has not been actively promoted in the media, and most churches and synagogues have not adequately conveyed it to their laymen. A second reason that knowledge of the historical approach has not reached the general public is that conservative religious leaders have aggressively opposed it.

Opposition to the Historical Approach

Throughout the history of the historical approach there has been strong opposition to its principles and methods. The record of hostility to its pioneers demonstrates the high price of progress. A long list could be compiled of scholars who suffered because of their honest efforts to advance intelligent understanding of the Bible. The treatment they have received has ranged from burning at the stake to dismissal from the clergy or professorship to denunciation and name-calling. John Haley in the nineteenth century supplied a good example of a bad practice; he charged that those persons who say that there are discrepancies in the Bible are "infidels."[52] After biblical research became centered in universities, conservative theologians tried to control the universities, and were critical of them when they could not dominate them. Today fundamentalism is the only major theological movement which rejects the historical approach almost completely. Other religious conservatives tend to oppose or at least not use those parts of it which lead to unorthodox conclusions.

Sometimes only a slightly unconventional application of

the historical approach aroused a lot of opposition, sometimes
from unexpected quarters. Edgar J. Goodspeed reported: "I
set forth an American translation [of the Bible], in 1923, and
was amazed at the storm of condemnation it incurred. Not
from my colleagues, or the clergy, but from newspaper editors all over the country, who had not noticed what had been
going on, and really thought nothing of significance had been
learned about the Bible since the King James Bible had made
its appearance three centuries before."[53]

Why have theological conservatives tended to oppose the
historical approach, or at least some essential elements of it?
The primary cause is fear—fear of its effects. The fear is
based on the belief that either the Bible itself or tradition
closely related to it is THE authority in religion. Therefore
whenever the historical approach upsets traditional interpretation of the Bible, it appears to be an evil which is undermining
the very foundation of religion. The tension between scholars
who want to pursue research, regardless of where it leads,
and those who fear the consequences, was epitomized in the
controversy between two famous textual critics of the nineteenth century, Westcott and Hort. Although they were inti-
mate friends, they disagreed strongly on this matter. While
the two men were collaborating in research on the text of the
New Testament, the timid Westcott became worried lest their
findings might weaken orthodox faith in the nature of divine
revelation. In 1860 he wrote to Hort for assurance that their
research would not lead to that result. Hort, however, replied that unless he was allowed to have complete intellectual
freedom, he would withdraw from the work. Westcott yield-
ed, and the two friends continued their project.[54] Intellectual
progress in religion comes from Hort's attitude, not from
Westcott's.

Detailed examination of fundamentalism and traditional
Jewish and Christian doctrines is outside the scope of this book.
We have not ignored them, however, because their advocates'
opposition to full study of the Bible has been a large factor in
hindering the development of the historical approach. Because
it has been so zealouly promoted by means of radio, television,
newspaper advertising, tracts, books, and the founding of
many sects, a few remarks about fundamentalism are in order.

The present writer was formerly a fundamentalist. In the interest of understanding we should recognize that both fundamentalists and historians are usually sincere. Biblical scholars are motivated by the ideal that religion should stand for truth. God and religion are intimately connected with "truth" in both the Old and New Testaments. We should remember, too, that religion is bigger than the Bible and is not dependent upon the truth of all or any part of it; above all, religion does not depend on the truth of every word of the Bible.

The Bible itself refutes the fundamentalist view of it. That the Bible contains errors and inconsistencies cannot be denied. And nowhere does the Bible state that we must believe every word of it. Such belief is not even included in its statements of what is vital in religion. According to the synoptic gospels, Jesus regarded the Two Commandments, the Decalogue, and giving to the poor as basic religion (Mark 10:17-21; 12:28-34). Matthew 5:17-19 and Luke 16:17 uphold the permanence of even details of the law, and have been used to defend the doctrine of the inerrancy of Scripture. The passages are weak support, for three reasons. First, they refer to only a portion of the Bible, the law, or Torah. Second, they probably originated in the church to defend the orthodox Jewish-Christian position that all Christians should continue to obey that law, in opposition to the view of Paul and his churches. Third, in the same chapter of Matthew (5:31-39) Jesus explicitly disagreed with three passages in the law (Deut. 24:1-4; Lev. 19:12; Exod. 21:24). If Jesus spoke these words, he certainly was not a fundamentalist! If he did not, the fact remains that one major section of the Bible, the Sermon on the Mount, specifically and intentionally rejects three passages in another major section, the law. Clearly the fundamentalist view cannot stand in the light of the testimony of the Bible itself, and should not be allowed to stand in the way of applying the historical approach. Growth from fundamentalism to a more mature understanding of the Bible and religion can be a painful personal experience, but it is well worth the cost.

Value of the Historical Approach

The numerous beneficial effects of the use of the histori-

cal approach to the Bible flow especially from two of its inherent characteristics. First, it is intellectually honest. Its
foundation is a sincere desire to understand the Bible more
accurately and a willingness to change interpretation of it in
the light of evidence. Second, it is self-correcting. It consists of scientific, historical methods which, when applied
more fully and more thoroughly, correct its earlier mistakes.
Thus it contains a built-in check against error, provided the
check is eventually used.

1. The most obvious beneficial effect is that the historical approach promotes understanding of the Bible. It achieves
this by studying the whole book—not just selected passages—,
by using historical methods, and by interpreting the Bible in
relation to its total environment, which automatically produces
a fuller understanding than any narrow approach. Such information can make the Bible "come to life." In the 1860s J. B.
Lightfoot's Cambridge University lectures on Galations were
enthusiastically received by students because Lightfoot introduced Paul's historical situation. In the past many important
passages were ignored because they did not support traditional doctrines; study of the whole Bible brings them into view.

The historical approach corrects past misinterpretation
of the Bible. Many examples could be given; these three are
major misunderstandings of its text. (a) The expectation that
Jesus will return in the twentieth century was based on a misunderstanding of many passages. More careful study demonstrated that New Testament writers expected his return in the
first or second century, not the twentieth. (b) Misunderstanding of the origin of John 8:44-47 caused Christians to think that
Jesus taught that Jews were sons of the devil and not of God,
and therefore Jews did not believe Jesus. Historical study
shows that the saying originated, not with Jesus, but with the
gentile-Christian author of John in the heat of the controversy
between Jews and Christians. (c) Misunderstanding of the
nature and origin of the Gospel of John also led to the belief
that Jesus taught that one must believe on him (John 8:24).
This passage conflicts with the synoptic gospels, where Jesus
never makes a statement of that type, and he even objects to
being called "good" (Mark 10:18). This synoptic tradition was
ignored; the origin of John's traditions in a Hellenistic church

was unknown; consequently, many people were taught that they were damned if they did not believe that Jesus was the Son of God. All three of these misunderstandings of the Bible have caused much ill will and tragedy in this world.

The historical approach has given many new insights into the nature and meaning of the Bible. These include recognition of the variety in it, the exact meaning of words and verses, the Bible's involvement with its environment, and its relation to the religious communities which produced it.

2. A second benefit derived from the historical approach is recognition of the fact that the book reflects intellectual and moral struggles which occurred within Judaism and Christianity. The belief that the Bible is a unity obscured this fact. The historical approach has disclosed that these struggles constitute one cause of the Bible's variety. Whereas the Pentateuch generally stresses the importance of sacrifices, Amos emphasized justice and righteousness, including fair treatment of the poor. In contrast to Ezra and Nehemiah's narrowness and intolerance of Gentiles, Second Isaiah and Jonah tried to move Judaism in the direction of internationalism. Contrast these two statements:

> When the Lord your God brings you into the land
> which you are entering to take possession of it, and
> clears away many nations before you, . . . and
> you defeat them; then you must utterly destroy
> them; you shall make no covenant with them, and
> show no mercy to them (Deut. 7:1-2).

> I will give you [Israel; verses 4-6b were inserted
> later] as a light to the nations, that my salvation
> may reach to the end of the earth (Isa. 49:6c).

If we try to make those statements agree with each other, we fail to grasp what was going on in Israel. Paul and his followers tried to free gentile Christians from observance of the Jewish law; orthodox Jewish Christians disagreed. The Christology of the author of the Gospel of John is incompatible with that of the synoptic gospels. Recognition of the intellectual conflicts gives us a far better understanding of the Bible.

3. The historical approach assists us in evaluating the teaching in the Bible so that we may select and apply that which is useful in a modern world. When we understand what a passage meant when it was written and for what historical situation it was intended, we are in a better position to judge its value today. If anyone thinks we should apply all of the Bible today, let him or her explain why we are not offering burnt sacrifices. Even in biblical times, evaluation and selection of Scripture was in progress. Often the conditions which produced the teaching ceased to exist later.

An important aspect of history to remember is the role played by controversy. Often a belief which originally was of secondary importance acquired primary importance later because there were disputes about it. Although Jesus probably believed that he was the Christ, that was not his main message, according to the synoptic gospels. But later the belief in Jesus' messiahship became THE basic Christian belief because Jews and Christians engaged in heated arguments about it. Similarly, later the Apostles' Creed omitted the ethics which originally were essential in Christianity, while it is concerned exclusively with defending beliefs which were being challenged. As a result of controversy, beliefs that are being argued about because their foundations are shaky, can be exalted above more important beliefs on which there is agreement! The more someone disagrees with us, the more important our beliefs seem to us—unfortunately.

4. The historical approach furnishes an incentive for further thorough research on the Bible and also on the history of religion. It encourages persons to really investigate instead of merely looking for evidence to "confirm" the Bible. The more we investigate historically, the more we realize that much remains to be discovered. After encountering the historical approach, many students have been induced to continue and become biblical scholars or historians of the ancient world.

5. A fifth value of the historical approach, closely related to the second, is that it greatly increases our understanding of history. It accomplishes this in two ways. Formerly some biblical narratives, descriptions, and sayings which are not historical were accepted at face value, thus producing a distorted view of history. Historical study exposes the real

nature of that material, so that we no longer accept as history some events that never happened and speeches that were never uttered. The second way that the historical approach has enlarged our knowledge of history is by providing information about the Bible's environment and background. With the aid of ancient literature, archaeology, and a more careful study of the Bible, we now have a more accurate understanding of what has actually happened in the past. By combining information from outside the Bible with evidence in it, we can reconstruct the early history of Jews and Christians, and we can see some of the interrelationships between their history and that of their neighbors. Our knowledge of secular history and especially of the history of religion has expanded enormously as historical study advanced.

6. Another virtue of the historical approach is that, in the long run, it decreases the tensions and ill will created by past misunderstanding of and divergent attitudes toward the Bible. Overemphasis on the importance of Scripture and the multitude of misinterpretations of it led to controversies between Jews and Christians, controversies within each of those religions, controversies between them and the secular world, and the formation of divisive sects and denominations. Historical study discloses that usually the issues were not that important, and often both sides were wrong anyway.

Historians believe that truth matters and therefore accurate interpretation of the Bible is important, but they do not feel that eternal life and death depend on biblical interpretation. Consequently, they tend to be tolerant and to favor ecumenism. This spirit extends to other religions and to secularism. Sometimes historians personally disagree with each other, but so far they have not burned each other at the stake as a result. The joint annual meetings of the American Academy of Religion and the Society of Biblical Literature, where Jews, Catholics, Protestants, members of other world religions, and independent secular scholars meet, is a model. They read papers to each other, respond to questions and criticisms afterwards, and demonstrate the congenial atmosphere that scholarship can create.

7. The historical approach to the Bible reduces the artificial wall between religion and secularism, a wall which nev-

er should have been constructed. A clear distinction between religion and secularism does not exist in the Bible, as historical study reveals. And neither is there a clear distinction between them today. Religion always has acquired information, ideas, and ethics from the secular world. Laws purported to have been received from the gods Yahweh and Shamash actually originated in the daily living of the people. A serious mistake made in modern times has been to imagine that the Bible must be unique and that a biblical ethic is of less value if it occurred also outside the Bible. The ethical importance of thoughts and motives, for example, is not lessened by the fact that it is found in ancient Greek philosophy (p. 280 above) as well as in the Bible (Ps. 19:14; Matt. 5:28). Secular knowledge has made many valuable contributions to the understanding of the Bible. Secularism is not an enemy; contrary to gnostic thought, "the world" is not inherently evil.

8. The most important benefit contributed by the historical approach is that it opens the way for the development of a more mature type of religion. Little growth could occur in this field while mankind was chained to the past and—worse yet—to erroneous ideas about the past. We must outgrow the notion that religion simply must be based on the Bible and only the Bible, for the notion retards the development of religion. To confine religion to the Bible is a case of thinking "too small." Religion deserves a broader base than that. The Bible can and should continue to contribute to religion, but it should not be allowed to inhibit progress.

We should not be disturbed by the idea that religion can and should change. All religions have changed very much in the past, including Judaism and Christianity. All other fields of culture have changed—why should religion be an exception? In what condition would we be today if we insisted that medicine be practiced just the way it was two millennia ago?

The historical approach frees our minds for intellectual progress in religion. With the Bible viewed in proper perspective, insights from it, other religions, ethics, psychology, and sociology can be combined to elevate the quality of religion so that religion can make greater contributions to the welfare of mankind.

NOTES

1. "Law" is the traditional English translation of the Hebrew word *torah*, but a more accurate translation is "instruction."

2. Tindal cited 1 Cor. 10:11; Rom. 13:11-12; Heb. 9:26; Jas. 5: 7-9; 1 John 2:18; 2 Pet. 3:12-13. He could have included 1 Cor. 16: 22; 1 Thess. 1:10; Rev. 22:20.

3. K. Barth, *The Epistle to the Romans*, p. 452.

4. P. Minear, *The Eyes of Faith*, p. 3.

5. In *The Journal of Bible and Religion* 28 (1960):197.

6. *CHB* [*The Cambridge History of the Bible*], vol. 1, p. 522; vol. 2, p. 108.

7. *CHB*, vol. 2, p. 388.

7a. The first serious study of the possibility that Hellenistic mystery religions may have influenced early Christianity was made by Isaac Casaubon, a Swiss classical scholar, while living in England (1614). He zealously opposed the sacramentalism of the Roman Catholic Church as derived from the mystery religions.

8. Cited from W. G. Kümmel, *The New Testament: The History of the Investigation of Its Problems*, p. 68.

9. E. G. Kraeling, *The Old Testament since the Reformation*, p. 54.

9a. In 1775 J. C. Doederlein, like Ibn Ezra in the 12th century, concluded that Isaiah 1-39 was written by a different author than was the rest of Isaiah.

10. Cited from Kümmel, op. cit., p. 79.

11. Ibid., p. 59.

12. Claus Westermann, in *Essays on Old Testament Hermeneutics*, ed. by C. Westermann, p. 41, n. 2.

13. A. Schweitzer, *The Quest of the Historical Jesus*, pp. 13-14.

14. Cited from Kümmel, op. cit., p. 81.

15. Ibid., p. 68.

16. A. Deissmann, *Bibelstudien*, p. 60; ET by H. Teeple.

17. J. Coppens, *The Old Testament and the Critics*, p. 10.

18. Cited from Kümmel, op. cit., p. 111.

19. W. R. Smith, *Lectures on the Religion of the Semites*, p. 4.

20. Kümmel, op. cit., p. 303.

20a. Gesenius used the history-of-religions approach to make an important contribution to Hebrew lexicology. He used Phoenician and Aramaic words in ancient inscriptions and literature to determine the meaning of similar terms in the Hebrew Scriptures.

21. Cited from Kümmel, op. cit., pp. 223-24.

22. Ibid., p. 225.

22a. Bultmann concluded that a Passion source also was used in chapters 18-20. Fortna and Teeple concluded that this material is mostly a portion of the Gospel of Signs source.

23. In *The Journal of Bible and Religion* 28 (1960):195.

24. In *Journal of Biblical Literature* 57 (1960):366.

25. See E. Käsemann, "The Problem of the Historical Jesus," in his *Essays on New Testament Themes*, pp. 15-47, and "Blind Alleys in the 'Jesus of History' Controversy," in his *New Testament Questions of Today*, pp. 23-65, especially p. 64.

26. N. Perrin, *Rediscovering the Religion of Jesus*, p. 233.

27. E. C. Colwell, *The Study of the Bible*, p. 104.

28. C. H. Talbert, *What Is a Gospel?*

29. H. M. Teeple, "Early Jewish-Christian Writing," *The Journal of Bible and Religion* 28 (1957):301-305.

30. R. H. Pfeiffer, *Introduction to the Old Testament*, rev. ed., p. 462.

31. R. Knierim, "Old Testament Form Criticism Reconsidered," *Interpretation* 27 (1973):435-67; D. A. Knight, "The Understanding of *'Sitz im Leben'* in Form Criticism," *Society of Biblical Literature Seminar Papers*, 1974, vol. 1, pp.105-25. See also the articles, with bibliographies, :Form Criticism, OT," and "Form Criticism, NT," in *IDB [The Interpreter's Dictionary of the Bible]*, Sup.

32. M. Burrows, *What Mean These Stones?*, p. 276.

33. Ibid., pp. 1-6.

34. See "Habiru" in *IDB*, Sup.

34a. 2 Cor. 11:24-25; Acts 6:9-14; 7:57-8:3; 13:45-50; 14:5,19; 17:5-7; 18:12; 21:27-31; 22:22; 23:12-15: Luke 6:23. Josephus (*Antiquities* 20.9.1) reports that the high priest Ananus had James, the brother of Jesus, stoned to death. Eusebius (*Hist. Eccl.* 2.23), quoting Hegesippus (an unreliable account), states that the "scribes and Pharisees" threw James down from a wall, then stoned him. Justin (*1 Apology* 31) reports that Simon Bar Kochba ordered that Christians be given cruel punishments if they would not deny that Jesus was the Christ. Antagonism between him and the Christians was inevitable, for he claimed that he was the Christ.

Persecution of apostles by Gentiles: Acts 12:1-5; 14:5; 16:19-24; 19:29; 21:33.

35. 2 Esdras 7:27; 2 Baruch 29:6-8.

35a. The Essenes at Qumran practised ritual bathings which "cleansed the flesh," while the Holy Spirit cleansed their souls and atoned for their sins (1QS 3:6-9). The spiritual cleansing was made possible by the repentance of the individual, not by the baptism. This was the case with John the Baptist's baptism too: "He [John] commanded the Jews to practice virtue, both as to righteousness toward one another and piety toward God [i.e., the Two Commandments], and so to come to baptism; for the washing would be acceptable to God if they used it not for the remission of sins, but for the purification of the body, assuming that the soul was thoroughly purified beforehand by righteousness" (Josephus, *Ant.* 18.5.2). In primitive Christianity, as in Judaism, repentance, not baptism, was the means to obtain God's forgiveness of sins (Acts 2:38). But later in Christianity baptism itself became the means (Acts 22:16; cf. discussion of baptism in our chapter 19).

The Essenes did not claim that baptism conferred the Spirit, and neither did John (Mark 1:8; John 1:33; Acts 19:2-3). The Essenes believed that on the last day before the new age, God will sprinkle his Spirit of truth on the Essenes to cleanse them and give them knowledge of himself (1QS 4:20-22). The early Christians applied this belief to themselves; the ultimate source for both groups was the prophecy in Joel 2, quoted in Acts 2. That belief, combined with the use of baptism as an initiation ritual, created the Jewish-Christian notion that baptism was the means of receiving the Spirit. Baptism was an initiation ceremony with the Pharisees, who baptized proselytes, and in some pagan mystery cults. The Jewish-Christian logic for introducing the idea that baptism conferred the Spirit must have been as follows: The last days are here and God is pouring out his Spirit on Christians, for we are the righteous remnant with whom God has made a new covenant; therefore the time when persons receive the Spirit is when they become Christians by being baptized.

36. See Carl Kraeling, *Anthropos*.

37. 1 Enoch 46:1-48:7; 62:2-63:12; 69:26-71:17.

38. Philo, *On Special Laws* 1. 65.

39. See H. M. Teeple, *The Mosaic Eschatological Prophet*.

40. See W. D. Davies, *Torah in the Messianic Age and/or the Age to Come*.

41. Although the prevailing view among scholars has been that Christian gnosticism grew out of Jewish gnosticism, very strong evidence indicates that the source was paganism and that Jewish gnosticism probably never existed: (1) The gnostic type of dualism between the spiritual and material worlds is an utter reversal of the Jewish thought of the day. It is improbable that beliefs so contrary to both Judaism and Christianity would suddenly become so prevalent in Christianity if Judaism were the source. Considering the wide expansion of Christianity among Gentiles in the second century, the rapid growth of Christian gnosticism is plausible if that philosophy's basic tenet was already present in paganism. Some biblical scholars tried in vain to relate gnosticism to the Dead Sea scrolls. The dualism of the Essenes was between truth and error, or light and darkness, but not between flesh and spirit. Unlike the gnostics, the Essenes did not regard flesh as inherently evil. (2) The parallels to Christian-gnostic dualism are found in pagan, not Jewish, literature. Some roots of gnosticism are in Platonism and Orphism, religious philosophies which taught that the soul is imprisoned in the body. Astralism is the source of the gnostic belief that demonic "archons" rule the planets. Gnosticism also has affinities with the Egyptian Hermetic religion. (3) The gnostics were hostile to virtually all aspects of Judaism: its God, its Scriptures, its people. Some pagans had become acquainted with Judaism; a few liked it, but many did not. A conjectural effort has been made to explain gnostic hostility to Judaism by assuming that the gnostics were a heretical Jewish sect. This conjecture is implausible, for even heretics usually retain some aspects of their former religion. (4) The gnostic use of Jewish materials has misled some biblical scholars into thinking that there was a Jewish gnosticism. Actually, gnostics revised the Jewish creation story and used other Jewish literature to discredit Judaism and promote their own beliefs. The use of an orthodox Jewish poem in the Christian gnostic hymn incorporated in the Prologue of the Gospel of John (see above, p. 122) has been misleading because scholars did not recognize that the Jewish features came from a different source than the gnostic features.

42. Even though the Son of Man sayings are in the third person, they definitely refer to Jesus. There are two basic reasons for believing that Jesus did not utter them: (1) It is improbable that a sane man would believe that he was the supernatural Son of Man who existed in heaven from the time of the beginning of the universe. (2) The sayings fit the situation in the early church (and hence originated there) when there was a crucial Christian need to demonstrate that Jesus was the Messiah who would come down from heaven. See H. M. Teeple, "The Origin of the Son of Man Christology," *Journal of Biblical Literature* 84 (1965):213-50.

43. See Adolf Deissmann, *Licht vom Osten*, 4th ed. (1923), p. 231.

44. Whether Jesus baptized or not is uncertain, but possible.
According to Matthew 3:2 and 4:17 John and Jesus preached the same
basic message, and in John's case, at least, baptism and the message
belonged together. According to John 3:22 and 4:1 Jesus baptized, but
later a scribe contradicted those verses by inserting 4:2.

45. Justin, *1 Apology* 61; Tertullian, *On Baptism* 5.

46. The explanation of the discrepancy in the Gospel of John between Jesus as the son of Joseph and Jesus as the incarnated Word is
that the author incorporated several sources which did not agree with
each other in Christology. Jesus is the son of Joseph in the Gospel
of Signs source (1:45; 6:42 is the author's own composition), but he
is the Word, the only-begotten of the Father, in the gnostic-Christian
hymn used in the Prologue.

47. Cited from Stephen L. Caiger, *Archaeology and the New Testament*, p. 169. For various pagan parallels to the canonical gospels,
see David L. Dungan and David R. Cartlidge, *Sourcebook of Texts for
the Comparative Study of the Gospels*.

48. In Abraham J. Festugière, "À Propos des Arétalogies d'Isis,"
Harvard Theological Review 42 (1949):209-234.

50. Cf. David L. Tiede, *The Charismatic Figure as Miracle Worker*.

51. A view clearly expressed in the Shepherd of Hermas, Parable
9.28.

52. John W. Haley, *An Examination of the Alleged Discrepancies
of the Bible*, p. x.

53. Cited from Balmer H. Kelly and Donald G. Miller, *Tools for
Bible Study*, p. 122.

54. Stephen Neill, *Interpretation of the New Testament: 1861-
1961*, p. 89.

BIBLIOGRAPHY

This bibliography is limited to pioneering works which contributed to the development of the historical approach to the Bible. Many of them contain some mistaken ideas, but all led biblical interpretation in the right direction in at least one important respect.

Abelard, Peter. Sic et Non [So and Not (So)]. 12th century.

Aland, Kurt, ed. Synopsis Quattuor Evangeliorum [Synopsis of the Four Gospels]. Stuttgart, 1964.

-----, ed. Vollständige Konkordanz zum griechischen Neuen Testament [A Complete Concordance to the Greek New Testament]. 2 vols. Berlin and New York, 1974-

Albright, William Foxwell. The Archaeology of Palestine. Harmondsworth (Eng.), 1949. Rev. ed., 1956.

Alt, Albrecht. Israel und Ägypten. Die politischen Beziehungen der Könige von Israel und Juda zu den Pharaonen [Israel and Egypt. The Political Relations of the Kings of Israel and Judah to the Pharaohs]. (BWANT 6) Leipzig, 1909.

Apostolic Fathers. The Apostolic Fathers. Tr. by Kirsopp Lake. (Loeb Classical Library) 2 vols. London/New York, 1912-13.

-----. The Apostolic Fathers: A New Translation and Commentary. Ed. by R. M. Grant. 6 vols. New York, 1964-68.

Astruc, Jean. Conjectures sur les Mémoires originaux dont il paroît que Moyse s'est servi pour composer le Livre de la Genese [Conjectures on the Original Memoirs which It Appears that Moses Used to Compose the Book of Genesis]. Paris, 1753.

Aune, David Edward. Early Christian Prophecy. Grand Rapids, 1982.

Auriol, Pierre. Compendium litteralis sensus totius sacrae scripturae [A Compendium of the Literal Sense of All Holy Scripture]. 1319.

Baly, Denis. The Geography of the Bible. 2d ed. New York, 1974.

Barrett, Charles K. The Holy Spirit and the Gospel Tradition. London, 1954.

-----, ed. The New Testament Background: Selected Documents. London, 1956.

Bauer, Bruno. Kritik der Evangelien und Geschichte ihres Ursprungs [Criticism of the Gospels and a History of Their Origin]. 2 vols. Berlin, 1850-51.

Bauer, Georg Lorenz. Entwurf einer Hermeneutik des Alten und Neuen Testaments [Sketch of a Hermeneutic of the Old and New Testaments]. Leipzig, 1799.

-----. Hebräische Mythologie des alten und neuen Testaments, mit Parallelen aus der Mythologie anderer Völker, vornehmlich der Griechen und Römer [Hebrew Mythology of the Old and New Testaments, with Parallels from the Mythology of Other Peoples, especially the Greeks and Romans]. Leipzig, 1802.

Bauer, Walter. A Greek-English Lexicon of the New Testament and Other Early Christian Literature. 2d ed. ET and revision by F. W. Gingrich and F. W. Danker of Bauer's 5th German ed. (1958). Chicago, 1979.

Baur, Ferdinand Christian. "Die Christuspartei in der korinthischen Ge-
meinde, . . . " [The Christ Party in the Corinthian Community, . . .].
In Tübinger Zeitschrift für Theologie 4 (1831):61 ff.

-----. Kritische Untersuchungen über die kanonischen Evangelien, ihr Verhältnis zueinander, ihren Charakter und Ursprung [Critical Investigations
about the Canonical Gospels, Their Relation to One Another, Their Character and Origin]. Tübingen, 1847.

-----. Die sogenannten Pastoralbriefe des Apostels Paulus aufs neue kritisch
untersucht [The So-called Pastoral Letters of the Apostle Paul again
Critically Examined]. Stuttgart and Tübingen, 1835.

Bengel, Johann Albrecht. Gnomon Novi Testamenti [Guide to the New Testa-
ment]. Ulm, 1742. 2d ed., 1763.

-----. Novum Testamentum Graecum . . . [Greek New Testament . . .].
Tübingen, 1734.

Betz, Hans Dieter. Galatians: A Commentary on Paul's Letter to the Churches
in Galatia. Philadelphia, 1979.

-----, ed. Plutarch's Ethical Writings and Early Christian Literature.
(SCHNT 4) Leiden, 1978.

-----, ed. Plutarch's Theological Writings and Early Christian Literature.
(SCHNT 3) Leiden, 1975.

Bewer, Julius A. The Literature of the Old Testament in Its Historical
Development. New York, 1922. 3d ed., rev. by E. G. Kraeling. New
York, 1963.

Bible. English. 1382. The Byble in Englyshe. Tr. by John Wycliffe. 1382.
[a manuscript Bible]

-----. English. 1611. The Holy Bible . . . London, 1611. [Authorized
Version]

-----. English. Revised. 1885. The Holy Bible, . . . Oxford, 1885.
[Revised Version]

-----. English. Revised Standard. 1973. The New Oxford Annotated Bible
with the Apocrypha. Revised Standard Version, Containing the 2d ed. of
the New Testament. Ed. by H. G. May and B. M. Metzger. New York,
1973.

-----. Old Testament. Hebrew. Biblica Hebraica. Ed. by Rudolf Kittel.
[periodically revised since]

-----. New Testament. Greek. Novum Testamentum Graece. 26th ed.
Rev. by Erwin Nestle and Kurt Aland. Stuttgart, 1979.

-----. New Testament. Polyglott. Nouum Instrumentu omne, . . . [The
Whole New Document, . . .]. 2 vols. Basil, 1516. [Greek & Latin]

-----. New Testament. Gospels. Harmonies. English. A Harmonie upon
the three Evangelists, Matthew, Mark and Luke, with the Commentarie
of M. Iohn Caluine [John Calvin]: faithfullie translated . . . by E. P.
[Eusebius Pagit]. London, 1584.

-----. New Testament. John. German. 1941. Bultmann. Das Evangelium
des Johannes [The Gospel of John]. Göttingen, 1941. ET of 17th ed.
(1963): The Gospel of John: A Commentary. Philadelphia, 1971.

-----. New Testament. Acts. Greek. 1920. The Beginnings of Christianity:
Part I, The Acts of the Apostles, ed. by F. J. Foakes-Jackson and Kir-

sopp Lake. 5 vols. London, 1920-33.

-----. New Testament. Epistles. Greek. 1935. A Third-century Papyrus
Codex of the Epistles of Paul, ed. by Henry A. Sanders. Ann Arbor, 1935.

-----. New Testament. Apocryphal books. English. 1924. The Apocryphal
New Testament, being the Apocryphal Gospels, Acts, Epistles and Apoca-
lypses with other Narratives and Fragments, newly tr. by Montagu R.
James. Oxford, 1924. Rev. ed., 1953.

-----. New Testament. Apocryphal books. English. 1963. New Testament
Apocrypha, by Edgar Hennecke. 3d ed. (1959) ed. by W. Schneemelcher.
ET rev. and ed. by R. McL. Wilson. 2 vols. London/Philadelphia,
1963-65.

Blackman, Edwin C. Marcion and His Influence. London, 1948.

Blair, Edward P. Jesus and the Gospel of Matthew. New York/Nashville,
1960.

Blass, Friedrich. Grammatik des neutestamentlichen Griechisch [Grammar
of New Testament Greek]. 4th ed., rev. by A. Debrunner. Göttingen,
1913. Eng. tr. and rev. of 9th/10th ed. by R. A. Funk: A Greek Grammar
of the New Testament and Other Early Christian Literature. Chicago,
1961.

Bornkamm, Günther, and others. Tradition and Interpretation in Matthew.
London/Philadelphia, 1963.

Bousset, (Johann Franz) Wilhelm. Die Hauptprobleme der Gnosis [The Major
Problems of Gnosis]. Göttingen, 1907.

-----. Kyrios Christos: Geschichte des Christusglaubens von den Anfängen
des Christentums bis Irenaeus [Lord Christ: The History of Christology
from the Beginnings of Christianity to Irenaeus]. Göttingen, 1913. ET
of 5th German ed.: Nashville, 1970.

Brandon, Samuel S. F. The Fall of Jerusalem and the Christian Church: A
Study of the Effects of the Jewish Overthrow of A.D. 70 on Christianity.
London, 1951. 2d ed., 1957.

-----. Jesus and the Zealots: A Study of the Political Factor in Primitive
Christianity. New York, 1967.

Breasted, James Henry. The Dawn of Conscience. New York/London, 1933.

Bretschneider, Karl Gottlieb. Probabilia de evangelii et epistolarum Iohannis
apostoli indole et origine eruditorum iudiciis modeste subjecit [Proba-
bility concerning the Mode and Origin of the Gospel and Letters of the
Apostle John, modestly offered for the judgment of the learned].
Leipzig, 1820.

Briggs, Charles Augustus. The Higher Criticism of the Hexateuch. New
York, 1892.

-----. Messianic Prophecy. The Prediction of the Fulfilment of Redemption
through the Messiah, . . . Edinburgh, 1886.

Bright, John. A History of Israel. Philadelphia, 1959. 3d rev. ed., 1981.

Brown, Francis. Assyriology: Its Use and Abuse in Old Testament Study.
New York, 1885.

-----, Samuel R. Driver, and Charles A. Briggs. (see Gesenius, H. F. W.)

Brunetière, Ferdinand. L'évolution des genres dans l'histoire de la littérature [The Evolution of the Types in the History of Literature]. Paris,
1890.

Bultmann, Rudolf K. Die Geschichte der synoptischen Tradition [The History of the Synoptic Tradition]. Göttingen, 1921. ET of 3d ed.: New York/ Oxford, 1963.

-----. The Gospel of John. (see: Bible. New Testament. John. German. 1941. Bultmann)

-----. "Johannesevangelium." In: Religion in Geschichte und Gegenwart. 3d Aufl., vol. 3, pp. 840-50. Tübingen, 1957.

Burrows, Millar. The Dead Sea Scrolls. New York, 1955.

-----. More Light on the Dead Sea Scrolls. New York, 1958.

Buttmann, Alexander. Grammatik des neutestamentlichen Sprachgebrauchs [Grammar of New Testament Language-usage]. Berlin, 1859.

Cadbury, Henry J. The Peril of Modernizing Jesus. New York, 1937.

-----. The Style and Literary Method of Luke. Cambridge, MA, 1920.

Calmet, Augustin. Dictionnaire historique et critique, chronologique, géographique et littéral de la Bible [Historical and Critical, Chronological, Geographical and Literal Dictionary of the Bible]. 2 vols. Paris, 1722; Supplement, 1728.

Calvin, John. [commentaries on individual books of the Bible] 1540-64.

Camilo dos Santos, E. An Expanded Hebrew Index for the Hatch-Redpath Concordance to the Septuagint. Jerusalem, 1973.

Cappel, Louis [Capellus]. Critica Sacra [Sacred Criticism]. Paris, 1650.

Carlston, Charles E. The Parables of the Triple Tradition. Philadelphia, 1975.

Casaubon, Isaac. De rebus sacris et ecclesiasticis exercitationes XVI [Sixteen Exercises concerning Sacred and Ecclesiastical Matters]. London, 1614.

Case, Shirley Jackson. Experience with the Supernatural in Early Christian Times. New York, 1929.

Cassels, Walter Richard. Supernatural Religion: An Inquiry into the Reality of Divine Revelation. 3 vols. London, 1874-77.

Castelli, David. Il Messia secondo gli Ebrei [The Messiah according to the Hebrews]. Florence, 1874.

Charles, Robert H., ed. The Apocrypha and Pseudepigrapha of the Old Testament. 2 vols. Oxford, 1913.

Charlesworth, James H., ed. The Old Testament Pseudepigrapha. New York, 1982.

Cludius, Hermann Heimart. Uransichten des Christenthums nebst Untersuchungen über einige Bücher des Neuen Testaments [Primitive Perspectives of Christianity, together with Researches on a Few Books of the New Testament]. Altona, 1808.

Colenso, John William. The Pentateuch and the Book of Joshua Critically Examined. 2 vols. London, 1862-79.

Coleridge, Samuel Taylor. Confessions of an Inquiring Spirit. London, 1840.

Collins, Adela Yarbro. The Combat Myth in the Book of Revelation. (Harvard Diss. in Religion 9) Missoula, 1976.

Collins, Anthony. Discourse of the Grounds and Reasons for the Christian Religion. London, 1724.

Colwell, Ernest C. The Greek of the Fourth Gospel. Chicago, 1931.

Conzelmann, Hans. The Theology of St Luke. Tr. from 2d German ed. London/New York, 1960.

Cook, Michael J. Mark's Treatment of the Jewish Leaders. (NovTSup 51) Leiden, 1978.

Crenshaw, James L., ed. Studies in Ancient Israelite Wisdom. New York, 1975.

Cross, Frank Moore. Canaanite Myth and Hebrew Epic: Essays in the History of the Religion of Israel. Cambridge, MA, 1973.

Cumont, Franz V. M. Les Religions orientales dans le paganisme romain [The Oriental Religions in Roman Paganism]. Paris, 1906. ET, 1911.

-----. Textes et monuments figurés relatifs aux mystères de Mithra [Texts and Figured Monuments pertaining to the Mysteries of Mithra]. 2 vols. Brussels, 1896-99.

Dautzenberg, G. Urchristliche Prophetie. Ihre Erforschung, ihre Voraussetzungen in Judentum und ihre Struktur im ersten Korintherbrief [Primitive Christian Prophecy: Its Investigation, Its Presuppositions, and Its Structure in 1 Corinthians]. Stuttgart, 1975.

Deissmann, Gustav Adolf. Bibelstudien [Bible Studies]. Marburg, 1895.

-----. Neue Bibelstudien [New Bible Studies]. Marburg, 1897. Combined ET: Bible Studies. Edinburgh, 1901.

-----. Licht vom Osten [Light from the East]. Tübingen, 1908. ET: Light from the Ancient East. London, 1910.

Descartes, René. Discours de la méthode [Discourse on Method]. Paris, 1637.

De Wette, Wilhelm M. L. Christliche Sittenlehre [Christian Ethics]. 2 vols. Berlin, 1819-23.

-----. Commentar über die Psalmen [Commentary on the Psalms]. Heidelberg, 1811

-----. Dissertatio Critica [Critical Dissertation]. Berlin, 1805.

-----. Lehrbuch der historisch kritischen Einleitung in die Bibel Alten und Neuen Testaments [Textbook of the Critical-historical Introduction to the Old and New Testaments in the Bible]. 2 vols. Berlin, 1817-26.

Dibelius, Martin. Aufsätze zur Apostelgeschichte [Essays on the Acts of the Apostles]. Göttingen, 1951. ET: London/New York, 1956.

-----. Die Formgeschichte des Evangeliums [The Form-history of the Gospel]. Tübingen, 1919. ET of 2d ed.: From Tradition to Gospel. New York, 1935.

-----. Die urchristliche Überlieferung von Johannes dem Täufer untersucht [The Primitive Christian Tradition about John the Baptist Investigated]. Göttingen, 1911.

Dieterich, Albrecht. Abraxas. Studien zur Religionsgeschichte des spätern Altertums [Abraxas. Studies in the History of Religion in Late Antiquity]. Leipzig, 1891.

-----. Eine Mithrasliturgie erläutert [A Mithras Liturgy Explained]. Leipzig, 1903.

Dittenberger, Wilhelm. Sylloge Inscriptionum Graecarum [A Collection of Greek Inscriptions]. 3d ed. 4 vols. Leipzig, 1915-24.

Dodd, Charles H. The Apostolic Preaching and Its Developments. London, 1936. 2d ed., 1944.

-----. The Bible and the Greeks. London, 1935.

Dölger, Franz Joseph. IXΘYC: Der heilige Fisch in den antiken Religionen und im Christentum [Ichthus (Fish): The Sacred Fish in Ancient Religions and in Christianity]. 3 vols. Münster, 1922-28.

Driver, Samuel Rolles. An Introduction to the Literature of the Old Testament. Edinburgh, 1891.

-----. A Treatise on the Use of the Tenses in Hebrew. Oxford, 1866.
[see Gesenius, H. F. W., for Hebrew lexicon Driver co-authored]

Duhm, Bernard. Das Buch Jeremia [The Book of Jeremiah]. Tübingen, 1901.

-----. Das Buch Jesaja [The Book of Isaiah]. Göttingen, 1892.

-----. Die Psalmen [The Psalms]. Tübingen, 1899.

-----. Die Theologie der Propheten als Grundlage für die innere Entwicklungsgeschichte der israelitischen Religion dargestellt [The Theology of the Prophets Presented as the Foundation for the Inner Historical Development of the Israelite Religion]. Bonn, 1875.

Dungan, David L., and David R. Cartlidge. Sourcebook of Texts for the Comparative Study of the Gospels. (Sources for Biblical Study 1) 3d ed. Missoula, 1973.

Edwards, Richard A. A Concordance to Q. (Sources for Biblical Study 7) Missoula, 1975.

-----. A Theology of Q: Eschatology, Prophecy, and Wisdom. Philadelphia, 1976.

Eichhorn, Albert. "Das Abendmahl im Neuen Testament" [The Lord's Supper in the New Testament]. Christliche Welt, sup. 36. Leipzig, 1898.

Eichhorn, Johann Gottfried. Allgemeine Bibliotek der biblischen Litteratur [Universal Library of Biblical Literature]. 10 vols. Leipzig, 1787-1801.

-----. Einleitung in das Alte Testament [Introduction to the Old Testament]. 3 vols. Leipzig, 1780-83.

-----. Einleitung in das Neue Testament [Introduction to the New Testament]. 2 vols. Leipzig, 1804-12.

-----. Einleitung in die apokryphischen Bücher des Alten Testament [Introduction to the Apocryphal Books of the Old Testament]. Leipzig, 1795.

Eichrodt, Walther. Theologie des Alten Testaments [Theology of the Old Testament]. Leipzig, 1933. ET of 6th ed.: London/Philadelphia, 1961.

Eissfeldt, Otto. The Old Testament: An Introduction. Tr. from the 3d German ed. (1964). New York, 1965.

Elijah Ben Asher, the Levite. Masoret Ha-Masorete [The Transmission of the Transmitted (Text)]. Venice, 1538.

Ellison, John W., comp. Nelson's Complete Concordance of the Revised Standard Version Bible. New York, 1957.

Encyclopedia of Archaeological Excavations in the Holy Land. Ed. by M. Avi-Yonah. 4 vols. Oxford/Englewood Cliffs, 1975-78.

Erasmus, Desiderius. Enchiridion Militis Christiani [Manual for the Christian Soldier]. Antwerp, 1504.

-----. (see also: Bible. New Testament. Polyglot)

Ernesti, Johann August. Institutio interpretis Novi Testamenti [Principles of Interpretation of the New Testament]. Leipzig, 1761.

Evanson, Edward. The Dissonance of the Four Generally Received Evangel-

ists, and the Evidence of Their Respective Authenticity Examined.
Ipswich, 1792.

Everett, Edward. Defence of Christianity against the Work of George B.
English. Boston, 1814.

Everling, Otto. Die paulinische Angelologie und Dämonologie. Ein biblisch-
theologischer Versuch [The Pauline Angelology and Demonology; A
Biblical-theological Essay]. Göttingen, 1888.

Farnell, Lewis R. The Cults of the Greek States. 5 vols. Oxford, 1896-1909.

Farrar, Frederic W. History of Interpretation. London, 1886.

Faure, Alexander. "Die alttestamentlichen Zitate im 4. Evangelium und die
Quellenscheidungshypothese" [The Old Testament Quotations in the Fourth
Gospel and the Source-separation Hypothesis]. Zeitschrift für die Neu-
testamentliche Wissenschaft 21 (1922):99-121.

Finegan, Jack. Light from the Ancient Past: The Archaeological Background
of the Hebrew-Christian Religion. Princeton, 1946. 2d ed., 1959.

Fischer, L. R. Ras Shamra Parallels: Texts from Ugarit and the Hebrew
Bible. Vol. 2 (Analecta Orientalia 50) Rome, 1975.

Fitzmeyer, Joseph A. "Some Notes on Aramaic Epistolography." Journal
of Biblical Literature 93 (1974): 201-25.

Flacius (Illyricus), Matthias. Clavis Scripturae [Key to Scripture]. Basil,
1567.

Foakes-Jackson, Frederick J. (see: Bible. N. T. Acts. Greek. 1920)

Foerster, Werner. Gnosis: A Selection of Gnostic Texts. 2 vols. New
York, 1972-74.

Fortna, Robert T. The Gospel of Signs: A Reconstruction of the Narrative
Source Underlying the Fourth Gospel. (SNTSMS 11) Cambridge, 1970.

Fosdick, Harry Emerson. A Guide to Understanding the Bible: The Development of Ideas within the Old and New Testaments. New York/London,
1938.

Fox, Adam. Plato and the Christians. London, 1957.

Francis, Fred O., and J. Paul Sampley, eds. Pauline Parallels. (Sources
for Biblical Study 9) Philadelphia/Missoula, 1975.

Frassen, Claude. Disquisitiones biblicae [Biblical Inquiries]. Paris, 1682.

Friedländer, Moritz. Die religiösen Bewegungen innerhalb des judentums im
zeitalter Jesu [The Religious Movements within Judaism in the Time of
Jesus]. Berlin, 1905.

Funk, Robert A. (see: Blass, Friedrich)

Gabler, Johann Philipp. De justo discrimine theologiae biblicae et dogmaticae
regundisque recte utriusque finibus [On the Proper Distinction between
Biblical and Dogmatic Theology and the Correct Determination of the Goals
of Each]. Altdorf, 1787.

Gaster, Theodor H., ed. The Dead Sea Scriptures. 3d ed. Garden City, 1976.

Gesenius, Heinrich Friedrich Wilhelm. Hebräisch-deutsches Handwörterbuch
über die Schriften des Alten Testaments [Hebrew-German Dictionary to
the Writings of the Old Testament]. 2 vols. Leipzig, 1810-1812.

-----. Hebräisches Elementarbuch. Es enthalt hebräische Grammatik [Ele-
mentary Book of Hebrew. It Contains Hebrew Grammar]. Halle, 1813.

-----. A Hebrew and English Lexicon of the Old Testament. Ed. by F.
Brown, S. R. Driver, and C. A. Briggs. Oxford, 1892.

Gevirtz, Stanley. Patterns in the Early Poetry of Israel. (Studies in Ancient
    Oriental Civilization 32) Chicago, 1963.
Glueck, Nelson. The Other Side of Jordan. New Haven, 1940.
Goguel, Maurice. La Naissance du Christianisme [The Birth of Christianity].
    Paris, 1946. ET: New York, 1953.
Goodenough, Erwin R. By Light, Light: The Mystic Gospel of Hellenistic
    Judaism. New Haven, 1935.
-----. Jewish Symbols in the Greco-Roman Period. 13 vols. New York/
    Princeton, 1953-68.
Gordon, Cyrus H. Introduction to Old Testament Times. Ventnor, NJ, 1953.
    Rev. ed., New York, 1958, entitled The World of the Old Testament.
Graf, Karl Heinrich. Die geschichtliche Bücher des Alten Testaments [The
    Historical Books of the Old Testament]. Leipzig, 1866.
Grant, Frederick C., comp. Hellenistic Religions. New York, 1953.
-----. Roman Hellenism and the New Testament. New York, 1962.
Grant, Robert M. Gnosticism: A Source Book of Heretical Writings from the
    Early Christian Period. New York, 1961.
-----. Gnosticism and Early Christianity. New York, 1959. Rev. ed., 1966.
-----. The Sword and the Cross. New York, 1955.
Gregory, Caspar Rene. The Canon and Text of the New Testament. New
    York, 1907.
Gressmann, Hugo, ed. Altorientalischer Texte und Bilder zum Alten Testa-
    ment [Ancient Oriental Texts and Pictures for the Old Testament]. 2
    vols. 2d ed. Berlin, 1926-27.
-----. Mose und seine Zeit [Moses and His Time]. (FRLANT 18) Göttingen,
    1913.
Griesbach, Johann Jakob. Novum Testamentum Graece [Greek New Testa-
    ment]. 2 vols. Halle, 1775-77.
-----. Synopsis Evangeliorum Matthäi Marci et Lucae . . . [Synopsis of the
    Gospels of Matthew, Mark, and Luke . . .]. Halle, 1776.
Groot, Hugo de [Grotius]. Annotationes in Novum Testamentum [Notes on
    the New Testament]. 3 vols. 1641-50.
Guillaume, Alfred. Prophecy and Divination among the Hebrews and Other
    Semites. London, 1938.
Gunkel, Johann F. Hermann. Ausgewählte Psalmen [Selected Psalms].
    Göttingen, 1904.
-----, and J. Begrich. Einleitung in die Psalmen: Die Gattungen der religiös-
    en Lyrik Israels [Introduction to the Psalms: The Genre of the Religious
    Lyric of Israel]. 2 vols. Göttingen, 1928-33.
Gunkel, Johann F. Hermann. Die Genesis [Genesis]. Göttingen, 1901.
-----. Schöpfung und Chaos in Urzeit und Endzeit: eine religionsgeschicht-
    liche Untersuchung über Gen 1 und ApJoh 12 [Creation and Chaos at the
    Beginning-time and End-time: A History-of-religion Investigation of
    Gen. 1 and Rev. 12]. Göttingen, 1895.
-----. Die Wirkungen des heiligen Geistes nach der populären Anschauung
    der apostolischen Zeit und nach der Lehre des Apostels Paulus [The
    Activities of the Holy Spirit according to the Popular View of the Apostolic
    Age and according to the Teaching of the Apostle Paul]. Göttingen, 1888.
Güttgemanns, Erhardt. Offene Fragen zur Formgeschichte des Evangeliums;

eine methodolische Skizze der Grundlagenproblematik der Form- und Redaktionsgeschichte [Open Questions about the Form Criticism of the Gospel; a Methodological Sketch of the Basic Problem of Form and Redaction
Criticism]. Munich, 1970.

Harnack, Adolf von. Beiträge zur Einleitung in das Neue Testament. 2.
Band, Sprüche und Reden Jesu: Die zweite Quelle des Mattäus und Lukas
[Contributions to an Introduction to the New Testament. Vol. 2, Sayings
and Speeches of Jesus: The Second Source of Matthew and Luke]. Leipzig, 1907. ET: The Sayings of Jesus: The Second Source of St. Matthew
and St. Luke. London/New York, 1908.

-----. Die Geschichte der altchristlichen Literatur bis Eusebius [The History
of Ancient Christian Literature until Eusebius]. 4 vols. Leipzig, 1893-
1904.

Harper, William Rainey. Introductory Hebrew Method and Manual. Chicago,
1885. Rev. ed. by J. M. P. Smith, New York, 1922.

Hatch, Edwin, and Henry A. Redpath. A Concordance to the Septuagint and
the Other Greek Versions of the Old Testament, including the Apocryphal
Books. 3 vols. Oxford, 1892-1900.

Hatch, Edwin. The Influence of Greek Ideas and Usages on the Christian
Church. (Hibbert Lectures, 1888) Oxford, 1900.

-----. The Organization of the Early Christian Churches. (Bampton Lectures, 1880) London/Oxford, 1881.

Hawkins, John C. Horae Synopticae [Synoptic Studies]: Contributions to the
Study of the Synoptic Problem. Oxford, 1899.

Heitmüller, Wilhelm. Taufe und Abendmahl bei Paulus: Darstellung und
religionsgeschichtliche Beleuchtung [Baptism and Lord's Supper according to Paul: Description and Religio-historical Illumination].
Göttingen, 1903.

Hempel, Johannes. Die althebräische Literatur und ihr hellenistisch-jü-
disches Nachleben [The Old Hebrew Literature and Its Hellenistic-
Jewish Later Life]. Wildpark-Potsdam, 1930.

Hengel, Martin. Judaism and Hellenism: Studies in their Encounter in Palestine during the Early Hellenistic Period. Tr. of 2d German ed., 1973.
2 vols. London/Philadelphia, 1974.

Hennecke, Edgar, and W. Schneemelcher. (see: Bible. New Testament.
Apocryphal books. English. 1963)

Herder, Johann Gottfried von. Christliche Schriften [Christian Writings].
4 vols. Riga, 1794-98.

-----. Vom Geist der Ebräischen Poesie [On the Spirit of Hebrew Poetry].
2 vols. Dessau, 1782-83.

Higgins, Godfrey. Anacalypsis: An Attempt to draw aside the Veil of the
Saitic Isis; or, an Inquiry into the Origin of Languages, Nations, and
Religions. 2 vols. London, 1833-36.

Hilgenfeld, Adolf. Die jüdische Apokalyptik in ihrer geschichtlichen Entwicklung.[Jewish Apocalyptic in Its Historical Development]. Jena, 1857.

Hobbes, Thomas. Leviathan. London, 1651.

Hölscher, Gustav. Geschichte der israelitisch-jüdischen Religion [History of
Israelite-Jewish Religion]. Giessen, 1922.

Holtzmann, Heinrich Julius. Die synoptischen Evangelien. Ihr Ursprung und ihr geschichtlicher Charakter [The Synoptic Gospels: Their Origin and Their Historical Character]. Leipzig, 1863.

Hooke, Samuel H. Babylonian and Assyrian Religion. Oxford, 1962.

-----, ed. Myth and Ritual. Oxford, 1933.

Hume, David. Dialogues concerning Natural Religion. London, 1779.

-----. Philosophical Essays concerning Human Understanding. London, 1748.

Ibn Ezra, Abraham. (see: Bible. Old Testament. Polyglot [at end of this bibliography])

Ilgen, Karl David. Die Urkunden des ersten Buchs von Moses in ihrer Urgestalt [The Documents of the First Book of Moses in Its Primitive Form]. Halle, 1798.

"The International Critical Commentary" [series]. 70 vols. Edinburgh, 1895-1951. [Listed in libraries under the names of the individual commentators] New editions and titles in the series: 1975-

The Interpreter's Dictionary of the Bible. 4 vols. New York/Nashville, 1962. Sup., 1976.

James, Montagu R. (see: Bible. New Testament. Apocryphal books. English. 1924)

Jastrow, Morris. Die Religion Babyloniens und Assyriens [The Religion of the Babylonians and Assyrians]. Giessen, 1912.

Johnson, Sherman. Jesus in His Own Times. New York, 1957.

Jowett, Benjamin. "The Interpretation of Scripture." In: Essays and Reviews, ed. by J. Parker. London, 1860.

Kabisch, Richard. Die Eschatologie des Paulus in ihren Zusammenhängen mit dem Gesamtbegriff des Paulus [The Eschatology of Paul in Its Connections with His Thought as a Whole]. Göttingen, 1893.

Kapelrud. Arvid S. The Ras Shamra Discoveries and the Old Testament. Norman, 1963.

Keil, Karl [Latinized as Carolus] A. G. De historia librorum interpretatione eiusque necessitate [On the Historical Interpretation of the Books [of the Bible] and Its Necessity]. Leipzig, 1788.

Kimhi, David. Book of Completeness. (ms. in Hebrew) 13th century.

-----. Book of Roots. (ms. in Hebrew) 13th century.

Kingsbury, Jack Dean. Matthew: Structure, Christology, Kingdom. Philadelphia, 1975.

Kittel, Gerhard. Geschichte der Hebräer [History of the Hebrews]. 2 vols. Gotha, 1888-93. 2d ed., 1909-12.

-----, ed. Theologisches Wörterbuch zum Neuen Testament. 9 vols. Stuttgart, 1932-73. ET: Theological Dictionary of the New Testament. 9 vols. Grand Rapids, 1964-74.

-----. (see also: Bible. Old Testament. Hebrew)

Klausner, Joseph. From Jesus to Paul. Tr. from Hebrew ed. New York, 1943.

-----. Jesus of Nazareth: His Life, Times, and Teaching. Tr. from Hebrew ed. New York, 1925.

-----. The Messianic Idea in Israel: From Its Beginning to the Completion of the Mishnah. Tr. from 3d Hebrew ed., 1950. New York, 1955.

Köhler, Ludwig, and Walter Baumgartner, et al. Hebräisches und Aramäisches Lexikon zum Alten Testament [Hebrew and Aramaic Lexicon to the Old Testament]. 3d ed. Leiden, 1967-

Kraeling, Carl Hermann. Anthropos and Son of Man: A Study in the Religious
    Syncretism of the Hellenistic Orient. New York, 1927.

Kuenen, Abraham. De Godsdienst van Israël [The Religion of Israel]. 2 vols.
    Haarlem, 1869-70.

-----. Historisch-kritisch onderzoek naar het ontstaan en de versameling van
    de boeken des Ouden Verbonds [Historical-critical Introduction to the Books
    of the Old Testament with regard to Their Origin and Collection]. 3 vols.
    Leiden, 1861-65.

Kümmel, Werner G. Introduction to the New Testament. Tr. from 17th Ger-
    man ed., 1973, by H. C. Kee. Nashville, 1975.

Lachmann, Karl. "De Ordine Narrationum in Evangeliis Synopticis" [Concern-
    the Order of the Narratives in the Synoptic Gospels]. In: Theologische
    Studien und Kritiken 8 (1835):570-90.

-----, ed. Novum Testamentum Graece et Latine [Greek and Latin New Testa-
    ment]. 2 vols. Berlin, 1842-50.

Lagarde, Paul de. "Über das Verhältnis des deutschen Staates zu Theologie,
    Kirche und Religion" [On the Relation of the German State to Theology,
    Church and Religion]. In: Deutsche Schriften, 5th ed., 1920.

Leclerc, Jean. Historia Ecclesiastica . . . [Church History . . .]. Am-
    sterdam, 1716.

Levita, Elijah. (see: Elijah Ben Asher, the Levite)

Liddell, Henry George, and Robert Scott. A Greek-English Lexicon, based
    on the German work of Francis Passow. Oxford, 1843.

Lietzmann, Hans. Ein Beitrag zur Mandäerfrage [A Contribution to the
    Mandaean Question]. Berlin, 1930.

-----. A History of the Early Church. 3d German ed. rev. and tr. by B.
    L. Woolf. 4 vols. London, 1953.

Lightfoot, Joseph Barber. The Apostolic Fathers. 3 vols. London, 1869-85.

Lightfoot, Robert Henry. History and Interpretation in the Gospels. London,
    1935.

-----. Locality and Doctrine in the Gospels. London, 1938.

Locke, John. An Essay concerning Human Understanding. London, 1690.

-----. Reasonableness of Christianity as Delivered in the Scriptures.
    London, 1695.

Lods, Adolphe. Histoire de la littérature hébraique et juive [History of He-
    brew and Jewish Literature]. Paris, 1950.

-----. The Prophets and the Rise of Judaism. ET of 1935 French ed.
    London, 1937.

Lohmeyer, Ernst. Das Evangelium des Markus [The Gospel of Mark].
    Göttingen, 1937.

-----. Galiläa und Jerusalem [Galilee and Jerusalem]. Göttingen, 1936.

-----. Kyrios Jesus: Eine Untersuchung zu Phil. 2:5-11 [Lord Jesus: An
    Investigation of Phil. 2:5-11]. Heidelberg, 1927/28.

Loisy, Alfred. L'Evangile et l'Eglise [The Gospel and the Church]. Paris,
    1902.

Lowth, Robert. De sacra Poesi Hebraeorum praelectiones academicae
    [Academic Lectures on the Sacred Poetry of the Hebrews]. Oxford,
    1753.

Lucius, Ludovicus. Dictionarium Novi Testamenti [Dictionary of the New
    Testament]. Basel, 1640.

Lücke, Friedrich. Grundriss der neutestamentlichen Hermeneutik und ihrer
    Geschichte. Zum Gebrauch für akademische Verlesungen [Outline of
    New Testament Hermeneutics and Its History. For Use for Academic
    Lectures]. Göttingen, 1817.

Luther, Martin, tr. Biblia, das ist, die gantze Heilige Schrift deutschend
    [The Bible, that is, the Whole Holy Scriptures translated into German].
    Wittenberg, 1522.

Mabillon, Jean. Acta Sanctorum [Acts of the Saints]. Paris, 1668.

-----. Traité des études monastiques [A Treatise on Monastic Studies].
    Paris, 1691.

Maimonides, Moses. Dux Neutrorum sive Dubiorum [Guide for the Per-
    plexed]. (ms.) 1190.

Mandelkern, Solomon. Veteris Testimenti concordantiae Hebraicae atque
    Chaldaicae [Hebrew and also Chaldean Concordance of the Old Testa-
    ment]. Leipzig, 1896.

Marbecke, John. A Concordance, that is to saie, a worke wherein by the
    order of the letters of the A.B.C. ye maie redely find any worde con-
    teigned in the whole Bible, so often as it is there expressed or mention-
    ed. London, 1550.

Marxsen, Willi. Mark the Evangelist. Tr. from 2d German ed., 1960.
    Nashville, 1969.

Mendenhall, George E. Law and Covenant in Israel and the Ancient Near
    East. Pittsburgh, 1955.

Merkel, Helmut. Die Widersprüche zwischen den Evangelien: Ihre polem-
    ische und apologetische Behandlung in der Alten Kirche bis zu Augustin
    [The Contradictions between the Gospels: Their Polemic and Apologetic
    Treatment in the Early Church until Augustine]. Tübingen, 1971.

Merrill, Selah. East of the Jordan: A Record of Travel and Observation in
    the Countries of Moab Gilead and Bashan during the Years 1875-77.
    New York, 1881.

Metzger, Bruce M. Introduction to the Apocrypha. New York, 1957.

-----. Manuscripts of the Greek Bible: An Introduction to Paleography.
    New York, 1981.

-----. The Text of the New Testament: Its Transmission, Corruption,
    and Restoration. 2d ed. New York, 1968.

Meyer, Heinrich August Wilhelm. Das Neue Testament Griechisch . . .
    und einem kritischen und exegetischen Kommentar [The Greek New
    Testament . . . and a Critical and Exegetical Commentary]. Göttingen,
    1829- . Later the series was (and is) published as: Kritisch-Exeget-
    ischer Kommentar über das Neue Testament.

Michaelis, Johann David. Einleitung in den göttlichen Schriften des Neuen
    Bundes [Introduction to the Divine Writings of the New Covenant].
    Göttingen. 1st ed., 1750. ET of 4th German ed., 1788: 5 vols. Cam-
    bridge, 1793-1801.

-----. Mosäisches Recht [Mosaic Law]. 6 vols.

Mills, John. Novum Testamentum Graecum . . . [Greek New Testament
    . . .]. Amsterdam, 1707.

Moffatt, James, ed. The Moffatt New Testament Commentary. 17 vols.
     New York, 1928-50.

Montefiore, Claude G. Rabbinic Literature and Gospel Teachings. London,
     1930.

Moore, George Foot. History of Religions. 2 vols. New York, 1925-26.

-----. Judaism in the First Centuries of the Christian Era: The Age of the
     Tannaim. 3 vols. Cambridge, MA, 1927-30.

Morrison, Clinton. An Analytical Concordance to the Revised Standard Ver-
     sion of the New Testament. Philadelphia, 1979.

Morton, Andrew Q., and James McLeman. Christianity and the Computer.
     London, 1964. (Pub. in New York, 1964, with title Christianity in the
     Computer Age)

Moulton, James Hope, and George Milligan. The Vocabulary of the Greek
     Testament, Illustrated from the Papyri and Other Non-literary Sources.
     London, 1914-29. [1 vol., issued in 8 parts]

Moulton, William F., and A. S. Geden. A Concordance to the Greek Testa-
     ment . . . Edinburgh, 1897.

Mowinckel, Sigmund. He that Cometh. Tr. from 1951 Norwegian ed. Ox-
     ford, 1956.

-----. Psalmenstudien [Psalms Studies]. 6 vols. Kristiania, 1921-24.

Nicholas of Lyra. Postilla Litteralis [According to the Literal (Sense)].
     Ms., 1322-31. Printed book: 5 vols. Rome, 1471-72.

Niebuhr, Barthold Georg. Römische Geschichte [Roman History]. 3 vols.
     Berlin, 1811-32.

Nilsson, Martin Persson. A History of Greek Religion. Tr. from Swedish
     ed. Oxford, 1925. 3d German ed.: Munich, 1967-

Noth, Martin. Geschichte Israels. 3d ed. Berlin, 1956. ET: The History
     of Israel. 2d ed. London/New York, 1960.

-----. Ueberlieferungsgeschichtliche Studien, II : Ueberlieferungsgeschicht-
     liche des Pentateuch [Tradition-history Studies, II: Tradition-history of
     the Pentateuch]. Stuttgart, 1948. ET: A History of the Pentateuchal
     Traditions. Englewood Cliffs, 1972.

Oesterley, William O. E. The Wisdom of Egypt and the Old Testament in the
     Light of the Newly Discovered 'Teaching of Amen-em-ope.' New York/
     Toronto, 1927.

Olrik, Axel. "Die epischen Gesetze der Volksdichtung" [The Epic Laws of
     Folk Poetry]. Zeitschrift für deutsches Altertum 51 (1909):1-12.

O'Neill, J. C. The Puzzle of 1 John: A New Examination of Origins. London,
     1966.

Overbeck, Franz. Studien zur Geschichte der alten Kirche [Studies in the
     History of the Early Church]. Leipzig, 1875.

-----. Über die Christlichkeit unserer heutigen Theologie [Concerning the
     Christ-likeness of Our Current Theology]. Leipzig, 1873.

The Oxford Bible Atlas. 2d ed. New York, 1974.

Paine, Thomas. The Age of Reason. Being an Investigation of True and
     Fabulous Theology. 3 vols. London/Paris, 1794-1807.

Papyrus Bodmer II: Evangile de Jean chap. 1-14. Ed. by Victor Martin.
     Cologny-Genève, 1956. Sup.: Evangile de Jean chap. 14-21. New ed.,
     ed. by Victor Martin and J. W. B. Barns. Cologny-Gèneve, 1962.

Papyrus Bodmer XIV-XV: Evangiles de Luc et Jean [Gospels of Luke and John].
    2 vols. Cologny-Genève, 1961.

Parker, Theodore. "The Transient and Permanent in Christianity." In: Theo-
    dore Parker: An Anthology, ed. by Henry Steele Commager. Boston, 1960.

Pedersen, Johannes. Israel: Its Life and Culture. 2 vols. London, 1926-40.

Perrin, Norman. Rediscovering the Teaching of Jesus. New York, 1967.

Pfeiffer, Robert H. History of New Testament Times; With an Introduction to
    the Apocrypha. New York, 1949.

-----. Introduction to the Old Testament. New York, 1941; rev. ed., 1948.

Pfleiderer, Otto. Das Urchristenthum, seine Schriften und Lehre, in ge-
    schichtlichem Zusammenhang beschrieben [Primitive Christianity, Its
    Writings and Doctrine Described in Historical Context]. 2d ed. Berlin,
    1902. ET: New York/London, 1906.

Pritchard, James B., ed. The Ancient Near East in Pictures. 2d ed.
    Princeton, 1954.

-----. Ancient Near Eastern Texts Relating to the Old Testament. 2d ed.
    Princeton, 1955.

Rad, Gerhard von. "Der Anfang der Geschichtsschreibung im Alten Israel"
    [The Beginnings of Historical Writing in Ancient Israel]. In: Archiv für
    Kulturgeschichte 32, Weimar, 1944, pp. 1-42.

-----. Das formgeschichtliche Problem des Hexateuchs [The Form-critical
    Problem of the Hexateuch]. Stuttgart, 1938.

Reimarus, Herman Samuel. Vom Zwecke Jesu und seiner Jünger [On the In-
    tentions of Jesus and His Disciples]. Braunschweig, 1778. ET: Reimar-
    us: Fragments, ed. by C. H. Talbert. Philadelphia, 1970.

Reitzenstein, Richard. Poimandres. Studien zur griechisch-ägyptischen und
    frühchristlicher Literatur [Poimandres: Studies on Greco-Egyptian and
    Early Christian Literature]. Leipzig, 1904.

Reland, Adrian. Palaestina ex monumentis veteribus illustrata [Palestine
    Illustrated by Ancient Monuments]. Trajecti Batavorum, 1709.

Renan, Joseph Ernest. La Vie de Jésus [The Life of Jesus]. Paris, 1863.

Reuchlin, Johann. De Rudimentis Hebraicis [On the Rudiments of Hebrew].
    Phorce, 1506.

Reuss, Eduard. Die Geschichte der heiligen Schriften Neuen Testaments
    [The History of the Holy Scriptures of the New Testament]. Halle, 1842.

Riddle, Donald W. Jesus and the Pharisees: A Study in Christian Tradition.
    Chicago, 1928.

-----. The Martyrs: A Study in Social Control. Chicago, 1931.

Robertson, Archibald T. A Grammar of the Greek New Testament in the
    Light of Historical Research. London/New York, 1914. 4th ed., 1923.

Robertson, David A. Linguistic Evidence in Dating Early Hebrew Poetry.
    (SBL Dissertation Series 3) Missoula, 1972.

Robinson, Edward. Biblical Researches in Palestine, Mount Sinai and Arabia
    Petraea. 3 vols. Halle/London/Boston, 1841.

Robinson, H. Wheeler. Inspiration and Revelation in the Old Testament.
    Oxford, 1946.

Robinson, James McConkey, ed. The Nag Hammadi Library in English.
    Leiden/New York/Toronto, 1977.

Rost, Leonhard. Die Überlieferung von der Thronnachfolge Davids [The

Tradition of Succession of the Throne of David]. Stuttgart, 1926.

Rückert, Leopold Immanuel. Commentar über die Briefe Pauli an die Römer [Commentary on Paul's Letters to the Romans]. Leipzig, 1831.

Russel, David S. The Method and Message of Jewish Apocalyptic: 200 BC-AD 100. London/Philadelphia, 1964.

Rylaarsdam, J. Coert. Revelation in Jewish Wisdom Literature. Chicago, 1944.

Sanders, Henry A. (see: Bible. New Testament. Epistles. Greek. 1935)

Sandmel, Samuel. The Genius of Paul: A Study in History. 2d ed. New York, 1970.

-----. The Hebrew Scriptures. New York, 1963.

Schleiermacher, Friedrich D. E. Hermeneutik und Kritik mit besonderer Beziehung auf das Neue Testament [Hermeneutics and Criticism with Special Relation to the New Testament]. In his Sämtliche Werke, vol. 1, Berlin, 1838.

-----. "Über den sogennanten ersten Brief des Paulos an den Timotheos. Ein kritisches Sendschreiben an J. C. Gass, 1807" [On the So-called First Letter of Paul to Timothy. A Critical Communication to J. C. Gass, 1807]. In his Sämtliche Werke, vol. 1, Berlin, 1838.

Schürer, Emil. Geschichte des jüdischen Volkes im Zeitalter Jesu Christi [A History of the Jewish People in the Time of Jesus Christ]. 2d ed. 2 vols. Leipzig, 1886-87 [superior to 1874 ed.]. ET, rev. and ed. by Geza Vermes [corrects Schürer's bias]: 2 vols. Edinburgh, 1973-79.

Schweitzer, Albert. "Das Messianitäts- und Leidensgeheimnis. Eine Skizze des Lebens Jesu" [The Mystery of Messiahship and Suffering. A Sketch of the Life of Jesus]. In his Das Abendmahl im Zusammenhang mit dem Leben Jesu und der Geschichte des Urchristentums. Leipzig, 1901. ET: The Mystery of the Kingdom of God. London, 1914.

-----. Von Reimarus zu Wrede: Eine Geschichte der Leben-Jesu-Forschung [From Reimarus to Wrede: A History of the Life-of-Jesus Research]. Tübingen, 1906. ET: The Quest of the Historical Jesus. London, 1910.

Sellin, Ernst. Alttestamentliche Religion im Rahmen der andern altorientalischen [Old Testament Religion in the Framework of Other Old Oriental (Religions)]. Leipzig, 1908.

Semler, Johann Salomo. Abhandlung von freier Untersuchung des Canon [Treatise on Free Investigation of the Canon]. 4 vols. Halle, 1771-75.

-----. Apparatus ad liberalem Novi Testamenti interpretationem [Apparatus for a Free Interpretation of the New Testament]. Halle, 1767.

-----. Vorbereitung zur theologischen Hermeneutik, zur weiteren Beförderung des Fleisses angehender Gottsgelehrten nebst Antwort auf die Tübingische Vertheidigung der Apocalypsis [Preparatory Study on Theological Hermeneutics, for the Promotion of Diligence among Beginning Learned Divines, together with a Reply to the Tübingen Defence of the Apocalypse]. Halle, 1769.

Simon, Richard. Histoire critique des principaux commentateurs du Nouveau Testament, depuis commençement du Christianisme jusques à nôtre temps

[Critical History of the Principle Commentators on the New Testament from the beginning of Christianity up to Our Time]. Rotterdam, 1693.

-----. Histoire critique des versions du Nouveau Testament, où l'on fait connoître quel a été l'usage de la lecture des Livres Sacres dans les principales Églises du monde [Critical History of the Versions of the New Testament, wherein Is Made Known what Has Been the Custom in the Reading of the Sacred Books in the Principle Churches of the World]. Rotterdam, 1690.

-----. Histoire critique du texte du Nouveau Testament, où l'on établit la Vérité des Actes sur lesquels la Réligion Chrêtienne est fondée [Critical History of the Text of the New Testament, wherein Is Established the Truth of the Acts on which the Christian Religion Is Founded]. Rotterdam, 1689.

-----. Histoire critique du Vieux Testament [Critical History of the Old Testament]. Amsterdam, 1680.

Smith, George Adam. Historical Geography of the Holy Land. London, 1894.

Smith, William Robertson. Lectures on the Religion of the Semites. London, 1889.

Spencer, John. De Legibus Hebraeorum, Ritualibus et earum Rationibus libri tres [Three Books on the Laws, Rituals, and Customs of the Hebrews]. Cambridge, 1685.

Spinoza, Baruch. Tractatus Theologico-Politicus [Theological-political Treatise]. Amsterdam, 1670.

Strauss, David Friedrich. Die christliche Glaubenslehre in ihrer geschichtlichen Entwicklung und im Kampfe mit der modernen Wissenschaft dargestellt [Christian Doctrine Presented in Its Historical Development and in Conflict with Modern Science]. 2 vols. Stuttgart, 1840-41.

-----. Das Leben Jesu kritisch bearbeitet [The Life of Jesus Treated Critically]. 2 vols. Tübingen, 1835-36.

Strong, James. The Exhaustive Concordance of the Bible: . . . New York/Cincinnati/Chicago, 1890.

Teeple, Howard M. The Literary Origin of the Gospel of John. Evanston, 1974.

-----. The Mosaic Eschatological Prophet. (JBL Mon. Series 10) Philadelphia, 1957.

Thayer, Joseph Henry. Greek-English Lexicon of the New Testament. New York/Edinburgh, 1886.

Thomas Aquinas, St. Catena Aurea [Golden Chain]. (ms.) 13th century.

Thompson, James Matthew. "The Composition of the Fourth Gospel." The Expositor, 8th series, 11 (1916):34-46.

-----. "The Structure of the Fourth Gospel." The Expositor, 8th series, 10 (1915):512-26.

Thompson, T. L. The Historicity of the Patriarchal Narratives: The Quest for the Historical Abraham. (BZAW 33) Berlin/New York, 1974.

Throckmorton, Burton H., Jr. Gospel Parallels: A Synopsis of the First Three Gospels. 2d ed. New York, 1957.

Titus, Eric L. "Did Paul Write 1 Corinthians 13?" Journal of Bible and Religion 27 (1959):299-302.

Toland, John. Nazarenus; or Jewish, Gentile and Mahometan Christianity.

London, 1718.

Toy, Crawford Howell. Quotations in the New Testament. New York, 1884.

Trench, Richard Chenevix. Synonyms of the New Testament. Cambridge, 1854.

Tromm, Abraham. Concordantiae graecae versionis vulgo dictae LXX interpretum [Greek Concordance to the Common Version Written by the Septuagint Translators]. Amsterdam/Utrecht, 1718.

Turretini, Jean Alphonse. De Sacrae Scripturae interpretandae methodo tractatus bipartitus, . . . [A Bipartite Tractate on the Method of Interpreting the Sacred Scriptures, . . .]. Trajecti Thuviorum, 1728.

Tyndale, William. The New Testament translated into English, with marginal notes, by William Tyndale. Cologne/Worms, 1525.

Urbach, Ephraim E. The Sages: Their Concepts and Beliefs. Tr. from 2d Hebrew ed., 1971. 2 vols. Jerusalem, 1975.

Usener, Hermann. Religionsgeschichtliche Untersuchungen I, Das Weinachtsfest [History-of-Religion Researches I: The Christmas Festival]. Bonn, 1889.

Valla, Lorenzo [Latinized as Laurentius]. In latinam Novi Testamenti interpretationem ex collatione graecorum exemplarium adnotationes apprime utiles [Especially Useful Comments on the Latin Translation of the New Testament, from a Collection of Greek Exemplars]. Ms., 1444; printed book, 1505.

Van Seters, John. Abraham in History and Tradition. New Haven, 1975.

Vatke, Wilhelm. Die biblische Theologie wissenschaftlich dargestellt: Die Religion des Alten Testaments nach den kanonischen Büchern entwickelt [Biblical Theology Scientifically Presented: The Religion of the Old Testament Developed according to the Canonical Books]. Berlin, 1835.

Weeden, Theodore J. Mark—Traditions in Conflict. Philadelphia, 1971.

Weimar, Peter. Untersuchungen zur Redaktionsgeschichte des Pentateuch [Investigations of the Redaction-History of the Pentateuch]. (BZAW 146) Berlin/New York, 1977.

Weiss, Johannes. Die Predigt Jesu vom Reiche Gottes [The Preaching of Jesus about the Kingdom of God]. Göttingen, 1892.

_____. Das Urchristentum [Primitve Christianity]. Göttingen, 1914. ET: The History of Primitive Christianity. Elmira, NY, 1937.

Weisse, Christian Hermann. Die evangelische Geschichte kritisch und philosophisch bearbeitet [The Gospel History Treated Critically and Philosophically]. 2 vols. Leipzig, 1838.

Weizsäcker, Carl. Das Apostolische Zeitalter der christlichen Kirche [The Apostolic Age of the Christian Church]. Freiburg, 1886.

Wellhausen, Julius. Die Composition des Hexateuchs und der historischen Bücher des Alten Testaments [The Composition of the Hexateuch and the Historical Books of the Old Testament]. Berlin, 1885.

-----. Einleitung in die drei ersten Evangelien [Introduction to the First Three Gospels]. Berlin, 1905.

-----. Das Evangelium Johannis [The Gospel of John]. Berlin, 1908.

-----. Geschichte Israels [History of Israel]. Berlin, 1878. [Later eds. entitled: Prolegomena zur Geschichte Israels]

Wendland, Paul. Geschichte der urchristliche Literaturformen [History of

Primitive Christian Literary Forms]. Tübingen, 1912.

-----. "Philo und die kynisch-stoiche Diatribe" [Philo and the Cynic-Stoic
    Diatribe]. In: Beiträge zur Geschichte der grieschen Philosophie und
    Religion, ed. by Wendland und Kern. Berlin, 1895.

Werner, Martin. Die Entstehung des christlichen Dogmas problemgeschicht-
    lich dargestellt [The Origin of Christian Dogma Presented as a Historical
    Problem]. Bern, 1941. ET: rev. Eng. tr. of 2d German ed., 1954: The
    Formation of Christian Dogma: An Historical Study of Its Problem. New
    York, 1957.

Westcott, Brooke Foss, and Fenton John Anthony Hort. The New Testament
    in the Original Greek. 2 vols. Cambridge/London, 1881-82.

The Westminster Historical Atlas to the Bible. Ed. by George Ernest Wright
    and Floyd Vivian Filson. Rev. ed. Philadelphia, 1956.

Wettstein, Johann Jakob. Novum Testamentum Graecum . . . [Greek New
    Testament . . .]. 2 vols. Amsterdam, 1951-52.

Widengren, George. Literary and Psychological Aspects of the Hebrew Pro-
    phets. Uppsala, 1948.

Wigram, George Vicesimus, ed. The Hebraist's Vade Mecum: a first attempt
    at a complete verbal index to the contents of the Hebrew and Chaldee
    Scriptures. London, 1867.

Wilke, Christian Gottlob. Der Urevangelist oder exegetisch kritische Un
    suchung über das Verwandtschaftsverhältniss der drei ersten Evangelien
    [The Original Evangelist, or Exegetical and Critical Research on the
    Kindred Relationship of the First Three Gospels]. Dresden/Leipzig,
    1838.

Willoughby, Harold R. Pagan Regeneration. Chicago, 1929.

Wilson, Robert McLean. Gnosis and the New Testament. Oxford/ Philadel-
    phia, 1968.

Winer, Georg Benedikt. Biblisches Realwoerterbuch [Biblical Dictionary].
    Leipzig, 1820.

-----. Grammatik des neutestamentlichen Sprachidioms [Grammar of
    New Testament Language-idiom]. Leipzig, 1822.

Witter, Henning Bernhard. Jura Israelitarum in Palaestinam terram
    Chananaeam, commentatione in Genesin . . . [Laws of the Israelites in
    the Palestinian-Canaanite Land, with a Commentary on Genesis . . .].
    Hildaeiae, 1711.

Wrede, Wilhelm. Das Messiasgeheimnis in den Evangelien. Zugleich ein
    Beitrag zum Verständnis des Markusevangeliums [The Messianic Secret
    in the Gospels; also a Contribution to the Understanding of the Gospel of
    Mark]. Göttingen, 1901.

-----. Paulus [Paul]. Tübingen, 1904.

Wycliffe, John. (see: Bible. English. 1382)

Young, Robert. Analytical Concordance to the Bible. New York, 1879; rev.
    ed., 1902.

ADD TO BIBLIOGRAPHY:

Bible. Old Testament. Polyglot [Hebrew and Aramaic]. [title in Hebrew]
    The Old Testament, with Aramaic Version (Targum) and the Commentaries
    of Rashi, Abraham Ibn Ezra, David Kimhi, and Others. 4 vols. Venice,
    1524-25.
Nickelsburg, George W. E., Jewish Literature Between the Bible and the Mish-
    nah: A Historical and Literary Introduction. Philadelphia, 1981.
North, Christopher R. The Old Testament Interpretation of History. London,
    1946.

NOTES:

Bible. Greek. 1707. Mills. (see: Mills, John)
Bible. German 1522. Luther. (see: Luther, Martin)
Bible. New Testament. Gospels. Greek. 1956. (see: Papyrus Bodmer II)
    [This is P^{66}]
Bible. New Testament. Gospels. Greek. 1961. (see: Papyrus Bodmer XIV-
    XV) [This is P^{75}]

The listing, "Bible. New Testament. Epistles. Greek. 1935. A Third Cen-
    tury Papyrus Codex . . . , ed. by Henry A. Sanders," is the listing of
    the Chester Beatty Papyrus, P^{46}.

Edgar J. Goodspeed compiled two important concordances to early Christian
    literature: Index Apologeticus and Index Patristicus.

PERSONAL NAME INDEX

Abbott, L., 34
Abelard, P., 51,54,65
Adrianos, 48
Aegidius of Viterbo, 60
Aland, K., 114,116,121
Albertus Magnus, 52,54
Albright, W.F., 126
Alcuin, 52
Allegro, J., 37
Alt, A., 127
Ambrose, 51
Ambrosiaster, 271
Ammonius Saccas, 48
Andrew of St. Victor, 56,58
Antiochus IV Epiphanes, 152
Antiochus VII Sidetes, 130
Aquila, 45,47
Aristotle, 53,54
Arminius, J., 66
Arndt, W. F., 116
Arnobius, 44
Astruc, J., 75
Augustine, 50,51,53,92
Aune, D.E., 135
Auriol, P., 52
Bacon, R., 56,58
Baldensperger, W., 136
Barrett, C.K., 135,137
Barth, K., 20,26,28,29,33
Barton, B., 35
Bauer, B., 91, 103
Bauer, G.L., 79
Bauer, W., 115,139,163
Baumgartner, W., 115
Baur, F.C., 32,89,95,98,101,104,
    105,143,258
Bede, 51
Bengel, J.A., 73
Bernard of Clairveaux, 53
Betz, H.D., 138
Bewer, J., 117
Billerbeck, P., 132
Blair, E., 123
Blass, F.W., 84,116
Bliss, F.J., 216
Bodmer, M., 113

Bonaventure, G.di F., 52
Bornkamm, G., 123
Bousset, W., 103,135,136,138,142
Bowyer, W.,Jr., 74
Brandon, S.G.F., 133,141
Breasted, J.H., 127
Bretschneider, K.G., 89
Briggs, C.A., 86,96,105,115
Brown, F., 86,94,105,115
Brunetière, F., 120
Bryennios, P., 97
Buckminster, J., 81, 105
Budge, E.W., 127
Bultmann, R., 122,124,139,143
Burgon, J.W., 85
Burney, C.F., 111
Burrows, M., 126,130,225
Buttmann, A., 87
Cadbury, H.J., 35,37,121,142
Cajetan, 17,65
Calmet, A., 75,88
Calvin, J., 5,20,64
Camilo dos Santos, E., 116
Cappel, L., 69
Carlstadt, 65
Carlston, C., 123
Cartlidge, D.R., 137,n.47
Casaubon, I., n.7a
Case, S.J., 139
Cassuto, U., 118,119
Castelli, D., 96
Celsus, 47
Champollion, J. F.
Charlemagne, 52
Charles, R.H., 131
Charlesworth, J.H., 131
Chivi of Balkh, 58
Chrysostom, J., 49,92
Chubb, T., 79
Clemen, C., 143
Clement of Alexandria, 31,44,49,53
Clement of Rome, 159
Cludius, H.H., 89
Cochlaeus, J., 63
Colenso, J.W., 95
Coleridge, S.T., 83

Colet, J., 59, 61
Collins, A., 75
Colwell, E.C., 34, 111, 152, 178
Conzelmann, H., 123
Copernicus, N., 68
Coppens, J., 86, 129
Couchard, P.-L., 103
Council of Trent, 14, 17, 23-24
Cowley, A.E., 86
Craig, C.T., 142
Cranmer, T., 63
Crenshaw, J., 119
Cromwell, O., 63
Cross, F.M., 127
Cullmann, O., 142
Cumont, F., 100, 138
Cyprian, 271
Danker, F.W., 116, 163
Dautzenberg, G., 135
Davidson, B., 87
Davies, W.D., n. 40
Debrunner, A., 116
Deissmann, A., 84, 143, 188, 189,
    n. 43
Democritus, 280
Denon, V., 78
Descartes, R., 67
De Wette, W., 20, 79, 88, 94
Dibelius, M., 123, 124, 136
Dieterich, A., 99, 137
Diodore of Tarsus, 49
Dionysius, 47
Dodd, C.H., 133, 136, 142
Doederlein, J.C., n. 9a
Dölger, J., 138
Dörpfeld, W., 215
Drews, A., 103
Driver, S.R., 86, 115
Duhm, B., 88, 90
Dungan, D., 137, n. 47
Eckermann, J., 122
Edwards, R., 122
Eichhorn, A., 97, 100
Eichhorn, J.G., 15, 75, 77, 79, 81,
    89, 92, 97
Eichrodt, W., 29, 129
Eissfeldt, O., 117
Eliezer ben Hyrcanus, 149
Elijah ben Asher, 60, 62

Ellison, J., 116
Engnell, 121
Erasmus, D., 60, 65
Ernesti, J.A., 12, 73, 81
Estienne, R., 61
Eusebius, 48, 75, 92, 282, n. 34a
Evanson, E., 77
Everett, E., 96, 105
Everling, O., 96
Farnell, L., 138
Fascher, E., 124
Faure, A., 122
Finegan, J., 130
Fisher, L.B., 127
Fitzmyer, J., 188
Flacius, M., 65
Foakes-Jackson, F.J., 121
Fortna, R.T., 122, n. 22a
Fox, A., 138
Francis, F.O., 144
Frankel, Z., 107
Frankfort, H., 127
Frederick the Great, 72
Friedländer, M., 132
Froben, J., 61
Funk, R.W., 116
Gabler, J., 15, 78, 79
Galileo, 68
Gardiner, S., 64
Gaster, T., 127, 132
Geden, A.S., 87, 116
Geiger, A., 107
Gersonides, 53
Gesenius, H.F.W., 86, n. 20a
Gevirtz, S., 118
Gingrich, F.W., 116, 163
Ginsberg, H.L., 118
Ginsburg, C.D., 86
Gladden, W., 34
Goguel, M., 124, 137
Goodenough, E.R., 132
Goodspeed, E.J., 105, 114, 133, 149,
    287
Gordon, C., 128
Graf, K., 89, 90
Grant, F.C., 122, 137, 139
Grant, R.M., 133, 136, 137
Gregory the Great, 51
Gregory, C.R., 74, 114, 167

Grenfell, B.P., 113
Gressmann, H., 120, 128
Griesbach, J.J., 74, 77
Grosseteste, R., 56
Grotius, H., 16, 70, 99
Gunkel, H., 96, 103, 120
Gutschmidt, A. von, 94
Güttgemann, E., 124
Haley, J.W., 92
Harnack, A. von, 34, 97, 101, 104, 122, 139, 143
Harper, W.R., 86, 105
Hase, K.A., 100
Hatch, E., 87, 98, 99, 140
Hawkins, J.C., 87
Hebert, A.G., 29
Hegel, G.W.F., 32
Heitmüller, W., 139
Hempel, J., 118
Hengel, M., 129, 141
Heracleon, 48
Herder, J.G., 76, 77, 80, 92
Herron, G., 34
Hess, J., 76
Heyne, C.G., 79
Higgins, G., 92
Hilgenfeld, A., 96
Hillel, 41, 49
Hirsch, S.R., 107
Hobbes, T., 16, 31, 67
Hölscher, G., 128
Holtzmann, H.J., 91, 101
Hooke, S.H., 127, 128
Hort, F.J.A., 85, 287
Hoskyns, E.C., 29
Hugh of St. Victor, 53, 56, 59
Ibn Ezra, 58
Ilgen, K.D., 76
Irenaeus, 279
Ishmael ben Elisha, 149
Jacob ben Chayim, 62
Jacobson, I., 106
James I, 68
James, E.O., 127
James, M.R., 134
Jastrow, M., 127
Jerome, 44, 46, 48, 50, 51
John XXIII, 25, 110
Johnson, S., 141

Josephus, n. 34a, 35a
Jowett, B., 83
Jülicher, A., 29
Justin, 27, 271, 276, 277, 280, n. 34a
Kabisch, R., 96
Kähler, M., 103
Kant, I., 72
Kapelrud, A.S., 127
Käsemann, E., 143, n. 25
Kautzsch, E.F., 86
Kee, H.C., 117
Keil, K., 15
Kennicott, B., 74
Kenyon, F., 157
Kenyon, K., 216
Kepler, J., 68
Kierkegaard, S., 33
Kingsbury, J.D., 123
Kittel, G., 116, 128
Kittel, R., 95, 112
Klausner, J., 129, 140, 144
Knierim, R., 120, 211, n. 31
Knight, D.A., 211, n. 31
Knox, J., 29
Knox, R., 115
Koch, J., 10
Köhler, L., 115, 124
Koppe, J.B., 90
Kraeling, C., n. 36
Kuenen, A., 88, 95
Kümmel, W.G., 103
Lachmann, K., 85, 90, 91
Lagarde, P. de, 17
Lake, K., 121, 133
Langton, S., 58
Layard, A.H., 93
Leclerc, J., 76
Leo XIII, 24
Lessing, G.E., 80
Levi ben Gershon, 53
Liddell, H.G., 87
Lietzmann, H., 117, 137, 138, 139
Lightfoot, J., 70
Lightfoot, J.B., 97
Lightfoot, R.H., 123
Locke, J., 67, 72, 75
Lods, A., 118, 128
Lohmeyer, E., 29, 123
Loisy, A., 106, 110, 143

Lowth, R., 77
Lucius, L., 70
Lücke, F., 11
Luther, M., 5, 14, 19, 23, 26, 62, 64
Mabillon, J., 71
Maimonides, 53, 54
Mandelkern, S., 87
Mariette, A., 93
Marksen, W., 123
Marsh, H., 81, 84
Martin, V., 113
McLeman, J., 121
Meek, T.J., 114
Mendenhall, G.E., 129, 221
Merbecke, J., 64
Merrill, S., 93
Metzger, B., 117
Meyer, H.A.W., 88, 117
Michaelis, J.D., 17, 81, 84
Milligan, G., 115
Mills, J., 73
Minear, P. 29, 30
Moffatt, J., 115
Montanus, A., 62
Montefiore, C., 132, 133
Moore, G.F., 132, 138
Mordecai ben Nathan, I., 58
More, T., 61, 63
Morgan, T., 79
Morgenstern, J., 128
Morrison, C., 116
Morton, A.Q., 121
Moulton, J.H., 115
Moulton, W.F., 87, 116
Mowinckel, S., 118, 120, 129
Napoleon, 78
Nestle, Eb. & Er., 114
Newton, I., 68
Nicholas of Lyra, 52, 56, 58
Niebuhr, B.G., 95
Nilsson, M., 138
Norden, E., 123, 138
North, C.R., 129
Noth, M., 120, 128, 209
Oesterley, W.O.E., 119
Olrik, A., 120
Origen, 25, 31, 44, 47, 48, 49, 53
Orlinsky, H.M., 115
Orr, J., 28

Osiander, A., 76
Overbeck, F., 97
Paine, T., 72
Paley, W., 83
Pantaenus, 49
Parker, T., 105
Pasor, G., 70
Paulus, H.E., 100
Pedersen, J., 129
Perrin, N., 143
Petrie, W.M.F., 216
Pfefferkorn, J., 63
Pfeiffer, R., 117, 207
Pfleiderer, O., 97, 144
Philo, 31, 34, 40, 53, 132
Pius X, 24, 110
Pius XII, 25, 110
Plato, 53, 138, 280
Pliny the Younger, 284
Plutarch, 138, 277 Porphyry, 47
Preuschen, E., 115
Pritchard, J., 128
Quentel, P., 63
Rad, G. von, 119, 120, 121
Rashi, 58
Rauschenbusch, W., 34
Rawlinson, H.C., 94
Redpath, H.A., 87
Reimarus, H., 77, 79, 102, 258
Reisner, G.A., 217
Reitzenstein, R., 137, 139
Renan, E., 102
Reuchlin, J., 63
Reuss, E., 89, 99
Riddle, D.W., 135, 136
Ritschl, A., 34
Roberts, C.H., 113
Robertson, A.T., 116
Robertson, D., 119
Robinson, E., 93, 105
Robinson, H.W., 129
Robinson, J.M., 134
Rossi, G. de, 74
Rost, L., 121
Rückert, L., 88
Russell, D.S., 132
Rylaarsdam, J.C., 119
Saadia ben Joseph, 55
Sampley, J.P., 144

Sanday, W., 122
Sandmel, S., 144
Schaeffer, C.F.A., 126
Schleiermacher, F.D.E., 16, 85, 89, 100
Schliemann, H., 93, 215
Schmidt, K., 124
Schonfield, H., 36
Schrader, E., 94
Schürer, E., 96
Schweitzer, A., 32, 79, 91
Scott, R., 87
Sellin, E., 128
Semler, J.S., 16, 72, 81
Seneca, 281
Shammai, 49
Simon, R., 24, 70
Smith, E., 93
Smith, G.A., 95
Smith, J.M.P., 114, 145
Smith, W.R., 92
Spencer, J., 71, 92
Spinoza, B., 31, 68
Steuernägel, C., 29
Strack, H., 132
Strauss, D.F., 32, 79, 101, 106
Strong, J., 87
Stuart, M., 105
Suetonius, 282
Symmachus, 45
Tacitus, 282, 283, 285
Talbert, C., 195
Tatian, 46
Teeple, H.M., 122, n. 22a, 39, 41
Tertullian, 44, 271
Thayer, J.H., 87
Theodore of Mopsuestia, 14, 48, 49
Theodoret, 92
Theodotion, 45, 47
Theodulf, 52
Thirlwall, C., 85
Thomas Aquinas, 52, 54
Thompson, J.M., 122
Thompson, T.L., 128
Thomsen, C., 216
Throckmorton, B., Jr., 121
Tiede, D.L., n. 50
Tindal, M., 12, 32, 79, n. 2
Tischendorf, C., 85

Titus, E.L., 123
Toland, J., 98
Torrey, C.C., 111
Toy, C.H., 91
Tregelles, S.P., 87
Trivet, N., 52, 58
Tromm, A., 74, 87
Tucker, G.M., 120
Turretini, J.A., 16, 78
Tyndale, W., 62
Urbach, E., 132
Usener, H., 99
Valla, L., 58
Van Seters, J., 128
Vatke, W., 89
Vogel, E.F., 89
Weeden, T., 123
Weiss, J., 102, 137
Weisse, C.H., 91
Weizsäcker, C., 99
Wellhausen, J., 89, 90, 92, 95, 106, 119, 135
Wendland, P., 99, 123, 138
Werner, M., 135
Wernle, P., 143
Westcott, B.F., 85, 287
Wettstein, J.J., 74, 114
Widengren, G., 121
Wigram, G.V., 87
Wilberforce, S., 106
Wilke, C.G., 91
Willoughby, H.R., 139
Wilson, E., 130
Wilson, R.M., 134, 137
Winckler, H., 126
Winer, J.G., 86, 88
Wise, I.M., 107
Witter, H.B., 75
Wrede, W., 91, 135, 141, 144
Wright, G.E., 126
Wycliffe, J., 52, 57
Young, F.W., 117
Young, R., 87, 160
Young, T., 78
Zahn, T., 89
Zeitlin, S., 130
Zeno, 280
Zwingli, H., 15, 26, 27, 64, 65

allegorical method, 31, 44
Arab influence, 54-56
archaeology, 78, 93-95, 126-28, 130-31, 188-89, chap. 15
authorship, 16-18, 46-47, 58-59, 65, 88-89, 95, 190
background of NT, Chr., 80, 97-99, 133-37, chap. 18
background of NT, gentile, 99-100, 137-140, chap. 19
background of NT, Jewish, 70-71, 96-97, 130-33, chap. 17
background of OT, 70, 71, 78, 92-96, 126-29, chap. 16
beliefs, 9-22
Bible, nature of, 7-9
canon, 17-18, 239
commentaries, 48, 52, 58, 64, 88, 117
concordances, 58, 75, 87, 116, 160
context, 42, 150-53
dictionaries, Bible, 75, 88
eschatology, Chr., 268-71
eschatology, Jewish, 242-53
ethics, 256-57, 280-81
form criticism, 120-21, 123-24, 211-12
fundamentalism, 10-14, 287-88
gentile Chr., 272-75
geographies, 58, 95
gnosticism, 44, 134
Greek influence, 56-57, chap. 19
historical approach, birth of, 80-82; growth of, 107-111, 124-25, 128, 145-46; in America, 104-105; opposition to, 286-88; principles of, chap. 9; value of, 288-93
historical situation, 59, 70-71, 77-80, 96
history, Chr., 258-67
history, Israelite, 226-33
history, Jewish, 240-42
ideology, Chr., 267-71
ideology, Jewish, 236-38
inspiration of Bible, 10-16, 72
interpretation of Bible, Chr., 5, 41-44, 51-52, 64-66, 83-84, 92, 95
interpretation of Bible, Jewish, 38-41, 50-51
intolerance, 65-66 (see also: scholars, persecution of)
introductions to Bible, 48-49, 77, 88
Israelites, ideological factors, 236-38; origin of, 226-27; political factors, 227-33; religious factors, 233-36
Israelites' environment, 238-39
Jesus, life of, 79-80, 100-104, 140-43
Jewish-Chr. relations, 54, 56, 60, 242, 255, 262-63
journal editors, 144-45
law (Torah), 253-57, 261-63
lexicology, 161-63
lexicons, 56, 61, 69-70, 86, 87, 115
linguistic study, 44-46, 55-57, 60-62, 63, 70, 73, 86-87, 111-12, 116, chap. 10
literary study, 46-49, 55-58, 62, 70-71, 75-77, 88-92, 117-21, chap. 12 (OT), chap. 13 (NT), chap. 14
literature, Chr., 97, 133-34, chap. 13
literature, Jewish, 70-71, 96, 130-33, chap. 12
literature, pagan, 281
Messiah, 246-53
miracles, 78, 199
modern knowledge, 20-22
modern life as guide, 33-36
"myth school," 79
Old Testament, Chr. use of, 18-20, 42-44, 64, 91
organization, church, 98, 264-65
pagan influence: on Israel, 233-36, 238; on Chr., 275-81
Paul, life of, 104, 143-44
philosophy, 31-33, 53-55, 67-68, 72, 279]81
problems, Chr., 268-71
prophecy, Chr., 264-66
prophecy, Jewish, 18-19, 180-82

redaction criticism, 89-91, 121-23, 203-11

Roman-Chr. relations, 282-85

Roman-Jewish relations, 240-42

scholars, persecution of, 49, 63, 70, 72-74, 95, 105-107

scholia, 51

schools and universities, 49-50, 52-53

science, 54-55, 68, 147

secular influence, 20-21, 71-72, 78-79, 82 (see also: science)

sensationalism, 36-37

Socinians, 67

source criticism, 75-76, 89-91, 119-22, 202-11

Spirit, Holy: as author of Bible, 10-16; as guide in interpretation, 25-27 (see also: prophecy)

structuralism, 212

textual study, 47-48, 57-58, 61-62, 69, 73-74, 83-86, 112-14, chap. 11

theology as guide, 27-30

tradition, 16, 23-25

translation, 45-46, 57, 62, 69, 84-85, 114-15, 164-65